lonely planet

USA's

NATIONAL PARKS

Contents

Plan Your Trip

USA's National Parks
Top 15......................... 4
Need to Know...........18
Month by Month......20
Get Inspired............. 23
Health & Safety 24
Clothing &
Equipment...............26
USA's National
Parks Overview 28
Best Hiking 36
Best Wildlife
Watching.................38
Best Family
Experiences............40
Best Adventures...... 42
USA's National
Parks by Region 44

California   47

Channel Islands 50
Death Valley 56
Joshua Tree 62
Classic Road Trip:
Palm Springs &
Joshua Tree Oases.......68
Kings Canyon...............74
Hike: Mist Falls 80
Classic Hike:
Rae Lakes Loop............84
Lassen Volcanic 88
Pinnacles.................... 94
Redwood..................... 96
Classic Road Trip:
Northern
Redwood Coast...........102
Sequoia.....................108
Hike: Monarch
Lakes.........................112

Hike: General Sherman
Tree to Moro Rock.......114
Yosemite..................... 118
Hike: Vernal &
Nevada Falls 124
Hike: Cathedral
Lakes...........................126
Classic Road Trip:
Yosemite, Sequoia
& Kings Canyon..........130

The
Southwest   137

Arches........................140
Big Bend 146
Classic Road Trip:
Big Bend
Scenic Loop................152
Bryce Canyon.............158
Drive: Scenic
Bryce Canyon.............162
Classic Hike:
Under the Rim Trail 168
Canyonlands 170
Capitol Reef 176
Drive: Highway 24 180
Carlsbad Caverns 184
Grand Canyon............186
Hike: Widforss Trail 192
Hike: Hermit Trail 193
Great Basin 196
Guadalupe
Mountains...................198
Mesa Verde 204
Petrified Forest 210
Saguaro 214
Zion............................216
Drive: Scenic
Zion Canyon 222

Classic Hike:
The Narrows:
Top Down....................226

Alaska
& the Pacific
Northwest   229

Crater Lake 232
Classic Road Trip:
Crater Lake Circuit.... 236
Denali......................... 242
Gates of the Arctic
& Kobuk Valley 254
Glacier Bay 260
Katmai 268
Kenai Fjords 274
Lake Clark 278
Mt Rainier..................280
Classic Road Trip:
Mt Rainier
Scenic Byways 284
North Cascades 292
Olympic 298
Classic Road Trip:
Olympic
Peninsula Loop.......... 304
Wrangell-St Elias 310

Rocky
Mountains   319

Black Canyon
of the Gunnison 322
Glacier 324
Hike: Hidden Lake
Overlook Trail............. 330
Hike: Highline Trail 331
Hike: Sun Point
to Virginia Falls 332

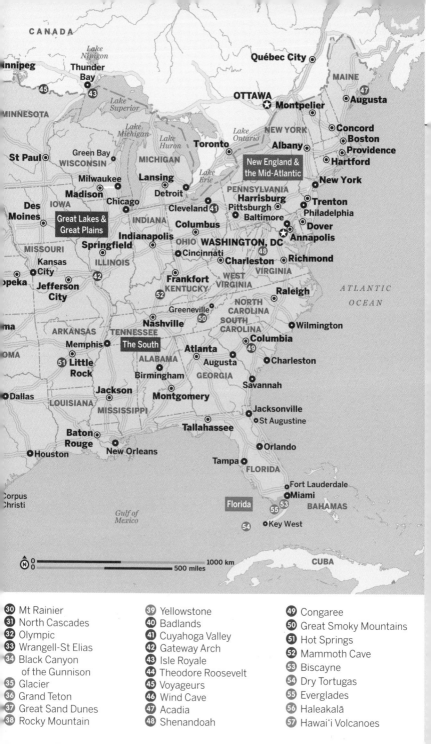

CANADA

Winnipeg
Thunder Bay
45
43
MINNESOTA
Lake Nipigon
Lake Superior
Lake Michigan
Lake Huron

Québec City
MAINE
OTTAWA
Montpelier
Augusta
47
NEW YORK

St Paul
Green Bay
WISCONSIN
MICHIGAN
Toronto
Lake Ontario
Concord
Boston
Albany
Providence
Hartford

Milwaukee
Madison
Chicago
Lansing
Detroit
Lake Erie
New York

**New England &
the Mid-Atlantic**

Des Moines
IOWA
Cleveland
41
PENNSYLVANIA
Harrisburg
Pittsburgh
Trenton
Philadelphia

**Great Lakes &
Great Plains**
INDIANA
Columbus
OHIO
Baltimore
Dover
Annapolis

Kansas City
Topeka
ILLINOIS
MISSOURI
Indianapolis
Springfield
Cincinnati
WASHINGTON, DC
48
Richmond
Charleston
VIRGINIA

Jefferson City
42
Frankfort
KENTUCKY
52
WEST VIRGINIA
Raleigh

Greeneville
50
NORTH CAROLINA

Nashville
TENNESSEE
SOUTH CAROLINA
Wilmington

ARKANSAS
Memphis
The South
Atlanta
Columbia
49
Charleston

51
Little Rock
ALABAMA
Augusta
GEORGIA

Oklahoma
Birmingham
Montgomery
Savannah

Dallas
Jackson
LOUISIANA
MISSISSIPPI
Tallahassee
Jacksonville
St Augustine

Baton Rouge
New Orleans
Orlando

Houston
Tampa
FLORIDA

Corpus Christi
Gulf of Mexico
Florida
Fort Lauderdale
Miami
55
53
BAHAMAS

54
Key West

ATLANTIC OCEAN

CUBA

N
0   500 miles
0   1000 km

30 Mt Rainier
31 North Cascades
32 Olympic
33 Wrangell-St Elias
34 Black Canyon
   of the Gunnison
35 Glacier
36 Grand Teton
37 Great Sand Dunes
38 Rocky Mountain

39 Yellowstone
40 Badlands
41 Cuyahoga Valley
42 Gateway Arch
43 Isle Royale
44 Theodore Roosevelt
45 Voyageurs
46 Wind Cave
47 Acadia
48 Shenandoah

49 Congaree
50 Great Smoky Mountains
51 Hot Springs
52 Mammoth Cave
53 Biscayne
54 Dry Tortugas
55 Everglades
56 Haleakalā
57 Hawai'i Volcanoes

Welcome to USA's National Parks

The USA's national parks are the very essence of America. These carefully protected natural enclaves reflect every facet of this vast, complex and magnificently diverse country.

National parks are America's big backyards. No cross-country road trip would be complete without a visit to at least one of these remarkable natural treasures, rich in unspoiled wilderness, rare wildlife and history.

The National Park Service (NPS) is responsible for the country's glorious parks, which are complemented by a slew of federally protected areas numbering in their thousands.

The parks represent American ideals at their best: the preservation of life and liberty, and the pursuit of happiness for all. That we are able to enjoy these special places today may seem like a matter of course, but the establishment of the national park system was no sure thing. Challenges have been present every step of the way, and many threatened to derail the entire experiment. But, until now, our best instincts have prevailed.

It is testimony to the NPS's diligent protective measures that the landscapes of many parks look much the same as they did centuries ago. From craggy islands off the Atlantic Coast, to prairie grasslands and buffalo herds across the Great Plains, to the Rocky Mountains raising their jagged teeth along the Continental Divide, and onward to the tallest trees on earth – coast redwoods – standing sentinel on Pacific shores, you'll never cease to be amazed by the USA's natural bounty.

In wildness is the preservation of the world.

– *Henry David Thoreau*

Yosemite National Park (p118)
JAVEN/SHUTTERSTOCK ©

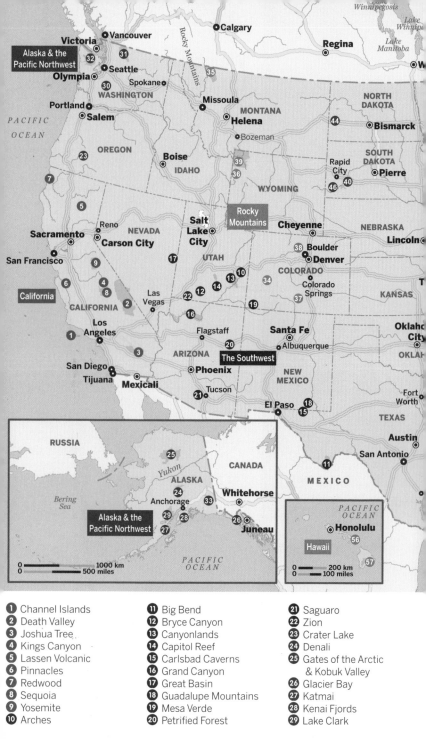

Winnipegosis

Lake Winnipeg
Lake Manitoba

○ Calgary

Rocky Mountains

● Regina

○ W

Victoria ● ○ Vancouver
31
Alaska & the Pacific Northwest
32
● Seattle
Olympia ○
30
WASHINGTON
Spokane ○
35

● Missoula

MONTANA
● Helena
44
● Bismarck

NORTH DAKOTA

Portland ○
● Salem
OREGON

○ Bozeman

● Boise
IDAHO

39
36

WYOMING

Rapid City ○
46 40
● Pierre
SOUTH DAKOTA

PACIFIC OCEAN

23

7

5

Reno ○
NEVADA
Sacramento ●
Carson City
San Francisco ●

Rocky Mountains

Salt Lake City ○

Cheyenne ○
NEBRASKA
Lincoln ○

38 Boulder ○
● Denver
COLORADO

9

6

4
8

California

CALIFORNIA
2

Las Vegas

UTAH

13 10

34

Colorado Springs ○

17

22 12

14

37

KANSAS

16

19

● Santa Fe

Los Angeles ●

Flagstaff ○

20

● Albuquerque

ARIZONA
The Southwest

Oklahoma City ○

San Diego ●
Tijuana ○
○ Mexicali

● Phoenix

3

NEW MEXICO

OKLA

21 ○ Tucson

El Paso ●
18
15

Fort Worth ○

TEXAS

RUSSIA

25

Yukon

CANADA

11

Austin ●

Bering Sea

24
Anchorage ○

29 28
27

ALASKA
33

Whitehorse ○

26
Juneau ●

MEXICO

San Antonio ●

Alaska & the Pacific Northwest

PACIFIC OCEAN

○ Honolulu

Hawaii

56

PACIFIC OCEAN

0 ___ 1000 km
0 ___ 500 miles

0 ___ 200 km
0 ___ 100 miles

57

1 Channel Islands
2 Death Valley
3 Joshua Tree
4 Kings Canyon
5 Lassen Volcanic
6 Pinnacles
7 Redwood
8 Sequoia
9 Yosemite
10 Arches

11 Big Bend
12 Bryce Canyon
13 Canyonlands
14 Capitol Reef
15 Carlsbad Caverns
16 Grand Canyon
17 Great Basin
18 Guadalupe Mountains
19 Mesa Verde
20 Petrified Forest

21 Saguaro
22 Zion
23 Crater Lake
24 Denali
25 Gates of the Arctic & Kobuk Valley
26 Glacier Bay
27 Katmai
28 Kenai Fjords
29 Lake Clark

Drive: Going-to-
the-Sun Road 333
Grand Teton.............. 336
Drive: Hole-in-One 342
Classic Hike:
Teton Crest Trail 346
Great Sand Dunes ... 348
Rocky Mountain....... 354
Yellowstone 362
Hike: Mt Washburn ... 368
Hike: Bunsen
Peak Trail....................370

**Great Lakes
& Great Plains 377**
Badlands 380
Cuyahoga Valley 382
Gateway Arch........... 384
Isle Royale 386
**Theodore
Roosevelt.................. 388**

Voyageurs................. 392
Wind Cave 394

**New England
& the
Mid-Atlantic 399**
Acadia......................402
Classic Road Trip:
Acadia 408
Shenandoah.............412

The South 417
Congaree 420
**Great Smoky
Mountains 422**
Hike: Alum
Cave Bluffs 428
Hike: Laurel Falls 429
Drive: Newfound
Gap Road 430

Drive: Roaring Forks
Motor Nature Trail...... 431
Classic Hike:
Charlies Bunion
& Kephart Loop 434
Hot Springs 436
Mammoth Cave 438

Florida 441
Biscayne 444
Dry Tortugas.............446
Everglades................448

Hawaii 453
Haleakalā 456
Hawai'i Volcanoes 466

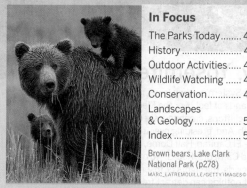

In Focus
The Parks Today........ 480
History 482
Outdoor Activities 488
Wildlife Watching 494
Conservation............. 499
Landscapes
& Geology 502
Index 508

Brown bears, Lake Clark
National Park (p278)
MARC_LATREMOUILLE/GETTY IMAGES©

Special Features
Diverse Landscapes.....92
Incredible
Rock Formations........ 212
Alaska's Historical
Monuments 252
Yellowstone's
Thermal Features....... 374
Great Plains
Wildlife 390
Hawaii's Other
Protected Areas 476

Plan Your Trip
USA's National Parks Top 15

EASTVILLAGE IMAGES/SHUTTERSTOCK ©

Yosemite Valley, Yosemite

In Yosemite (p118), the National Park System's crown jewel, massive granite rock formations tower thousands of feet over the Merced River. Wild creeks plummet from the clifftops, creating a spectacle of waterfalls unlike anywhere on earth. And, presiding over it all, iconic and mighty sentinels of rock – El Capitan, Half Dome, the Royal Arches, the Three Brothers and Cathedral Rocks. No matter what you hear about the summer crowds, the sights of Yosemite Valley are so astonishing that almost nothing can detract from the experience. Left: Yosemite Falls (p120); Right: Bear cub

WITHDRAWN

Glacier

1

Going-to-the-Sun Road, Glacier

Going-to-the-Sun Rd (p333) in Glacier National Park offers steely-nerved motorists the drive of their life. Chiseled out of the mountainside and punctuated by some of the sheerest and most vertiginous drop-offs in the US, this 53-mile, vista-laden strip of asphalt offers drivers access to some of the most astounding sights in the Rockies.

2

Sunset, Grand Canyon

Of all the places to watch the sunset in the world, few can measure up to the Grand Canyon (p186). Lipan Point is one of the finest spots to do it. Or, if you're feeling lazy, simply grab a drink and a porch swing on the patio of El Tovar lodge, where you can watch the sunset in style.

Snake River, Grand Teton

Spilling down from Jackson Lake beneath the mighty Teton Range, the wild and scenic Snake River (p338) offers some of the most dramatic mountain scenery in the country. Not only are its waters the perfect place to gawk at the Tetons themselves (including the 13,775ft Grand Teton), but they're prime for wildlife watching. Numerous outfitters offer float trips ranging from gentle to giant water. No matter which you choose, prepare to be awed.

Rock Climbing, Joshua Tree

Whether you're a rock-climbing novice or a bouldering goddess, you'll find heaven above earth when you take to the granite in Joshua Tree (p62). With more than 8000 established climbing routes, this is truly one of the world's rock meccas. There are classes for beginners, and the 400-plus climbing formations offer endless fun for seasoned enthusiasts. Amid the giant boulders and sweaty climbers, the bizarre Joshua trees themselves lend the scenery an otherworldly character.

TUPUNGATO/SHUTTERSTOCK ©

Longs Peak, Rocky Mountain

Whether you hike to the top of its 14,259ft summit or just ogle its glaciated slopes from below, Longs Peak (p356) is truly a feast for the eyes. Those who attempt the ascent via the Keyhole Route must first brave the hair-raising Ledges, before conquering the Trough and inching across the Narrows, which finally give way to the (whew!) Homestretch.

6

The Narrows, Zion

Check your claustrophobia at the door and prepare to get wet on this hike up the Virgin River into a 2000ft-deep slot canyon (p216). As you make your way upriver, the cliffs press inward, towering higher and higher until, finally, you reach Wall Street, where the width of the canyon narrows to under 30ft.

7

Wildlife Watching, Yellowstone

No matter how many nature shows you've seen, nothing can prepare you for the first time you spot a moose in the wild. And in Yellowstone (p362), if you don't see a moose – or a bison or a herd of elk or a bear – you probably have your eyes closed. On par with the Galápagos, the Serengeti and Brazil's Pantanal, Yellowstone is one of the world's premier wildlife-watching destinations. Big mammals are everywhere. The knowledge that grizzlies, wolves and mountain lions are among them simply adds to the rush.

JESS KRAFT/SHUTTERSTOCK ©

IMP TRAVELLER/SHUTTERSTOCK ©

9

Sunrise, Cadillac Mountain, Acadia

Catching the country's 'first sunrise' from the top of Cadillac Mountain (p403) is, hands down, one of the finest ways to kick off a day. At 1530ft, Cadillac Mountain is the highest point on Maine's Mount Desert Island, and the views over the Atlantic are sublime. The island is one of the easternmost points in the USA, and, while it's technically not the *first* place that catches the morning sun, we prefer to do what everyone else up top does at sunrise: ignore the technicalities and bliss out.

FILIP FUXA/SHUTTERSTOCK ©

PEERASITH PATRICK TRIRATPADOONGPHOL/SHUTTERSTOCK ©

CAVAN IMAGES/GETTY IMAGES ©

Bryce Amphitheater, Bryce Canyon

Proof that nature has a wild imagination, hoodoos are one of the strangest formations on the planet. From the rim of southern Utah's Bryce Amphitheater (p158) you can look down upon thousands of these bizarre, ancient rock spires as they tower out of the so-called Silent City, a conglomeration of hoodoos so vast that you'd be forgiven for thinking you'd landed on another planet.

10

Hoh Rain Forest, Olympic

Embrace the rain! It's what makes this temperate rainforest (p298), in all its Tolkienesque beauty, one of the greenest places in North America. With an average rainfall of up to 170in (that's 14ft), it is also one of the wettest. This tremendous amount of water creates a forest covered in mosses, lichens and ferns, with a canopy so dense the forest floor seems trapped in the perpetual lowlight of dusk. Pack your rain jacket and watch for the Roosevelt elk.

Paddling, Everglades

The country's third-largest national park (p448) is a paddler's paradise, with kayak and canoe 'trails' meandering through mangrove swamps and freshwater marshes that teem with wildlife. Crocodiles, alligators, turtles, cormorants, herons, egrets and fish are just some of the wildlife that boaters come across while paddling around this subtropical park. Thanks to the National Park Service's handy (and free) kayak and canoe trail maps, navigating the waters is fairly straightforward.

CHERI ALGUIRE/SHUTTERSTOCK ©

Cliff Palace, Mesa Verde

This grand engineering achievement, the largest cliff dwelling in North America (p204), has 217 rooms and 23 kivas, and once provided shelter for 250 to 300 Ancestral Puebloans. To access it, visitors must climb down a stone stairway and four 10ft ladders, as part of an hour-long ranger-led tour. It's a great place to puzzle out the clues left by its former inhabitants – who vacated the site in AD 1300 for reasons still not fully understood.

13

SERGEY YECHIKOV/SHUTTERSTOCK ©

Kayaking, Glacier Bay

Blue-water paddling – kayaking in Alaskan coastal areas, which are characterized by extreme tidal fluctuations, cold water and the possibility of high winds and waves – is the means of escape into areas such as Muir Inlet in Glacier Bay (p260). Everywhere you turn, a tide-water glacier seems to be calving in this grand park, where you may also see humpback whales, black bears, seals and bald eagles.

14

CRACKERCLIPS STOCK MEDIA/SHUTTERSTOCK ©

Wildflower Season, Mt Rainier

Mt Rainier (p280) is covered in glaciers, and the high meadows are blanketed in snow for nearly nine months of the year. Once the snow finally melts and the meadows are exposed, wildflowers explode into bloom. Avalanche lilies, beargrass, bog orchids, wood nymphs and dozens of other flowers turn the slopes of the Cascade's highest mountain into a rainbow of color.

15

USA'S NATIONAL PARKS TOP 15 PLAN YOUR TRIP

Plan Your Trip
Need to Know

When to Go

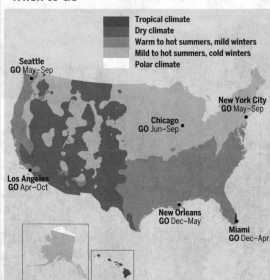

Tropical climate
Dry climate
Warm to hot summers, mild winters
Mild to hot summers, cold winters
Polar climate

Seattle
GO May–Sep

New York City
GO May–Sep

Chicago
GO Jun–Sep

Los Angeles
GO Apr–Oct

New Orleans
GO Dec–May

Miami
GO Dec–Apr

High Season (mid-Jun–mid-Sep)

- High-country sectors in the Rockies, Sierras and Cascades are guaranteed to be open.

- July and August are crowded; reservations are a must.

Shoulder (May–mid-Jun & mid-Sep–Oct)

- Waterfalls in Yosemite and Great Smoky Mountains are at their peak in spring.

- High-elevation roads are still closed in spring.

Low Season (Nov–Apr)

- Cross-country skiing and snowshoeing are excellent in the Rockies and Sierras.

- High season for the subtropical Everglades.

Entry Fees

7-day pass from free to per vehicle/pedestrian $35/20.

America the Beautiful Annual Pass

$80 per vehicle valid for all national parks for 12 months from purchase. Buy through National Park Service (☎888-275-8747, ext 3; www.nps.gov).

ATMs

Most parks have at least one ATM; widely available in gateway towns.

Credit Cards

Major credit cards widely accepted; Forest Service, BLM and other campgrounds accept cash and/or checks only.

Cell Phones

Coverage inside parks is spotty at best.

Wifi

Some park lodges have wireless. Outside the parks, most cafes and hotels offer free wireless. Chain hotels sometimes charge.

Tipping

Tip restaurant servers 15–20%; porters $2 per bag; hotel maids $2 to $5 per night.

Advance Planning

Twelve months before Reserve campsites and historic lodge accommodations.

Six months before Reserve hotel rooms in satellite towns if visiting in summer. Book flights.

Three months before Start training if planning to backpack. If you haven't reserved sleeping arrangements, do so.

One month before Secure rental car. Take your own car in for a safety inspection and tune-up if planning a long drive.

Useful Websites

Lonely Planet (www.lonelyplanet.com/usa) Destination information, hotel bookings, traveler forum and more.

National Park Service (NPS; www.nps.gov) Gateway to America's greatest natural treasures, its national parks.

RoadsideAmerica.com (www.roadsideamerica.com) All those weird roadside attractions!

The National Parks (www.pbs.org/nationalparks) Online portal of Ken Burn's national park PBS classic.

Accommodations

Campsites Reservation and first-come, first-served sites both available in all parks. Flush toilets are common, hot showers are not. Full hookups for RVs usually found outside parks.

Park Lodges Wonderful experience. Usually lack TV; some have wi-fi.

B&Bs Available in gateway towns outside parks; often excellent and usually include wi-fi.

Hotels Occasionally inside parks; most in gateway towns. Nearly all have wi-fi.

Arriving at a National Park

Camping If you're going for a first-come, first-served site, head straight to the campground. Try to arrive no later than mid-morning Friday.

Daily Costs

Budget: Less than $150

- Camping & RV sites: $15–45
- Park entrance fee: free-$35
- Cheap self-catering food or cafe/diner meal $6-15
- Free park shuttles

Midrange: $150–250

- Double room in midrange hotel: $100–250
- Popular restaurant dinner for two: $30–60
- Car hire per day: from $30

Top end: More than $250

- Double room in a top-end hotel: from $200
- Dinner in a top restaurant: $60–100

Information Pick up a park newspaper at the entry kiosk and hang onto it; they're packed with useful information.

Parking People not spending the night inside a park will find parking difficult. Arrive early, park and take free shuttles whenever possible.

Visitor Centers Best places to start exploring the parks. Purchase books and maps, ask rangers questions, check weather reports and trail and road conditions.

Getting Around

Car Most convenient way to travel between the parks. A few park roads are gravel. Traffic inside some parks can be horrendous.

Park Shuttles Many parks have excellent shuttle systems with stops at major visitor sites and trailheads.

Bicycles Some parks have rentals. Good for getting around developed areas. Elsewhere, roads can be steep and shoulders narrow.

Plan Your Trip
Month by Month

January & February

Strap on your snowshoes or cross-country skis and enjoy the white winter magic in Yellowstone, Glacier and Grand Teton. Joshua Tree is lovely, and the subtropical Everglades are sublime.

⚘ Snowshoeing

Leave the crowds behind and take to the trails in snowshoes. Seeing the high-elevation and northern parks when they're blanketed in snow is a magical experience. Rangers at some of the parks even host guided snowshoe hikes.

March

The biting cold of winter fades from the desert parks, and wildflowers begin to bloom at lower elevations. Snow activities are still good at high elevations.

⚘ Frozen Dead Guy Days

Join the living in Nederland, CO (near Rocky Mountains National Park) and celebrate a dead guy – a Norwegian named Grandpa Bredo Morstoel – who is cryogenically frozen in a local lab, patiently awaiting reanimation. The festival (www.frozendeadguydays.org) includes music and coffin races.

April

Wildflowers are in full swing at lower elevations, and waterfalls begin pumping at full force with the beginning of the snowmelt. Weather in the desert parks is beautiful.

☉ Spring Wildflowers

Wildflowers put on dazzling springtime displays at the lower-elevation parks, especially at Death Valley, Shenandoah, Great Smoky Mountains, Zion and sometimes Joshua Tree. Check the National Park Service websites for wildflower walks, talks and celebrations.

☉ Yosemite Waterfalls

Most people who visit Yosemite in July and August have no idea – until they get there – that the Valley's famous falls are but a trickle of their springtime selves. April, May and June are the best months to see the falls in full force (pictured).

23

🏃 National Park Week

For an entire week every April, admission to the national parks is free. Exactly which week it will fall on is announced early in the year. Many parks also host free activities.

May

Temperatures in Zion, Bryce, Grand Canyon, Yosemite, Death Valley and Joshua Tree are delightful. The summer crowds have yet to materialize, waterfalls are at their peak, and river and stream levels are high.

☆ Joshua Tree Music Festival

Over a long weekend, numerous bands rock Joshua Tree Lake Campground during a family-friendly indie music fest (www.josh uatreemusicfestival.com). It's followed by a soulful roots celebration in mid-October.

June

It's still possible to beat the crowds of summer in early June. By late June, the parks are jammed but the weather is stellar in many of them. Upper-elevation roads are still closed in the Sierras and Rocky Mountains.

★ Best Events

Cody Stampede, July
Spring Wildflowers, April
Joshua Tree Music Festival, May
Grand Teton Music, July
Frozen Dead Guy Days, March

☆ Utah Shakespeare Festival

Near Zion National Park, Cedar City kicks off its three-month-long Shakespeare Festival (www.bard.org) in late June. Activities include top-notch performances, classes, literary seminars, magic shows and more.

July

High elevation sectors of the Rockies, Sierras and Cascades begin opening. It's prime hiking time in the high-country, where wildflowers are at their peak. Desert parks, including Grand Canyon, are sweltering.

☉ Cody Stampede

In Yellowstone's gateway communities, rodeo is the major cultural event of the year.

Cowboys take to the saddle throughout June, July and August in various communities. The largest rodeos are the Cody Stampede (www.codystampederodeo.com; pictured p21) and the Wild West Yellowstone Rodeo (www.yellowstonerodeo.com).

✢ North American Indian Days
In the second week of July, head to the Blackfeet Indian Reservation, immediately east of Glacier National Park, for traditional drumming, dancing and the annual crowning of the year's Miss Blackfeet. The four day festival (www.blackfeetcountry.com) is a wonderful display of Blackfeet traditions.

☉ Summer Wildflowers
In high-elevation parks such as Glacier, Rocky Mountain, Mt Rainier, Yellowstone, Grant Teton and parts of Yosemite, wildflowers bloom intensely during the short growing season between snows.

✢ Grand Teton Music Festival
Over 40 classical music concerts are held throughout the Jackson Hole region. Everything from children's concerts to full orchestras are on the menu. Concerts take place almost nightly throughout July and into August. See www.gtmf.org for calendars and to purchase tickets.

August
Hello crowds! It's the height of summer, it's blazing hot, and every hotel and campsite is reserved. First-come-first-served campgrounds are your best bet. Head to the high-country, where the weather is superb.

✢ Christmas in August
Join the caroling in one of the parks' oddest celebrations, Yellowstone's Christmas in August (celebrated on the 25th). The event dates back to the turn of the last century, when a freak August snowstorm stranded a group of visitors in the Upper Geyser Basin.

September
The crowds begin to thin out and by the end of the month things are pretty quiet. If you don't mind brisk evenings, this can be a beautiful time to visit the parks. High-country sectors close by the end of the month.

✢ Mountain Life Festival
Participate in hearth cooking demonstrations and help make historic farm staples like hominy, apple butter, apple cider and soap. The event is celebrated every year in mid-September at the Mountain Farm Museum in Great Smoky National Park.

October
From Yosemite to the Great Smoky Mountains, fall color is nothing short of fabulous in many of the parks. Crowds are nonexistent and the temperatures are dropping quickly. High-elevation sectors are closed.

✢ Pioneer Days
On the third weekend in October, the town of Twentynine Palms, near Joshua Tree National Park, celebrates Pioneer Days (www.visit29.org) with an Old West-themed carnival featuring a parade, arm-wrestling and a giant chili dinner.

November
Winter is creeping in quickly. The best parks to visit are those in southern Utah, Arizona and the California deserts, where the weather is cool but still beautiful.

✢ Death Valley '49ers
In early or mid-November, Furnace Creek hosts this historical encampment (www.deathvalley49ers.org), featuring cowboy poetry, campfire sing-alongs and a gold-panning contest. Show up early to watch the pioneer wagons come thunderin' in.

December
Winter is well under way in most of the parks. High-elevation roads and park sectors are closed, and visitor center and business hours are reduced. Think snowshoeing and cross-country skiing.

✢ National Audubon Society Christmas Bird Count
Every year around Christmastime, thousands of people take to the wilds to look for and record birds for the Audubon Society's annual survey. Many of the parks organize a count and rely on volunteers to help. Check www.nps.gov for information.

Plan Your Trip
Get Inspired

NICOLASDECORTE/SHUTTERSTOCK ©

Read

Our National Parks (1901)
The words of John Muir inspired a nation to embrace national parks.

Ranger Confidential (2010)
Former park ranger Andrea Lankford tells you what it takes to fill a ranger's shoes.

Lost in My Own Backyard (2004) Chuckle your way around Yellowstone with Tim Cahill.

A Sand County Almanac (1949) Aldo Leopold's nature classic embodies the conservation ethic that lies at the heart of our national parks.

In the National Parks (2010) Reading Ansel Adams is the next best thing to being there.

Watch

American Experience: Ansel Adams (2004) Inspire your snapshots with this PBS documentary.

Vacation (1983) Perfect comedy kick-starter for any family vacation.

Into the Wild (2007) Follow Chris McCandless as he kisses his possessions goodbye and hitchhikes to Alaska.

Wild (2014) A recently divorced woman throws caution to the wind to undertake a hike of self-discovery on the Pacific Crest Trail.

The National Parks, America's Best Idea (2009) Ken Burns' 12-hour PBS miniseries is a must.

Listen

Classic Old-Time Fiddle (2007) Perfect fiddle compilation for trips to Great Smoky Mountains and Shenandoah.

Joshua Tree (1987) Crank up this U2 classic, whether you're heading to Joshua Tree or not.

Beautiful Maladies (1998) Nothing spells 'road trip' like a good Tom Waits tune.

This Land is Your Land: The Asch Recordings, Vol. 1 (1997) Woodie Guthrie sings everything from 'This Land is Your Land' to 'The Car Song'.

Anthology of American Folk Music (1952) Dig into the blues, folk and country roots of America with Harry Smith's iconic collection.

Joshua Tree National Park (p62)

Plan Your Trip
Health & Safety

Before You Go

If you require medications bring them in their original, labeled containers. A signed and dated letter from your physician describing your medical conditions and medications, including generic names, is a good idea. If carrying syringes or needles, a physician's letter is a necessity.

Some of the walks in this book are physically demanding and most require a reasonable level of fitness, even the easy or moderate walks. If you're aiming for the demanding walks, training is essential.

If you have any medical problems, or are concerned about your health in any way, it's a good idea to have a full checkup before you start walking.

In the Parks

Visiting city dwellers will need to keep their wits about them in order to minimize the chances of suffering an avoidable accident or tragedy. Dress appropriately, tell people where you are going, plan a hike that matches your skills and experience and,

above all, respect the wilderness and the inherent dangers that it conceals.

Crime is far more common in big cities than in sparsely populated national parks. Nevertheless, use common sense: lock valuables in the trunk of your vehicle, especially if you're parking it at a trailhead overnight, and never leave anything worth stealing in your tent.

Walk Safety – Basic Rules

○ Allow plenty of time to accomplish a walk before dark, particularly when daylight hours are shorter.

○ Study the route carefully before setting out, noting the possible escape routes and the point of no return (where it's quicker to continue than to turn back). Monitor your progress during the day against the time estimated for the walk, and keep an eye on the weather.

○ It's wise not to walk alone. Always leave details of your intended route, number of people in your group and expected return time with someone responsible before you set off, and let that person know when you return.

o Before setting off, make sure you have a relevant map, compass and whistle, and that you know the weather forecast for the area for the next 24 hours. In the Rockies always carry extra warm, dry layers of clothing and plenty of emergency high-energy food.

Avalanches

Avalanches are a threat during and following storms, in high winds and during temperature changes, particularly when it warms in spring. Educate yourself about the dangers of avalanches before setting out into the backcountry. Signs of avalanche activity include felled trees and slides.

If you are caught in an avalanche, your chance of survival depends on your ability to keep yourself above the flowing snow and your companions' ability to rescue you. The probability of survival decreases rapidly after half an hour, so the party must be self-equipped, with each member carrying an avalanche beacon, a sectional probe and a collapsible shovel.

Altitude

To prevent acute mountain sickness:

o Ascend slowly – have frequent rest days, spending two to three nights at each rise of 3281ft (1000m). If you trek to a high alti-tude, acclimatization takes place gradually and you are less likely to be affected than if you fly directly to high altitude.

o It is always wise to sleep at a lower altitude than the greatest height reached during the day, if possible. Also, once above 9843ft (3000m), care should be taken not to increase the sleeping altitude by more than 984ft (300m) per day.

★ Water Purification

To ensure you are getting safe, clean drinking water in the backcountry you have three basic options:

Boiling Water is considered safe to drink if it has been boiled for at least a minute.

Chemical Purification You can choose from various chlorine or iodine products on the market. Read the instructions carefully first, be aware of expiration dates and check you are not allergic to either chemical.

Filtration Devices can pump water through microscopic filters and take out potentially harmful organisms. If carrying a filter, take care it doesn't get damaged in transit, read the instructions carefully and always filter the cleanest water you can find.

o Drink extra fluids. The mountain air is dry and cold and moisture is lost as you breathe; evaporation of sweat may occur unnoticed and result in dehydration.

o Eat light, high-carbohydrate meals for more energy.

o Avoid alcohol and sedatives.

Rescue & Evacuation

If someone in your group is injured or falls ill and can't move, leave somebody with them while another one or more goes for help. They should take clear written details of the location and condition of the victim, and of helicopter landing conditions. If there are only two of you, leave the injured person with as much warm clothing, food and water as it's sensible to spare, plus the whistle and torch. Mark the position with something conspicuous – an orange bivvy bag, or perhaps a large stone cross on the ground.

Mesa Arch (p171), Canyonlands National Park

Plan Your Trip
Clothing & Equipment

Deciding what gear is essential for a trip and what will only weigh you down is an art. Don't forget essentials, but be ruthless when packing, since every ounce counts when you're lugging your gear up a steep mountain or kayaking down a sweltering hot channel in the Everglades.

Layering

A secret of comfortable walking is to wear several layers of light clothing, which you can easily take off or put on as you warm up or cool down. Most walkers use three main layers: a base layer next to the skin; an insulating layer; and an outer-shell layer for protection from wind, rain and snow.

For the upper body, the base layer is typically a T-shirt of synthetic fabric or merino wool. The insulating layer retains heat next to your body, and is usually a (windproof) fleece jacket or sweater. The outer shell consists of a waterproof jacket that also protects against cold wind.

For the lower body, the layers generally consist of either shorts or loose-fitting trousers, thermal underwear ('long johns') and waterproof overtrousers.

When purchasing outdoor clothing, one of the most practical fabrics is merino wool – it's warm, breathable and moisture-wicking. Plus it's not as prone to retaining odors (a fact sure to be appreciated by your hiking companions).

Sun Protection

In the desert and at high altitude you can sunburn in less than an hour, even through cloud cover. Use sunscreen (with a SPF of 30 or higher), especially on skin not typically exposed to sun, reapply it regularly, and wear long sleeves. Be sure to apply sunscreen to young children and to wear wide-brimmed hats.

Waterproof Shells

Jackets should be made of a breathable, waterproof fabric, with a hood that is roomy enough to cover headwear, but that still allows peripheral vision. Other handy accessories include a large map pocket and a heavy-gauge zip protected by a storm flap.

Waterproof pants are best with slits for pocket access and long leg zips so that you can pull them on and off over your boots.

Footwear

Running shoes are OK for walks that are graded easy or moderate. However, you'll probably appreciate, if not need, the support and protection provided by hiking boots for more demanding walks.

Buy boots in warm conditions or go for a walk before trying them on, so that your feet can expand slightly, as they would on a hike. It's also a good idea to carry a pair of sandals to wear at night or at rest stops, or when fording waterways.

Gaiters help to keep your feet dry in wet weather and on boggy ground; they can also deflect small stones or sand and maintain leg warmth. The best are made of strong fabric, with a robust zip protected by a flap, and secure easily around the foot.

Walking socks should be free of ridged seams in the toes and heels.

Backpack & Daypacks

For day walks, a day pack (30L to 40L) will usually suffice, but for multiday walks you will need a backpack of between 45L and 90L capacity. Even if the manufacturer claims your pack is waterproof, use heavy-duty liners.

Bear Spray

Most of the hikes/activities in the parks are also in bear country. As a last resort, bear spray (pepper spray) has been used effectively to deter aggressive bears, and park authorities often recommend that you equip yourself with a canister when venturing into backcountry. Be sure to familiarize yourself

with the manufacturer's instructions before use, and only use as a last resort (ie on a charging bear approximately 30ft to 50ft/9m to 15m away from you). Most shops in or around the parks stock bear spray, which sells for approximately US$45; some rent it by the day. It is best kept close at hand on a belt around your waist.

Tent

A three-season tent will fulfill most walkers' requirements. The floor and the outer shell, or fly, should have taped or sealed seams and covered zips to stop leaks. The weight can be as low as 2.2lb (1kg) for a stripped-down, low-profile tent, and up to 6.6lb (3kg) for a roomy, luxury, four-season model.

Dome- and tunnel-shaped tents handle windy conditions better than flat-sided tents.

Map & Compass

You should always carry a good map of the area in which you are walking, and know how to read it. Before setting off on your walk, ensure that you are aware of the contour interval, the map symbols, the magnetic declination (difference between true and grid north), plus the main ridge and river systems in the area and the general direction in which you are heading. On the trail, try to identify major landforms such as mountain ranges and valleys, and locate them on your map to familiarize yourself with the geography.

Buy a compass and learn how to use it. The attraction of magnetic north varies in different parts of the world, so compasses need to be balanced accordingly. Compass manufacturers have divided the world into five zones. Make sure your compass is balanced for your destination zone. There are also 'universal' compasses on the market that can be used anywhere in the world.

Grand Canyon National Park (p186)

Plan Your Trip
USA's National Parks Overview

NAME	STATE	ENTRANCE FEE
Acadia National Park (p402)	Maine	7-day pass per vehicle $30
Arches National Park (p140)	Utah	7-day pass per vehicle $30
Badlands National Park (p380)	South Dakota	7-day pass per vehicle $20
Big Bend National Park (p146)	Texas	7-day pass per vehicle $25
Biscayne National Park (p444)	Florida	Free
Black Canyon of the Gunnison National Park (p322)	Colorado	7-day pass per vehicle $20
Bryce Canyon National Park (p158)	Utah	7-day pass per vehicle $35
Canyonlands National Park (p170)	Utah	7-day pass per vehicle $30
Capitol Reef National Park (p176)	Utah	7-day pass per vehicle $15
Carlsbad Caverns National Park (p184)	New Mexico	3-day pass per adult/child $12/free
Channel Islands National Park (p50)	California	Free
Congaree National Park (p420)	South Carolina	Free

DESCRIPTION	GREAT FOR...
The only national park in New England encompasses an unspoiled wilderness of undulating coastal mountains, towering sea cliffs, surf-pounded beaches and quiet ponds.	
Giant sweeping arcs of sandstone frame snowy peaks and desert landscapes; explore the park's namesake formations in a red-rock wonderland.	
This otherworldly landscape, softened by its rainbow hues, is a spectacle of sheer walls and spikes stabbing the dry air.	
Traversing Big Bend's 1252 sq miles, you come to appreciate what 'big' really means. This is a land of incredible diversity, and vast enough to allow a lifetime of discovery.	
A portion of the world's third-largest reef sits here off the coast of Florida, along with mangrove forests and the Florida Keys.	
No other canyon in America combines the narrow openings, sheer walls and dizzying depths of the Black Canyon.	
Bryce Canyon's sights are nothing short of otherworldly: repeated freezes and thaws have eroded soft sandstone and limestone into a landscape that's utterly unique.	
A forbidding and beautiful maze of red-rock fins, bridges, needles, spires, craters, mesas and buttes, Canyonlands is a crumbling, decaying beauty – a vision of ancient earth.	
Giant slabs of chocolate-red rock and sweeping yellow sandstone domes dominate the landscape of Capitol Reef, which Freemont Indians called the 'Land of the Sleeping Rainbow.'	
Scores of wondrous caves hide under the hills at this unique national park. The cavern formations are an ethereal wonderland of stalactites and fantastical geological features.	
Tossed like lost pearls off the coast, the Channel Islands are California's last outpost of civilization; the islands have earned themselves the nickname 'California's Galápagos.'	
The lush trees growing here are some of the tallest in the eastern USA, forming one of the highest temperate deciduous forest canopies left in the world.	

NAME	STATE	ENTRANCE FEE
Crater Lake National Park (p232)	Oregon	7-day pass per vehicle $25
Cuyahoga Valley National Park (p382)	Ohio	Free
Death Valley National Park (p56)	California	7-day pass per vehicle $35
Denali National Park (p242)	Alaska	7-day pass per adult/child $10/free
Dry Tortugas National Park (p446)	Florida	7-day pass per person $15
Everglades National Park (p448)	Florida	7-day pass per vehicle $25
Gates of the Arctic & Kobuk Valley National Parks (p254)	Alaska	Free
Gateway Arch National Park (p384)	Missouri	Free
Glacier Bay National Park (p260)	Alaska	Free
Glacier National Park (p324)	Montana	7-day pass per vehicle $35
Grand Canyon National Park (p186)	Arizona	7-day pass per vehicle $35
Grand Teton National Park (p336)	Wyoming	7-day pass per vehicle $35
Great Basin National Park (p196)	Nevada	Free
Great Sand Dunes National Park (p348)	Colorado	7-day pass per vehicle $20
Great Smoky Mountains National Park (p422)	North Carolina & Tennessee	Free

DESCRIPTION	GREAT FOR...
The gloriously blue waters of Crater Lake reflect surrounding mountain peaks like a giant dark-blue mirror, making for spectacular photographs and breathtaking panoramas.	
Along the winding Cuyahoga River, between Cleveland and Akron, this park is one of Ohio's nicest surprises.	
The name itself evokes all that is harsh and hellish, yet closer inspection reveals water-sculpted canyons, windswept sand dunes, palm-shaded oases, jagged mountains and wildlife aplenty.	
The park is probably your best chance in the Interior (if not in the entire state) of seeing a grizzly bear, moose or caribou.	
Your efforts to get here (by boat or plane only) will be rewarded with amazing snorkeling, diving, bird-watching and stargazing.	
This is not just a wetland, or a swamp, or a lake, or a river, or a prairie, or a grassland – it is all of the above.	
These parks are part of a contiguous wilderness harboring no roads and a population of precisely zero.	
The USA's newest national park is also one of its smallest, but its main attraction, the Gateway Arch, is the largest manmade monument in the US.	
Seven tidewater glaciers spill out of the mountains and fill the sea with icebergs of all shapes, sizes and shades of blue.	
Glacier is the only place in the lower 48 states where grizzly bears still roam in abundance, and smart park management has kept the place accessible yet at the same time authentically wild.	
The Grand Canyon embodies the scale and splendor of the American West, captured in its dramatic vistas and inner canyons.	
Simply put, this is sublime and crazy terrain, crowned by the dagger-edged Grand (13,770ft).	
Rising abruptly from the desert, and dominating Great Basin National Park, 13,063ft Wheeler Peak creates an awesome range of life zones and landscapes within a very compact area.	
Landscapes collide in a shifting sea of sand at Great Sand Dunes National Park, making you wonder whether a spaceship has whisked you to another planet.	
The iconic Great Smoky Mountains National Park offers visitors a chance to experience deep, mysterious old-growth forests.	

NAME	STATE	ENTRANCE FEE
Guadalupe Mountains National Park (p198)	Texas	7-day pass per adult/child $5/free
Haleakalā National Park (p456)	Hawaii	7-day pass per vehicle $25
Hawai'i Volcanoes National Park (p466)	Hawaii	7-day pass per vehicle $25
Hot Springs National Park (p436)	Arkansas	Free
Isle Royale National Park (p386)	Michigan	1-day pass per person $7
Joshua Tree National Park (p62)	California	7-day pass per vehicle $30
Katmai National Park (p268)	Alaska	Free
Kenai Fjords National Park (p274)	Alaska	Free
Kings Canyon National Park (p74)	California	7-day pass per vehicle $35
Lake Clark National Park (p278)	Alaska	Free
Lassen Volcanic National Park (p88)	California	7-day pass per vehicle $25 ($10 in winter)
Mammoth Cave National Park (p438)	Kentucky	Free; cave tours $6-60
Mesa Verde National Park (p204)	Colorado	7-day pass per vehicle $15-20
Mount Rainier National Park (p280)	Washington	7-day pass per vehicle $30
North Cascades National Park (p292)	Washington	Free

DESCRIPTION	GREAT FOR...
Guadalupe Mountains National Park is a Texas high spot, both literally and figuratively. At 8749ft, Guadalupe Peak is the highest point in the Lone Star State.	
It's impossible not to be awed by the raw beauty of this ancient place, a haven for wildlife and surefooted hikers.	
This fantastic park dramatically reminds you that nature is very much alive and in perpetual motion.	
Hot Springs borders a city that has made an industry out of the park's major resource: mineral-rich waters.	
This is certainly the place to go for peace and quiet; the 1200 moose creeping through the forest are all yours.	
Like figments from a Dr Seuss book, Joshua trees welcome visitors to this park where the Sonora and Mojave Deserts converge.	
Stand spine-tinglingly close to 1000lb brown bears, who use their formidable power to paw giant salmon out of the river.	
Crowning this park is the massive Harding Ice Field; from it, tidewater glaciers pour down, carving the coast into fjords.	
Kings Canyon is one of North America's deepest canyons, plunging over 8000ft.	
An awesome array of tundra-covered hills, mountains, glaciers, coastline, the largest lakes in the state, and two active volcanoes.	
Anchoring the southernmost link in the Cascades' chain of volcanoes, this alien landscape bubbles over with roiling mud pots, noxious sulfur vents, steamy fumaroles, colorful cinder cones and crater lakes.	
With hidden underground rivers and more than 400 miles of explored terrain, the world's longest cave system shows off sci-fi-looking stalactites and stalagmites up close.	
Shrouded in mystery, Mesa Verde is a fascinating, if slightly eerie place, with a complex of cliff dwellings, some accessed by sheer climbs.	
Mt Rainier (elevation 14,411ft) is the USA's fourth-highest peak (outside Alaska) and arguably its most awe-inspiring.	
The lightly trodden North Cascades National Park has no settlements, no overnight accommodations and one unpaved road.	

NAME	STATE	ENTRANCE FEE
Olympic National Park (p298)	Washington	7-day pass per vehicle $30
Petrified Forest National Park (p210)	Arizona	7-day pass per vehicle $20
Pinnacles National Park (p94)	California	7-day pass per vehicle $30
Redwood National Park (p96)	California	Free
Rocky Mountain National Park (p354)	Colorado	7-day pass per vehicle $35
Saguaro National Park (p214)	Arizona	7-day pass per vehicle $15
Sequoia National Park (p108)	California	7-day pass per vehicle $35
Shenandoah National Park (p412)	Virginia	7-day pass per vehicle $30
Theodore Roosevelt National Park (p388)	North Dakota	7-day pass per vehicle $30
Voyageurs National Park (p392)	Minnesota	Free
Wind Cave National Park (p394)	South Dakota	Free
Wrangell-St Elias National Park (p310)	Alaska	Free
Yellowstone National Park (p362)	Wyoming	7-day pass per vehicle $35
Yosemite National Park (p118)	California	7-day pass per vehicle $35
Zion National Park (p216)	Utah	7-day pass per vehicle $35

DESCRIPTION	GREAT FOR...
Home to one of the world's only temperate rainforests, this notoriously wet national park is as 'wild' and 'west' as it gets.	
Home to an extraordinary array of fossilized ancient logs and the multicolored sandscape of the Painted Desert.	
Pinnacles National Park is a study in geologic drama, with craggy monoliths, sheer-walled canyons and ancient volcanic remnants.	
The world's tallest living trees have been standing here from time immemorial; prepare to be impressed.	
Rocky Mountain National Park showcases classic alpine scenery, with wildflower meadows and serene mountain lakes set under snowcapped peaks.	
An entire army of the majestic saguaro plant is protected in this two-part desert playground.	
With trees as high as 20-story buildings, this is an extraordinary park with soul-sustaining forests and vibrant wildflower meadows.	
In spring and summer the wildflowers explode; in fall the leaves burn bright; and in winter a beautiful hibernation period sets in.	
Wildlife abounds in these surreal mounds of striated earth; sunset is particularly evocative as shadows dance across the lonely buttes.	
Voyageurs National Park is an outstanding mix of land and waterways formed from earthquakes, volcanoes and glaciers.	
Beneath the mixed-grass prairie and pine forest lies one of the world's longest, most complex cave systems.	
Comprising more than 20,000 sq miles of brawny ice-encrusted mountains, this is the second-largest national park in the world.	
The real showstoppers here are the geysers and hot springs, but at every turn this land of fire and brimstone breathes, belches and bubbles like a giant kettle on the boil.	
It's hard to believe so much natural beauty can exist in the one place. The jaw-dropping head-turner of USA national parks, Yosemite garners the devotion of all who enter.	
From secret oases of trickling water to the hot-pink blooms of a prickly pear cactus, Zion's treasures turn up in the most unexpected places.	

Plan Your Trip
Best Hiking

Top left: Highline Trail (p331), Glacier National Park; Top right: Angels Landing (p218), Zion National Park; Bottom: Vernal Fall (p125), Yosemite National Park

Nothing encapsulates the spirit of the national parks like hiking. Thousands of miles of trails zigzag the parks, accessing their most scenic mountain passes, highest waterfalls and quietest corners.

Highline Trail, Glacier
The ultimate high country traverse in the shadow of the great Continental Divide.

Grandview Trail, Grand Canyon
A rugged and steep trail with switchbacks of cobblestone and epic canyon views.

Teton Crest Trail
There's no let-up in the jagged mountain scenery on this 40-mile romp through Wyoming's greatest hits.

Vernal & Nevada Falls, Yosemite
Take in unmatched views of Yosemite's most stunning waterfalls.

Angels Landing, Zion
Exposed scrambling and unrivaled panoramas on a chain-assisted climb to heaven.

Cascades Pass Trail, North Cascades
High-altitude scenery at its best in the lightly trodden Pacific Northwest wilderness.

Plan Your Trip
Best Wildlife Watching

Above: Anhinga, Everglades National Park (p448); Top right: Brown bears, Katmai National Park (p268); Bottom right: Wolf, Glacier National Park (p324)

North America is home to creatures both great and small and the USA's national parks are by far the best places to see them.

Park Rd, Denali
One of the best places to spot wildlife in Alaska, this road takes you into the heart of Denali.

Oxbow Bend, Grand Teton
Moose, elk, bald eagles, trumpeter swans, blue herons and more can be seen at this special place in Grand Teton.

Brooks Camp, Katmai
Watch brown bears pluck salmon straight from the falls in this ursine paradise.

Anhinga Trail, Everglades
Spot alligators soaking up the sun and watch for the trail's namesake birds as they spear their prey with their razor-sharp bills.

Glacier
Your best chance of seeing a grizzly in the Lower 48, as well as 70 other mammals including cougars and wolverines.

Plan Your Trip
Best Family Experiences

Top left: Hoh Rain Forest (p298), Olympic National Park; Top right: Mammoth Cave National Park (p438); Bottom: Cadillac Mountain (p403), Acadia National Park

There's something inherently gratifying about bringing kids to a national park, most of which offer educational programs and activities designed to engage children in the environments around them.

Rock Climbing, Yosemite
The world's holy grail of rock climbing is made accessible to all at Yosemite Mountaineering School. It is a gold mine of opportunity.

Cave Tour, Mammoth Cave
Longer than any other known cave, with vast interior cathedrals, bottomless pits and strange, undulating rock formations.

Sand Sledding, Great Sand Dunes
Landscapes collide here in a shifting sea of sand – you might wonder whether a spaceship has whisked you to another planet.

Wildlife Watching, Denali
The whole North American ecosystem viewable from the seat of a slow-moving park bus.

Hoh Rain Forest, Olympic Peninsula
Enter a hobbit-like world of huge mossy trees and giant dripping ferns, and let your imagination run wild in this very old and very wet rainforest.

Sunrise, Acadia
It'll be worth getting everyone out of bed to see the US's first sunrise (October to March; still among the first the rest of the year!)

Plan Your Trip
Best Adventures

LEFT: GALYNA ANDRUSHKO/SHUTTERSTOCK ©; TOP RIGHT: PACIFIC NORTHWEST PHOTO/SHUTTERSTOCK ©; BOTTOM RIGHT: JONATHAN ASH/SHUTTERSTOCK ©

Above: Mt Rainier National Park (p280); Top right: Rafting the Colorado River (p186), Grand Canyon National Park; Bottom right: Canyoneering in Zion National Park (p218)

With environments ranging from the subtropics of the Everglades to the glacial snowfields of the Pacific Northwest, the USA's national parks have no shortage of spectacular settings for a bit of adventure.

Rafting, Grand Canyon
Rafting this stretch of the Colorado River is a virtual all-access pass to the Grand Canyon, in all its wildness, peace and ancient glory.

Mountaineering, Mt Rainier
The snowcapped summit and forest covered foothills boast numerous hiking trails, huge swaths of flower-carpeted meadows, and an alluring conical peak that presents a formidable challenge for aspiring climbers.

Canyoneering, Zion
Rappelling 100ft over the lip of a sandstone bowl, tracing a slot canyon's sculpted curves, staring up at a ragged gash of blue sky – canyoneering is beautiful, dangerous and sublime all at once.

Paddling, Everglades
Paddle the 99-mile Wilderness Waterway, a labyrinth of mangroves, swamps and the waterways of the Ten Thousand Islands.

Nordic Skiing & Snowshoeing, Grand Teton
Enjoy some winter fun when the crowds have gone home in Wyoming from hair-raising ski-mountaineering on Grand Teton to groomed cross-country trails in the foothills.

USA's
National Parks
BY REGION

Rocky Mountains (p319)
Gasp at high country views and explore frontier history, pristine lakes, natural geysers and celebrity ski resorts.

Alaska & the Pacific Northwest (p229)
Eleven massive parks inhabit the snow-capped periphery of America from magical Crater Lake to the Gates of the Arctic.

California (p47)
Cruise by the surf-tossed Pacific and reach for the sky in the Sierra Nevada on your way through nine national parks.

Hawaii (p453)
Volcanoes, subtropical forests, coral reefs, and unique island wildlife: Hawaii introduces you to the diverse flavors of Oceania.

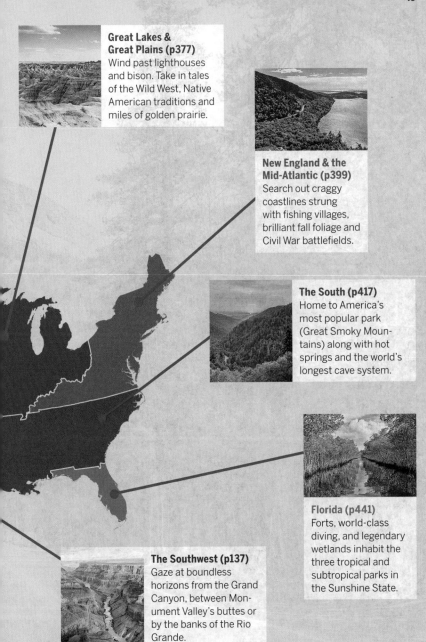

**Great Lakes &
Great Plains (p377)**
Wind past lighthouses
and bison. Take in tales
of the Wild West, Native
American traditions and
miles of golden prairie.

**New England & the
Mid-Atlantic (p399)**
Search out craggy
coastlines strung
with fishing villages,
brilliant fall foliage and
Civil War battlefields.

The South (p417)
Home to America's
most popular park
(Great Smoky Moun-
tains) along with hot
springs and the world's
longest cave system.

Florida (p441)
Forts, world-class
diving, and legendary
wetlands inhabit the
three tropical and
subtropical parks in
the Sunshine State.

The Southwest (p137)
Gaze at boundless
horizons from the Grand
Canyon, between Mon-
ument Valley's buttes or
by the banks of the Rio
Grande.

In This Chapter

Channel Islands 50
Death Valley 56
Joshua Tree 62
Kings Canyon 74
Lassen Volcanic 88
Pinnacles 94
Redwood 96
Sequoia 108
Yosemite 118

California

From misty forests to sun-kissed beaches, the Golden State is an all-seasons outdoor playground with more national parks than anywhere else in the United States. California has it all: the arid expanses of the Mojave Desert reach almost to the Pacific's underwater kelp forests, while mighty redwoods line the northern coast. Hike among desert wildflowers in spring, dive into the Pacific in summer, mountain bike through fall foliage and ski down wintry mountains.

Don't Miss

o Roaming from waterfalls to granite monoliths in Yosemite Valley (p118)

o Gazing up at gigantic trees in Redwood (p96)

o Being awed by Death Valley's dunes and mountains (p56)

o Exploring otherworldly Lassen Volcanic National Park (p88)

o Toiling up stairs to reach Sequoia's spectacular Moro Rock (p110)

o Hiking or climbing at subalpine Tuolumne Meadows (p121)

When to Go

Summer's high season (June to August) sees prices rise by 50% or more in many parks. But it's low season in the hot desert regions.

Crowds and prices drop during the shoulder seasons (April to May and September to October). It's wetter in spring and drier in autumn, but generally mild at these times.

Winter (November to March) is peak season in SoCal's deserts. But elsewhere it's low season, with room rates lowest along the coast. In the mountains, expect chilly temperatures, rainstorms and heavy snow.

Previous page: Yosemite National Park (p118)
SUNDRY PHOTOGRAPHY/SHUTTERSTOCK ©

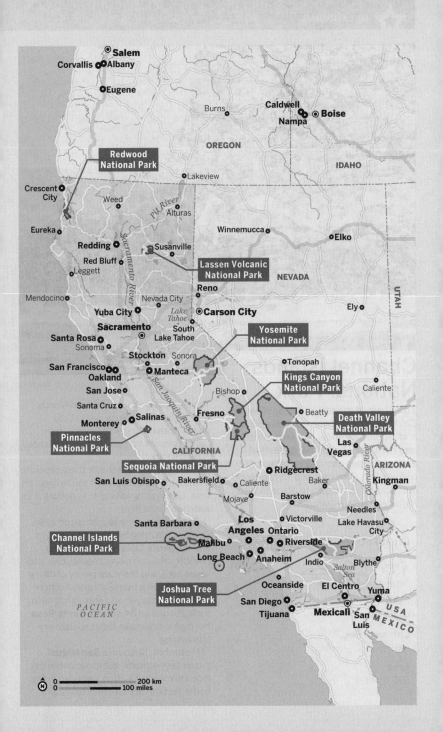

Sea lions

Channel Islands National Park

This chain of islands off the Southern California coast is rich in unique flora and fauna, tide pools and kelp forests, and home to 23 endemic terrestrial animal species and 578 varieties of native plant. This raw, end-of-the-world landscape is an inspiring place to hike, kayak and whale-watch.

The archipelago's four northern islands, San Miguel, Santa Rosa, Santa Cruz and Anacapa, along with tiny southern Santa Barbara, comprise Channel Islands National Park.

Anacapa Island, actually three separate islands, is the best option if you're short on time. Go kayaking, diving, tide-pooling and watch sea lions here.

Santa Cruz is the largest island at 96 sq miles, claiming two mountain ranges and the park's tallest peak, Mt Diablo (2450ft). You can swim, snorkel, dive and kayak here, and there are plenty of hiking options starting from Scorpion Anchorage. Beach, canyon and grasslands hiking trails abound on 84-sq-mile **Santa Rosa**, but high winds make water sports very challenging.

Meanwhile, 14-sq-mile **San Miguel** guarantees solitude, but its westernmost location means it's often shrouded in fog. Some sections are off-limits to visitors.

Great For...

State
California

Entrance Fee
Free

Area
390 sq miles

TRAVEL STOCK/SHUTTERSTOCK ©

Bat star and orange cup corals, Santa Cruz Island; Overleaf: Anacapa Island

 Channel Islands History

Originally, the Channel Islands were inhabited by Chumash tribespeople, who were forced to move to mainland Catholic missions by Spanish military forces in the early 1800s. The islands were subsequently taken over by Mexican and American ranchers during the 19th century and the US military in the 20th century, until conservation efforts began in the 1970s and '80s.

Scenic & Whale-Watching Cruises

The main provider of boats for Channel Islands visits is Island Packers (p54), with day trips and overnight camping excursions available. Boats mostly set out from Ventura but a few go from nearby Oxnard. It also offers wildlife cruises year-round, including seasonal whale-watching from late December to mid-April (gray whales) and mid-May through mid-September (blue and humpback whales).

Water Sports

Aquasports (☎805-968-7231; www.islandkay aking.com) offers day and overnight kayaking trips to Santa Cruz, Anacapa and along the coast near Santa Barbara, led by professional naturalists. Book ahead to rent kayaks and SUPs from **Channel Islands Kayak Center** (☎805-984-5995; www.cikayak.com; 1691 Spinnaker Dr, Ventura; ⊙by appointment only). It can also arrange a private guided kayaking tour of Santa Cruz or Anacapa.

Wildlife & Nature

Human beings have left a heavy footprint. Erosion was caused by overgrazing livestock, rabbits fed on native plants, and the US military even used San Miguel as a practice bombing range. In 1969 an offshore oil spill engulfed the northern islands.

But the future isn't all bleak. Brown pelicans have rebounded on West Anacapa and Santa Barbara, while on San Miguel, native vegetation has returned a half-century after overgrazing sheep were removed.

Essential Information

When to Go
In summer, island conditions are hot, dusty and bone-dry. Better times to visit are during the spring wildflower bloom or in early fall, when the fog clears. Winter can be stormy, but it's also great for wildlife-watching, especially whales.

Sleeping & Eating
Each island has a primitive year-round **campground** (reservations 877-444-6777; www.recreation.gov; tent sites $15) with pit toilets and picnic tables. Water is only available on Santa Cruz Island. Advance reservations are required for all island campsites.

There's nowhere to buy food on the islands so bring a picnic (and take out all your trash).

Visitor Center
Channel Islands National Park Visitor Center (Robert J Lagomarsino Visitor Center; 805-658-5730; www.nps.gov/chis; 1901 Spinnaker Dr, Ventura; 8:30am-5pm) is on the mainland at the far end of Ventura Harbor. A free video gives some background.

Getting There & Around
You can access the national park by taking a boat from Ventura or Oxnard or a plane from Camarillo. Trips may be canceled anytime due to high surf or weather conditions. Reservations are essential for weekends, holidays and summer trips. **Island Packers** (805-642-1393; http://islandpackers.com; 1691 Spinnaker Dr, Ventura; Channel Island day trips from $59, wildlife cruises from $68) offers regularly scheduled boat services.

The open seas on the boat ride out to the Channel Islands may feel choppy to land-lubbers. To avoid seasickness, sit outside on the lower deck, keep away from the diesel fumes in the back, and focus on the horizon.

Alternatively, you can take a scenic flight to Santa Rosa or San Miguel with **Channel Islands Aviation** (805-987-1301; www.flycia.com; 305 Durley Ave, Camarillo). ∎

Humpback whale off Channel Islands

THIERRYHENNET/GETTY IMAGES ©

Zabriskie Point

Death Valley National Park

The name evokes all that is harsh, hot and hellish – a punishing, barren and lifeless place. Yet closer inspection reveals that nature is putting on a truly spectacular show: singing sand dunes, boulders moving across the desert floor, extinct volcanic craters, stark mountains rising to 11,000ft and plenty of wildlife.

Great For...

State
California

Entrance Fee
7-day pass per car/motorcycle/person on foot or bicycle $35/25/15

Area
5270 sq miles

Dramatic Viewpoints

Southeast of Furnace Creek is **Zabriskie Point**, for spectacular views across golden badlands eroded into pleats and gullies. It was named for a manager of the Pacific Coast Borax Company and also inspired the title of Michelangelo Antonio's 1970s movie. Early morning is the best time to visit.

Twenty miles south is 5475ft-high **Dante's View**, gazing out on the entire southern Death Valley basin from the top of the Black Mountains. On very clear days, you can simultaneously see the highest (Mt Whitney) and lowest (Badwater) points in the contiguous USA. Allow about 1½ hours for the round-trip from the turnoff at Hwy 190.

Scenic Drives

About 9 miles south of Furnace Creek, the 9-mile, one-way **Artists Drive** scenic loop offers 'wow' moments around every turn; it's best done in the late afternoon when exposed minerals and volcanic ash make the hills erupt in fireworks of color.

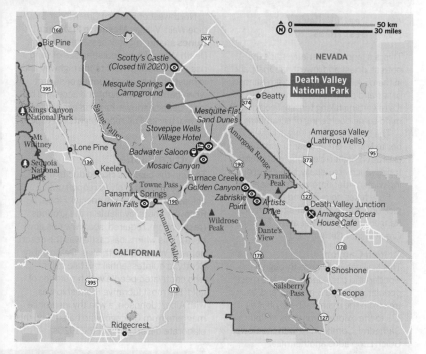

Dante's View

Death Valley's Best Hikes

This is a land of superlatives: it's the hottest, driest and lowest national park in the USA. There are also palm-shaded oases and plenty of endemic wildlife, so it's rewarding hiking terrain if you don't mind some bouldering or scrambling.

The best time for hiking is November to March. Steer clear in summer, except on higher-elevation mountain trails, which are usually snowed in during winter. Adequate water is essential.

Easy hikes do exist, and families can pick up a free fun-for-all-ages *Junior Ranger Activity Booklet* at the Furnace Creek Visitor Center (p60).

Golden Canyon

This trail network winds through a wonderland of golden rocks. The most popular route is a 3-mile out-and-back trek from the main trailhead off Hwy 178 to the oxidized iron cliffs of Red Cathedral. Combining it with the Gower Gulch Loop adds another mile.

Wildrose Peak

This moderate-to-strenuous trail begins near the charcoal kilns off Wildrose Canyon Rd and ascends to Wildrose Peak (9064ft), which has a stunning vista. The 8.4-mile round-trip hike is best in spring or fall.

Mosaic Canyon Trail

West of Stovepipe Wells Village, a 2.3-mile gravel road leads to Mosaic Canyon, where you can hike and scramble past smooth multihued rock walls. Colors are sharpest at midday.

Darwin Falls

This natural-spring-fed year-round cascade plunges into a gorge, embraced by willows that attract migratory birds. Look for the (unmarked) turnoff about 0.75 miles west of Panamint Springs, then follow the dirt road for 2.5 miles to the parking area. The 1-mile hike to the first waterfall requires some climbing over rocks and crossing small streams.

Northwest of Furnace Creek, near Stovepipe Wells Village, **Mesquite Flat Sand Dunes** are the most accessible dunes in Death Valley. This undulating sea of sand rises to 100ft high next to the highway and is most photogenic at sunrise or sunset when bathed in soft light and accented by long, deep shadows. Keep an eye out for animal tracks. Full-moon nights are especially magical.

Scotty's Castle

Though the castle is closed due to flood damage and not likely to reopen until at least 2020, there are special 'Flood Recovery Tours' available in the grounds (reservations required, see www.nps.gov/deva). This whimsical castle was the desert home of Walter E Scott, alias 'Death Valley Scotty,' a quintessential tall-tale teller who captivated people with his stories of gold. His most lucrative friendship was with Albert Johnson, a wealthy insurance magnate from Chicago, who bankrolled this elaborate desert oasis in the 1920s.

CHECUBUS/SHUTTERSTOCK ©

NADIA YONG/SHUTTERSTOCK ©

Top: Mesquite Flat Sand Dunes; Bottom: Scotty's Castle

Essential Information

Sleeping

Camping is plentiful but if you're looking for a place with a roof, in-park options are limited, pricey and often booked solid in springtime. Alternative bases are the gateway towns of Beatty (40 miles from Furnace Creek), Lone Pine (40 miles), Death Valley Junction (30 miles) and Tecopa (70 miles). Options a bit further afield include Ridgecrest (120 miles) and Las Vegas (140 miles).

Death Valley National Park Campgrounds (www.nps.gov/deva; campsites free-$36) The National Park Service (NPS) operates nine campgrounds on a first-come, first-served basis (exception: Furnace Creek between mid-October and mid-April). Campsites fill by midmorning on some weekends, especially during the spring wildflower bloom.

Mesquite Springs Campground (760-786-3200; www.nps.gov/deva; Hwy 190; per site $14) In the northern reaches of the park, this first-come, first-served campground has 30 spaces. At an elevation of 1800ft, it's also a lot cooler than the desert floor. Sites come with fire pits and tables, and there's water and flush toilets.

Stovepipe Wells Village Hotel (760-786-2387; www.deathvalleyhotels.com; 51880 Hwy 190, Stovepipe Wells; RV sites $33.30, r $140-210; ✳@🔔🏊) The 83 rooms at this private resort have beds draped in quality linens and accented with cheerful Native American–patterned blankets. There's a small pool and the on-site cowboy-style restaurant serves breakfast and dinner daily, with lunch available in the next-door saloon.

Eating & Drinking

There are restaurants and stores for stocking up on basic groceries and camping supplies in Furnace Creek, Stovepipe Wells Village and Panamint Springs. Hours vary seasonally; some close in summer.

Amargosa Opera House Cafe (760-852-4432; www.amargosacafe.org; Death Valley Junction; mains $9-19, pie per slice $5; ⊙8am-3pm Mon, Fri, Sat & Sun, 6:30-9pm Sat) ✔ This charmer in the middle of nowhere gets you ready for a day in Death Valley with hearty breakfasts or healthy sandwiches, but truly shows off its farm-to-table stripes at dinnertime on Saturdays. Combine with a tour of (or show at) the late Marta Becket's kooky opera house. Excellent coffee to boot.

Badwater Saloon (760-786-2387; www.death valleyhotels.com; 51880 Hwy 190, Stovepipe Wells Village; ⊙11:30am-9pm or later) Light meals and bar snacks are served at this colorful bar with Old West knickknacks, cold draft beer and Lynyrd Skynyrd on the jukebox.

Information

Furnace Creek is Death Valley's commercial hub, with the park's main visitor center, a general store, gas station, post office, ATM, wi-fi, golf course, lodging and restaurants.

There is no public transportation to Death Valley. Coming from Las Vegas, it's about 120 miles via Hwy 160 or 140 miles via I-95 and Hwy 373. Coming from Hwy 395, you can reach Furnace Creek in about 100 miles from Lone Pine via Hwy 190 or in 120 miles from Ridgecrest via Hwys 178 and 190. From I-15, get off at Baker and head 115 miles north via Hwy 127.

Gas is available 24/7 at Furnace Creek and Stovepipe Wells Village and from 7am to 9:30pm in Panamint Springs. Prices are much higher than outside the park, especially at Panamint.

Cell towers provide service at Furnace Creek and Stovepipe Wells but there's little to no coverage elsewhere in the park.

Visitor Center

Furnace Creek Visitor Center (760-786-3200; www.nps.gov/deva; ⊙8am-5pm; 🔔) has engaging exhibits on the park's ecosystem and the indigenous tribes as well as a gift shop, clean toilets, (slow) wi-fi and friendly rangers to answer questions and help you plan your day. Check the schedule for ranger-led activities. ■

Top left: Stovepipe Wells Village Hotel store; Top right: Death Valley NP Campground; Bottom: Furnace Creek Visitor Center

S. BORISOV/SHUTTERSTOCK ©

Joshua Tree National Park

Taking a page from a Dr Seuss book, the whimsical Joshua trees (actually tree-sized yuccas) welcome visitors to this park at the transition zone between two deserts. Rock climbers know 'JT' as California's best place to climb, hikers seek out shady oases, and mountain bikers are hypnotized by desert vistas.

Great For...

State
California

Entrance Fee
7-day pass per car/motorcycle/person on foot or bike $30/25/15

Area
1235 sq miles

Hiking

Just about anyone can enjoy a clamber on the cluster of rocks at the **Hidden Valley Trail**. An easy 1-mile trail loops around and back to the parking lot and picnic area.

For immersion into the Wonderland of Rocks, a striking rock labyrinth, embark on the challenging, 8-mile one-way **Boy Scout Trail** linking Indian Cove and Park Blvd (near Quail Springs picnic area). Arrange for pick-up at the other end.

The moderate 3-mile **Fortynine Palms Oasis Trail** allows an escape from the crowds; the trailhead is at the end of Canyon Rd that veers off 29 Palms Hwy/Hwy 62.

Cycling

Bikes are not permitted on hiking trails, but only on public paved and dirt roads that are also open to vehicles, including 29 miles of backcountry. Popular routes include challenging **Pinkham Canyon Rd**, starting from the Cottonwood Visitor Center, and the long-distance **Black Eagle Mine Rd**,

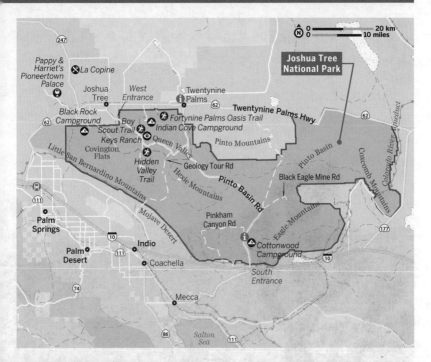

Boy Scout Trail

 Prophetic Trees

It was Mormon settlers who named the Joshua trees because the branches stretching up toward heaven reminded them of the biblical prophet Joshua pointing the way to the promised land. In springtime, the trees send up a huge single cream-colored flower.

6.5 miles further north. **Queen Valley** has a gentler set of trails with bike racks along the way, so people can lock up their bikes and go hiking, but it's busy with cars, as is the bumpy, sandy and steep **Geology Tour Rd**. There's also a wide-open network of dirt roads at **Covington Flats**.

Rock Climbing

JT's rocks are famous for their rough, high-friction surfaces; from boulders to cracks to multipitch faces, there are more than 8000 established routes. Some of the most popular climbs are in the Hidden Valley area.

Joshua Tree Rock Climbing School (☑760-366-4745; www.joshuatreerockclimbing. com; 63439 Doggie Trail, Joshua Tree; 1-day course from $195) and **Vertical Adventures** (☑949-854-6250, 800-514-8785; www.verticaladven tures.com; courses from $155; ⊙Sep-May) offer guided climbs and climbing instruction.

Left: Covington Flats;
Right: Fortynine Palms Oasis Trail

Essential Information

Sleeping

Unless you're day-tripping from Palm Springs, set up camp inside the park or base yourself in the desert communities linked by 29 Palms Hwy/Hwy 62 along the park's northern perimeter. Twenty-nine Palms and Yucca Valley have mostly national chain motels, while pads in Joshua Tree have plenty of charm and character.

Camping

Of the park's eight campgrounds, only **Cottonwood** (Pinto Basin Rd; per site $20) and **Black Rock Canyon** (Joshua Lane; per site $20) have potable water, flush toilets and dump stations. **Indian Cove** (Indian Cove Rd; per site $20) and Black Rock accept reservations from October through May. The others are first-come, first-served and have pit toilets, picnic tables and fire grates. None have showers, but there are some at **Coyote Corner** (6535 Park Blvd; ☉9am-6pm) in Joshua Tree. Details are available at www.nps.gov/jotr or ☎760-367-5500.

Between October and May, campsites fill by Thursday noon, especially during the springtime bloom. If you arrive too late, there's overflow camping on Bureau of Land Management (BLM) land north and south of the park as well as in private campgrounds.

Backcountry camping is allowed 1 mile from any road or 500ft from any trailhead. There is no water in the park, so bring one to two gallons per person per day for drinking, cooking and personal hygiene. Campfires are prohibited to prevent wildfires and damage to the fragile desert floor. Free self-registration is required at a backcountry board inside the park, where you can also leave your car.

Lodgings

Sacred Sands (☎760-424-6407; www.sacredsands.com; 63155 Quail Springs Rd, Joshua Tree; studio/ste $339/369, 2-night minimum; ❋�☎) ✎ In an isolated, pin-drop-quiet spot, these two desert-chic suites are the ultimate romantic retreat, each with a private outdoor shower, hot tub, sundeck and earthen straw-bale walls. There are astounding views across the desert hills and into the national park. Owners Scott and Steve are gracious hosts. It's 4 miles south of 29 Palms Hwy (via Park Bl), 1 mile west of the park entrance.

Eating

La Copine (www.lacopinekitchen.com; 848 Old Woman Rd, Flamingo Heights; mains $10-16; ☉9am-3pm Thu-Sun) It's a long road from Philadelphia to the high desert, but that's where Nikki and Claire decided to take their farm-to-table brunch cuisine from pop-up to brick and mortar. Their roadside bistro serves zeitgeist-capturing dishes such as the signature salad with smoked salmon and poached egg, homemade crumpets and gold milk turmeric tea. Expect a wait on weekends.

Drinking & Entertainment

Joshua Tree Coffee Company (☎760-974-4060; www.jtcoffeeco.com; 61738 29 Palms Hwy/Hwy 62, Joshua Tree; ☉7am-6pm) Organic and locally roasted, this spotless outfit makes some of the best coffee in JT. It's sold in places around the valley but roasted right here in the little hipster cafe with outdoor seating.

Pappy & Harriet's Pioneertown Palace (☎760-365-5956; www.pappyandharriets.com; 53688 Pioneertown Rd, Pioneertown; mains $6-15; ☉11am-2am Thu-Sun, from 5pm Mon) For local color, toothsome BBQ, cheap beer and kick-ass live music, drop in at this textbook honky-tonk in Pioneertown, a movie set turned living town. Monday's open-mike nights (admission free) are legendary and often bring out astounding talent. From Thursday to Saturday, local and national talent takes over the stage.

Getting There & Away

Joshua Tree has three park entrances. Access the west entrance from the town of Joshua Tree, the north entrance from Twentynine Palms and the south entrance from I-10. The park's northern half harbors most of the attractions.

Top left: Coyote Corner; Top right: Pappy & Harriet's Pioneertown Palace; Bottom: Indian Cove

CLASSIC ROAD TRIPS

Palm Springs & Joshua Tree Oases

Southern California's deserts can be brutally hot, barren places – escape to Palm Springs and Joshua Tree National Park, where shady fan-palm oases and date gardens await.

Duration 2–3 days

Distance 170 miles

Best Time to Go
February to April for spring wildflower blooms and cooler temperatures.

Essential Photo
Sunset from Keys View.

Best for Solitude
Hike to the Lost Palms Oasis.

❶ Palm Springs

Hollywood celebs have always counted on Palm Springs as a quick escape from LA. Today, this desert resort town shows off a trove of well-preserved mid-Century Modern buildings. Stop at the **Palm Springs Visitors Center** (☎760-778-8418, 800-347-7746; www.visitpalmsprings.com; 2901 N Palm Canyon Dr; ☺9am-5pm), inside a 1965 gas station by modernist Albert Frey, to pick up a self-guided architectural tour map. Then drive uphill to clamber aboard the **Palm Springs Aerial Tramway** (☎760-325-1391, 888-515-8726; www.pstramway.com; 1 Tram Way; adult/child $26/17, parking $5; ☺1st tram

up 10am Mon-Fri, 8am Sat & Sun, last tram down 9:45pm daily, varies seasonally), which climbs nearly 6000 vertical feet from the hot Sonoran Desert floor to the cool, even snowy San Jacinto Mountains in less than 15 minutes. Back down on the ground, drive south on Palm Canyon Dr, where you can hop between art galleries, cafes, cocktail bars, trendy restaurants and chic boutiques. For a dose of culture, check out the latest exhibit at the excellent **Palm Springs Art Museum** (☎760-322-4800; www.psmuseum. org; 101 Museum Dr; adult/student $12/5, all free 4-8pm Thu; ☺10am-5pm Sun-Tue & Sat, noon-9pm Thu & Fri).

The Drive » Drive north out of downtown Palm Springs along Indian Canyon Dr for 7 miles, passing over the I-10. Turn right onto Dillon Rd, then after 2.5 miles turn left onto Palm Dr, which heads north into central Desert Hot Springs.

❷ Desert Hot Springs

In 1774 Spanish explorer Juan Bautista de Anza was the first European to encounter the desert Cahuilla tribe. Afterward, the Spanish name Agua Caliente came to refer to both the indigenous people and the natural hot springs, which still flow restoratively through the town of Desert Hot Springs (www.visitdeserthotsprings.com), where hip boutique hotels have appeared atop healing waters bubbling up from deep below. Imitate Tim Robbins in Robert Altman's film *The Player* and have a mud bath at **Two Bunch Palms Spa Resort** (☎760-676-5000; www.twobunchpalms.com/spa; 67425 Two Bunch Palms Trail; day-spa package from $195; ☺by reservation 9am-7pm Tue-Thu, 9am-8:30pm Fri, 8am-8:30pm Sat, 8am-7pm Sun & Mon) ✿, which sits atop an actual oasis. Bounce between a variety of pools and sunbathing areas, but maintain the code of silence (actually, whispers only).

The Drive » Head west on Pierson Blvd back to Indian Canyon Dr. Turn right and drive northwest through the dusty outskirts of Desert Hot Springs. Turn right onto Hwy 62 Eastbound toward Yucca Valley; after about 4 miles, turn right onto East Dr and look for signs for Big Morongo Canyon Preserve.

❸ Big Morongo Canyon Preserve

An oasis hidden in the high desert, Big Morongo Canyon Preserve is a bird-watching hot spot. Tucked into the Little San Bernardino Mountains, this stream-fed riparian habitat is flush with cottonwood and willow trees. Nearly 250 bird species have been identified here, including over 70 that use the area as breeding grounds. Tramp along wooden boardwalks through marshy woodlands as hummingbirds flutter atop flowers and woodpeckers hammer away.

The Drive » Rejoin Hwy 62 Eastbound past Yucca Valley, with its roadside antiques, vintage shops, art galleries and cafes, to the town of Joshua Tree about 16 miles away, which makes a good place to base yourself for the night. At the

intersection with Park Blvd, turn right and drive 5 miles to Joshua Tree National Park's west entrance. Make sure you've got a full tank of gas first.

❹ Hidden Valley

It's time to jump into **Joshua Tree National Park**, a wonderland of jumbo rocks interspersed with sandy forests of Joshua trees (related to agave plants). Revel in the scenery as you drive along the winding park road for about 8 miles to the Hidden Valley picnic area. Turn left and drive past the campground to the trailhead for **Barker Dam**. Here a kid-friendly nature trail loops for just over a mile past a pretty little artificial lake and a rock incised with Native American petroglyphs. If you enjoy history and Western lore, check with the national park office whether ranger-led walking tours of nearby **Keys Ranch** (☎760-367-5500; www.nps.gov/jotr; tour adult/child $10/5; ⊗tour schedules vary) are offered during

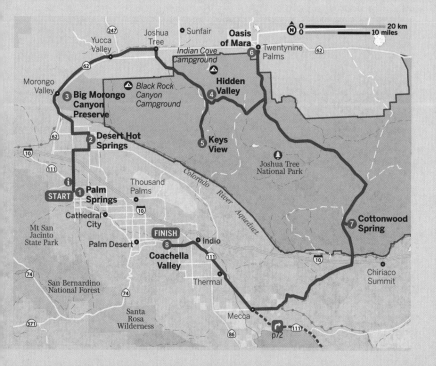

your stay. Pioneer homesteaders tried their hand at cattle ranching, mining and desert farming here in the 19th century.

The Drive » Backtrack to Park Blvd, turn left and head south again past jumbled rock formations and fields of spiky Joshua trees. Take the well-signed right turn toward Keys View. You'll pass several trailheads and roadside interpretive exhibits over the next 5.5 miles leading up to the viewpoint.

❺ Keys View

Make sure you embark at least an hour before sunset for the drive up to Keys View (5185ft), where panoramic views look into the **Coachella Valley** and reach as far south as the shimmering Salton Sea or, on an unusually clear day, Mexico's Signal Mountain. Looming in front of you are **Mt San Jacinto** (10,800ft) and **Mt San**

Gorgonio (11,500ft), two of Southern California's highest peaks, often snow-dusted even in spring. Down below snakes the shaky **San Andreas Fault**.

The Drive » Head back downhill to Park Blvd. Turn right and wind through the park's Wonderland of Rocks (where boulders call out to scampering kids and serious rock jocks alike), passing more campgrounds. After 10 miles, veer left to stay on Park Blvd and drive north for 8 miles toward the town of Twentynine Palms onto Utah Trail.

❻ Oasis of Mara

Drop by Joshua Tree National Park's **Oasis Visitor Center** (www.nps.gov/jotr; 74485 National Park Dr, Twentynine Palms; ☺8:30am-5pm) for its educational exhibits about Southern California's desert fan palms. These palms are often found growing along

Top: Oasis Visitor Center; Bottom Left: Keys View; Bottom Right: Ladder-backed woodpecker

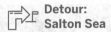

Detour: Salton Sea

Start: ❼ Cottonwood Spring

Driving along Hwy 111 southeast of Mecca, it's a most unexpected sight: California's largest lake in the middle of its largest desert. It was created by accident in 1905 when spring flooding breached irrigation canals built to bring water from the Colorado River to the farmland in the Imperial Valley. Marketed to mid-20th-century tourists as the 'California Riviera' with beachfront vacation homes, the Salton Sea has been mostly abandoned because agricultural runoff has increased the lake's salinity to the point where few fish species can survive. An even stranger sight is folk-art **Salvation Mountain** (☎760-624-8754; www.salvationmountain inc.org; 603 E Beal Rd, Niland; donations accepted; ☉dawn-dusk), an artificial hill covered in acrylic paint and found objects and inscribed with Christian religious messages. It's outside Niland, about 3 miles east of Hwy 111 en route to Slab City.

fault lines, where cracks in the earth's crust allow subterranean water to surface. Outside the visitor center, a gentle half-mile nature trail leads around the **Oasis of Mara**, where Serrano peoples once camped. Ask for directions to the trailhead off Hwy 62 for the 3-mile, round-trip hike to **Fortynine Palms Oasis**, where a sun-exposed dirt trail marches you over a ridge, then drops you into a rocky gorge, doggedly heading down past barrel cacti toward a distant speck of green.

The Drive » Drive back south on Utah Trail and re-enter the park. Follow Park Blvd south, turning left at the first major junction onto Pinto Basin Rd for a winding 30-mile drive southeast to Cottonwood Spring.

❼ Cottonwood Spring

On your drive to Cottonwood Spring, you'll pass from the high Mojave Desert into the lower Sonoran Desert. At the **Cholla Cactus Garden**, handily labeled specimens burst into bloom in spring, including unmistakable ocotillo plants, which look like green octopus tentacles adorned with flaming scarlet flowers. Turn left at the Cottonwood Visitor Center for a short drive east past the campground to Cottonwood Spring. Once used by the Cahuilla, who left behind archaeological evidence such as mortars and clay pots, the springs became a hotbed for gold mining in the late 19th century. The now-dry springs are the start of the moderately strenuous 7.5-mile round-trip trek out to **Lost Palms Oasis**, a fan-palm oasis blessed with solitude and scenery.

The Drive » Head south from Cottonwood Springs and drive across the I-10 to pick up scenic Box Canyon Rd, which burrows a hole through the desert, twisting its way toward the Salton Sea. Take 66th Ave west to Mecca, then turn right onto Hwy 111 and drive northwest ('up valley') toward Indio.

❽ Coachella Valley

The hot but fertile Coachella Valley is the ideal place to find the date of your dreams – the kind that grows on trees, that is. Date farms let you sample exotic-sounding varieties like halawy, deglet noor and zahidi for free, but the signature taste of the valley is a rich date shake from certified-organic **Oasis Date Gardens** (www.oasisdate.com) or the 1920s pioneer **Shields Date Garden** (www.shieldsdate garden.com). ∎

Cottonwood Spring

General Grant Tree Trail

Kings Canyon National Park

Rugged Kings Canyon offers true adventure to those who crave verdant trails, rushing streams and gargantuan rock formations. The camping, backcountry exploring and climbing are superb, and Kings Canyon Scenic Byway twists through some of California's most dramatic scenery.

Great For...

State
California

Entrance Fee
7-day pass per vehicle/person on foot or bicycle $35/20

Area
721 sq miles

❶ General Grant Grove

This sequoia grove off Generals Hwy is astounding. The paved half-mile **General Grant Tree Trail** is an interpretive walk that visits a number of mature sequoias, including the 27-story **General Grant Tree**. This giant holds triple honors as the world's second-largest living tree, a memorial to US soldiers killed in war and the nation's official Christmas tree since 1926. The nearby **Fallen Monarch**, a massive, fire-hollowed trunk you can walk through, has been a cabin, hotel, saloon and stables.

To escape the bustling crowds, follow the more secluded 1.5-mile **North Grove Loop**, which passes wildflower patches and bubbling creeks as it gently winds underneath a canopy of stately sequoias, evergreen pines and aromatic incense cedars.

The magnificence of this ancient sequoia grove was nationally recognized

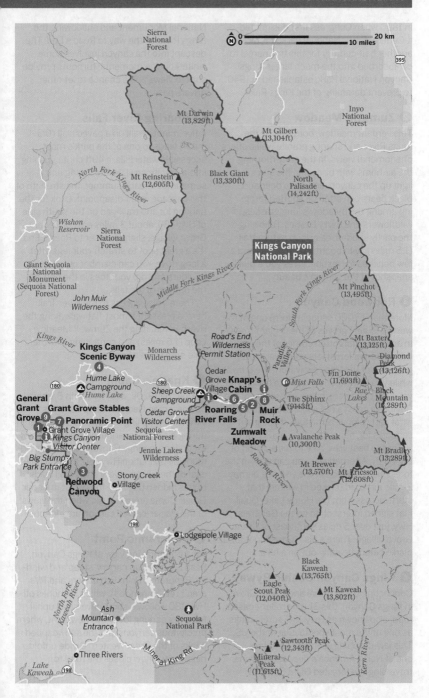

in 1890 when Congress first designated it General Grant National Park. It took another half-century for this tiny parcel to be absorbed into the much larger Kings Canyon National Park, established in 1940 to prevent damming of the Kings River.

❷ Zumwalt Meadow

This verdant meadow, bordered by the Kings River and soaring granite walls, offers phenomenal views. In the early morning, the air hums with birdsong, the sun's rays light up the canyon, and mule deer and black bears can often be spotted foraging among the meadow's long grasses, wildflowers and berry bushes. Following the partly shaded, easy loop nature trail (1.5 miles), with boardwalk sections and a few benches for resting, gives you a quick snapshot of the canyon's beauty.

❸ Redwood Canyon

More than 15,000 sequoias form one of the world's largest groves of these giant trees. In an almost-forgotten corner of the park, this secluded forest lets you revel in the grandeur of the trees away from the crowds while you hike mostly moderate trails. What you won't find here, however, are any of the California coast's redwood trees – that's what early pioneers mistook these giant sequoias for, hence the erroneous name.

For the best view, hike to the summit of Big Baldy. Alternatively, you can walk in the forest via trailheads at the end of a bumpy 2-mile dirt road (closed in winter) that starts across from the Hume Lake/Quail Flat signed intersection on the Generals Hwy, just over 5 miles southeast of Grant Grove Village. There's also a good spot for a picnic before heading out on a hike.

❹ Kings Canyon Scenic Byway

Connecting Grant Grove and Cedar Grove in Kings Canyon, this 31-mile roller-coaster road, also known as Hwy 180, surely ranks as one of the most spectacular in the US. This jaw-dropping scenic drive enters one of North America's deepest canyons, traversing the forested Giant Sequoia National Monument and shadowing the Kings River all the way to Road's End. The descent into the canyon involves some white-knuckle moments; turnouts provide superb views and a chance to let other drivers pass.

❺ Roaring River Falls

A five-minute walk on a paved trail (0.3 miles) leads to one of the park's most accessible waterfalls, a 40ft chute gushing into a granite bowl. In late spring and sometimes in early summer, the strength of this cascade won't disappoint. Look for the parking lot and trailhead on the south side of Hwy 180, about 3 miles east of Cedar Grove Village, slightly closer to Road's End. It's a great spot to stretch your legs after a long drive. You can clamber over the boulders and dip your toes in the pool at the bottom of the falls.

There's also access to the River Trail here, a pleasant almost-flat walk along the riverbed reaching the Zumwalt Meadow Loop (1.6 miles) and continuing a further mile onto Road's End.

❻ Knapp's Cabin

During the 1920s, wealthy Santa Barbara businessman George Knapp built this simple wood-shingled cabin to store gear in during his extravagant fishing and camping excursions in Kings Canyon. From a signed roadside pullout on Hwy 180, about 2 miles east of the village, a very short trail leads to this hidden building, the oldest in Cedar Grove. Come around dusk, when the views of the glacier-carved canyon are glorious.

❼ Panoramic Point

For a breathtaking view of Kings Canyon, head 2.3 miles up narrow, steep and winding Panoramic Point Rd (trailers and RVs aren't recommended), which branches off Hwy 180. Follow a short paved trail uphill from the parking lot to the viewpoint, where precipitous canyons and the snowcapped peaks of the Great Western Divide unfold below you. Snow closes the road to

KINGS CANYON NATIONAL PARK **77**

vehicles during winter, when it becomes a cross-country ski and snowshoe route.

Hikers may access the road when snow levels are low. From the visitor center in Grant Grove, follow the paved side road east, turning left after 0.1 miles, then right at the John Muir Lodge.

⑧ Muir Rock

On excursions to Kings Canyon, John Muir would allegedly give talks on this large, flat river boulder, a short walk from the Road's End parking lot and less than a mile past Zumwalt Meadow. A sandy river beach here is taken over by gleeful swimmers in midsummer. Don't jump in when the raging waters, swollen with snowmelt, are dangerous. Ask at the Road's End ranger station (p82) if conditions are calm enough for a dip.

⑨ Horseback Riding

Just north of General Grant Grove in Kings Canyon, pint-sized **Grant Grove Stables** (☏559-335-9292; Hwy 180; trail rides from $40; ⊙mid-Jun–early Sep) is a summer-only operation offering one- and two-hour trail rides. Short and overnight rides (reservations required) are available from **Cedar Grove Pack Station** (☏559-565-3464; www.facebook.com/CedarGrovePackStation; Cedar Lane, Cedar Grove; 1/2hr ride $40/75, overnights (2-night minimum) from $350; ⊙late May–mid-Oct).

Zumwalt Meadow; Overleaf: Panoramic Point

NATALIEJEAN/SHUTTERSTOCK ©

Hike Mist Falls

TRY MEDIA/SHUTTERSTOCK ©

A satisfying long walk along the riverside and up a natural granite staircase highlights the beauty of Kings Canyon. The waterfall is thunderous in late spring and possibly into early summer, depending on the previous winter's snowpack.

Duration 3–5 hours

Distance 9.2 miles round-trip

Difficulty Moderate

Start & Finish Road's End

Nearest Town/Junction
Cedar Grove Village

Transportation Car

Bring plenty of water and sunscreen on this hike, which gains 600ft in elevation before reaching the falls. Get an early morning start because the return trip can be brutally hot on summer afternoons, and also to beat the crowds of big families.

The trail begins just past the Road's End wilderness permit station (p82), crossing a small footbridge over **Copper Creek**. Walk along a sandy trail through sparse cedar and pine forest, where boulders rolled by avalanches are scattered on the canyon floor. Keep an eye out for black bears. Eventually the trail enters cooler, shady and low-lying areas of ferns and reeds before reaching a well-marked, three-way junction with the Woods Creek Trail, just shy of 2 miles from Road's End.

Turn left (north) toward Paradise Valley and begin a gradual climb that runs parallel to powerful cataracts in the boulder-saturated Kings River. Stone-framed stairs lead to a granite knob overlook, with wide southern views of **Avalanche Peak** and the

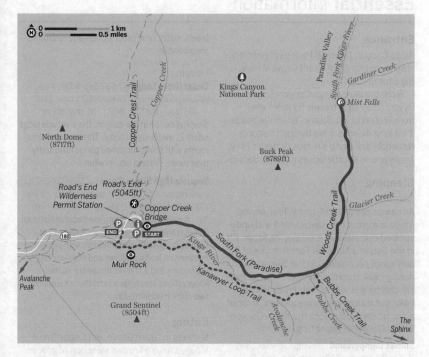

oddly pointed **Sphinx**, another mountain peak, behind you.

Follow cairns up the rock face and continue briefly through shady forest to reach **Mist Falls**, one of the park's largest waterfalls, with a fine spray to cool down warm hikers. Warning: don't wade above the waterfall or swim below it due to the danger of rockfall and swift water currents, especially during snowmelt runoff. In late summer, the river downstream from the falls may be tame enough for a dip – use your own best judgment, however.

Retrace your steps, around 2.5 miles downhill, to the three-way trail junction. Instead of returning directly to Road's End, you can bear left and cross the bridge over the **Kings River** (pictured), briefly joining the Bubbs Creek Trail. After less than a quarter-mile, turn right onto the untrammeled Kanawyer Loop Trail, which is mostly

flat. After crossing **Avalanche Creek** (you may need to wade through or cross via a makeshift bridge), the tree canopy opens up to show off sprawling talus slopes along the Kings Canyon's southern walls.

Muir Rock and its late-summer swimming hole come into view across the river before you make a short climb to the River Trail junction. Turn right and walk across the red footbridge, below which is another favorite late-summer swimming hole. Follow the path back to the paved highway, turning right to walk back to the Road's End parking lot.

Essential Information

Entrance

Kings Canyon National Park's only entrance station, not far from Grant Grove Village, is Big Stump.

From the west, Kings Canyon Scenic Byway (Hwy 180) travels 53 miles east from Fresno to Big Stump. From the south, it's a long 46-mile drive through Sequoia National Park along sinuous Generals Hwy. There are no shuttle buses in Kings Canyon.

Sleeping

Camping

All campsites are first-come, first-served. There are great free, uncrowded and unde-veloped campgrounds off Big Meadows Rd in the Sequoia National Forest, some of the only empty campsites in the Sierra Nevada during peak summer season. Free roadside car camping is also allowed near Hume Lake, but no campfires are allowed without a permit (available from the Kings Canyon Visitor Center in Grant Grove).

Sunset Campground (www.nps.gov/seki; Hwy 180; tent & RV sites $22; ⊘late May-early Sep) Grant Grove's biggest campground has 157 sites and is a five-minute walk from the village. Ranger campfire programs run in summer. Two large group sites are also available (with space for 15 to 30 people). Flush toilets, water, bear-proof lock-ers, fire rings and picnic benches are available.

Hume Lake Campground (www.recreation.gov; Hume Lake Rd; tent & RV sites $27; ⊘mid-May–mid-Sep) Almost always full, this campground operated by California Land Management offers around 65 relatively uncrowded, shady campsites at 5250ft. It's on the lake's northern shore and has picnic tables, campfire rings, flush toilets and drinking water. Reservations are highly recommended.

Sheep Creek Campground (www.nps.gov/seki; Hwy 180; tent & RV sites $18; ⊘late May–mid-Sep) Just a short walk west of the visitor center and village, Cedar Grove's second-biggest camp-ground, with 111 sites, has shady waterfront loops that are especially popular with RVers. Flush

toilets, water, bear-proof lockers and restrooms are available.

Lodgings

Cedar Grove Lodge (☑559-565-3096; www. visitsequoia.com; 86724 Hwy 180; r from $147; ⊘mid-May–mid-Oct; ❀🖭) The only indoor sleeping option in the canyon, this riverside lodge offers 21 motel-style rooms. Three ground-floor rooms with shady furnished patios have spiffy river views, TVs and kitchenettes.

Sequoia High Sierra Camp (☑866-654-2877; www.sequoiahighsierracamp.com; off Forest Rte 13S12; tent cabins for 2 $500; ⊘early Jun–mid-Sep) A mile's hike deep into the Sequoia National Forest is this off-the-grid, all-inclusive resort. Canvas bungalows are spiffed up with pillow-top mattresses, feather pillows and cozy wool rugs. Restrooms and a shower house are shared. Reservations are required and there's usually a two-night minimum stay.

Eating

Markets in Grant Grove and Cedar Grove Villages have a limited selection of grocer-ies. Each village also has a restaurant, the best being **Grant Grove Restaurant** (Hwy 180; mains $8-30; ⊘7-10am, 11:30am-3:30pm & 5-9pm late May-early Sep, until 8pm Apr-late May & early Sep-Oct; 🖭) 🍴.

Information

Cedar Grove Visitor Center (☑559-565-3793; Hwy 180; ⊘9am-5pm late May-late Sep) Small, seasonal visitor center in Cedar Grove Village.

Kings Canyon Visitor Center (☑559-565-4307; Hwy 180; ⊘9am-5pm) The park's main facility in Grant Grove Village.

Road's End Wilderness Permit Station (Hwy 180; ⊘usually 7am-3:30pm late May-late Sep) Dispenses wilderness permits, rents bear-proof canisters and sells a few trail guides and maps between late May and late September. It's 6 miles east of Cedar Grove Village, at the end of Hwy 180.

DAVID H. CARRIERE/GETTY IMAGES ©

General Grant Grove

Rae Lakes Loop

The best backpacking loop in Kings Canyon traverses some of the Sierra Nevada's finest landscapes. The route takes in sun-blessed forests and meadows, crosses one mind-bending pass and skirts a chain of jewel-like lakes beneath the Sierra crest, joining the famous John Muir Trail partway along.

Duration 5 days

Distance 42 miles

Difficulty Hard

Start & Finish Road's End

Nearest Town Cedar Grove Village

Transportation Car

For good reason, this five-day hike is one of the park's most popular trails. Note: one of the bridges on this trail has washed out, making the trail impossible to complete unless you trek at the height of summer when the South Fork of the Kings River is at its lowest.

DAY 1: Road's End to Middle Paradise Valley (7 miles)

The Rae Lakes Loop kicks off with a 4.5-mile hike along the Woods Creek Trail from **Road's End** (5045ft) to **Mist Falls**. Rocky switchbacks lead into the shadier forest. The trail levels out at **Paradise Valley**, less than 2 miles north. The Kings River's South Fork flows through forested meadows,

inviting you to linger at the backpacker campsites in **Lower Paradise Valley** (6600ft). Continue through mixed-conifer forest just over a mile further to **Middle Paradise Valley** (6700ft).

DAY 2: Middle Paradise Valley to Woods Creek (9 miles)

The trail gradually ascends alongside a grassy meadow before dropping back to the river in **Upper Paradise Valley** (6800ft). Forested campsites appear before the confluence of the Kings River's South Fork and Woods Creek, about 1.5 miles from Middle Paradise Valley.

The South Fork Kings River Bridge above Paradise Valley washed out during the winter of 2016–17. At the time of writing, construction of a replacement bridge was due to begin in 2019. It may be possible to cross this section of river in late summer, after a hot spell, when water levels are at their lowest. However, proceed with caution – crossing the South Fork of the Kings River can be extremely hazardous. The trail steadily ascends through a valley above Woods Creek. Less than 4 miles from the river crossing, the trail rolls into **Castle Domes Meadow** (8200ft).

The trail re-enters pine forest. At the signposted **John Muir Trail (JMT) junction** (8500ft), turn right and cross Woods Creek on the suspension bridge. Backpacker campsites sprawl south of the bridge.

DAY 3: Woods Creek to Middle Rae Lake (8 miles)

Heading south, the JMT rolls easily across open slopes along the west side of Woods Creek's South Fork. Crossing a small stream, the trail rises over rocky terrain to a small meadow. At the next crossing, a bigger stream cascades over a cleft in the rock. Foxtail pines dot the dry slope above the trail as it continues up to **Dollar Lake** (10,220ft), about 3.5 miles from the Woods Creek crossing. There's a striking view of **Fin Dome** (11,693ft) above Dollar Lake (camping strictly prohibited).

Skirting Dollar Lake's west shore, the JMT continues up to arrive at larger **Arrowhead Lake** (10,300ft) and enchanting **Lower Rae Lake** (10,535ft). The gently rolling trail crosses several small side streams and passes a spur trail to a seasonal ranger station. Continue to the signed turnoff for campsites above the eastern shore of **Middle Rae Lake** (10,540ft).

DAY 4: Middle Rae Lake to Junction Meadow (8 miles)

Return to the JMT and turn right (south). Walk along the northern shore of **Upper Rae Lake** (10,545ft). Cross the connector stream between the lakes. At a signed trail junction, keep straight ahead on the JMT, which continues south up well-graded switchbacks above the west side of Upper Rae Lake. More switchbacks take you to a tarn-filled basin, from where Glen Pass is visible ahead on the dark, rocky ridgeline. The trail passes several small mountain lakes, then rises to narrow **Glen Pass**

(11,978ft), almost 3 miles from Middle Rae Lake.

Gravelly but well-graded switchbacks take you down from Glen Pass toward a pothole tarn. Filter water here – the next reliable water is not until the Bullfrog Lake outlet a few miles ahead. Head down the canyon until the trail swings south, then contours high above Charlotte Lake. A connector trail to Kearsarge Pass appears about 2.5 miles from Glen Pass, after which you'll soon reach a four-way junction with the main Charlotte Lake (northwest) and Kearsarge Pass (northeast) Trails. Continue straight (south).

At the head of Bubbs Creek, cross a low rise and then start descending, passing a junction. The scenic descent twice crosses the outlet from Bullfrog Lake to reach **Lower Vidette Meadow** (9480ft). Leaving the JMT, turn right (southwest) and follow the trail down Bubbs Creek past campsites and crossing several streams and a large rockslide. The trail drops to Bubbs

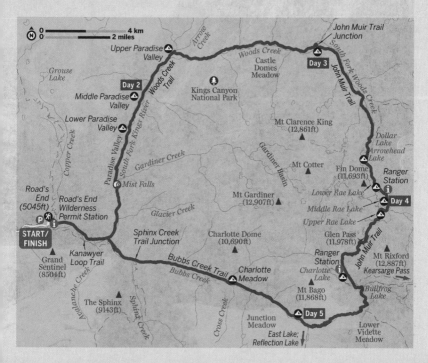

Creek, continuing to aspen-filled **Junction Meadow** (8500ft). Past the signed junction with the East and Reflection Lakes Trails, you'll find grassy campsites.

DAY 5: Junction Meadow to Road's End (10 miles)

The Bubbs Creek Trail meanders down the valley to Charlotte Creek, about 3.5 miles from Junction Meadow, continuing creek-side downhill for three more miles to the **Sphinx Creek Trail junction** (6240ft).

Continuing straight ahead, the Bubbs Creek Trail descends steeply, providing sweeping views. At the canyon floor, the trail crosses braided Bubbs Creek over wooden footbridges. Just beyond the steel **Bailey Bridge** is the Paradise Valley Trail junction. Turn left (west) and retrace your steps from day one for less than 2 miles to **Road's End**. ■

Top: Glen Pass; Bottom Left: Paradise Valley Trail; Bottom Right: Mist Falls

ROOM THE AGENCY/ALAMY STOCK PHOTO ©

STRAYSTONE/SHUTTERSTOCK ©

Bumpass Hell boardwalk

Lassen Volcanic National Park

Offering a glimpse into the earth's fiery core, this alien landscape bubbles over with roiling mud pots, noxious sulfur vents, steamy fumaroles, colorful cinder cones and crater lakes. The region was once a meeting point for Native American tribes; some indigenous people still work closely with the park.

Great For...

State
California

Entrance Fee
7-day entry per vehicle $25 ($10 in winter)

Area
166 sq miles

The dry, smoldering, treeless terrain within this national park stands in stunning contrast to the cool, green conifer forest that surrounds it. That's the summer; in winter tons of snow ensure you won't get too far inside its borders. Still, entering the park from the southwest entrance is to suddenly step into another world.

Hwy 89, the road through the park, wraps around **Lassen Peak** on three sides and provides access to dramatic geothermal formations, pure lakes, gorgeous picnic areas and remote hiking trails.

Hiking

In total, the park has 150 miles of hiking trails, including a 17-mile section of the Pacific Crest Trail. Experienced hikers can attack the **Lassen Peak Trail**; it takes at least 4½ hours to make the 5-mile round-trip but the first 1.3 miles up to the Grandview viewpoint is suitable for families. The 360-degree view from the top is stunning,

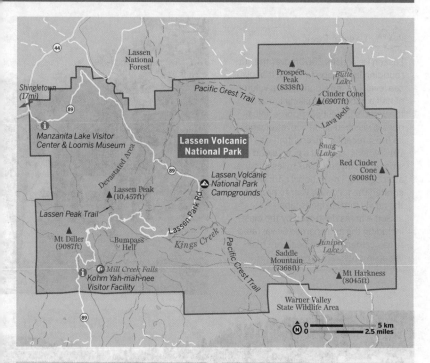

Lassen Peak Trail

Essential Information

From the north on Hwy 89, you won't see many gas/food/lodgings signs after Mt Shasta City. Aside from the eight developed **campgrounds** (☑518-885-3639, reservations 877-444-6777; www.recreation.gov; tent & RV sites $12-24) in the park, there are many more in the surrounding Lassen National Forest. The nearest hotels and motels are in Chester, which accesses the south entrance of the park. There are some basic services near the split of Hwy 89 and Hwy 44, in the north.

There are a few basic places to eat in the small towns surrounding the park but, for the most part, you'll want to pack provisions.

Lassen Peak

Lassen Peak rises 2000ft over the surrounding landscape to 10,457ft above sea level. Lassen's dome has a volume of half a cubic mile, making it one of the world's largest plug-dome volcanoes. Classified as an active volcano, its most recent large eruption was in 1915, when it spewed a giant cloud of smoke, steam and ash 7 miles into the atmosphere. The national park was created the following year to protect the newly formed landscape.

Some areas destroyed by the blast, including the aptly named Devastated Area northeast of the peak, are making an impressive recovery.

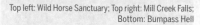
Top left: Wild Horse Sanctuary; Top right: Mill Creek Falls;
Bottom: Bumpass Hell

even if the weather is a bit hazy. Early in the season you'll need snow and ice-climbing equipment to reach the summit.

Near the Kom Yah-mah-nee Visitor Facility, a gentler 2.3-mile trail leads through meadows and forest to **Mill Creek Falls**. Further north on Hwy 89, you'll recognize the roadside sulfur works by its bubbling mud pots, hissing steam vent, fountains and fumaroles.

Bumpass Hell

At Bumpass Hell a moderate 1.5-mile trail and boardwalk lead to an active geothermal area, with bizarrely colored pools and billowing clouds of steam. The road and trails wind through cinder cones, lava and lush alpine glades, with views of Juniper Lake, Snag Lake and the plains beyond. Most of the lakes at higher elevations remain partially and beautifully frozen in summer.

Wild Horse Sanctuary

Since 1978 the **Wild Horse Sanctuary** (☎530-474-5770; www.wildhorsesanctuary.com; 5796 Wilson Hill Rd, Shingletown; ⏰10am-4pm Wed & Sat) FREE has been sheltering horses and burros that would otherwise have been destroyed. You can visit its humble visitor center on to see these lovely animals, or even volunteer for a day with advance arrangement. To see them on the open plains, take a two- to three-day weekend pack trip in spring or summer. Shingletown lies 20 miles to the west of the park. ∎

Diverse Landscapes

From snowy peaks to scorching deserts, and golden-sand beaches to misty redwood forests, California is home to a bewildering variety of ecosytems, flora and fauna.

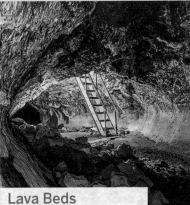

Lava Beds National Monument

Lava flows, cinder and spatter cones, volcanic craters, lava tubes... This was the site of the Modoc War, and ancient Native American petroglyphs are etched into rocks and pictographs painted in caves.

Santa Monica Mountains National Recreation Area

The northwestern-most stretch of the Santa Monica Mountains National Recreation Area is where nature gets bigger and wilder, with jaw-dropping red-rock canyons, and granite outcrops with sublime sea views.

Channel Islands

The Channel Islands have been California's last outpost of civilization ever since seafaring Chumash people established villages on these remote rocks. Marine life thrives here, from coral reefs to giant elephant seals.

Point Reyes National Seashore

This windswept peninsula juts 10 miles out to sea on an entirely different tectonic plate than the mainland, protecting over 100 sq miles of beaches, lagoons and forested hills.

Muir Woods National Monument

Wander among an ancient stand of the world's tallest trees at 550-acre Muir Woods National Monument. Easy hiking trails loop past thousand-year-old coast redwoods at Cathedral Grove.

CHERI ALGUIRE/SHUTTERSTOCK ©

Pinnacles National Park

Named for the towering rock spires that rise abruptly out of the chaparral-covered hills, Pinnacles National Park preserves forests of oak, sycamore and buckeye, wildflower-strewn meadows, and caves. The rocky spires at the heart of the park are the eroded remnants of a long-extinct volcano.

Great For...

State
California

Entrance Fee
7-day pass per car/motorcycle/person on foot or bicycle $30/25/15

Area
42 sq miles

Hiking

Moderate loops of varying lengths and difficulty ascend into the High Peaks and include thrillingly narrow clifftop sections. In the early morning or late afternoon, you may spot endangered California condors soaring overhead. Get an early start to tackle the 9-mile round-trip trail to the top of **Chalone Peak**.

Rangers lead guided full-moon hikes and stargazing programs on some weekend nights, usually in spring or fall. Call ☎831-389-4485 to reserve or check for last-minute vacancies at the visitor center.

Talus Caves

Among the park's biggest attractions are its two talus caves, formed by piles of boulders. **Balconies Cave** is almost always open for exploration. It's pitch-black inside and not for claustrophobes. A flashlight is essential and be prepared to get lost a bit.

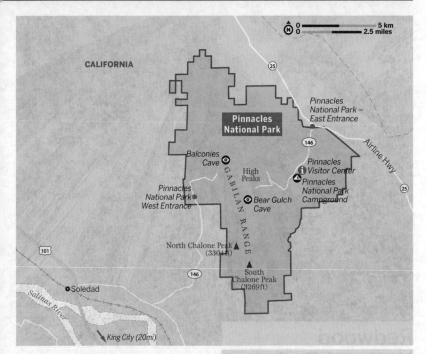

It's along a 2.5-mile hiking loop from the west entrance. Nearer the east entrance, **Bear Gulch Cave** is closed seasonally, so as not to disturb a resident colony of Townsend's big-eared bats.

Climbing

Pinnacles is popular for rock climbing, but has unique conditions due to its relatively soft rock. The most popular areas for climbing are **Bear Gulch**, **Discovery Wall** and the **High Peaks**. Spring and fall are the best seasons, with dry, comfortable weather. Winter climbing can also be good, but expect chilly conditions in the shade. Summer tends to be oppressively hot. For route information, visit the Friends of Pinnacles website (www.pinnacles.org). ∎

Essential Information

There is no road connecting the two sides of the park. To reach the less-developed **west entrance** (⏰7:30am-8pm), exit Hwy 101 at Soledad and follow Hwy 146 northeast for 14 miles. The **east entrance** (⏰24hr), for the visitor center and campground, is accessed via lonely Hwy 25 in San Benito County, southeast of Hollister and northeast of King City.

On the park's east side, the popular, family-oriented **Pinnacles National Park Campground** (☎831-389-4538; www.recreation.gov; 5000 Hwy 146; tent/RV sites $23/36; ⛱) has over 130 sites (some with shade), drinking water, coin-op hot showers, fire pits and an outdoor pool.

WILDNERDPIX/SHUTTERSTOCK ©

Redwood National Park

In the upper reaches of California's northwestern Pacific coast, Redwood National Park houses some of the world's tallest trees, which predate the Roman Empire by over 500 years. Alongside, there's a verdant mix of coastal, riverine and prairie wildlands. Prepare to be impressed.

Great For...

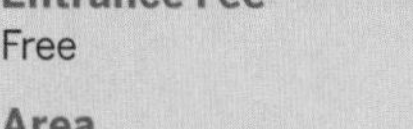

State
California

Entrance Fee
Free

Area
172 sq miles

The national park is seamlessly intertwined with three state parks (Prairie Creek Redwoods, Del Norte Coast Redwoods and Jedediah Smith Redwoods SP), all jointly administered by the National Park Service and the California Department of Parks and Recreation.

Hiking

A network of trails passes through the park's variety of landscapes, offering hiking experiences for all fitness levels.

After picking up a map at the **Thomas H. Kuchel Visitor Center** (707-465-7765; www.nps.gov/redw; Hwy 101, Orick; 9am-5pm Apr-Oct, to 4pm Nov-Mar), you'll have a suite of choices for hiking. The 1-mile kid-friendly loop trail at **Lady Bird Johnson Grove** is a good choice, or you might want to get lost in the secluded serenity of **Tall Trees Grove**.

Most popular with hikers is the 0.7-mile loop into **Fern Canyon**, along a creekside

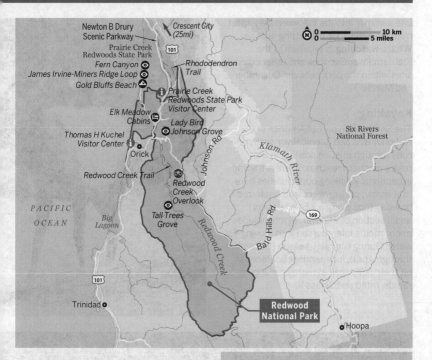

path framed by fern-covered cliff faces. The 6.3-mile **Rhododendron Trail** is especially scenic between mid-May and early June when flamboyant pink and red rhododendrons tower as high as 35ft above the trail. For a classic loop through some of the park's most majestic redwoods, followed by a short jaunt along the Pacific Ocean and a return walk along a 19th-century gold-mining trail, take the 9-mile **James Irvine-Miner's Ridge Loop**.

Stock up on water, muesli bars and similar if you are planning on hiking. Although there are some small towns dotted around, there are very few stores for buying provisions.

Wildlife & Nature

The massive stands of first-growth California coastal redwoods (*Sequoia sempervirens*) here, draped in moss and ferns, tower up to 379ft tall. In among the trees, wildlife-watching opportunities abound,

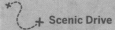

Scenic Drive

Just north of Orick is the turnoff for the 8-mile **Newton B Drury Scenic Parkway**, which runs parallel to Hwy 101 through untouched ancient redwood forests. The parkway is a not-to-miss short detour off the freeway where you can view the magnificence of these trees. Numerous trails branch off from roadside pullouts, including family-friendly options and trails that fit ADA (American Disabilities Act) requirements, such as Big Tree Wayside and Revelation Trail.

One key attraction is the park's resident population of **Roosevelt elk**, which can be seen grazing in the prairie lands at the heart of Prairie Creek Redwoods and along the coast near Gold Bluffs Beach. The males are especially impressive from late summer into the fall, when they sport massive antlers for the rutting season. **Whale-watching** is excellent at the Klamath River Overlook and other coastal sites within the park between December and March.

Kayaking

The Smith River, part of America's National Wild and Scenic River system, runs through pristine scenery in the park's northern reaches. There are some exceptional kayaking opportunities here. In summer, park rangers lead organized half-day trips along a 3.5-mile, class I and II section of the river, which includes minor rapids interspersed with moving flat water. During the rainy season (December through April), independent boaters can pit their skills against more challenging rapids, rated up to class V.

Top left: Roosevelt elk; Top right: Fern Canyon;
Bottom: Lady Bird Johnson Grove

Essential Information

Sleeping

There is an excellent choice of campsites, several with tent pitches beside the pristine Smith River. **Gold Bluffs Beach** (Prairie Creek Redwoods State Park; tent sites $35) sits between 100ft cliffs and wide-open ocean (no reservations). Spotless and bright **Elk Meadow Cabins** (866-733-9637; www.redwoodadventures.com; 7 Valley Green Camp Rd, Orick; cabins $169-299;) has equipped kitchens and all the mod-cons are in a perfect mid-parks location. Expect to see elk on the lawn in the mornings. Cabins sleep six to eight people.

Information

Unlike most national parks, Redwood does not have a main entrance and only charges fees in some sections, most notably the Gold Bluffs Beach and Fern Canyon area. The park's widely dispersed sites of interest are signposted along the main highway, with side roads and parking lots providing access. It's imperative to pick up the free map at the park headquarters in **Crescent City** (707-465-7306; www.nps.gov/redw; 1111 2nd St; 9am-5pm Apr-Oct, to 4pm Nov-Mar) or at the information center in Orick. Rangers here issue permits to visit Tall Trees Grove and loan bear-proof containers to backpackers.

For in-depth redwood ecology, buy the excellent official park handbook. The **Redwood Parks Association** (www.redwoodparksassociation.org) provides good information on its website, including detailed descriptions of all the park's hikes.

Tall Trees Grove

CLASSIC ROAD TRIPS

Northern Redwood Coast

Hug a 700-year-old tree, stroll moody coastal bluffs and drop in on roadside attractions of yesteryear on this trip through verdant redwood parks and personality-packed villages.

Duration 3–4 days

Distance 150 miles

Best Time to Go
April to October for usually clear skies and the region's warmest weather.

Essential Photo
Misty redwoods clinging to rocky Pacific cliffs at Del Norte Coast Redwoods State Park.

Best Scenic Drive
Howland Hill Rd through dense old-growth redwood forests.

❶ Samoa Peninsula
Even though this trip is about misty primeval forest, the beginning is a study of opposites: the grassy dunes and wind-swept beaches of the 10-mile long Samoa Peninsula. At the peninsula's south end is **Samoa Dunes Recreation Area**, part of a 34-mile-long dune system that's the largest in Northern California. While it's great for picnicking or fishing, the wildlife viewing is also excellent.

The Drive » Head north on Hwy 101 from Eureka, passing myriad views of Humboldt Bay. Fifteen miles north of Arcata, take the first Trinidad exit.

❷ Trinidad
Perched on an ocean bluff, cheery Trinidad somehow manages an off-the-beaten-path feel despite a constant flow of visitors. The free town map at the information kiosk will help you navigate the town's cute little shops and several fantastic hiking trails, most notably the **Trinidad Head Trail** with superb coastal views and excellent whale-watching (December to April). If the weather is nice, stroll the exceptionally beautiful cove at **Trinidad State Beach**; if not, make for the **HSU Telonicher Marine Laboratory** (707-826-3671; www.humboldt. edu/marinelab; 570 Ewing St; $1; 9am-4:30pm Mon-Fri year-round, plus 10am-5pm Sat & Sun mid-Sep–mid-May) . It has a touch tank, several aquariums (look for the giant Pacific octopus), an enormous whale jaw and a cool three-dimensional map of the ocean floor.

The Drive » Head back north of town on Patrick's Point Dr to hug the shore for just over 5 miles.

❸ Patrick's Point State Park
Coastal bluffs jut out to sea at 640-acre Patrick's Point State Park, where sandy beaches abut rocky headlands. Easy access to dramatic coastal bluffs makes this a best bet for families, but visitors of any age will find a feast for the senses as they climb rock formations, search for breaching whales, carefully navigate tide pools and listen to barking sea lions and singing birds. The park also has **Sumêg**, an authentic reproduction of a Yurok village, with hand-hewn redwood buildings. In the native plant garden you'll find species for making traditional baskets and medicines. The 2-mile **Rim Trail**, a former Yurok trail around the bluffs, circles the point with access to huge rocky outcrops. Don't miss **Wedding Rock**, one of the park's most romantic spots, or **Agate Beach**, where lucky visitors spot (but don't take, since that's illegal) bits of jade and sea-polished agate.

The Drive » Make your way back out to Hwy 101 through thick stands of redwoods. North another five minutes will bring you

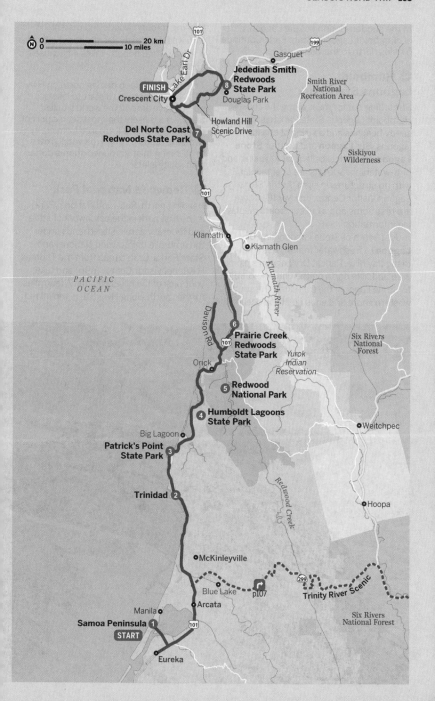

0 ——— 20 km
0 ——— 10 miles

101

Gasquet

199

Jedediah Smith Redwoods State Park

Smith River National Recreation Area

FINISH
Crescent City

8
Douglas Park

Howland Hill Scenic Drive

Del Norte Coast Redwoods State Park

7

101

Siskiyou Wilderness

101

Klamath

Klamath Glen

PACIFIC OCEAN

Davison Rd

Klamath River

6

Prairie Creek Redwoods State Park

Six Rivers National Forest

Orick

Yurok Indian Reservation

5

Redwood National Park

4

Humboldt Lagoons State Park

Big Lagoon

Patrick's Point State Park

3

Weitchpec

Trinidad

2

Redwood Creek

McKinleyville

Hoopa

Blue Lake

p107

299

Trinity River Scenic

Manila

Arcata

Samoa Peninsula

1

Six Rivers National Forest

START

101

Eureka

to the sudden clearing of Big Lagoon, part of Humboldt Lagoons State Park. Continue 6 miles north to the visitor center.

❹ Humboldt Lagoons State Park

Stretching out for miles along the coast, Humboldt Lagoons State Park has long, sandy beaches and a string of coastal lagoons. **Big Lagoon** and prettier **Stone Lagoon** are both excellent for kayaking and bird-watching. Sunsets are spectacular, with no structures in sight. At the Stone Lagoon Visitor Center, on Hwy 101, there are restrooms and a bulletin board displaying information.

Just south of Stone Lagoon, tiny **Dry Lagoon** (a freshwater marsh) has a fantastic day hike. Park at Dry Lagoon's picnic area and hike north on the unmarked trail to Stone Lagoon; the trail skirts the southwestern shore and ends up at the ocean, passing through woods and marshland rich with wildlife. Mostly flat, it's about 2.5 miles one way – and nobody takes it because it's unmarked.

The Drive » Keep driving north on Hwy 101. Now, at last, you'll start to lose all perspective among the world's tallest trees. This is likely the most scenic part of the entire trip; you'll emerge from curvy two-lane roads through redwood groves to stunning mist-shrouded shores dotted with rocky islets.

❺ Redwood National Park

Heading north, Redwood National Park is the first park in the patchwork of state and federally administered lands under the umbrella of Redwood National and State Parks. Grab a map from the Thomas H Kuchel Visitor Center (p96) and take your pick of the hikes on offer. A few miles further north along Hwy 101, a trip inland

RANDY ANDY/SHUTTERSTOCK ©

Top: Sumêg; Bottom left: Wedding Rock; Bottom right: Memorial lighthouse, Trinidad

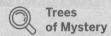

Trees of Mystery

As you pass through Klamath, it's hard to miss the giant statues of Paul Bunyan and Babe the Blue Ox towering over the parking lot at Trees of Mystery – a shameless, if lovable, tourist trap. It has a gondola running through the redwood canopy, and a surprisingly wonderful museum that has an outstanding collection of Native American arts and artifacts.

At Tour Thru Tree, also in Klamath, you can squeeze through a tree and check out the emus.

on Bald Hills Rd will take you to **Lady Bird Johnson Grove**, with its 1-mile kid-friendly loop trail, or get you lost in the secluded serenity of **Tall Trees Grove**. To protect the latter grove, a limited number of cars per day are allowed access; get permits at the visitor center. This can be a half-day trip itself, but you're well rewarded after the challenging approach (a 6-mile rumble on an old logging road behind a locked gate, then a moderately strenuous 4-mile round-trip hike).

The Drive » Back on Hwy 101, less than 2 miles north of Bald Hills Rd, turn left onto Davison Rd, which trundles for 7 miles (mostly unpaved) out to Gold Bluffs Beach.

❻ Prairie Creek Redwoods State Park

The short stroll to **Gold Bluffs Beach** will lead you to the best spot for a picnic. Past the campground, you can take a longer hike beyond the end of the road into **Fern Canyon**, whose 60ft, fern-covered, sheer rock walls are seen in *The Lost World: Jurassic Park*. This is one of the most photographed spots on the North Coast – damp and lush, all emerald green – and totally worth getting your toes wet to see.

Back on Hwy 101, head two miles further north and exit onto the 8-mile **Newton B Drury Scenic Parkway**, which runs parallel to the highway through magnificent, untouched ancient redwood forests.

Family-friendly nature trails branch off from roadside pullouts, including the wheelchair-accessible Big Tree Wayside, and also start outside the **Prairie Creek Redwoods State Park Visitor Center** (☏707-488-2039; www.parks.ca.gov; Newton B Drury Scenic Pkwy; ⊗9am-5pm May-Sep, to 4pm Wed-Sun Oct-Apr), including the Revelation Trail for visually impaired visitors.

The Drive » Follow the winding Newton B Drury Scenic Pkwy with views of the east and its layers of ridges and valleys. On returning to Hwy 101, head north to Klamath, with its bear bridge. Del Norte Coast Redwoods State Park is just a few minutes further north.

❼ Del Norte Coast Redwoods State Park

Marked by steep canyons and dense woods, half the 6400 acres of this park are virgin redwood forest, crisscrossed by 15 miles of hiking trails. Even the most jaded of redwood-watchers can't help but be moved. Tall trees cling precipitously to canyon walls that drop to the rocky, timber-strewn coastline. It's almost impossible to get to the water, except via gorgeous but steep **Damnation Creek Trail** or **Footsteps Rock Trail**. The former may be only 4 miles long, but the 1100ft elevation change and cliffside redwoods make it the park's best hike (temporarily closed since mid-2015). The trailhead is at an unmarked parking pullout along Hwy 101 near mile marker 16.

The Drive » Leaving Del Norte Coast Redwoods State Park and continuing on Hwy 101, you'll enter dreary little Crescent City, a fine enough place to gas up or grab a bite, but not worth stopping at for long. About 4 miles northeast of town, Hwy 199 splits off from Hwy 101; follow it northeast for 6 miles to Hiouchi.

❽ Jedediah Smith Redwoods State Park

The final stop on the trip is loaded with worthy superlatives – the northernmost park has the densest population of redwoods and the last natural undammed, free-flowing river in California, the sparkling

Smith. All in all Jedediah Smith Redwoods State Park is a jewel. The redwood stands here are so dense that few hiking trails penetrate the park, so drive the outstanding 10-mile **Howland Hill Rd**, which cuts through otherwise inaccessible areas, heading back toward Crescent City.

The Drive » It's a rough, unpaved road, and it can close if there are fallen trees or washouts, but you'll feel as if you're visiting from Lilliput as you cruise under the gargantuan trunks. To spend the night, reserve a site at the park's fabulous campground tucked along the banks of the Smith River. ∎

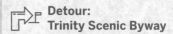

Detour:
Trinity Scenic Byway

Start: ❶ Samoa Peninsula

If you've got an extra couple of days, cut inland on Hwy 299 from Arcata and get lost in the wild country of California's northern mountains.

Cruising this secluded corner of California you'll pass majestic peaks, tranquil inland lakes and historic mountain towns, experiencing both rugged nature and plush hospitality.

Jedediah Smith Redwoods State Park

SIMON DANNHAUER/SHUTTERSTOCK ©

General Sherman Tree

Sequoia National Park

With trees as high as 20-story buildings and as old as the Bible, this extraordinary park has five-star geological highlights, soul-sustaining forests and wildflower meadows. Gaze at dagger-sized stalactites in a 10,000-year-old cave, climb 350 steps to admire the Great Western Divide or drive through a hole in a 2000-year-old log.

Great For...

State
California

Entrance Fee
7-day pass per car/motorcycle $35/20

Area
631 sq miles

❶ General Sherman Tree

By volume the largest living tree on earth, the massive General Sherman Tree rockets into the sky and waaay out of the camera frame. Pay your respects to this giant (which measures more than 100ft around at its base and 275ft tall) via a paved, wheelchair-accessible path from the upper parking lot off Wolverton Rd. The trail cleverly starts at the height of the tree's tip (14 stories high) and descends 0.5 miles to its base.

❷ Giant Forest

This 3-sq-mile grove protects the park's most gargantuan tree specimens, including the General Sherman. Join the Congress Trail, a paved 2-mile pathway that takes in General Sherman, the Washington Tree (the world's second-biggest sequoia) and the see-through Telescope Tree. Hint: take your time on the steep walk back up from

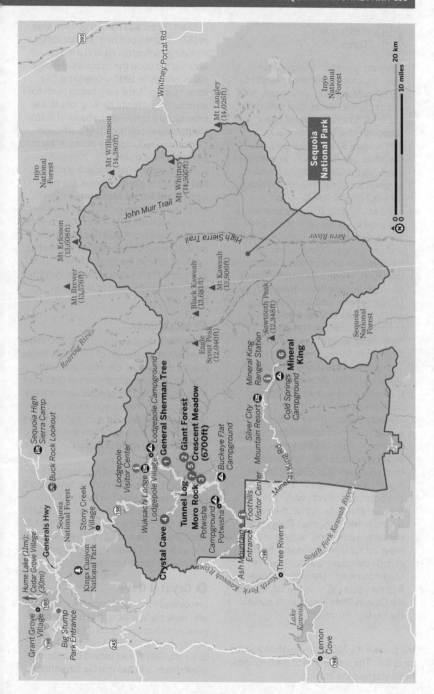

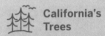

California's Trees

California is a region of superlative trees: the oldest (bristlecone pines of the White Mountains live to nearly 5000 years old), the tallest (coast redwoods reach 380ft) and the largest (giant sequoias of the Sierra Nevada exceed 36ft across). Sequoias are unique to California, adapted to survive in isolated groves on the Sierra Nevada's western slopes in Yosemite, Sequoia and Kings Canyon National Parks.

An astounding 20 native species of oak grow in California, including live (evergreen) oaks with holly-like leaves and scaly acorns. Other common trees include the aromatic California bay laurel, whose long slender leaves turn purple. Rare native trees include Monterey pines and Torrey pines, gnarly species that have adapted to harsh coastal conditions such as high winds, sparse rainfall and sandy, stony soils. Torrey pines only grow at Torrey Pines State Reserve near San Diego and in the Channel Islands, California's hot spot for endemic plant species.

Heading inland, the Sierra Nevada has three distinct eco-zones: the dry western foothills covered with oak and chaparral; conifer forests starting from an elevation of 2000ft; and an alpine zone above 8000ft. Almost two dozen species of conifer grow in the Sierra Nevada, with mid-elevation forests home to massive Douglas firs, ponderosa pines and, biggest of all, the giant sequoia. Deciduous trees include the quaking aspen, a white-trunked tree with shimmering leaves that turn pale yellow in the fall, helping the Golden State live up to its name in the Eastern Sierra.

the grove – it's 7000ft in elevation and the air is thin. The 5-mile Trail of the Sequoias helps you lose the crowds.

Giant Forest was named by John Muir in 1875. At one point over 300 buildings, including campgrounds and a lodge, encroached upon the sequoias' delicate root systems. In 1997, recognizing this adverse impact, the park began to remove structures and resite parking lots. It also introduced a convenient, seasonal visitor shuttle, significantly cutting traffic congestion and reducing the potential harm to these majestic trees.

For a primer on the intriguing ecology and history of giant sequoias, the pint-sized **Giant Forest Museum** (☑559-565-4480; www.nps.gov/seki; 47050 Generals Hwy, cnr Crescent Meadow Rd; ⊙9am-4:30pm winter, 9am-6pm summer) 🌿 FREE has hands-on exhibits about the life stages of these big trees, which can live for more than 3000 years, and the fire cycle that releases their seeds and allows them to sprout on bare soil.

❸ Moro Rock

A quarter-mile staircase climbs 350 steps (over 300ft) to the top of Sequoia's iconic granite dome at an elevation of 6725ft, offering mind-boggling views of the Great Western Divide. This spectacular vantage point is sometimes obscured by thick haze, especially during summer. Historical photos at the trailhead show the rock's original rickety wooden staircase, erected in 1917.

From the Giant Forest Museum, the trailhead is 2 miles up narrow, twisty Moro Rock–Crescent Meadow Rd. The free seasonal shuttle bus (summer only) stops at the small parking lot, which is often full. Alternatively, park at Giant Forest Museum and walk the 1.7 miles along Crescent Meadow Rd to the trailhead.

❹ Crystal Cave

Discovered in 1918 by two park employees who were going fishing, this unique **cave** (www.recreation.gov; Crystal Cave Rd, off Generals Hwy; tours adult/child/youth from $16/5/8; ⊙late May-Sep) 🌿 was carved by an underground river and has marble formations estimated to be 10,000 years old. The cave is also a unique biodiverse habitat for spiders, bats and tiny aquatic insects that are found nowhere else on earth.

Tours fill up quickly, especially on weekends, so buy tickets online at least a month before your trip.

❺ Crescent Meadow

Said to have been described by John Muir as the 'gem of the Sierra,' this lush meadow is buffered by a forest of firs and giant sequoias. High grass and summer wildflowers are good excuses for a leisurely loop hike (1.3 miles), as is watching black bears snack on berries and rip apart logs to feast on insects.

The meadow is almost 3 miles down Moro Rock–Crescent Meadow Rd, best accessed by the free seasonal shuttle bus. The road closes to all traffic after the first snowfall and doesn't reopen until spring, but you can still walk to it – snowshoes or cross-country skiing may be needed.

❻ Mineral King

A scenic subalpine valley at 7500ft, Mineral King is Sequoia's backpacking mecca and a good place to find solitude. Gorgeous and gigantic, its glacially sculpted valley is ringed by massive mountains, including the jagged 12,348ft Sawtooth Peak. The area is reached via Mineral King Rd – a slinky, steep and narrow 25-mile road not suitable for RVs or speed demons; it's usually open from late May through October. Plan on spending the night unless you don't mind driving the three-hour round-trip.

❼ Tunnel Log

Visitors can drive through a 2000-year-old tree, which fell naturally in 1937. It once stood 275ft high with a base measuring 21ft in diameter. Regular sedans and small cars fit through the gap, or it's just as fun to walk through the 17ft-wide, 8ft-high arch cut into the tree by the Civilian Conservation Corps (CCC).

Tunnel Log

Hike Monarch Lakes

HUDSON FLEECE/ALAMY STOCK PHOTO ©

A marmot-lover's paradise! This exceptionally scenic out-and-back high-country route reaches two alpine lakes below jagged Sawtooth Peak. Although it's not very long, the trail can be breathtakingly steep.

A steep climb kicks off this higher-altitude trek. At the Timber Gap Trail junction just over 0.5 miles in, you can see Mineral King Rd back below and snow-brushed peaks looking south. Turn right, following the signs for Sawtooth Pass. Corn lilies and paintbrush speckle **Groundhog Meadow**, named for the whistling marmots that scramble around the granite rocks seemingly everywhere you look during this hike.

Leaving the meadow, rock-hop across burbling **Monarch Creek**. On its far bank, a shady wooded spot is the perfect place for a picnic lunch. From there, begin ascending a stretch of loose and lazy

Duration 4–6 hours

Distance 8.4 miles

Difficulty Hard

Start & Finish Sawtooth/Monarch trailhead parking area

Nearest Town Silver City

switchbacks with goose-bump views. It's a slow, steady climb through red fir and pine forest that won't leave you too winded, though you'll feel the altitude the higher you climb. Blue grouse may be spotted on the hillsides.

At about 2.5 miles, there's a signed junction for the Crystal Lake Trail, which takes a hard and steep right. Bear left and continue straight up toward Sawtooth Pass instead. After flipping to the opposite side of the ridgeline, the trail rounds

Chihuahua Bowl, an avalanche-prone granite basin named after a Mexican mining region. The tree line wavers and fades away, opening up gorgeous views of Monarch Creek canyon, Timber Gap and the peaks of the Great Western Divide.

The distinctive pitch of Sawtooth Peak (12,348ft) is visible ahead. A walk through a large talus field and some stream crossings brings you to **Lower Monarch Lake** (10,400ft), where round-topped Mineral Peak (11,615ft) points up directly south. The maintained trail stops here, but **Upper Monarch Lake** (10,640ft) can be reached by a steep trail heading up the hillside. Established backpacker campsites are by the lower lake; for overnight camping, a wilderness permit is required.

When you're ready, retrace your steps to return. If you're looking for extremely challenging cross-country treks with some steep drop-offs and rock scrambling required, detour up scree-covered **Sawtooth Pass** (11,725ft) or make an alternate return route via **Crystal Lake** (10,900ft). Ask for route advice and safety tips at the Mineral King Ranger Station first.

Note: Mineral King Rd, the winding route up to the Sawtooth/Monarch trailhead, is closed during winter (usually between October and June). Hardcore hikers with snow gear may attempt to trek the snow-covered road from Three Rivers to the trailhead (around 25 miles), but it's not recommended.

Hike General Sherman Tree to Moro Rock

CHECUBUSI/SHUTTERSTOCK ©

A deviation from the popular Congress Trail Loop, this rolling one-way hike takes in huge sequoias, green meadows and the pinnacle of Moro Rock. Expect stretches of blissful solitude and potential black bear sightings.

Keep in mind that hiking this route in one direction is possible only when the free seasonal park shuttle buses are running, usually from late May until late September.

From the General Sherman parking lot and shuttle stop off Wolverton Rd, just east of the Generals Hwy, a paved trail quickly descends through towering sequoias. At an overlook on the way down, you'll get the best view of the **General Sherman Tree**. After walking up to the giant's trunk, turn around and walk downhill on the western branch of the Congress Trail Loop. (If you end up on the eastern branch by mistake, jog right then left

Duration 3–4 hours

Distance 6 miles one way

Difficulty Moderate

Start Wolverton Rd parking lot/ shuttle stop

Finish Moro Rock parking lot/ shuttle stop

Nearest Town Lodgepole Village

at two minor trail junctions that appear about 0.5 miles south of the General Sherman Tree.)

At a five-way junction by the **McKinley Tree**, continue straight ahead south on the dirt trail toward **Cattle Cabin**. Pass the hollow-bottom **Room Tree** and the pretty cluster of the **Founders Group** as you walk through tufts of ferns and corn lilies. Approaching the bright green strip of

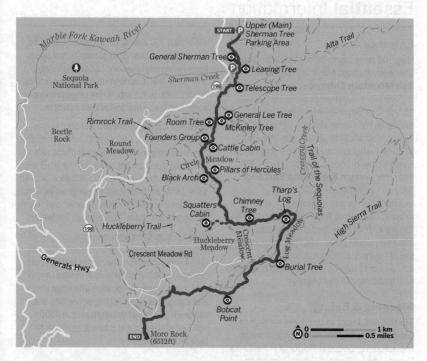

'C'-shaped **Circle Meadow**, there are no more crowds and all you can hear is the breeze and birdsong. Trace the eastern edge of the meadow toward another well-named tree group, the **Pillars of Hercules**. Stand between them and look up for a heroic view.

The trail then passes the huge charred maw of the **Black Arch** tree. Continue south, veering slightly right and then left at the next two trail junctions. At a three-way intersection, lush Crescent Meadow finally comes into view. Go straight at this junction and the next one to continue or make a 0.6-mile round-trip detour to the **Squatters Cabin** by going right on the trail marked 'Huckleberry Meadow.' On the north side of Crescent Meadow stands the hollow-bodied **Chimney Tree**. Continue east past **Tharp's Log**, which once was a pioneer cabin, then turn right (south) on

a paved trail along the east side of **Log Meadow**.

Before reaching the Crescent Meadow parking lot, head left then right onto the signed High Sierra Trail, heading west for more marvelous ridge views. Stop at **Bobcat Point** overlook to take in the Great Western Divide and Kaweah Canyon. In 0.2 miles, cross Crescent Creek on a log to join the Sugar Pine Trail. Go left (west) and follow it for 0.9 miles to **Moro Rock** (pictured). Climb the granite dome for some of the park's best views, then return to your starting point via shuttle buses (the gray route leaves from Moro Rock and goes to Giant Forest Museum, from where the green route goes to General Sherman).

Essential Information

Entrances

Hwy 198 runs north from Visalia through Three Rivers past Mineral King Rd to the **Ash Mountain Entrance** (Generals Hwy, via Sierra Dr; car/person (walk-in)/motorcycle $30/15/25). Beyond here, the road continues as the Generals Hwy, a narrow and windy road snaking all the way into Kings Canyon National Park, where it joins the Kings Canyon Scenic Byway (Hwy 180) near the western **Big Stump Entrance** (Hwy 180; entry per car $30).

There are no gas stations in the park proper; fill up your tank before you arrive in the park. Those in need can find **gas** (559-305-7770; 64144 Hume Lake Rd; pumps 24hr (credit card only after hours), market 8am-noon & 1-5pm) at Hume Lake year-round (11 miles north of Grant Grove Village).

Sleeping & Eating

There's one lodge in the main section of the park proper. Two other lodges are in the adjoining Sequoia National Forest and Grant Grove Village in Kings Canyon has a couple of options. Otherwise, camping is the easiest and most inexpensive way to go.

There's a snack bar at Lodgepole Village, plus a market for camping supplies. Basic supplies are also available at the small store in Stony Creek Lodge (closed between November and April). Park restaurants are limited to Wuksachi and Stony Creek. The town of Three Rivers has more variety and quality.

Camping

Lodgepole, Potwisha and Buckeye Flat campgrounds in the national park and both Stony Creek campgrounds in the national forest offer reservations (essential in summer); most other campgrounds are first-come, first-served. Campfires are allowed only in existing fire rings.

Lodgepole Campground (www.nps.gov/seki; Lodgepole Rd; tent & RV sites $22; mid-Apr–late Nov) Closest to the Giant Forest area, with more than 200 closely packed sites, this place fills quickly because of its proximity to Kaweah River swimming holes and Lodgepole Village amenities. The 16 walk-in sites are more private. Flush toilets, picnic tables, fire rings, drinking water and bear-proof lockers are available.

Potwisha Campground (www.recreation.gov; Generals Hwy; tent & RV sites $22; year-round) Popular campground with decent shade near swimming spots on the Kaweah River. It's 3 miles northeast of the Ash Mountain Entrance, with 42 sites. There are flush toilets, bear-proof lockers, picnic benches and fire pits. Reservations (highly recommended) taken May through September.

Cold Springs Campground (www.nps.gov/seki; Mineral King Rd; tent sites $12; late May-late Oct) A short walk from the ranger station, Cold Springs has 40 sites (nine walk-in sites) and is a peaceful, creekside location with ridge views and a gorgeous forest setting of conifers and aspens. If you spend the night here at 7500ft, you'll be well on your way to acclimatizing for high-altitude hikes.

Lodgings

Silver City Mountain Resort (559-561-3223; www.silvercityresort.com; Mineral King Rd; cabins with/without bath from $205/165, largest cabin from $495; late May-late Oct;) The only food-and-lodging option anywhere near these parts, this rustic, old-fashioned place rents everything from cute and cozy 1950s-era cabins to modern chalets sleeping up to eight. It's 3.5 miles west of the ranger station. Minimum two-night booking may be required.

Wuksachi Lodge (information 866-807-3598, reservations 317-324-0753; www.visitsequoia.com; 64740 Wuksachi Way; r $220-325;) Built in 1999, Wuksachi Lodge is the park's most upscale option. But don't get too excited: the wood-paneled atrium lobby has an inviting stone fireplace and forest views, but the motel-style rooms are fairly generic, with coffeemakers, minifridges, oak furniture and thin walls. The location near Lodgepole Village, however, can't be beat. ∎

General Sherman Tree

MIMI DITCHIE PHOTOGRAPHY/GETTY IMAGES ©

Half Dome

Yosemite National Park

From the emerald-green Yosemite Valley to the giant sequoias catapulting into the air at Mariposa Grove, this place inspires a sense of reverence. Four million visitors wend their way to the country's third-oldest national park annually – and this head-turning park garners the devotion of all who enter.

Great For...

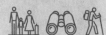

State
California

Entrance Fee
7-day pass per car/motorcycle/person on foot or bicycle $35/30/20

Area
1169 sq miles

❶ Yosemite Valley

The park's crown jewel, spectacular meadow-carpeted Yosemite Valley stretches 7 miles long, bisected by the rippling Merced River and hemmed in by some of the most majestic chunks of granite anywhere on earth. Ribbons of water, including some of the highest waterfalls in the US, fall dramatically before crashing in thunderous displays.

It's also where you'll find amenities in Yosemite and Curry Villages, the visitor center, museum, theater and the Ansel Adams Gallery.

❷ Half Dome

Yosemite's most distinctive natural monument is 87 million years old and has a 93% vertical grade – the sheerest cliff in North America. Climbers come from around the world to grapple with its legendary north face, but good hikers can reach its summit via a 17-mile round-trip trail from Yosemite

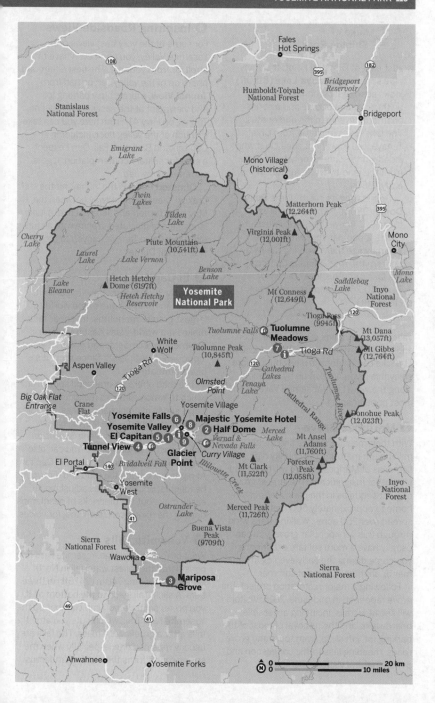

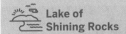

Lake of Shining Rocks

Just east of Olmsted Point, the shiny blue surface of **Tenaya Lake** (8150ft) looks absolutely stunning framed by thick stands of pine and a series of smooth granite cliffs and domes. The lake takes its name from Chief Tenaya, the Ahwahneechee chief who aided white soldiers, only to be driven from the land by white militias in the early 1850s.

Dominating its north side is **Polly Dome** (9806ft). The face nearest the lake is known as Stately Pleasure Dome, a popular spot with climbers – you may see them working their way up from the road. Sloping up from the lake's south shore are Tenaya Peak (10,266ft) and Tresidder Peak (10,600ft).

Valley. The trail gains 4900ft in elevation and has cable handrails for the last 200yd. The hike can be done in a day but is more enjoyable if you break it up by camping along the way (Little Yosemite Valley is the most popular spot).

❸ Mariposa Grove

With their massive stature and multi-millennium maturity, the chunky high-rise sequoias of Mariposa Grove will make you feel rather insignificant. The largest grove of giant sequoias in the park, Mariposa is home to approximately 500 mature trees spread over 250 acres. Walking trails wind through this very popular grove; you can usually have a more solitary experience if you come during the early evening in summer or anytime outside of summer.

Following a major restoration project, the grove reopened in mid-June, 2018. Visitors will see new trails, including accessible boardwalks, and the removal of most of the parking lot, gift shop, tram tours and grove roads, meaning less traffic congestion and a more natural visitor experience.

❹ Inspiring Roadside Views

For some of the very best views over Yosemite Valley, you don't even have to stroll far from your car. The best all-around photo op of the valley can be had from **Tunnel View**, a large, busy parking lot and viewpoint at the east end of Wawona Tunnel, on Hwy 41. From here you can take in much of the valley floor, including El Capitan and Bridalveil Fall. Don't expect a spot for solitary contemplation; it gets extremely crowded.

Olmsted Point is the 'honey, hit the brakes!' viewpoint, midway between the May Lake turnoff and Tenaya Lake: a lunar landscape of glaciated granite with a stunning view down Tenaya Canyon to the back side of Half Dome.

❺ El Capitan

At nearly 3600ft from base to summit, El Capitan ranks as one of the world's largest granite monoliths. Its sheer face makes it a world-class destination for experienced climbers, and one that wasn't 'conquered' until 1958. Since then, it's been inundated.

The road offers several good spots from which to watch climbers reckoning with El Cap's series of cracks and ledges, including the famous 'Nose' – like the Valley View turnout and the pullout along Southside Dr just east of Bridalveil Fall. You can also park on Northside Dr, just below El Capitan. At night, park along the road and dim your headlights; once your eyes adjust, you'll easily make out the pinpricks of headlamps dotting the rock face. Listen, too, for voices.

❻ Yosemite Falls

West of Yosemite Village, Yosemite Falls is considered the tallest waterfall in North America, dropping 740m (2425ft) in three tiers. A slick trail leads to the bottom or, if you prefer solitude, you can clamber up the Yosemite Falls Trail, which puts you atop the falls after a grueling 3.4 miles. The falls are usually mesmerizing, especially when the spring runoff turns them into thunderous cataracts, but are reduced to a trickle by late summer.

❼ Tuolumne Meadows

About 55 miles from Yosemite Valley, 8600ft Tuolumne Meadows is the largest subalpine meadow in the Sierra. Blanketed in snow for most of the year, the meadow explodes to life in summer, when the wildflowers, taking full advantage of the short growing season, fill the grassy expanse with color. Hikers and climbers will find a paradise of options.

The 200ft scramble to the top of Pothole Dome – preferably at sunset – gives you great views of the meadow. Park along Tioga Rd, then follow the trail around the dome's west side and up to its modest summit. It's a fairly quick trip and well worth the effort.

Tuolumne is far less crowded than the valley, though the area around the campground, lodge store and visitor center gets busy, especially on weekends. Altitude can make breathing harder than in the valley, and nights can be nippy, so pack warm clothes.

Tuolumne Meadows sits along Tioga Rd (Hwy 120) west of the park's Tioga Pass Entrance. The **Tuolumne Meadows Hikers' Bus** (☏209-372-1240; www.travelyosemite.com) makes the trip along Tioga Rd once daily in each direction, and can be used for one-way hikes. There's also a free **Tuolumne Meadows Shuttle** (one-way adult/child 5-12yr $9/4.50; ⏱7am-7pm Jun–mid-Sep), which travels between the Tuolumne Meadows Lodge and Olmsted Point, including a stop at Tenaya Lake.

Yosemite Falls

CHRISTIAN/500PX ©

Left: Majestic Yosemite Hotel;
Right: Glacier Point

❽ Majestic Yosemite Hotel

The elegant Majestic Yosemite Hotel has
drawn well-heeled tourists through its towering doors since 1927. Originally named
the Ahwahnee, the hotel was built on the
site of a former Ahwahnee–Miwok village.
A visit to Yosemite Valley is hardly complete
without a stroll through the **Great Lounge**
(aka the lobby), which is handsomely
decorated with leaded glass, sculpted tile,
Native American rugs and Turkish kilims. If
the hotel's lobby looks familiar, perhaps it's
because it inspired the lobby of the Overlook Hotel, the ill-fated inn from Stanley
Kubrick's *The Shining*.

❾ Glacier Point

If you drove, the views from 7214ft Glacier Point might make you feel like you
cheated – superstar sights present themselves without your having made barely any
physical effort. A quick mosey up from the
parking lot and you'll find the entire eastern
Yosemite Valley spread out before you,
from Yosemite Falls to Half Dome, as well
as the distant peaks that ring Tuolumne
Meadows. Half Dome looms practically at
eye level, and if you look closely you can
spot hikers on its summit.

Hike Vernal & Nevada Falls

BAS VERMOLEN/GETTY IMAGES ©

If you can only do a single day hike in Yosemite – and it's springtime – make this the one. Not only are Vernal and Nevada Falls two of Yosemite's most spectacular waterfalls, but Yosemite Falls and Illilouette Fall both make appearances in the distance from select spots on the trail.

There are two ways to hike this loop: up the **Mist Trail** and down the **John Muir Trail** (in a clockwise direction) or vice versa. It's easier on the knees to go for the clockwise route. The granite slabs atop Nevada Fall make for a superb lunch spot (as close to the edge as you want), with the granite dome of **Liberty Cap** (7076ft) towering above.

From the Happy Isles shuttle stop, cross the road bridge over the Merced River, turn right at the trailhead and follow the riverbank upstream. As the trail steepens,

Duration 4–6 hours

Distance 5.4-mile round-trip

Difficulty Moderate–difficult

Start & Finish Vernal & Nevada Falls/ John Muir trailhead

Nearest Junction Happy Isles

Transportation Valley Visitor Shuttle (shuttle stop 16)

watch over your right shoulder for Illilouette Fall (often dry in summer), which peels over a 370ft cliff in the distance. From a lookout, you can gaze west and see Yosemite Falls. After 0.8 miles you arrive at the **Vernal Fall footbridge**, which offers the first view of 317ft Vernal Fall upstream.

Shortly beyond the Vernal Fall footbridge (just past the water fountain and restrooms), you'll reach the junction of the

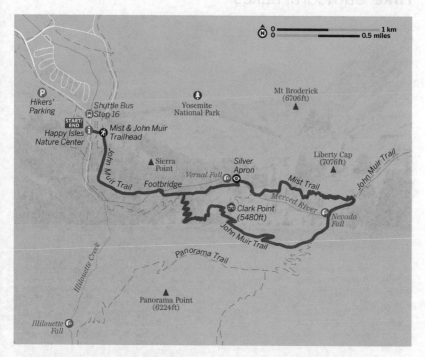

John Muir and Mist Trails. To do the trail clockwise, hang a left and shortly begin the steep 0.3-mile ascent to the top of **Vernal Fall** (pictured) by way of the Mist Trail's granite steps. If it's springtime, prepare to get drenched in spray – wear some waterproof clothing!

Above the falls, the Merced whizzes down a long ramp of granite known as the **Silver Apron** and into the deceptively serene Emerald Pool before plunging over the cliff. *Don't enter the water:* underwater currents in Emerald Pool have whipped many swimmers over the falls.

From above the apron, it's another 1.3 miles via granite steps and steep switchbacks to the top of the Mist Trail, which meets the John Muir Trail, about 0.2 miles northeast of the falls. From this junction, it's 2.5 miles back to Happy Isles via the Mist Trail or 4 miles via the John Muir Trail.

Shortly after joining the John Muir Trail, you'll cross a footbridge (elevation 5907ft) over the Merced. Beneath it, the river whizzes through a chute before plummeting 594ft over the edge of **Nevada Fall**. Nevada Fall is the first of the series of steps in the **Giant Staircase**, a metaphor that becomes clear when viewed from afar at Glacier Point. Plant yourself on a slab of granite for lunch and views, and be prepared to fend off the ballsy Steller's jays and squirrels.

Returning back from Nevada Fall along the John Muir Trail offers a fabulous glimpse of Yosemite Falls. The trail passes the Panorama Trail junction and traverses a cliff, offering awesome views of Nevada Fall. Soon you'll reach **Clark Point** and a junction that leads down to the Mist Trail. From here it's just over 2 miles downhill, through Douglas firs and canyon live oaks to Happy Isles.

Hike Cathedral Lakes

MARKMANDERSONFILMS/SHUTTERSTOCK ©

Easily one of Yosemite's most spectacular hikes, this steady climb through mixed conifer forest ends with glorious views of Cathedral Peak from the shores of two shimmering alpine lakes.

Lower Cathedral Lake (9289ft) sits within a mind-blowing glacial cirque, a perfect amphitheater of granite capped by the iconic spire of nearby **Cathedral Peak** (10,911ft). From the lake's southwest side, the granite drops steeply away, affording views as far as Tenaya Lake, whose blue waters shimmer in the distance. Although it's only about two hours to this lower lake, you could easily spend an entire day exploring the granite slopes, meadows and peaks surrounding it. Continuing to the **Upper Cathedral Lake** (9585ft) adds less than an hour to the hike and puts the round-trip walk at 8 miles, including the stop at Cathedral Lake. Admittedly,

Duration 3–6 hours

Distance 8-mile round-trip (upper lake)

Difficulty Moderate

Start & Finish Cathedral Lakes trailhead

Nearest Town Tuolumne Meadows

Transportation Tuolumne Meadows hikers' bus (shuttle stop 7)

the upper lake is less spectacular when measured against the lower lake, but by all other standards it's utterly sublime.

Parking for the Cathedral Lake trailhead is along the shoulder of Tioga Rd, 0.5 miles west of Tuolumne Meadows Visitor Center. Due to the popularity of this hike, parking spaces fill up fast, so arrive early or take the free shuttle. Camping is allowed at the lower lake (despite what

YOSEMITE NATIONAL PARK **127**

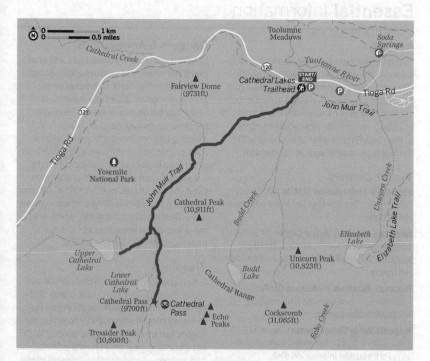

some maps show), but be absolutely certain you're 100ft from the water *and* the trail, and that you choose an already impacted site to prevent further damage. Better yet, camp somewhere near the upper lake or off the pass.

From the Cathedral Lake trailhead on Tioga Rd, the hike heads southwest along the John Muir Trail. Almost immediately, it begins to climb through forest of lodgepole pine, mountain hemlock and the occasional whitebark pine. After ascending over 400ft, the trail levels out and a massive slab of granite – the northern flank of Cathedral Peak – slopes up from the left side of the trail. Soon you'll see Fairview Dome (9731ft) through the trees to your right.

Before long, the trail begins its second ascent, climbing nearly 600ft before leveling off and affording outstanding views of

Cathedral Peak. Three miles from the trailhead, you'll hit the junction that leads 0.5 miles southwest to Cathedral Lake. This trail crosses a stunning **meadow** (turn around as you cross it for the head-on view of Cathedral Peak) before arriving at the granite shores of the lake. Be sure to follow the trail around the lake and take in the views from the southwest side.

To visit the upper lake, backtrack to the main trail, turn right (southeast) and, after about 0.5 miles, you'll hit the lake. If you wish to stretch the hike out even further, you can continue past the upper lake to **Cathedral Pass** (9700ft), where you'll be rewarded with a stellar side view of Cathedral Peak and Eichorn Pinnacle (Cathedral's fin-like west peak). This side trip adds about 0.6 miles to the trip.

Essential Information

Access

Yosemite is accessible year-round from the west (via Hwys 120 W and 140) and south (Hwy 41), and in summer from the east (via Hwy 120 E). Roads are plowed in winter, but snow chains may be required at any time. In 2006 a mammoth rockslide buried part of Hwy 140, 6 miles west of the park; traffic there is restricted to vehicles under 45ft.

Visitor Centers

Big Oak Flat Information Station (209-372-0200; 8am-5pm late May-Oct) Has a wilderness permit desk.

Tuolumne Meadows Visitor Center (209-372-0263; 9am-6pm Jun-Sep) Information desk, bookstore and small exhibits on the area's wildlife and history.

Tuolumne Meadows Wilderness Center (209-372-0309; 8am-5pm late May–mid-Oct) Issues wilderness permits.

Yosemite Valley Visitor Center (209-372-0200; 9035 Village Dr, Yosemite Village; 9am-5pm) Park's busiest information desk.

Yosemite Valley Wilderness Center (209-372-0745; Yosemite Village; 8am-5pm May-Oct) Permits, maps and backcountry advice.

Information

Upon entering the park, you'll receive an NPS map and a copy of the seasonal *Yosemite Guide* newspaper. The official NPS website (www.nps.gov/yose) has comprehensive information. For recorded park information, call 209-372-0200.

Stores in Yosemite Village, Half Dome Village and Wawona all have ATMs, as do the Yosemite Valley Lodge and the Majestic Yosemite Hotel.

Fill your tank year-round at Wawona or Crane Flat inside the park (you'll pay dearly), at El Portal on Hwy 140 just outside its western boundary, or at Lee Vining at the junction of Hwys 120 and 395 outside the park in the east.

Dangers & Annoyances

Landslides frequently close trails and steep paths get slippery after rains and flooding.

Avoid direct contact and exposure to animal droppings, especially rodents, and never touch a dead one. Avoid sleeping on the ground; always use a cot, hammock, sleeping bag or other surface. Follow park rules on proper food storage and utilize bear-proof food lockers when parked overnight.

Mountain lion sightings are uncommon, but if you see one, do not run; rather, attempt to scare it away by shouting and waving your arms. Do the same for coyotes, which are more frequently seen. Report sightings to park dispatch (209-372-0476).

Sleeping

Reservations for the seven campgrounds within the park that aren't first-come, first-served are handled by Recreation.gov, up to five months in advance. Competition for sites is fierce from May to September. Without a booking, your only chance is to hightail it to an open campground or proceed to one of four campground reservation offices in Yosemite Valley, Wawona, Big Oak Flat and Tuolumne Meadows.

All noncamping reservations within the park are handled by **Aramark/Yosemite Hospitality** (888-413-8869; www.travel yosemite.com) and can be made up to 366 days in advance; reservations are critical from May to early September. Rates – and demand – drop from October to April.

Other park visitors overnight in nearby gateway towns like Fish Camp, Midpines, El Portal, Mariposa and Groveland; however, commute times into the park can be long.

Eating

The **Village Store** (Yosemite Village; 8am-8pm, to 10pm summer) has the best selection (including health-food items and some organic produce), while stores at Half Dome Village, Wawona, Tuolumne Meadows and the Yosemite Valley Lodge are more limited. ∎

Yosemite Valley Visitor Center

Yosemite, Sequoia & Kings Canyon

Drive up into the lofty Sierra Nevada, where glacial valleys and ancient forests overfill the windshield scenery. Go climb a rock, pitch a tent or photograph wild-flowers and wildlife.

Duration 5–7 days

Distance 450 miles

Best Time to Go
April and May for waterfalls; June to September for full access.

Essential Photo
Yosemite Valley from panoramic Tunnel View.

Best Scenic Drive
Kings Canyon Scenic Byway to Cedar Grove.

❶ Tuolumne Meadows

These are the Sierra Nevada's largest sub-alpine meadows, with fields of wildflowers, bubbling streams, ragged granite peaks and cooler temperatures at an elevation of 8600ft. Note that the route crossing the Sierra and passing by the meadows, **Tioga Rd** (a 19th-century wagon road and Native American trading route), is completely closed by snow in winter. It usually reopens in May/June and remains passable until October or November.

Nine miles west of the meadows, a sandy half-moon beach wraps around **Tenaya Lake**, tempting you to brave some of the park's coldest swimming. A few minutes further west, stop at **Olmsted Point**, over-looking a lunar-type landscape of glaciated granite.

The Drive » From Tuolumne Meadows it's 50 miles to Yosemite Valley, following Tioga Rd (Hwy 120), turning south onto Big Oak Flat Rd, then east onto El Portal Rd.

❷ Tunnel View

For your first, spectacular look into Yosemite Valley, pull over at Tunnel View, a vista that has inspired painters, poets, natural-ists and adventurers for centuries. On the right, Bridalveil Fall swells with snowmelt in late spring, but by late summer it's a mere whisper. Spread below you are the pine forests and meadows of the valley floor, with the sheer face of El Capitan rising on the left and, in the distance straight ahead, iconic granite Half Dome.

The Drive » Merge carefully back onto eastbound Wawona Rd, which continues downhill into Yosemite Valley, full of con-fusingly intersecting one-way roads. Drive east along the Merced River on Southside Dr past the Bridalveil Fall turnoff. Almost 6 miles from Tunnel View, turn left and drive across Sentinel Bridge to Yosemite Village's day-use parking lots. Ride free shuttle buses that circle the valley.

❸ Yosemite Valley

At busy Yosemite Village, start inside the Yosemite Valley Visitor Center (p128), with its thought-provoking history and nature displays and free *Spirit of Yosemite* film screenings. At the nearby **Yosemite Museum** (www.nps.gov/yose; 9037 Village Dr, Yosemite Village; ⊙9am-5pm summer, 10am-4pm rest of year, often closed noon-1pm) 🖋 FREE, Western landscape paintings are hung beside Native American baskets and beaded clothing.

The valley's famous waterfalls are thun-derous cataracts in May, but mere trickles by late July. Triple-tiered **Yosemite Falls** is North America's tallest, while **Bridalveil Fall** is hardly less impressive. A strenuous, often slippery staircase beside Vernal Fall

Tuolumne Meadows

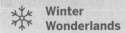

❄️ Winter Wonderlands

When the temperature drops and the white stuff falls, there are still tons of fun outdoor activities around the Sierra Nevada's national parks. In Yosemite, strap on some skis or a snowboard and go tubing downhill off Glacier Point Rd; plod around Yosemite Valley on a ranger-led snowshoe tour; or just try to stay upright on ice skates at Half Dome Village. Further south in Sequoia and Kings Canyon National Parks, the whole family can go snowshoeing or cross-country skiing among groves of giant sequoias. Before embarking on a winter trip to the parks, check road conditions on the official park websites or by calling ahead. Don't forget to put snow tires on your car, and always carry tire chains too.

leads you, gasping, right to the top edge of the waterfall, where rainbows pop in clouds of mist. Keep hiking up the same Mist Trail to the top of **Nevada Fall** for a heady 5.5-mile round-trip trek.

The Drive » Use Northside Dr to loop round and join Wawona Rd again. Follow Wawona Rd/Hwy 41 up out of the valley. After 9 miles, turn left onto Glacier Point Rd at the Chinquapin intersection, driving 15 more miles to Glacier Point.

❹ Glacier Point

In just over an hour, you can zip from Yosemite Valley up to head-spinning Glacier Point. Note that the final 10 miles of Glacier Point Rd is closed by snow in winter, usually from November through April or May. During winter, the road remains open as far as the Yosemite Ski & Snowboard Area, but snow tires and tire chains may be required.

Rising over 3000ft above the valley floor, dramatic Glacier Point (7214ft) practically puts you at eye level with Half Dome. On your way back from Glacier Point, take time out for a 2-mile hike up **Sentinel Dome** or out to **Taft Point** for incredible 360-degree valley views.

The Drive » Drive back downhill past Yosemite Ski & Snowboard Area, turning left at the Chinquapin intersection and winding south through thick forest on Wawona Rd/Hwy 41. After almost 13 curvy miles, you'll reach Wawona, with its lodge, visitor center, general store and gas station, all on your left.

❺ Wawona

At Wawona, a 45-minute drive south of the valley, drop by the **Pioneer Yosemite History Center** (☎209-372-0200; www.nps. gov/yose/planyourvisit/upload/pyhc.pdf; rides adult/child $5/4; ☉24hr, rides 10am-2pm Wed-Sun Jun-Sep) FREE, with its covered bridge, pioneer-era buildings and historic Wells Fargo office. On summer evenings, imbibe a civilized cocktail in the lobby lounge of the **Big Trees Lodge** (☎reservations 888-413-8869; www.travelyosemite.com; 8308 Wawona Rd; r with/without bath from $220/150; ☉mid-Mar–late Nov & mid-Dec–early Jan; 🛜🏊), where pianist Tom Bopp often plays tunes from Yosemite's bygone days.

The Drive » By car, follow Wawona Rd/Hwy 41 south for 4.5 miles to the park's south entrance, where you must leave your car at the new parking lot. A free shuttle will take you to Mariposa Grove.

❻ Mariposa Grove

Wander giddily around the Mariposa Grove, home to 500 giant sequoias. Nature trails wind through this popular grove, but you can only hear yourself think above the noise of vacationing crowds during the early morning or evening.

The Drive » From Yosemite's south entrance station, it's a 115-mile, three-hour trip to Kings Canyon National Park. Follow Hwy 41 south 60 miles to Fresno, then slingshot east on Hwy 180 for another 50 miles, climbing out of the Central Valley back into the mountains. Keep left at the Hwy 198 intersection, staying on Hwy 180 toward Grant Grove.

❼ Grant Grove

North of Big Stump entrance station in Grant Grove Village, turn left and wind

Mariposa Grove

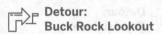

Detour:
Buck Rock Lookout

Start: ⑧ Cedar Grove

To climb one of California's most evocative fire lookouts, drive east of the Generals Hwy on Big Meadows Rd into the Sequoia National Forest between Grant Grove and the Giant Forest. Follow the signs to staffed **Buck Rock Fire Lookout** (☏559-901-8151; www.buckrock.org; ☉10am-4pm mid–May-Oct). Constructed in 1923, this active fire lookout allows panoramic views from a dollhouse-sized cab lording it over the horizon from 8500ft atop a granite rise, reached by 172 spindly stairs. It's not for anyone with vertigo. Opening hours may vary seasonally, and the lookout closes during lightning storms and fire emergencies.

Glacier Point and Half Dome

Detour: Crystal Cave

Start: **❾** **Giant Forest**

Off the Generals Hwy, about 2 miles south of the Giant Forest Museum, turn right (west) onto twisting 6.5-mile-long Crystal Cave Rd for a fantastical walk inside 10,000-year-old **Crystal Cave** (www.recreation.gov; ⊗late May–Sep; tours adult/child/youth from $16/5/8), carved by an underground river. Stalactites hang like daggers from the ceiling, and milky-white marble formations take the shape of ethereal curtains, domes, columns and shields. Bring a light jacket – it's 50°F (10°C) inside the cave. Buy tour tickets a month or more in advance online at www.recreation.gov; during October and November, tickets are only sold in person at the Giant Forest Museum and Foothills Visitor Center. Tour tickets are not available at the cave itself.

downhill to Grant Grove, where you'll see some of the park's landmark giant sequoia trees. You can walk right through the Fallen Monarch, a massive, fire-hollowed trunk that's done duty as a cabin, hotel, saloon and horse stable.

The Drive » Kings Canyon National Park's main visitor areas, Grant Grove and Cedar Grove, are linked by the narrow, twisting, 30-mile Kings Canyon Scenic Byway (Hwy 180). Hwy 180 from the Hume Lake turnoff to Cedar Grove is closed during winter (usually mid-November through mid-April).

❽ Cedar Grove

Hwy 180 plunges down to the Kings River, where roaring white water ricochets off the granite cliffs of North America's deepest canyon, technically speaking. Pull over partway down at the **Junction View** overlook for an eyeful, then keep rolling down along the river to **Cedar Grove Village**. East of the village, **Zumwalt Meadow** is the place for spotting birds, mule deer and black

bears. Starting from **Road's End**, a very popular day hike climbs 4 miles each way to **Mist Falls**, which thunders in late spring.

The Drive » Backtrack from Road's End nearly 30 miles up Hwy 180. Turn left onto Hume Lake Rd. Curve around the lake past swimming beaches and campgrounds, turning right onto 10 Mile Rd. At Hwy 198, turn left and follow the Generals Hwy (often closed from January to March) south for about 23 miles to the Wolverton Rd turnoff on your left.

❾ Giant Forest

Park off Wolverton Rd and walk downhill to reach the world's biggest living tree, the **General Sherman Tree**. By car, drive 2.5 miles south along the Generals Hwy to the **Giant Forest Museum**. Starting outside the museum, Crescent Meadow Rd makes a 6-mile loop into the Giant Forest, passing right through **Tunnel Log**. Note: Crescent Meadow Rd is closed to traffic by winter snow; during summer, ride the free shuttle buses around the loop road.

The Drive » Narrowing, the Generals Hwy drops for more than 15 miles into the Sierra Nevada foothills, passing Amphitheater Point and exiting the park beyond Foothills Visitor Center. Before reaching the town of Three Rivers, turn left on Mineral King Rd, a dizzyingly scenic 25-mile road (partly unpaved, no trailers or RVs allowed and closed in winter) that switchbacks up to Mineral King Valley.

❿ Mineral King Valley

Navigating over 700 hairpin turns, it's a winding 1½-hour drive up to the glacially sculpted **Mineral King Valley** (7500ft). Trailheads into the high country begin at the end of Mineral King Rd, where historic private cabins dot the valley floor flanked by massive mountains. Your final destination is just over a mile past the ranger station, where the valley unfolds all of its hidden beauty, and hikes to granite peaks and alpine lakes beckon.

Note that Mineral King Rd is typically open only from late May through late October. ∎

Top left: Zumwalt Meadow; Top right: Giant Forest Museum; Bottom: Upper Yosemite Falls

In this chapter
Arches 170
Big Bend ....
Bryce Canyon 158
Canyonlands 170
Capitol Reef 176
Grand Canyon 188

THE SOUTHWEST

In This Chapter

Arches...................................140
Big Bend...............................146
Bryce Canyon......................158
Canyonlands.......................170
Capitol Reef........................176
Carlsbad Caverns...............184
Grand Canyon.....................186
Great Basin..........................196
Guadalupe Mountains.........198
Mesa Verde..........................204
Petrified Forest...................210
Saguaro...............................214
Zion......................................216

The Southwest

The Southwest is America's untamed playground, luring travelers with giant arches, desert mesas, canyons and ancient petroglyphs. Whether you're admiring a giant cactus or the polished walls of a narrow slot canyon, one thing's clear: water rules all here.

Trace the Colorado River to find a string of desert jewels: Arches, Canyonlands and the Grand Canyon. Further west are neck-craning Zion and Bryce's surreal hoodoos. A network of scenic drives links the most beautiful sites.

Don't Miss

o Feeling minuscule in front of the Grand Canyon (p186)

o Driving Big Bend's scenic roads (p152)

o Witnessing Island in the Sky's enthralling views (p170)

o Rambling to rock formations in Arches National Park (p140)

o River-splashed hiking in Zion's fabled Narrows (p216)

o Delving into Mesa Verde's ancient mysteries (p204)

When to Go

In summer (June to August), temperatures soar well above 100°F and national parks are at maximum capacity; higher elevations bring cool relief. Fall is the best time to go, with colorful scenes, cooler temperatures and lighter crowds on the Grand Canyon South Rim.

National parks in Utah and northern Arizona clear out as the snow arrives from December to March, though it's busy on the slopes in Utah, Colorado and New Mexico.

Previous page: Grand Canyon National Park (p186)
AMINCAH/SHUTTERSTOCK ©

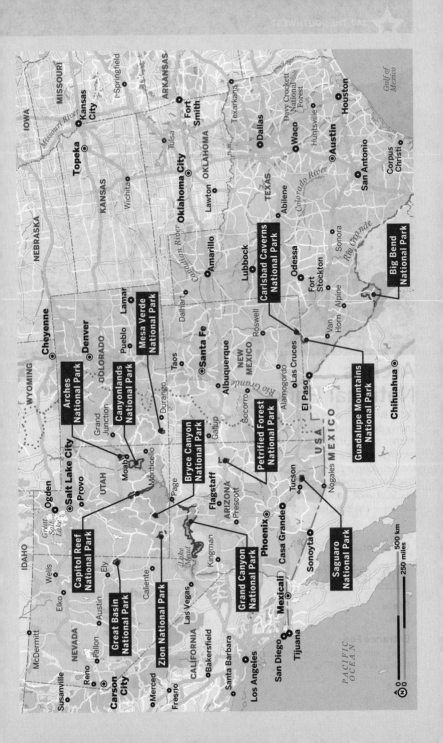

CHECUBUS/SHUTTERSTOCK ©

Double O Arch

Arches National Park

Giant sweeping arcs of sandstone frame snowy peaks and desert landscapes at Arches National Park. It's the highest density of rock arches on earth: more than 2500 in a 119-sq-mile area. You'll lose perspective on size at some, such as 290ft-wide Landscape Arch. Others are tiny – the smallest is only 3ft across.

Great For...

State
Utah

Entrance Fee
7-day pass per car/motorcycle/person on foot or bicycle $30/25/15

Area
119 sq miles

To hit all the highlights, follow the paved **Arches Scenic Drive**. It's packed with photo ops and short walks to arches and iconic landmarks. The full 43-mile drive (including spurs) takes two to three hours if you're not taking any hikes.

❶ Delicate Arch

You've seen this arch before: it's the unofficial state symbol, stamping nearly every Utah tourist brochure. The best way to experience it is from beneath. Park near **Wolfe Ranch**, a well-preserved 1908 pioneer cabin. From there a footbridge crosses **Salt Wash** (near Native American rock art) and marks the beginning of the moderate-to-strenuous, 3-mile round-trip trail to the arch itself. The trail ascends slickrock, culminating in a wall-hugging ledge before reaching the arch.

Ditch the crowds by passing beneath the arch and continuing down the rock by several yards to where there's a great

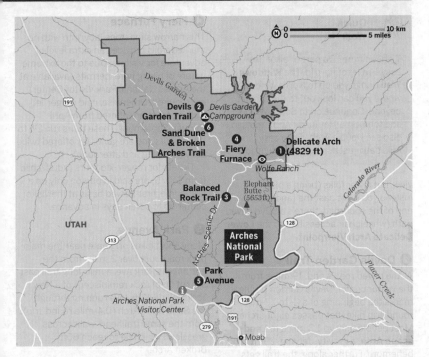

Delicate Arch

view, but fewer folks (bring a picnic). If instead you drive past the ranch to the end of the spur road, there's a 50yd paved path (wheelchair accessible) to the **Lower Delicate Arch Viewpoint**.

❷ Devils Garden Trail

At the paved road's end, 19 miles from the visitor center, Devils Garden trailhead marks the beginning of a 2- to 7.7-mile round-trip hike that passes eight arches. Most people only go 1.3 miles to **Landscape Arch**, a gravity-defying, 290ft-long behemoth. Further along, the trail gets less crowded, growing rougher and steeper toward **Double O Arch** and **Dark Angel Spire**.

The optional, difficult **Devils Garden Primitive Loop** has narrow-ledge walking and serious slickrock hiking. Ask rangers about conditions before attempting it.

❸ Balanced Rock Trail

A 3577-ton boulder atop a leaning pedestal, Balanced Rock shoots from the earth like a fist. The pedestal is made of soft Dewey Bridge mudstone, which erodes faster than the rock above. Eventually, this pedestal will snap, and the boulder will come crashing down.

While you can see the formation clearly from the trailhead, the easy, 0.3-mile loop allows you to grasp its actual size (55ft to the top of the pedestal, 128ft to the top of the rock). There is wheelchair access to the viewpoint.

❹ Fiery Furnace

This narrow sandstone labyrinth with no marked trails provides an extra level of adventure for visitors. Due to the extreme nature of hiking here, permits (available at the Arches National Park Visitor Center) are required. Otherwise, paid ranger-led walking tours are offered from April through September. These tours run 2½ to three hours and are generally offered twice daily (morning and afternoon).

Tickets for ranger-led tours (adult/child from $10/5) are sold in person only on a first-come, first-served basis at the visitor center up to seven days in advance.

❺ Park Avenue

Many short hikes originate near the main park road. Just over 2 miles from the entrance is Park Ave, a mile-long trail past a giant fin of rock reminiscent of a New York skyline. Kids love running through the Sand Dune Arch (0.4-mile round-trip); from the same trailhead, walk across grassland for 1 mile to reach 60ft Broken Arch.

❻ Sand Dune & Broken Arches Trail

From the Sand Dune Arch parking area, follow the trail through deep sand between narrow stone walls that are the backmost fins of **Fiery Furnace**. In less than 0.25 miles you'll arrive at **Sand Dune Arch**, which looks something like a poodle kissing a polar bear. Resist the temptation to climb or jump off the 8ft arch. From here you can bear left to return to your car or bear right across open grassland en route to Broken Arch. At the next fork (the start of the loop trail), grasses give way to piñon pines and junipers along a gentle climb to **Broken Arch**. The treat here is the walk *through* the arch atop a slickrock ledge. Wear rubber-soled shoes or boots, or you may have trouble climbing to the arch.

This 2.4-mile loop is a good trail for kids, especially the first section.

Devils Garden trail

Essential Information

Sleeping & Eating

There's stiff competition for camping in the park but there are plenty of campgrounds throughout the region and lodging galore in Moab. No food is available in the park; Moab is the place to stock up or dine out.

Devils Garden Campground (☎877-444-6777; www.recreation.gov; Arches National Park; tent & RV sites $25) Surrounded by red rock and scrubby piñons, the park's only campground is 19 miles from the Arches National Park Visitor Center. From March to October, sites are available by reservation. Book months ahead.

Information

In summer arrive by 9am, when crowds are sparse and temperatures bearable, or visit after 7pm and enjoy a moonlight stroll. July highs average 100°F (38°C); carry at least one gallon of water per person if hiking. Two rugged back roads lead into semi-solitude, but 4WD is recommended – ask at the visitor center. Cell phones do not work in most of the park.

Arches National Park Visitor Center (☎435-719-2299; www.nps.gov/arch/planyourvisit/hours.htm; Arches National Park; ⊙7:30am-5pm) Has Arches canyoneering and climbing permits (also available at archespermits.nps.gov). You can watch an informative video, check ranger-led activity schedules and pick up your Fiery Furnace tickets.

Getting There & Around

As yet the park has no shuttle system and no public buses so most visitors arrive in cars. Ongoing road-widening efforts mean delays are possible.

Several outfitters in Moab run motorized park tours. **Moab Adventure Center** (☎866-904-1163, 435-259-7019; www.moab adventurecenter.com; 225 S Main St; half-day tours from $85) and **Adrift Adventures** (☎800-874-4483, 435-259-8594; www.adrift. net; 378 N Main St; half-day tours from $90) have scenic-drive van tours. ∎

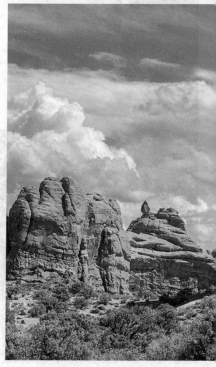

Top left: Broken Arch; Top right: Long-nosed leopard lizard; Bottom: Balanced Rock

Balanced Rock

Big Bend National Park

When you're traversing Big Bend's 1252 sq miles, you come to appreciate what 'big' really means. It's a land of incredible diversity, vast enough to allow a lifetime of discovery, yet laced with enough well-placed roads and trails to permit short-term visitors to see a lot in two to three days.

Great For...

State
Texas

Entrance Fee
7-day pass per car/motorcycle/person on foot or bicycle $25/20/12

Area
1252 sq miles

Scenic Drives

With 110 miles of paved road and 150 miles of dirt road, scenic driving is easily the park's most popular activity.

Old Maverick Road

The 23-mile stretch between the west entrance and park headquarters is notable for its desert scenery and wildlife. Just west of Basin Junction, a side trip on the gravel Grapevine Hills Rd leads to fields of oddly shaped, highly eroded boulders.

Ross Maxwell Scenic Drive

This 30-mile route leaves Maverick Dr midway between the west entrance and park headquarters. The Chisos Mountains provide a grand panorama, and the big payoff is the view of Santa Elena Canyon and its 1500ft sheer rock walls.

Rio Grande Village Drive

This 21-mile drive leads from park head-quarters toward the Sierra del Carmen

Santa Elena Canyon

Starry Nights

Big Bend has taken major steps to reduce light pollution in the last few years, installing LED lights and retrofitting outdoor light sources on more than 280 buildings and in other developed areas. These steps make it easier to see stars in the night sky. The International Dark Sky Association awarded the park a gold-tier certification in 2012, and the park shares the honor with only a dozen or so other parks worldwide.

Check the *Paisano*, the park's seasonal newspaper, for a list of celestial events, from solstices to meteor showers, that may occur during your visit. Evening ranger talks may cover night skies, with a telescope provided for celestial viewing.

range, running through the park toward Mexico. The best time to take this drive is at sunrise or sunset, when the mountains glow brilliantly with different hues.

Hiking

With more than 150 miles of trails to explore, it's no wonder hiking is big in Big Bend. The **Chisos Basin Loop Trail** (1.8 miles) offers nice views of the basin and a relatively large amount of shade, while the popular **Lost Mine Trail** (4.8 miles) has views that just get better and better as you climb over 1000ft in elevation.

The **Hot Springs Historic Walk** (0.75 miles) passes historic buildings and Native American pictographs painted on rock walls on its way to a stone tub brimming with 105°F (41°C) water.

The fascinating desert **Grapevine Hills Trail** (2.2 miles), near Panther Junction, accesses Balanced Rock, a much-photographed formation of three acrobatic boulders that form an inverted-triangle 'window.'

River Trips

The Rio Grande has earned its place among the top North American river trips for both rafting and canoeing. Rapids up to class IV alternate with calm stretches that are perfect for wildlife-viewing, photography and just plain relaxation.

Trips on the river can range from several hours to several days. **Boquillas Canyon** is the longest and most tranquil of the park's three canyons and is best for intermediate to advanced boaters and canoeists with camping skills. **Colorado Canyon** is just upriver from the park and, depending on the water level, has lots of white water. **Mariscal Canyon** is noted for its beauty and isolation, and **Santa Elena Canyon** is a classic float featuring the class IV Rock Slide rapid.

Guided floats cost about $145 per person per day ($79 for a half-day), including all meals and gear (except a sleeping bag for overnighters). **Big Bend River Tours** (432-371-3033, 800-545-4240; www.bigbendrivertours.com; 23331 FM 170; half-/full day river trip $75/135) offers saddle-paddle tours with half a day each rowing and horseback riding.

Bird-Watching

Over 450 bird species have been spotted in the park; prime sites include Rio Grande Valley, the Sam Nail Ranch, the Chisos Basin and Castolon near Santa Elena Canyon. The Big Bend region may be best known for its peregrine falcons, which, while still endangered, have been making a comeback. The current number of falcon nests is not known, but there are some within the park.

The **Rio Grande Village Nature Trail** (0.75 miles) is a good short trail for birding and photography. Beginning at campsite 18 at the Rio Grande Village campground, the trail passes through dense vegetation before emerging in the desert for a view of the Rio Grande.

Canoeing, Rio Grande

DAVID NEVALA/GETTY IMAGES ©

Essential Information

Sleeping & Eating

Tent campers or smaller RVs that don't require hookups can use the three main campgrounds; some take reservations but some are first-come, first-served.

Chisos Lodge Restaurant (Lodge Dining Room; www.chisosmountainslodge.com; Chisos Mountain Lodge; lunch $7-12, dinner $10-22; ⏱7-10am, 11am-4pm & 5-8pm) Run by concessionaire Forever Resorts, this is the only full-service restaurant in the park. It offers breakfast, lunch and dinner and has a small bar. Otherwise, bring your own food or buy snacks and basic groceries at one of the park's convenience stores.

Cottonwood Campground (www.nps.gov/bibe; tent sites $14) Set beneath cottonwood trees near Castolon, the 24-site Cottonwood Campground provides a subdued and shady environment along the river with no generators or idling vehicles to ruin the ambience. No hookups and no dump station. Pit toilets and water are available. No reservations.

Maps

Readily available at the entrances and visitor centers, the free National Park Service (NPS) *Big Bend* map is adequate for most visitors to the park. You'll also find summaries and mileage information about popular trails in the *Paisano*, the free park newspaper. The visitor centers also sell trail guides. Serious backpackers or anyone looking to hike the less-developed trails will want to pick up a topographic map.

Visitor Centers

In addition to the park headquarters and visitor center at **Panther Junction** (Main Visitor Center; ☏432-477-1158; www.nps.gov/bibe; ⏱9am-5pm), visitor centers are found in **Chisos Basin** (☏432-477-2264; ⏱8:30am-noon & 1-4pm) and at **Persimmon Gap** (☏432-477-2393; ⏱9:30-11:30am & 12:30-4pm).

Safety

Don't underestimate the heat; this is the desert, after all. Drink lots of water, and take plenty with you when you hike.

Most snakes keep a low profile in daylight, when you're unlikely to see them. Night hikers should stay on the trail and carry a flashlight. Big Bend's scorpions are not deadly, but you should still get prompt attention if you're stung. Shake out boots or shoes before putting them on.

Getting There & Away

There is no public transportation to, from or within the park. The closest buses and trains run through Alpine, 108 miles northwest of Panther Junction. The nearest major airports are 230 miles northeast in Midland and 325 miles northwest in El Paso.

You'll find gas at the service stations at **Panther Junction** (☏432-477-2294; ⏱convenience store 7am-6:30pm May-Sep, 8am-5:30pm Jun-Aug, pumps 24hr) and **Rio Grande Village** (☏432-477-2293; ⏱8am-7pm Oct-May, to 5pm Jun-Sep).

Note that the border patrol has checkpoints for vehicles coming from Big Bend. If you're not a US citizen, presenting your passport will help avoid delays (ie prove you're not coming from Mexico).

Top left: Painted bunting; Top right: Claret cup cactus; Bottom: Stargazing at Balanced Rock

CLASSIC ROAD TRIPS

Big Bend Scenic Loop

Big Bend National Park and the endless vistas straight out of an old Western are reason enough to make this trip. But you'll also have plenty of fun along the way, exploring quirky small towns, minimalist art and astronomy parties.

Duration 5–7 days

Distance 690 miles

Best Time to Go

Best between February and April – before the heat sets in.

Essential Photo

Prada Marfa, a quirky roadside art installation.

Best for Outdoors

McDonald Observatory's nighttime star parties.

❶ El Paso

Start your trip in El Paso, a border city that's wedged into a remote corner of west Texas. While here, take advantage of the great Mexican food you can find all over the city – it's right across the river from Mexico – and enjoy El Paso's many free museums. Downtown, the **El Paso Museum of Art** (☏915-212-0300; www.epma. art; 1 Arts Festival Plaza; �)9am-5pm Tue-Sat, to 9pm Thu, noon-5pm Sun) **FREE** has a terrific Southwestern collection, and the engaging modern pieces round out the display nicely.

Another one you shouldn't miss is the **El Paso Holocaust Museum** (☏915-351-0048; www.elpasoholocaustmuseum.org; 715 N Oregon St; ☉9am-5pm Tue-Fri, 1-5pm Sat & Sun) **FREE**. It may seem a little anachronistic in a predominately Hispanic town, but it hosts amazingly thoughtful and moving exhibits that are imaginatively presented for maximum impact.

To the west, you'll find several good restaurants and watering holes in the new and developing Montecillo commercial and residential district.

The Drive » Head east on I-10 for two hours, then turn onto TX 118 toward Fort Davis. The area is part of both the Chihuahuan Desert and the Davis Mountains, giving it a unique setting where the endless horizons are suddenly interrupted by rock formations springing from the earth.

❷ Fort Davis

Here's why you'll want to plan on being in Fort Davis on either a Tuesday, Friday or Saturday: to go to an evening star party at **McDonald Observatory** (☏432-426-3640; www.mcdonaldobservatory.org; 3640 Dark Sky Dr; day pass adult/child 6-12yr/under 6yr $8/7/free; ☉visitor center 10am-5:30pm). The observatory has some of the clearest and darkest skies in North America, not to mention some of the most powerful telescopes – a perfect combination for gazing at stars, planets and assorted celestial bodies, with astronomers on hand to explain it all.

Besides that, nature lovers will enjoy **Davis Mountains State Park**, and history buffs can immerse themselves at the 1854 **Fort Davis National Historic Site** (☏432-426-3224; www.nps.gov/foda; Hwy 17; adult/child under 16yr $7/free; ☉8am-5pm), a well-preserved frontier military post that's impressively situated at the foot of Sleeping Lion Mountain.

The Drive » Marfa is just 20 minutes south on TX 17, a two-lane country road where tumbleweeds bounce slowly by and congregate around the barbed-wire fences.

McDonald Observatory

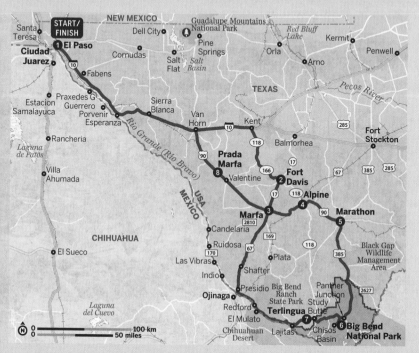

❸ Marfa

Marfa got its first taste of fame when Rock Hudson, Elizabeth Taylor and James Dean came to town to film the 1956 film *Giant*. It's since served as a film location for movies like *There Will Be Blood* and *No Country for Old Men*.

But these days, this tiny town with one stoplight draws visitors from around the world for a different reason: its art scene. Donald Judd single-handedly put Marfa on the art-world map in the 1980s when he used a bunch of abandoned military buildings to create one of the world's largest permanent installations of minimalist art at the **Chinati Foundation** (☎432-729-4362; www.chinati.org; 1 Calvary Row; adult/student Full Collection Tour $25/10, Selections Tour $20/10; ⊘9am-4:30pm Wed-Sun, tours 10am, 10:30am, 11am, 11:30am).

Art galleries are sprinkled around town, exploring everything from photography to sculpture to modern art. **Ballroom Marfa** (☎432-729-3600; www.ballroommarfa.org; 108 E San Antonio St; suggested donation $5; ⊘10am-6pm Wed-Sat, to 3pm Sun) is a great gallery to catch the vibe. Try not to visit on a Monday or Tuesday, when many businesses are closed.

The Drive » Alpine is about 30 minutes east of Marfa on Hwy 90/67.

❹ Alpine

The biggest little town in the area, Alpine is the county seat, a college town (Sul Ross University is here) and the best place to stock up on whatever you need before you head down into the Chihuahuan Desert.

Stop by the **Museum of the Big Bend** (☎432-837-8143; www.museumofthebigbend.com;

Top: Ballroom Marfa; Bottom left: Cemetery, Terlingua; Bottom right: Wagon, Fort Davis

STEVENS FREMONT/GETTY IMAGES ©

JEN MCCORMACK/SHUTTERSTOCK ©

VINCENT K HO/SHUTTERSTOCK ©

Mysterious Lights

The Marfa Lights that flicker beneath the Chinati Mountains have captured the imagination of many a traveler over the decades, with accounts of mysterious lights that appear and disappear on the horizon that go all the way back to the 1800s. Numerous studies have been conducted to explain the phenomenon, but the only thing scientists all agree on is that they have no idea what causes the apparition.

Catch the show at the Marfa Lights Viewing Area, on the south side of the road between Marfa and Alpine. From the platform, look south and find the red blinking light (that one's real). Just to the right is where you will (or won't) see the Marfa Lights doing their ghostly thing.

---

400 N Harrison St; donations accepted; ⏰9am-5pm Tue-Sat, 1-5pm Sun) **FREE** to brush up on the history of the Big Bend region. But don't expect it to be dry and dusty. The multimedia exhibits are big and eye-catching, and display-reading is kept to a minimum. Most impressive? The enormous replica wing bone of the Texas pterosaur found in Big Bend – the largest flying creature ever found – with an estimated wing span of more than 50ft – along with the intimidatingly large re-creation of the whole bird that's big enough to snatch up a fully grown human to carry off for dinner.

The Drive » Keep heading east. In 15 miles, look south for the the guerrilla art installation *Target Marathon,* a fun nod to Prada Marfa. In another 15 miles you'll reach the seriously tiny town of Marathon (*mar*-a-thun). The views aren't much during this stretch of the drive, but Big Bend will make up for all that.

❺ Marathon

This tiny railroad town has two claims to fame. It's the closest town to Big Bend's north entrance – providing a last chance to fill up your car and your stomach – and it's got the **Gage Hotel** (📞432-386-4205; www.gagehotel.com; 102 NW 1st St/Hwy 90; r $229-279; ✸@🛜✸), a true Texas treasure that's worth a peek, if not an overnight stay.

The Drive » Heading south on US-385, it's 40 miles to the northern edge of Big Bend, and 40 more to get to the Chisos Basin, the heart of the park. The flat road affords miles and miles of views for most of the drive.

❻ Big Bend National Park

Talk about big. At 1252 sq miles, this national park (p146) is almost as big as the state of Rhode Island. Some people duck in for an afternoon, hike a quick trail and leave, but we recommend staying at least two nights to hit the highlights.

Seventeen miles south of the Persimmon Gap Visitor Center, pull over for the **Fossil Discovery Exhibit**, which spotlights the dinosaurs and other creatures that inhabited this region beginning 130 million years ago.

The Drive » From the west park entrance, turn left after 3 miles then follow the signs for Terlingua Ghost Town, just past Terlingua proper. It's about a 45-minute drive from the middle of the park.

❼ Terlingua

Quirky Terlingua is a unique combination: it's both a ghost town and a social hub. When the local cinnabar mines closed down in the 1940s, the town dried up and blew away like a tumbleweed, leaving buildings that fell into ruins.

But the area has slowly repopulated, businesses have been built on top of the ruins, and locals gather here for two daily rituals. In the late afternoon, everyone drinks beer on the porch of **Terlingua Trading Company** (📞432-371-2234; http://terlinguatradingco.homestead.com; 100 Ivey St; ⏰10am-9pm). And after the sun goes down, the party moves next door to **Starlight Theatre** (📞432-371-3400; www.thestarlighttheatre.com; 631 Ivey Rd; mains

$10-27; ⊙5pm-midnight Sun-Fri, to 1am Sat), where there's live music every night.

Come early enough to check out the fascinating **stone ruins** (from the road – they're private property) and the old **cemetery**, which you're welcome to explore.

The Drive » Continue west on Rte 170, also known as the River Road, for a gorgeous drive along the Rio Grande inside Big Bend Ranch State Park. In 60 miles or so you'll reach Presidio. Head north on US-67 to return to Marfa, then cut west on US-90.

❽ Prada Marfa

So you're driving along a two-lane highway out in the middle of nowhere, when suddenly a small building appears in the distance like a mirage. You glance over and see...a Prada store? Known as the 'Prada Marfa' (although it's really closer to Valentine) this art installation set against the backdrop of dusty west Texas is a tongue-in-cheek commentary on consumerism. You can't go in, but you're encouraged to window shop or snap a photo. ∎

Terlingua Trading Company

BLAINE HARRINGTON III/GETTY IMAGES ©

MARGARET.W/SHUTTERSTOCK ©

Thor's Hammer

Bryce Canyon National Park

The high altitude of Bryce Canyon National Park, which hugs the eastern edge of an 18-mile plateau, sets it apart from southern Utah's other national parks. Famous for its otherworldly sunset-coloured spires punctuated by tracts of evergreen forest, this is one of the planet's most exquisite geological wonders.

Great For...

State
Utah

Entrance Fee
7-day pass per car/motorcycle/person on foot or bicycle $35/30/20

Area
56 sq miles

❶ Bryce Point

If you stop nowhere else along the scenic drive, be sure to catch the stunning views from Bryce Point. You can walk the rim above Bryce Amphitheater for awesome views of the Silent City, an assemblage of hoodoos so dense, gigantic and hypnotic that you'll surely begin to see shapes of figures frozen in the rock. Be sure to follow the path to the actual point, a fenced-in promontory that juts out over the forested canyon floor, 1000ft below. The extension allows a broad view of the hoodoos. This rivals any overlook in the park for splendor and eye-popping color. An interpretive panel tells the story of Ebenezer Bryce, the Mormon pioneer for whom the canyon was named, and his wife Mary.

❷ Natural Bridge

Natural Bridge is an extremely popular stop, and with good reason: a stunning span of eroded, red-hued limestone juts

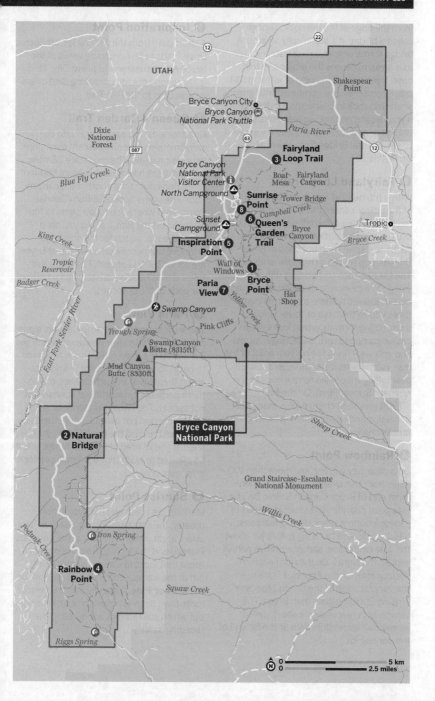

from the edge of the overlook. Though called a bridge, it's technically an arch. A bridge forms when running water, such as a stream, causes the erosion. In this case, freezing and thawing of water inside cracks and crevices, combined with gravity, shattered rock to create the window. Even if you're tight on time, squeeze this stop onto your agenda. There is also a viewpoint to see Natural Bridge from above at Scenic Drive Mile 12.5.

❸ Fairyland Loop Trail

With a trailhead at Fairyland Point north of the visitor center, this 8-mile round-trip makes for a beautiful half-day hike (four to five hours). The sorbet-colored, sand-castle-like spires and hoodoos of Bryce Canyon pop up like a Dr Seuss landscape. The tall hoodoos and bridges unfold best if you go in a clockwise direction. At around mile 4, you will run into a side trail that takes you to the base of Tower Bridge, a crumbling formation that looks like a castle, complete with drawbridge, turrets and goblins. This is the bottom point of the trail. From there, it's a rather long ascent over rolling moon-like terrain back to the rim near Sunset Point. On the trail there's a 700ft elevation change, plus many additional ups and downs, making this a good fitness challenge.

❹ Rainbow Point

On a clear day you can see more than 100 miles from this overlook at the southern-most end of Bryce Canyon Scenic Dr. The viewpoint provides jaw-dropping views of canyon country. Giant sloping plateaus, tilted mesas and towering buttes jut above the vast landscape, and interpretive panels explain the sights. On the northeastern horizon look for the Aquarius Plateau – the very top step of the Grand Staircase – rising 2000ft higher than Bryce. The viewpoint is reached on a short, paved, wheelchair-accessible path at the far end of the parking lot.

❺ Inspiration Point

A short path from the parking lot, off Scenic Drive, leads to jaw-dropping views of the Bryce Amphitheater and Silent City. This is also a top spot for stargazing, and offers easy access to the Rim Trail.

❻ Queen's Garden Trail

Good for kids, the easiest trail into the canyon makes a gentle descent over slop-ing erosional fins. The moderate 1.8-mile out-and-back hike passes elegant hoodoo formations but stops short of the canyon floor. The trail is accessed from Sunrise Point, from where you follow signs to the trailhead off the Rim Trail. As you drop below the rim, watch for the stark and primitive bristlecone pines, which at Bryce are about 1600 years old. These ancient trees' dense needles cluster like foxtails on the ends of the branches.

❼ Paria View

Three miles north of Swamp Canyon, signs point to the Paria View viewpoint, which lies 2 miles off the main road. This is *the* place to come for sunsets. Most of the hoodoo amphitheaters at Bryce face east, making them particularly beautiful at sunrise, but not sunset. The amphitheater here, small by comparison but beautiful nonetheless, faces west toward the Paria River water-shed. If you're tired of RVs and buses, you'll be pleased to learn that this small overlook is for cars only.

❽ Sunrise Point

Marking the north end of Bryce Amphi-theater, the southeast-facing Sunrise Point offers great views of hoodoos, the Aquarius Plateau and the Sinking Ship, a sloping mesa that looks like a ship's stern rising out of the water. Keep your eyes peeled for the **Limber Pine**, a spindly pine tree whose roots have been exposed through erosion, but which still remains anchored to the receding sand.

Natural Bridge

Drive Scenic Bryce Canyon

The scenic drive winds south for 17 miles and roughly parallels the canyon rim, climbing from 7894ft at the visitor center to 9115ft at Rainbow Point, the plateau's southern tip at road's end. Snowstorms may close the road in winter. Check at the visitor center for current road conditions.

Duration 2 hours

Distance 34 miles

Start & Finish Bryce Canyon National Park Visitor Center

Nearest Town/Junction Bryce

Head directly to **Rainbow Point** (a 35-minute drive; pictured), then stop at the scenic overlooks as you return to avoid left-hand turns into the turnouts. Visit Rainbow Point via a short, paved, wheelchair-accessible path at the far end of the parking lot.

At the other end of the parking lot another short, paved, wheelchair-accessible trail leads to **Yovimpa Point**, one of the park's windiest spots. The southwest-facing view reveals more forested slopes and less eroding rock.

Just north of Mile 16, at 8750ft, the small **Black Birch Canyon** overlook shows precipitous cliffs roadside.

Higher than the previous stop, **Ponderosa Canyon** offers long vistas like those at Rainbow Point. One of the best stops at this end of the park, the **Agua Canyon** viewpoint overlooks two large formations of precariously balanced, top-heavy hoodoos. Park at **Natural Bridge** to view a stunning span of eroded, red-hued limestone. The stop at **Farview Point** offers a grand view of giant plateaus,

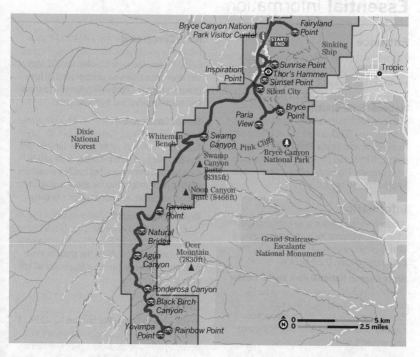

blue-hued mesas and buttes. The over-look at **Swamp Canyon** sits in a forested dip between two ridgelines. Three miles north, turn right and follow signs to **Paria View** (p160).

At **Bryce Point** (p158), you can wonder at the natural architecture of Bryce Amphitheater and take in the hoodoos the **Silent City**, standing like melting sandcastles in shades of coral, magenta, ocher and white against a deep-green pine forest background.

At **Inspiration Point** a short ascent up a paved path takes you to another overlook into Bryce Amphitheater. The Silent City is most compelling from here. The hoodoos feel closer, and you can make out more details on the canyon floor.

Views at **Sunset Point** are as good as they get, but don't expect solitude. This

point is known for **Thor's Hammer**, a big square-capped rock balanced atop a spindly hoodoo. Don't be fooled by the name of this point. Because it faces east, sunrises are better here than sunsets.

At the north end of Bryce Amphitheater, **Sunrise Point** (p160) offers great views.

End your driving tour at the visitor center or head to **Fairyland Point**. To reach the point, drive a mile north of the entrance gate, then a mile east of the main road. Fairyland Point is a less-visited spot with wooded views north toward the Aquarius Plateau. Here you can see hoodoos at all stages of evolution, from fin to crumbling tower, and start the Fairyland Loop Trail.

Essential Information

Entrance

The nearest town is Bryce Canyon City, just 3 miles north of the park. Tropic is 11 miles northeast on Hwy 12.

Take advantage of the **Bryce Canyon National Park Shuttle** (☑435-834-5290; www.nps.gov/brca/planyourvisit/shuttle.htm; ⊙hours vary) FREE, a free service between Ruby's Inn and Bryce Point, with buses every 15 minutes between 8am and 8pm in high season. Parking at the visitor center is limited to one hour.

Information

A booth at the park's sole entrance distributes a park brochure with a driving map and facilities information as well as the park newspaper, the *Hoodoo*.

Bryce Canyon National Park Visitor Center (☑435-834-5322; www.nps.gov/brca; Hwy 63; ⊙8am-8pm May-Sep, 8am-6pm Oct & Apr, 8am-4:30pm Nov-Mar; ⊛) Issues backcountry permits for overnight travel on a first-come, first-served basis.

Safety

Hydration stations throughout the park offer free water bottle refills (rangers recommend a gallon of water per person per day in summer).

If there is lightning, crouch low to the ground and avoid stand-alone trees. If there's flooding, head to higher ground.

Backcountry travelers can get free bear-proof cans at the visitor center. Never cook or store food in your tent, especially in the backcountry. Never leave designated trails.

Sleeping

The park has one lodge and two campgrounds. Most travelers stay just north of the park in Bryce Canyon City, near the Hwy 12/63 junction, or 11 miles east in Tropic.

There are limited vacation rentals near the park, but extend your search by about 20 miles and you'll find plenty of options.

North Campground (☑877-444-6777; www.recreation.gov; Bryce Canyon Rd; tent/RV sites $20/30) Near the visitor center, the 101 sites at this enormous trail-side campground all have campfire rings. A short walk takes you to showers, a coin laundry and a general store.

Sunset Campground (☑877-444-6777; www.recreation.gov; Bryce Canyon Rd; tent/RV site $20/30; ⊙Apr-Sep) Just south of Sunset Point, this 102-site campground offers more shade than North Campground but has few amenities beyond flush toilets. Inquire about availability at the visitor center, and secure your site early.

Bryce Canyon Resort (☑800-834-0043; www.brycecanyonresort.com; cnr Hwys 12 & 63; r $189, cabins $250; ⊛⊜⊠) Four miles from the park, this is a great option. While the grounds leave much to be desired, there's a modernist-kitsch appeal to the rooms.

Eating

Bryce Canyon Lodge Restaurant (☑435-834-5361; Bryce Canyon Rd; breakfast & lunch $10-20, dinner $10-35; ⊙7am-10pm Apr-Oct) ✿ While service may lag, meals deliver, with the excellent regional cuisine ranging from fresh green salads to bison burgers, braised portobellos and steak. All food is made on-site and the certified green menu offers only sustainable seafood.

Ebenezer's Barn & Grill (☑800-468-8660; www.ebenezersbarnandgrill.com; 1000 S Hwy 63; dinner show $32-38; ⊙7pm mid-May–Oct) A big BBQ dinner here comes with a kitschy but good-natured evening of country and western music (drinks not included). Options include salmon, steak, pulled pork or chicken served with beans and cornbread. Reservations are necessary.

Travelers with Disabilities

The national park's multi-use trail is a paved trail perfect for visitors with restricted mobility, though a few sections may be too steep for solo wheelchair users. The visitor center is wheelchair accessible.

Top left: Bryce Canyon Motel; Top right: Squirrel; Bottom: Sunset Campground

Under the Rim Trail

This hike skirts beneath cliffs, through amphitheaters and amid pines and aspens. Rangers prefer visitors hike south to north, but you can do it either way. Permits ($5 per person) are obtained at the visitor center. This is a one-way hike, so consider leaving a car at one or both ends.

Duration 3 days

Distance 22.9 miles

Difficulty Moderate–hard

Start Rainbow Point

Finish Bryce Point

Nearest Towns Tropic, Panguitch

DAY 1: Bryce Point to Right Fork Swamp Canyon Campsite (4–6 hours, 10.5 miles)

From **Bryce Point** the trail descends steeply almost due east, then swings south. After 0.5 miles you'll wind down to a ridge and over the next 0.5 miles **Rainbow Point** comes into view. Two miles in you'll pass the **Hat Shop**, its gray boulder caps perched atop spindly conglomerate stands.

At the base of this descent, 2.8 miles from Bryce Point, is the **Right Fork Yellow Creek campsite**. Follow the left (east) bank of the creek for half a mile, then cross it and bear south. As the trail turns west, you'll pass the **Yellow Creek group campsite**.

A quarter-mile further, you'll reach **Yellow Creek**. The trail climbs toward the Pink Cliffs and Paria View, 1000ft above, and soon crosses the creek; cairns point the way. Another 0.25 miles brings you to the **Yellow Creek campsite**. It's a great spot to watch the sunset.

From here you'll turn southwest up a short, steep hill. The trail undulates for about 2 miles, crossing a slope between two amphitheaters. After 1.5 miles the trail drops into Pasture Wash. Follow cairns to the south edge of the wash and look for a sharp uphill turn. The view will reward your effort.

Descend into the valley to the junction with the **Sheep Creek Connecting Trail**, which climbs 2 miles to the scenic drive. A well-marked spur leads 0.5 miles south to the **Sheep Creek campsite** (closed when we last visited due to bear activity); you can usually find water here.

From the junction, the trail climbs 150ft – crossing from the Sheep Creek amphitheater to the Swamp Canyon amphitheater – then descends into Swamp Canyon. On the left (southeast), in a clearing among large ponderosa pines, is the **Right Fork Swamp Canyon campsite**; water is sometimes available in upper Swamp Canyon, 100yd west of the campsite.

DAY 2: Right Fork Swamp Canyon Campsite to Natural Bridge Campsite (1½–2½ hours, 4.6 miles)

Three hundred feet past the campsite is the junction with the mile-long Swamp Canyon Connecting Trail. From the connecting trail junction, you'll climb steadily south, then turn west up switchbacks. Just beyond, at 8200ft, is the **Swamp Canyon campsite**. You'll sometimes find water 0.25 miles up the Whiteman Connecting Trail.

Beyond camp, the trail descends to the base of Farview Cliffs. From here you'll skirt **Willis Creek** for a mile until it turns southeast. Bear south and west.

The trail ducks into Dixie National Forest for 0.25 miles, then curves sharply east to climb an eroded sandstone slope southwest of Willis Creek. At the top, the sandy trail offers gorgeous views of the **Pink Cliffs**.

Descend to a southern tributary of Willis Creek and continue 0.5 miles to the **Natural Bridge campsite**, which lacks water.

DAY 3: Natural Bridge Campsite to Rainbow Point (3–5 hours, 7.8 miles)

Half a mile out of camp, the trail traverses a sage meadow toward Agua Canyon. Due to floods you now need to hike up the canyon 0.75 miles, then switchback up the canyon's south ridge. When in doubt, follow the cairns. Atop this ridge, the Agua Canyon Connecting Trail climbs 1.6 miles to the scenic drive. This is one of the hardest stretches of the trail, with fallen trees and washouts.

From the connecting trail junction, you'll descend into Ponderosa Canyon, then zig-zag to South Fork Canyon. Past the head of the canyon, you'll reach the **Iron Spring campsite**. Amid a grove of aspens 600ft up canyon (southwest) from the campsite, **Iron Spring** supplies year-round water. The turnoff for the spring lies 100yd north of the campsite.

The trail dips to cross both arms of Black Birch Canyon. After clambering over the lower slopes of a northwest-jutting promontory, you'll enter the southernmost amphitheater of Bryce Canyon's Pink Cliffs.

The trail traces the hammer-shaped ridge below Rainbow Point. Ascend the final 1.5 miles up the back (south) side of the amphitheater to the rim. You'll cross the Riggs Spring Loop Trail, 100yd east of the **Rainbow Point** parking lot. ∎

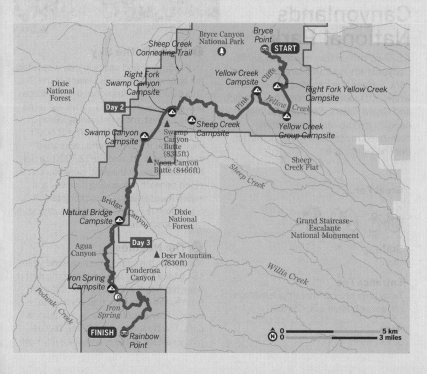

ED RESSEL/SHUTTERSTOCK ©

Mesa Arch

Canyonlands National Park

A 527-sq-mile vision of ancient earth, Canyonlands is Utah's largest national park. Serpentine canyons tipped with white cliffs loom high over the Colorado and Green Rivers. Skyward-jutting needles and spires, deep craters, blue-hued mesas and majestic buttes dot the landscape.

Great For...

State
Utah

Entrance Fee
7-day pass per car/motorcycle/person on foot or bicycle $30/25/15

Area
527 sq miles

❶ Island in the Sky

You'll comprehend space in new ways atop the appropriately named Island in the Sky. This 6000ft-high flat-topped mesa drops precipitously on all sides, providing some of the longest, most enthralling vistas of any park in southern Utah. The 11,500ft Henry Mountains bookend panoramic views in the west, and the 12,700ft La Sal Mountains are to the east. Here you can stand beneath a sparkling blue sky and watch thunderheads inundating far-off regions while you contemplate applying more sunscreen.

❷ The Needles

Named for the spires of orange-and-white sandstone jutting skyward from the desert floor, the Needles District is so different from Island in the Sky that it's hard to believe they're both in the same national park. The Needles receives only half as many visitors as the Island since it's more remote – though only 90 minutes from Moab – and there are fewer roadside attractions (but most are well worth the hike). The payoff is huge: peaceful solitude and the opportunity to participate in, not just observe, the vastness of canyon country. Morning light is best for viewing the rock spires.

Get among them on the **Chesler Park/ Joint Trail Loop**, an awesome 11-mile route across desert grasslands, past towering red-and-white-striped pinnacles and between deep, narrow slot canyons, some only 2ft across. Elevation changes are mild, but the distance makes it an advanced day hike.

❸ Mesa Arch

Canyonlands' most photographed arch is one of the best places to watch the sunrise – though don't expect to be alone. A moderately easy walk up a gentle rise brings you to the arch, an elegant sweep of Navajo sandstone that dramatically frames

the La Sal Mountains. A thousand feet below, the basin extends in layers of red, brown, green and tan.

❹ The Maze

A 30-sq-mile jumble of high-walled canyons, the Maze is a rare preserve of true wilderness for hardy backcountry veterans. The colorful canyons are rugged, deep and sometimes completely inaccessible. Many of them look alike and it's easy to get turned around – hence the district's name. (Think topographic maps and GPS.) Rocky roads absolutely necessitate reliable, high-clearance 4WD vehicles. Plan on spending at least three days. If you're at all inexperienced with four-wheel driving, stay away.

❺ Horseshoe Canyon

Far west of Island in the Sky, Horseshoe Canyon shelters one of the most impressive collections of millennia-old rock art in the Southwest. The centerpiece is the

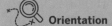

Orientation

The Colorado and Green Rivers form a Y dividing the park into separate districts, inaccessible to one another from within the park. Cradled atop the Y, Island in the Sky (30 miles, 45 minutes from Moab) is the most developed and visited district due to its ease of access. Its viewpoints look down into the incredible canyons of The Needles and The Maze.

Great Gallery and its haunting Barrier Canyon–style pictographs from between 2000 BC and AD 500. The heroic, bigger-than-life-size figures are magnificent. Artifacts recovered here date back as far as 9000 BC. The gallery lies at the end of a 6.5-mile round-trip hiking trail descending 750ft from a dirt road. Plan on six hours. Rangers lead hikes here on Saturday and Sunday from April through October; contact the Hans Flat Ranger Station for times.

❻ Mountain Biking on White Rim Road

Blazed by uranium prospectors in the 1950s, primitive **White Rim Road** encircling Island in the Sky is the top choice for mountain-biking trips. This 70-mile route is accessed near the visitor center via steeply descending Shafer Trail Rd. It generally takes three to four days by bike. Since the route lacks any water sources, cyclists should team up with a 4WD support vehicle or travel with a Moab outfitter.

Other trails include the moderate-level 27-mile **Salt Creek Canyon Trail** loop, a favorite for archaeology junkies for its rock art, and the 32-mile **Elephant Hill** round trip. This route is the most well-known and technically challenging in the state, with steep grades and tight turns – smell the burning brakes and clutches. (Don't try this as your first mountain-bike adventure.)

Top left: Island in the Sky; Top right: Narrow canyons, Needles District; Bottom: Mountain biking White Rim Rd

Essential Information

Sleeping & Eating

Many visitors sleep in nearby Moab. Canyonlands' campgrounds in the Needles and Island in the Sky districts are extremely popular.

At Island in the Sky sites are first-come, first-served. Backcountry camping in the Island is mostly open-zone (not in prescribed areas), but is still permit-limited. Visitors can reserve some campsites and all group sites at the Needles. Backcountry camping, in prescribed areas only, is quite popular, so it's hard to secure an overnight permit without advance reservation.

There are no restaurants in the park. Bring your own provisions and plenty of water.

Squaw Flat Campground (☑435-719-2313; www.nps.gov/cany/planyourvisit/camping.htm; tent & RV sites $20; ☺year-round) This first-come, first-served, 26-site campground 3 miles west of the Needles Visitor Center fills up every day from spring to fall. It has flush toilets and running water, but no showers and no hookups. Opt for side A, where many sites (12 and 14, for example) are shaded by juniper trees and cliffs.

Willow Flat Campground (☑435-719-2313; tent & RV sites $15; ☺year-round) Seven miles from the Island in the Sky Visitor Center, the first-come, first-served, 12-site Willow Flat Campground has vault toilets but no water or hookups. Bring firewood and don't expect shade.

Information

Island in the Sky (☑435-259-4712; www.nps.gov/cany; Hwy 313; ☺8am-6pm Mar-Oct, 9am-4:30pm Nov-Feb) and the **Needles** (☑435-259-4711; Hwy 211; ☺8am-6pm Mar-Oct, 9am-4:30pm Nov-Feb) have visitor centers. The information center in **Moab** (☑435-259-8825; http://discovermoab.com/visitor-center/; 25 E Center St; ☺8am-7pm; ☎) also covers the park.

The easiest way to tour Canyonlands is by car. Traveling between districts takes two to six hours, so plan to visit no more than one per day. ∎

Top left: Island in the Sky; Top right: Shafer Canyon Overlook; Bottom: Needles District

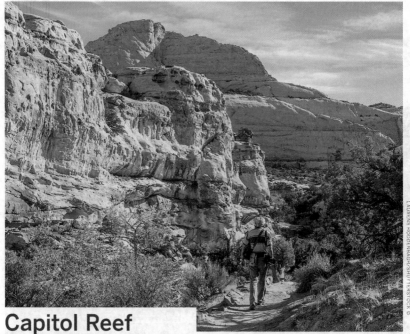

LAURENS HOODENBAGH/SHUTTERSTOCK ©

Capitol Reef National Park

Hickman Bridge Trail

Native Americans once called this colorful landscape the Land of the Sleeping Rainbow. The park's centerpiece is Waterpocket Fold, a 100-mile-long buckle in the earth's crust, and it's known for enormous domes – one of which echoes Washington, DC's Capitol Dome.

Capitol Reef harbors fantastic hiking trails, rugged 4WD roads and 1000-year-old Fremont petroglyph panels. At the park's heart grow the shady orchards of the Fruita Rural Historic District, a Mormon settlement dating back to the 1870s. Most services, including food, gas and medical aid, are in the town of Torrey, 11 miles west.

Scenic Drives

The rolling, mostly paved **Capitol Reef Scenic Drive** follows the Waterpocket Fold. It's a geology diorama come to life, with arches, hoodoos, canyon narrows and other unique features easily within view, plus day-hiking opportunities, too. The best of the route is its last 2 miles between the narrow sandstone walls of Capitol Gorge. It'll knock your socks off. Pay admission at the visitor center or self-service kiosk. The 9.3-mile road starts at the Scenic Dr fee station, just south of Fruita Campground.

Great For...

State
Utah

Entrance Fee
7-day pass per car/motorcycle/person on foot or bicycle $15/10/7

Area
378 sq miles

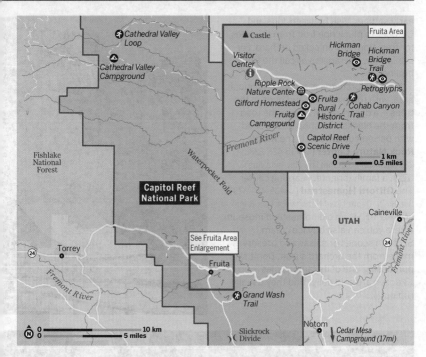

To continue south past Pleasant Creek, a 4WD vehicle is advised.

Long-distance mountain bikers and 4WDers love the 58-mile **Cathedral Valley Loop**, starting 18.6 miles east of the visitor center. The bumpy, roughshod backcountry road explores the remote northern area of the park and its alien desert landscapes, pierced by giant sandstone monoliths eroded into fantastic shapes. Before starting, check conditions at the visitor center and purchase an interpretive route guide.

Hiking

Along Scenic Dr, a good dirt road leads to the **Grand Wash Trail** (2.25 miles, easy), a flat hike between canyon walls that, at one point, tower 80 stories high but are only 15ft apart. You can follow an offshoot of level slickrock to the cool Cassidy Arch (2 miles) or continue further to link with other trails.

Often overlooked, the moderate 1.7-mile **Cohab Canyon Trail** deters crowds with a

steep climb at the beginning, but exploring a hidden canyon and the views from atop Capitol Reef are worth every sweaty step. Starting across the road from Fruita Campground, the trail makes a 0.25-mile ascent atop a rocky cliff. From there it levels out through a desert wash, beside small slot canyons.

The popular **Hickman Bridge Trail** (1 mile, moderate) includes a canyon stretch, a stunning natural bridge and wildflowers in spring. Mornings are coolest; it starts about 2 miles east of the visitor center off Hwy 24.

Fruita Rural Historic District

Fruita (*froo*-tuh) is a cool, green oasis, where shade-giving cottonwoods and fruit-bearing trees line the Fremont River's banks. The first Mormon homesteaders arrived here in 1880; Fruita's final resident left in 1969. Among the historic buildings, the NPS maintains 2700 cherry, apricot, peach, pear and apple trees planted by early settlers. Visit between June and October to pluck ripe fruit from the trees, for free, from any unlocked orchard. For availability, ask rangers or call the fruit hotline.

Near the orchards is a wonderful picnic area, with roaming deer and birds in the trees – a desert rarity. Across the road from the blacksmith shop (just a shed with period equipment) is the **Ripple Rock Nature Center** (☏435-425-2233; 281 Scenic Dr; ⊙1-5pm late May–mid-Aug) FREE, a family-oriented learning center. The **Gifford Homestead** (☏435-425-3791; Scenic Dr, Capitol Reef National Park; ⊙8am-5pm Mar-Oct) is an old homestead museum where you can also buy ice cream, Scottish scones or salsas and preserves made from the orchard's fruit. Don't skip purchasing one of its famous pies – up to 13 dozen are sold daily (and they usually run out!).

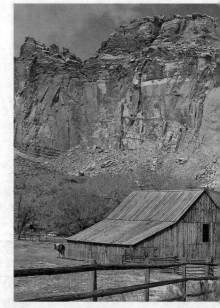

Top left: Gifford Homestead; Top right: Rock climbing;
Bottom: Petroglyphs

TOP LEFT: OLOS/SHUTTERSTOCK © TOP RIGHT: LEE COHEN/GETTY IMAGES ©

Petroglyphs

East of the visitor center on Hwy 24, look
for the roadside petroglyphs; these are the
carvings that convinced archaeologists that
the Fremont Indians were a distinct group.
Follow the roadside boardwalk to see
several panels.

Rock Climbing

Technical rock climbing is allowed without
permits. Note that Wingate Sandstone can
flake unpredictably. Follow clean-climbing
guidelines, and take all safety precautions.
For details, check with rangers or see www.
nps.gov/care.

Drive Highway 24

EDMUND LOWE PHOTOGRAPHY/SHUTTERSTOCK ©

This easy, winding route gives you a taste of everything that Capitol Reef offers: striking geology, dramatic desert overlooks, ancient Native American petroglyphs, early Western settlers' sites and hiking trails for stretching your legs.

Duration 1–4 hours

Distance 22 miles

Start Torrey

Finish Orientation pullout

From Torrey, head east into Capitol Reef on Hwy 24. There is no entrance station; driving this route is free. Be sure to stop at turnouts along the way to read interesting geologic interpretive panels. Then pull over at **Chimney Rock** (pictured), the towering reddish-brown rock formation 7 miles east of Torrey. If you're in great shape, consider hiking the strenuous 3.6-mile loop for wide-open clifftop views of Capitol Reef.

A half-mile east of Chimney Rock, turn right toward Panorama Point and drive 0.8 miles along a graded dirt road to the **Gooseneck Overlook**. An easy 0.1-mile walk from the parking area over rock slabs

takes you to this viewpoint above Sulphur Creek, which twists through the canyon in elegant S-curves. Though the observation platform is fenced in, much of the area around it is open – watch your little ones! From the parking area it's an easy 0.4-mile stroll to **Sunset Point**, where the ambient light on the cliffs and domes is best for photographers in the late afternoon.

Another 2.4 miles further east on Hwy 24, you'll arrive at the well-signed turnoff to Capitol Reef's visitor center (p182), just north of the Fruita Rural Historic District and the paved **Scenic Drive**. Rising majestically just north of this junction is the snaggle-toothed **Castle**; an interpretive panel details its geologic history.

East of the visitor center, Hwy 24 skirts the Fremont River, the surrounding rock growing paler and more yellow as you approach the park's Navajo sandstone domes. Peer through the windows of the historic **Fruita school**, 0.8 miles east of the visitor center, before stopping at the **ancient petroglyphs** 0.2 miles further east. Created by the Fremont Culture, these carvings helped convince archaeologists that the Fremont culture was distinct from that of Ancestral Puebloans. The boardwalk is wheelchair-accessible. Bring binoculars or a camera with a zoom lens.

Stop at the turnout 0.8 miles east of the petroglyphs for views of **Capitol Dome**, a giant sandstone dome that vaguely resembles the US Capitol, as it appeared in

1850. This parking area beside the Fremont River is where you'll find the trailheads for **Hickman Bridge** and the more strenuous Rim Overlook and Navajo Knobs route. On the south side of Hwy 24 is an alternate trailhead for **Cohab Canyon**, while 2.7 miles further east is the end of the Grand Wash.

About 4 miles east of Hickman Bridge, on your right, stop to peer through the window of the one-room 1882 **Behunin Cabin**, once home to a Mormon settler's family of 13. On the north side of the highway, 0.7 miles east of the cabin, you'll pass a waterfall. Swimming is not allowed here; numerous accidents and even drownings have occurred. At the park's eastern orientation pullout, just over 9 miles from the visitor center, are restrooms and an information kiosk. It's on the north side of the intersection with Notom-Bullfrog Rd.

Essential Information

Orientation

The narrow park runs north–south following the Waterpocket Fold. A little over 100 miles southwest of Green River, Hwy 24 traverses the park. Capitol Reef's central region is the Fruita Rural Historic District. To the far north lies Cathedral Valley, the least-visited section; toward the south you can cross over into Grand Staircase–Escalante National Monument on the Burr Trail Rd.

Dangers & Annoyances

Occasional summer thunderstorms pose a serious risk of flash flooding. Always check weather with rangers at the **Visitor Center** (☑435-425-3791; www.nps.gov/care; cnr Hwy 24 & Scenic Dr; ☺8am-6pm Jun-Aug, 8am-4:30pm Sep-May).

Remember that Capitol Reef has little shade. Drink at least one quart of water for every two hours of hiking and wear a hat. Summer temperatures can exceed 100°F (38°C) at the visitor center (5400ft), but it's cooler than Moab. If it's too hot, ascend to Torrey (10°F/6°C cooler) or Boulder Mountain (30°F/17°C cooler). Bugs bite in May and June.

Sleeping & Eating

The nearest motel lodgings are in Torrey.

The park has one large campground and several small ones. Free primitive camping is possible year-round at **Cathedral Valley Campground** (☑435-425-3791; www.nps.gov/care/planyourvisit/primitivecampsites.htm; cnr Hartnet & Cathedral Rds; ☺year-round) FREE, at the end of River Ford Rd, and at **Cedar Mesa Campground** (☑435-425-3791; www.

nps.gov/care/planyourvisit/primitivecampsites.htm; Notom-Bullfrog Rd;☺year-round) FREE, where five first-come, first-served free sites lack water, but have pit toilets, fire grates and picnic tables, as well as great views east along the fold. It's 30 miles south of Hwy 24.

Visitors can get a slice of pie or ice cream at the general store in the park; otherwise head east toward Torrey for multiple dining options.

Getting There & Around

Capitol Reef has no public transportation system. Aside from Hwy 24 and Scenic Dr, park routes are dirt roads that are bladed only a few times a year. In summer you may be able to drive Notom-Bullfrog Rd and the Burr Trail in a regular passenger car. Remote regions like Cathedral Valley will likely require a high-clearance 4WD vehicle. Check weather and road conditions with rangers before heading out.

Bicycles are allowed on all park roads but not trails. Cyclists and hikers can arrange drop-off/pick-up shuttle services ($1 to $2 per mile) with **Hondoo Rivers & Trails** (☑435-425-3519; www.hondoo.com; 90 E Main St, Torrey; ☺9am-9pm) in Torrey.

Inquire about ranger-led programs, watch the short film, then ooh and aah over the 64-sq-ft park relief map at the visitor center. The bookstore sells several interpretive trail and driving tour maps as well as area-interest books and guides. ■

Top left: Capitol Reef NP entrance; Top right: Capitol Dome; Bottom: Grand Staircase–Escalante National Monument

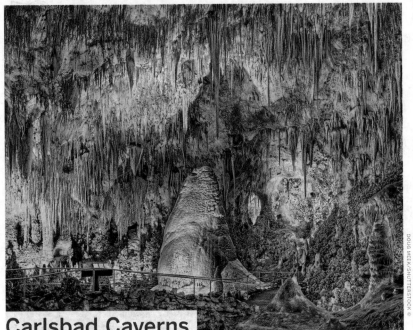

DOUG MEEK/SHUTTERSTOCK ©

Carlsbad Caverns National Park

Elaborately carved by the slow hand of time, the magnificent underground rooms and passageways of Carlsbad Caverns feel like they belong in another realm. The portals to this magical place? An elevator that drops the length of the Empire State Building or, more enjoyably, a spooky 1.25-mile subterranean walk.

Great For...

State
New Mexico

Entrance Fee
3-day pass adult/child $12/free

Area
73 sq miles

While a cave might not sound quite as sexy as redwoods, geysers or the Grand Canyon, there's no question that this one measures up on the national parks' jaw-droppingly ginormous scale. The Big Room is an underground room 1800ft long (that's the equivalent of 11 American football fields), 255ft high and over 800ft below the surface, where you're free to walk an intricate loop trail (1.25 miles) past a pick of amazing sights, including the world's largest stalagmite and the ever-popular Bottomless Pit. Wear a sweatshirt: the temperature is 56°F year-round.

Cave Tours

Self-guided and guided ($7 to $20, reserve ahead) tours are available. For a look at the wilder side of Carlsbad, sign up for the moderately challenging 5½-hour **Slaughter Canyon** guided tour. Among the highlights: the 89ft-high Monarch, one of the world's tallest limestone columns. Adventurers will

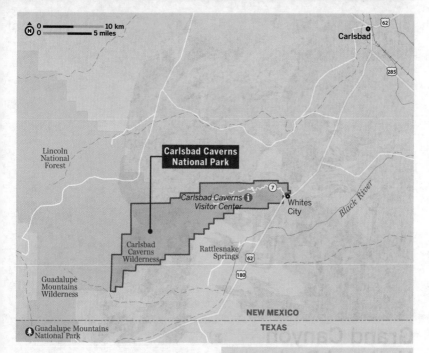

enjoy the three-hour **Lower Cave** ranger-led tour, which takes in an amazing array of formations, including the stalactite-filled 'Texas toothpick.' Descent is by 60ft of ladders and a knotted rope at the cave's entrance. The 1-mile ranger-led tour of **Kings Palace**, which lasts 90 minutes, takes you through three underground chambers, including the Big Room and some of the deepest caverns open to the public.

Bat Watching

From May through October, hundreds of thousands of Brazilian free-tailed bats roost in the caves. Their nightly exodus happens just after dusk when the bats take to the Chihuahuan Desert in search of food. You can watch them set off from the amphitheater near the cave entrance. Around sunset from late May through October you can attend the **Bat Flight Program**, a short and free ranger talk describing these fascinating mammals.

Essential Information

The park is in the southeastern corner of New Mexico. The closest major airport is El Paso (145 miles southwest). From Roswell, NM, about 100 miles north, follow US 285 south to US 62/180 west. From El Paso, the **visitor center** (⏱8am-7pm late May-early Sep, to 5pm rest of year) is 155 miles to the northeast via US 62/180 east.

Stargazing

The night sky is exceptionally dark in this remote corner of New Mexico – seeing the Milky Way and hundreds of stars and constellations is not to be missed. The park schedules ranger-led Night Sky programs on select dates each month from June through October. The walks are free but limited to 25 people. Registration is required. Check the park calendar for other stargazing events. ■

STUDIO BARCELONA/SHUTTERSTOCK ©

Grand Canyon National Park

There is nothing like arriving at the edge of the Grand Canyon and taking it all in – the immensity, the depth, the light. The canyon embodies the scale and splendor of the American West, captured in dramatic vistas, dusty trails and stories of exploration, preservation and exploitation.

Great For...

State
Arizona

Entrance Fee
7-day pass per car/motorcycle/person
on foot or bicycle $35/30/20

Area
1904 sq miles

❶ Hiking Rim to Rim

There's no better way to fully appreciate the grand of Grand Canyon than hiking through it, rim to rim. The classic corridor route descends the North Rim on the North Kaibab Trail, includes a night at Phantom Ranch or Bright Angel Campground at the bottom of the canyon, crosses the Colorado River and ascends to the South Rim on Bright Angel Trail. A popular alternative rim-to-rim route is to descend from the South Rim on the South Kaibab Trail and ascend via the North Kaibab Trail.

❷ Rafting the Colorado River

Considered the trip of a lifetime by many river enthusiasts, rafting the Colorado is a wild ride down a storied river, through burly rapids, past a stratified record of geologic time and up secretive side canyons. Though riding the river is the initial attraction, the profound appeals of the trip reveal themselves each day and night in

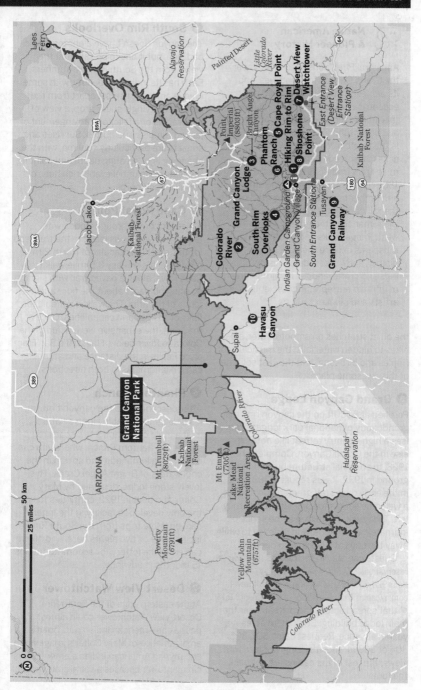

Native American & Pioneer History

Ancestral Puebloans lived in and near the Grand Canyon for centuries, and its pioneer history is full of wild and eccentric characters who wrangled this intimidating expanse for profit and adventure. Their stories echo in the weathered trails they built to access terraced fields; the iconic mule-train traditions that lured 18th-century tourists; and the stone and timber buildings constructed by the railroads in their effort to codify the romance of the American Southwest. Ranger talks and South Rim museums explore the park's native history, showcase indigenous dwellings and crafts, and tell inspiring tales of intrepid entrepreneurs, scientists, artists and pioneer tourists.

the quiet stretches on smooth water, side hikes to hidden waterfalls, the musicality of ripples and birdsong, and the vast solitude of this awesome place.

❸ Grand Canyon Lodge

Perched at 8000ft on the canyon rim, this granddaddy of national park lodges promises a high-country retreat like nothing else in the Grand Canyon. Completed in 1928, the original structure burned to the ground in 1932. It was rebuilt in 1937, and in the early days staff greeted guests with a welcome song and sang farewell as they left. Today, you'll find that same sense of intimate camaraderie, and it's easy to while away the days at a North Rim pace.

Guests can stay in the **cabins** (✐advance reservations 877-386-4383, same-day reservations 928-638-2611; www.grandcanyonforever. com; r/cabins from $141/155; ☺May 15–Oct 15) ✐ that spread across the plateau near the main lodge building. Book them at least a year in advance. Request cabin 301, 305, 306 or 309 for mesmerizing Western Rim views; the rest of the cabins are set back in the forest.

❹ South Rim Overlooks

The canyon doesn't have a photographic bad side, but it has to be said that the views from the South Rim are stunners. Each has its individual beauty, with some unique angle that sets it apart from the rest – a dizzyingly sheer drop, a view of river rapids or a felicitous arrangement of jagged temples and buttes. Sunrises and sunsets are particularly sublime, with the changing light creating depth and painting the features in unbelievably rich hues of vermilion and purple.

❺ Cape Royal Point

A pleasant drive through woods with teasing canyon views leads to the trailhead for this most spectacular of North Rim overlooks. It's an easy 0.5-mile walk to Cape Royal along a paved trail with signs pointing out facts about the flora and fauna of the area. The walk is suitable for folks of all ages and capabilities. Once at the point, the expansive view includes the Colorado River below, Flagstaff's San Francisco Peaks in the distance and stunning canyon landmarks in both directions.

❻ Phantom Ranch

After descending to the canyon bottom, it's a delight to ramble along a flat trail, past a mule corral and a few scattered cabins to Phantom Ranch, where you can relax with a lemonade and splash in the cool waters of Bright Angel Creek. This lovely stone lodge, designed by Mary Colter and built in 1922, continues to be the only developed facility in the inner canyon. Mule trips from the South Rim include one or two nights here, and hikers can enter the lottery for accommodations 15 months in advance.

❼ Desert View Watchtower

At the eastern edge of the South Rim, Desert View Watchtower could almost pass as an American Indian ruin, but it's an amalgamation of Mary Colter's imagination and myriad American Indian elements. This circular tower encases a spiral stairway that winds five stories to the top floor, with walls featuring a Hopi mural and graphic symbols from various American Indian tribes. From its many windows on all sides, you can see mile upon magnificent mile of canyon ridges, desert expanse, river and sky.

⑧ Shoshone Point

For a leisurely walk away from the South Rim circus, hiking through the ponderosa to Shoshone Point does the trick. The soundtrack to this mostly flat 1-mile walk is that of pine needles crunching underfoot and birdsong trilling overhead, and lacy shadows provide cover from the sun. Upon reaching the rim, you'll trace the edge for a short while to the stone point jutting out over the canyon depths. Shoshone Point, or the picnic area at the end of the trail, is perfect for a peaceful lunch.

⑨ Grand Canyon Railway

Things start out with a bang at the Wild West shootout in Williams, and then the 'sheriff' boards the train to make sure everything's in its place. Is it hokey? Maybe a little. Fun? Absolutely. Riding the historic Grand Canyon Railway to the South Rim takes a bit longer than if you were to drive, but you avoid traffic and disembark relaxed and ready to explore the canyon. The train drops you off a few minutes from the historic El Tovar and canyon rim.

⑩ Havasu Canyon

The people of the blue-green waters, as the Havasupai call themselves, take their name from the otherworldly turquoise-colored waterfalls and creek that run through the canyon. Due to limestone deposits on the creekbed, the water appears sky-blue, a gorgeous contrast to the deep red of the canyon walls. The only ways into and out of Havasu Canyon are by foot, horse or helicopter, but those who make the 10-mile trek are richly rewarded by the magic of this place, epitomized by spectacular **Havasu Falls**.

Grand Canyon Railway

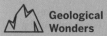

Geological Wonders

One look at the russet hues of the canyon walls and the park's spires and buttes, and you can't help but wonder about the hows and whys of the canyon's formation. Luckily for laypeople with rock-related questions, the South Rim has answers, primarily at **Yavapai Point and Geology Museum** (☏928-638-7890; www.nps.gov/grca/planyour visit/yavapai-geo.htm; Rim Trail, Grand Canyon Village Historic District; ⊗8am-7pm Mar-May & Sep-Nov, to 6pm Dec-Feb, to 8pm Jun-Aug; 🚌Kaibab/Rim) FREE and the **Trail of Time installation** (Rim Trail, Grand Canyon Village Historic District; 🚌Village), and both rims offer geology talks and walks given by the park's knowledgeable rangers. For a more DIY experience, hike into the canyon with a careful eye for fossilized marine creatures, animal tracks and ferns.

Top left: Phantom Ranch; Top right: Grand Canyon rafting; Bottom: Havasu Falls

TOP LEFT: FREDLYFISH4/SHUTTERSTOCK. TOP RIGHT: PACIFIC NORTHWEST PHOTO/SHUTTERSTOCK ©

Hike Widforss Trail

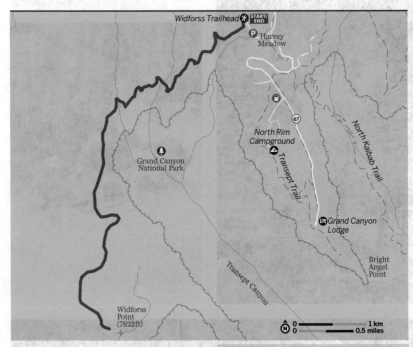

Meandering through shady forests of mixed conifer, old-growth ponderosa pine and quaking aspen punctuated by carpets of lupine, the Widforss Trail rolls past the head of The Transept and out to Widforss Point. Although it's a relatively popular day hike, people disperse quickly, and you likely won't see more than a few other explorers.

To reach the trailhead, turn onto the dirt road just south of the Cape Royal Rd turnoff, continuing a mile to the Widforss Trail parking area. After a 15-minute climb, the **Transept** comes into view. For the next 2 miles, enjoy wide views of the canyon to one side and meadows and woods to the other.

Halfway into the hike, the trail veers away from the rim and dips into gullies of lupines and ferns. The canyon doesn't come into view again until the end. Stops

Duration 6 hours

Distance 10 miles

Difficulty Moderate

Start & Finish Widforss trailhead

along the self-guided trail (brochures are often available at the trailhead, but get one at the visitor center just in case) end at mile 2.5, and many turn around here for a shorter option. Though any given hill is slight, the rolling terrain adds up, and you'll climb and descend about 1100ft over the course of the full 10-mile round-trip. Bring plenty of water.

The trail is named for Gunnar Widforss, an early-20th-century artist who painted many of America's national parks. He spent his final years living at the Grand Canyon and is buried on the South Rim.

Hike Hermit Trail

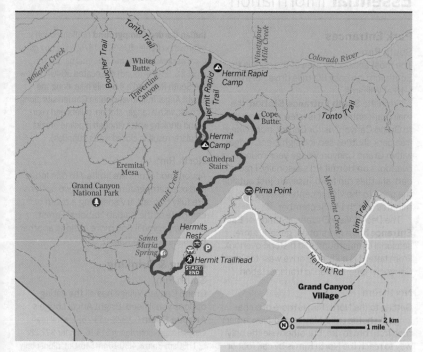

Tracing the path of the Hermit, this steep but rewarding out-and-back hike leads to a backcountry campground on the site of one of the park's earliest tourist accommodations.

Duration 2 days

Distance 18.4 miles

Difficulty Hard

Start & Finish Hermit trailhead

From the trailhead, a steep, rocky path descends 2 miles to **Santa Maria Spring**. The trail levels for a mile or so before zigzagging over loose rocks. The trail hasn't seen a maintenance crew in over 80 years; at the Supai section, hikers will need to scramble over rocks.

After descending the Redwall via extremely steep, compressed switchbacks, the **Cathedral Stairs**, the Hermit eventually hits the cross-canyon Tonto Trail (6.4 miles from the trailhead, at 3210ft).

Turn left (west) to merge with the Tonto; in 1 mile you'll reach the stone remnants of the old Hermit Camp (2800ft). Beyond the ruins, the cliff-rimmed backcountry campground (with pit toilets and seasonal water)

makes a glorious place to sleep. It's another 1.5 miles to the Colorado River; follow your nose down the creek.

At the river, the canyon walls are exquisite black Vishnu schist shot through with veins of pink Zoroaster granite. **Hermit Rapid**, a major Colorado River rapid, marks the confluence of Hermit Creek and the Colorado. There's a backcountry campground, but no facilities.

On day two, to return to Hermits Rest, retrace your steps for the arduous climb back to the trailhead. For a longer wilderness excursion, with advanced backcountry permits, you can pick up the eastbound Tonto and intercept the Bright Angel.

Essential Information

Park Entrances

South Rim

The most accessible area of the park is the South Rim, an easy 60-mile drive north of I-40 at Williams.

From the **South Entrance Station**, the main park entrance, it is a few miles north to Grand Canyon Visitor Center, from where free park shuttles service sights and lodges within Grand Canyon Village year-round and overlooks on Hermit Rd seasonally. Free park shuttles run from Tusayan, just outside the park, to the visitor center every 20 minutes March 1 to September 30.

The Desert View Entrance Station or **East Entrance** has a gas station, general store, seasonal campground and historic overlook. From here, it is a 25-mile drive west to Grand Canyon Village; no public transportation.

North Rim

Getting to the North Rim is more of a challenge. A shuttle (mid-May to mid-November) runs from rim to rim, but otherwise the only way to reach the North Rim is by car, foot or bicycle. It's about 12 miles to North Rim services from the **North Rim Entrance Gate**.

Sleeping

South Rim

Lodges and campgrounds mostly cluster in the tourist hub of Grand Canyon Village, with the best are along the rim in the Historic District. The common areas at the **El Tovar** (☑advanced reservations 888-297-2757, reservations within 48hr 928-638-3283; www. grandcanyonlodges.com; r/ste from $228/461) ooze old-world national park glamor.

Below the rim, there is one lodge, three designated campgrounds, and multiple backcountry primitive campsites.

Phantom Ranch (contact as per El Tovar; dm $49, cabin d $142, available by lottery; ❄) Bunks at this camp-like complex on the canyon floor are in cabins sleeping two to 10 people. Meals must be reserved when booking. Phantom is accessible by mule trip, on foot or via raft on the Colorado River.

Indian Garden Campground (☑Backcountry Information Center 928-638-7875; www.nps.gov/ grca; backcountry permit $10, plus per person per night $8; ⊙year-round) ✈ Located 3040ft below the South Rim, and a 4.6-mile hike along the Bright Angel Trail, lovely Indian Garden sits along a creek, with a ranger station, toilets and year-round drinking water (though pipeline breaks regularly result in closed water supplies).

North Rim

Accommodations are limited to one lodge and one campground. If these two options are fully booked, try snagging a cabin or campsite at the Kaibab National Forest. Otherwise, you'll find more options another 60 miles north in Kanab, UT.

Eating & Drinking

South Rim

Grand Canyon Village has all the eating options you'll need. Bright Angel Lodge's **Arizona Room** (☑928-638-2631; www.grand canyonlodges.com; lunch $13-16, dinner $22-28; ⊙11:30am-3pm & 4:30-10pm Feb-Oct, dinner only Nov-Jan; 🚌Village) and **Harvey House Cafe** (mains $13-21; ⊙6am-4:30pm & 5-10pm; 🚌Village westbound) are among the few table-service restaurants on the South Rim, though several bars serve small plates and snacks.

North Rim

Food options are limited to the Grand Canyon Lodge dining room, takeout from Deli in the Pines, or the paltry offerings at the general store. Bring your own groceries and plan on picnics or cookouts.

Visitor Centers

Grand Canyon Visitor Center (South Rim; ☑park headquarters 928-638-7888; www.nps. gov/grca; Grand Canyon Village; ⊙9am-5pm; 🚌Village, 🚌Kaibab/Rim, 🚌Tusayan Mar 1-Sep 30) The South Rim's main visitor center; on the plaza here, bulletin boards and kiosks display information about ranger programs, the weather, tours and hikes. ∎

El Tovar Hotel

PAMELA MARCELIN/SHUTTERSTOCK ©

Bristlecone pine

Great Basin National Park

With rugged mountain slopes and ancient trees, Great Basin is a gorgeous place to ponder your insignificance. Its bristlecone pines began growing when Egypt's Great Pyramid was still under construction. You'll also find stone arches, thousand-year-old wall paintings and an underground cavern.

Great For...

State
Nevada

Entrance Fee
Free

Area
121 sq miles

Perched 1 mile above sea level in the craggy Snake Range, the park marks the eastern endpoint of the Loneliest Road, which stretches across the white-hot center of Nevada along US 50.

Lehman Caves

This colossal marble cavern features a staggering collection of formations, including stalactites, stalagmites, helictites, flowstone, popcorn and more than 300 rare shields. Local rancher Absalom Lehman is credited with discovering the caves in 1865. The only way to view them today is by guided tour. Take your pick of two tours: the 60-minute **Lodge Tour** (adult/child $9/5) or the slightly more demanding 90-minute **Grand Palace Tour** (adult/child $11/6), which takes in the famous Parachute Shield. Advance reservations recommended. Note that the temperature inside the caves is a constant 50°F (10°C): bring a sweater.

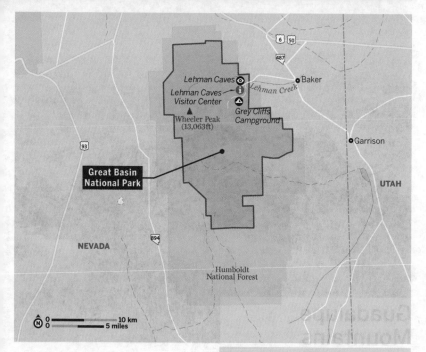

Wheeler Peak Scenic Drive

Rising abruptly from the desert floor to a height of 13,063ft, Wheeler Peak is the tallest mountain in the Snake Range. Its slopes can be explored along the paved 12-mile Wheeler Peak Scenic Drive. Starting at the Lehman Caves Visitor Center, the sinuous road climbs past pinyon pines, a mountain mahogany wilderness and a mixed-conifer forest. At Mile 11 it passes white-barked aspens in a subalpine forest. It's said to be the same ecological diversity as driving from Baker, NV, to Canada's frozen Yukon thousands of miles north.

Stargazing

Cloudless nights in Great Basin offer an extravaganza of stars, and these exceptional stargazing conditions earned the park an International Dark Sky Park designation in 2016. Five planets can be seen with the naked eye, plus the Andromeda Galaxy, the Milky Way and meteor showers. In early September the park hosts its

Essential Information

The park is in eastern Nevada, near the Utah border. The closest major airport is Salt Lake International Airport (235 miles northeast). There is no public transportation to the park.

With the exception of campsites at Grey Cliffs Campground, campgrounds are all first-come, first served. Lower Lehman Creek Campground is the only one open year-round.

Lehman Caves Visitor Center (☏775-234-7331; www.nps.gov/grba; 5500 NV-488, Baker; ⊙ 8am-4:30pm, tours 8:30am-4pm) Caves tour bookings and national park information; 5 miles outside the town of Baker, which is 63 miles east of Ely.

annual three-day **Astronomy Festival**, with volunteer astronomers, evening programs, loads of telescopes for star viewing and a night-sky photography workshop. ■

CHRISTOPHER DNH/SHUTTERSTOCK ©

Guadalupe Mountains National Park

This is a Texas high spot, both literally and figuratively. At 8749ft, Guadalupe Peak is the highest point in the Lone Star State. More than half the park is a federally designated wilderness area and the fall foliage in McKittrick Canyon is the best in west Texas.

Great For...

State
Texas

Entrance Fee
7-day pass per adult/child $5/free

Area
135 sq miles

We won't go so far as to call it Texas' best-kept secret, but even many Texans aren't aware of the Guadalupe Mountains National Park. It's just this side of the Texas–New Mexico state line and a long drive from practically everywhere in the state.

The NPS has deliberately curbed development to keep the park wild. There are no restaurants or indoor accommodations and only a smattering of services and programs (so plan ahead to keep your gas tank full and your cooler stocked).

McKittrick Canyon Trail

Deservedly one of the park's most popular walks, this 3.4-mile one-way hike on a mostly level day-use trail ends at a scenic grotto. You'll pass the historic **Pratt Cabin** along the way. The cabin was built in 1932 by petroleum geologist Wallace Pratt, who later donated the land to the NPS; it

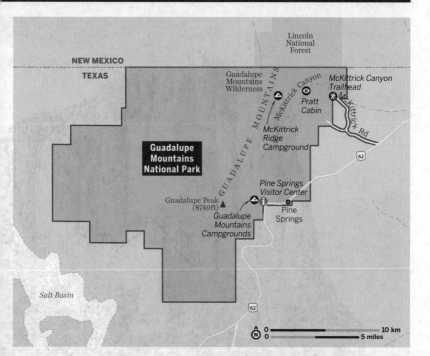

remains furnished as the Pratt family left it. Surrounded by colorful leaves, it's at its most scenic in the fall.

The hike is 15.2 miles round-trip if you climb to the McKittrick Ridge Campground, with a gain of about 2700ft. The entrance road to the trailhead is 7 miles east of the Pine Springs Visitor Center on Hwy 62/180.

Fossil Reef

A geologist's dream, the park sits amid the world's most extensive exposed fossil reef. In fact, the mountains contain the world's best example of a 260- to 270-million-year-old exposed rock layer, the Guadalupian Global Stratotype.

The reef began to grow 250 million years ago, when an immense tropical ocean covered parts of Texas, New Mexico and Mexico. Over a period of five million years, lime-secreting marine organisms built the

horseshoe-shaped reef to a length of 400 miles. After the sea evaporated, the reef was buried in sediment for millions more years, until a mountain-building geological uplift revealed part of it as the Guadalupe Mountains.

Fall Colors

McKittrick Canyon's fall colors are glorious from early October through mid-November, and while nights can be chilly, daytime is warmly sublime. But be aware that autumn weekends are by far the busiest time and there may be a wait of several hours to enter the canyon.

Left: El Capitan peak; Right: Sage thrasher

Park History

Until the mid-19th century, the Guadalupe Mountains were used exclusively by Mescalero Apaches, who hunted and camped in the area. Members of this tribe, who called themselves Nde, became the hunted starting in 1849, when the US Army began a ruthless 30-year campaign to drive them from the area. The mid-19th century also marked the brief tenure of the Butterfield Overland Mail Route, a revolution in American communications and transportation whereby a letter could move 2700 miles from St Louis to San Francisco via El Paso, Tucson and Los Angeles in a then-breathtaking 25 days. Guadalupe Mountains National Park was established in 1972.

Essential Information

Time

Unlike most of the rest of Texas, the park is in Mountain Time Zone, as are El Paso and Carlsbad Caverns National Park.

Sleeping & Eating

If you want to stay in the area, there aren't a lot of options. Camp in the park, bring your own food, and...that's it.

If camping doesn't appeal and you want to spend more than a day exploring the park, you can drive 45 minutes to Whites City, NM, a resort town with over 100 motel rooms and two RV parks.

There are even fewer eating options than sleeping options here – in other words, zero. Plan on bringing food, either to tide you over till you can get to Whites City (which has a couple of mediocre restaurants), or to sustain you throughout your stay without having to cross state lines.

Note that no wood or charcoal fires are allowed within the park; propane stoves or grills are permitted, however.

Guadalupe Mountains Campgrounds (☑915-828-3251; www.nps.gov/gumo; tent & RV sites $8) The park's campgrounds are first-come, first-served – unless you have a group of 10 or more, in which case you can reserve a group camping spot up to 60 days in advance (for $3 per person). Campsites fill up during spring break, and several nights a week in the summer, although visitors arriving by early afternoon will usually find a site. The most convenient campgrounds are at Pine Springs, right along Hwy 62/180 near the visitor center; if it looks full, look for the 'campground host' sign for directions to overflow spots. If all the sites are full, RVs are permitted to park overnight at the nearby state highway picnic areas.

Visitor Center

Information, restrooms and drinking water are available at the **Pine Springs Visitor Center** (☑915-828-3251; www.nps.

gov/gumo; ⊗8am-4:30pm). You'll also find water, restrooms and outdoor exhibits in McKittrick Canyon; the Dog Canyon Ranger Station has information, restrooms and water. Visit the park website to download a map of the park before you visit.

Getting There & Away

Guadalupe Mountains National Park is on Hwy 62/180, 110 miles east of El Paso and 55 miles southwest of Carlsbad, NM. The closest gas stations are 35 miles in either direction on Hwy 62/180 and the closest services are in Whites City, NM, 45 minutes northeast of the park entrance on Hwy 62/180. ∎

Top left: Pratt Cabin; Top right: Yucca; Bottom: McKittrick Canyon

SOPOTNICKI/SHUTTERSTOCK ©

Mesa Verde National Park

More than 700 years after its inhabitants disappeared, Mesa Verde retains an air of mystery. It's a wonderland for adventurers of all sizes, who can clamber up ladders to carved-out dwellings, see rock art and delve into the secrets of ancient America.

Great For...

State
Colorado

Entrance Fee
7-day pass per car $15–20, per motorcycle $10–15, per person on foot or bicycle $7–10

Area
81 sq miles

❶ Cliff Palace

This grand engineering achievement provided shelter for 250 to 300 people. Springs across the canyon, below Sun Temple, were most likely their primary water sources. The use of small 'chinking' stones between the large blocks is strikingly similar to Ancestral Puebloan construction at distant Chaco Canyon.

The only way to see it is to take the hour-long ranger-led tour ($5), retracing the steps taken by the Ancestral Puebloans – visitors must climb down a stone stairway and five 10ft ladders.

❷ Balcony House

On the east side of the Cliff Palace Loop is an adventure that will challenge anyone's fear of heights or small places. You'll be rewarded with outstanding views of Soda Canyon, 600ft below the sandstone overhang that once served as the ceiling for

Balcony House

Trail Safety

Given the historical nature of the park, backcountry access is specifically forbidden and fines are imposed on anyone caught wandering off designated trails or entering cliff dwellings without a ranger.

When hiking in Mesa Verde always carry water and avoid cliff edges. Trails can be muddy and slippery after summer rains and winter snows, so wear appropriate footwear. Most park trails, except the Soda Canyon Trail, are strenuous and involve steep elevation changes. Hikers must register at the respective trailheads before venturing out.

35 to 40 rooms. Tickets are required for the one-hour guided tours ($5).

❸ Chapin Mesa

The largest concentration of Ancestral Puebloan sites is at Chapin Mesa, where you'll see the densely clustered **Far View Site** and the large **Spruce Tree House** – check ahead, as the latter may be closed due to safety concerns about rockfalls. It's worth touring the **Chapin Mesa Museum** (📞970-529-4475; www.nps.gov/meve; Chapin Mesa Rd; admission incl with park entry; 🕗8am-6:30pm Apr–mid-Oct, to 5pm mid-Oct–Apr); staff here provide information on weekends when the park headquarters is closed.

❹ Wetherill Mesa

This is the second-largest concentration of Ancestral Puebloan sites. Visitors may enter stabilized surface sites and two cliff dwellings, including the **Long House**, open from late May through August. A strenuous place to visit, it is only reached as part of a ranger-led guided tour organized from the visitor center ($5). Access involves climbing three ladders – two at 15ft and one at 4ft.

❺ Skiing & Snowshoeing the Cliff Palace Loop Rd

Winter is a special time in Mesa Verde. The crowds disperse and the cliff dwellings sparkle in the snow. Certain park roads have been designated for cross-country skiing and snowshoeing when weather permits. Before setting out, check the current snow conditions by calling the park headquarters.

The Cliff Palace Loop Rd is a relatively flat 6-mile loop located off the Mesa Top Loop Rd. The road is closed to vehicles after the first snowfall, so you won't have to worry about vehicular traffic. Park at the closed gate and glide 1 mile to the Cliff Palace overlook, continuing on past numerous other scenic stopping points.

In addition to the Cliff Palace Loop Rd, the Morefield Campground Loop Rds offer multiple miles of relatively flat terrain. The campground itself is closed in winter, but skiers and snowshoers can park at the gate and explore to their heart's content.

Long House

Essential Information

Sleeping

There are plenty of accommodations options in nearby Cortez and Mancos, and Mesa Verde can be easily visited as a day trip from Durango.

Morefield Campground (📞970-529-4465; www.visitmesaverde.com; Mile 4; tent/RV sites $30/40; ⊗May–early Oct) 🐾 The park's camping option, located 4 miles from the entrance gate, has hundreds of regular tent sites on grassy grounds conveniently located near Morefield Village. The village has a general store, a gas station, a restaurant, showers and a laundry. It's managed by Aramark. Dry RV campsites (without hookup) cost the same as tent sites.

Far View Lodge (📞970-529-4421, toll-free 800-449-2288; www.visitmesaverde.com; Mile 15; r $124-177; ⊗mid-Apr–Oct; ❄🤖) Perched on a mesa top 15 miles inside the park entrance, this tasteful Pueblo-style lodge has 150 Southwestern-style rooms, some with kiva fireplaces. Don't miss sunset over the mesa from your private balcony. Standard rooms don't have air-con (or TV) and summer daytimes can be hot. You can even bring your dog for an extra $10 per night.

Eating

There's fine dining, a small market and a cafe in the park, but campers will be happiest if they come stocked with provisions.

Metate Room (📞800-449-2288; www.visit mesaverde.com; Mile 15, Far View Lodge; mains $20-36; ⊗7-10am & 5:30-9:30pm Apr–mid-Oct, 5-7:30pm mid-Oct–Mar) 🐾 With an award in culinary excellence, this upscale restaurant in the Far View Lodge offers an innovative menu inspired by Native American food and flavors.

Visitor Centers

The huge **Mesa Verde Visitor & Research Center** (📞970-529-4465; www.nps.gov/meve; ⊗7:30am-7pm Jun–early Sep, 8am-5pm early Sep–mid-Oct & mid-Apr–May, closed mid-Oct–mid-Apr; 🤖) has water, wi-fi and bathrooms, in addition to information desks selling tickets for tours of Cliff Palace, Balcony House or Long House. It also displays museum-quality artifacts.

Getting There & Around

The Mesa Verde National Park entrance is off US 160, midway between Cortez and Mancos. Most people visit with a private car or motorcycle but there are some operators running tours to and around the national park from Durango, 36 miles to the east.

Vehicular transport is necessary to get to the sites from the front park gate as well as to travel between them. ∎

Top left: Pictograph, Long House; Top right: Anasazi pottery; Bottom: Kiva (a ceremonial room)

EKATERINA POKROVSKY/SHUTTERSTOCK ©

Painted Desert

Petrified Forest National Park

This national park is an extraordinary sight: the Painted Desert here is strewn with fossilized logs predating the dinosaurs. Up to 6ft in diameter, they're strikingly beautiful, with extravagantly patterned cross-sections of wood glinting in ethereal pinks, blues and greens.

Great For...

State
Arizona

Entrance Fee
7-day pass per car/person on foot, motorcycle or bicycle $20/10

Area
170 sq miles

Ancient Trees

The 225-million-year-old 'trees' of Petrified Forest National Park are fossilized logs scattered over a vast area of semidesert grassland. Trees arrived in this area via major floods, only to be buried beneath silica-rich volcanic ash before they could decompose. Groundwater dissolved the silica, carried it through the logs and crystallized into solid, sparkly quartz mashed up with iron, carbon, manganese and other minerals. Uplift and erosion eventually exposed the logs.

Souvenir hunters filched thousands of tons of petrified wood before Teddy Roosevelt made the forest a national monument in 1906 (it became a national park in 1962). Scavenge today and you'll be looking at fines and even jail time.

Scenic Drive

Straddling the I-40, the park has an entrance at exit 311 off I-40 in the north,

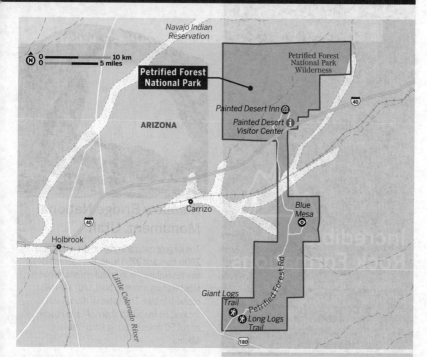

and another off Hwy 180 in the south. A 28-mile, paved scenic road links the two. To avoid backtracking, westbound travelers should start in the north, eastbound ones in the south.

The drive has about 15 pullouts, some with short trails. Two trails near the southern entrance allow close-ups of the petrified logs: the 0.6-mile **Long Logs Trail**, which has the largest concentration, and the 0.4-mile **Giant Logs Trail**, which sports the park's largest log. A highlight in the center section is the 3-mile loop drive (Blue Mesa Scenic Rd) out to **Blue Mesa**, where you'll be treated to 360-degree views of spectacular badlands, log falls and logs balancing atop hills with the leathery texture of elephant skin.

Painted Desert Inn

Redesigned in the 1940s by Mary Colter, the architect behind similar Hopi-style buildings in Grand Canyon Village, this

Essential Information

The 28-mile road through the park runs between I-40 in the north and Hwy 180 in the south.

Camping requires a free permit. The closest lodging is in Holbrook. Food service is very limited.

Painted Desert Visitor Center (☑928-524-6228; www.nps.gov; 1 Park Rd, Petrified Forest National Park; ☺8am-5pm) Good for information and access/camping permits, with a video describing how the logs were fossilized.

1930s adobe lodge is now a **museum** (☑928-524-6228; www.nps.gov; 1 Park Rd; ☺9am-4pm) **FREE**, decorated with murals by Hopi artist Fred Kabotie. After narrowly avoiding demolition, it was made a National Historic Landmark in 1987. ∎

Incredible Rock Formations

Grottoes, arches, a palette of red, rust and orange... The spellbinding rock formations at the heart of desert national parks transform adventure travelers into budding geologists.

Rainbow Bridge National Monument, Utah

The largest natural bridge in the world, at 290ft high and 275ft wide, this sacred Navajo site resembles the graceful arc of a rainbow. Most visitors arrive by boat, with a 2-mile round-trip hike. The national monument is located on the south shore of Lake Powell, about 50 miles by water from Wahweap Marina.

Glen Canyon National Recreation Area, Arizona–Utah

In the 1960s, the construction of a massive dam flooded Glen Canyon, forming Lake Powell, a recreational playground. Fifty years later this is still an environmental hot-button topic, but generations of Western families have grown up boating here. Water laps against stunning, multihued cliffs that rise hundreds of feet; narrow channels and tributary canyons twist off in every direction.

Natural Bridges National Monument, Utah

Forty miles west of Blanding via Hwy 95, this monument became Utah's first NPS land in 1908. The highlight is a dark-stained, white-sandstone canyon containing three easily accessible natural bridges. The oldest, the Owachomo Bridge, spans 180ft but is only 9ft thick. The flat 9-mile Scenic Drive loop is ideal for biking.

Hoodoos, Bryce Canyon

Hoodoos are freestanding pinnacles that have developed from side-eroding fins; layers disintegrate at different rates, creating an irregular profile. The bizarre formations are shaped as runoff over the canyon rim carves parallel gullies with narrow rock walls, the fins. Siltstone layers alternating with resilient limestone bands give them strength as they erode into towering hoodoos.

Chiricahua National Monument, Arizona

Rain, thunder and wind have chiseled volcanic rocks into fluted pinnacles, natural bridges, gravity-defying balancing boulders and soaring spires reaching skyward like totem poles carved in stone. The remoteness made Chiricahua a favorite hiding place of Apache warrior Cochise and his men. Today it attracts birds and wildlife, including bobcats, bears, deer, coatis and javelinas.

DMITRY VINOGRADOV/500PX ©

Saguaro National Park

Saguaros are an iconic symbol of the American Southwest, and an entire army of these majestic cactus plants is protected in this two-part desert playground. Established in 1933, Saguaro National Monument was the first federal monument created to protect a specific plant.

Great For...

State
Arizona

Entrance Fee
7-day pass per vehicle/motorcycle/person on foot or bicycle $15/10/5

Area
143 sq miles

The park is divided into two distinct sections. Petroglyphs, nature trails and saguaro groves grab the spotlight in the **Tucson Mountain District** on the western edge of Tucson. Thirty miles east, the **Rincon Mountain District** unfurls across six eco-zones, stretching from low-lying desert to the summits of isolated mountain ranges known as 'sky islands.'

Hiking

More than 165 miles of hiking trails crisscross the park. In the eastern district, the 1-mile round-trip **Freeman Homestead Trail** leads to a grove of massive saguaros. The 5.6-mile round-trip **Douglas Spring Trail** ascends from saguaros to desert grasslands and a seasonal waterfall in the Rincon Mountain foothills. For a full-fledged desert adventure, tackle the steep and rocky **Tanque Verde Ridge Trail**, which climbs to the summit of Tanque Verde peak (7049ft) and returns, for an 18-mile adventure.

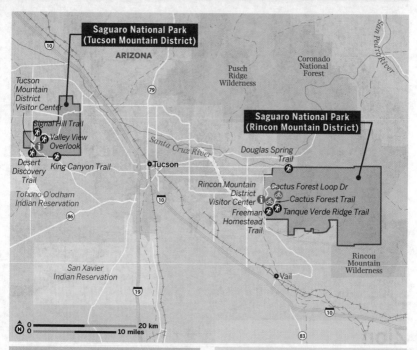

ARIZONA

Tucson
Mountain
District
Visitor Center

Signal Hill Trail

Valley View
Overlook

Desert
Discovery
Trail   King Canyon Trail

Tohono O'odham
Indian Reservation

San Xavier
Indian Reservation

Pusch
Ridge
Wilderness

Coronado
National
Forest

Santa Cruz River

Tucson

Saguaro National Park
(Rincon Mountain District)

Douglas Spring
Trail

Rincon Mountain
District
Visitor Center

Cactus Forest Loop Dr

Cactus Forest Trail

Freeman
Homestead
Trail

Tanque Verde Ridge Trail

Rincon
Mountain
Wilderness

Vail

San Pedro River

0   20 km
0   10 miles

Cactus Facts

Saguaros (sah-wah-ros) grow slowly, taking almost a century before they begin to assume their typical many-armed appearance. The best time to visit is April, when the cacti begin blossoming with lovely white blooms.

Don't refer to the limbs of the saguaro as branches. As park docents will quickly tell you, the mighty saguaro grows arms, not lowly branches.

Two easy but rewarding hikes in the western district are the 0.8-mile sunset-worthy **Valley View Overlook** and the almost half-mile **Signal Hill Trail**, which leads to scores of ancient petroglyphs. For a more strenuous trek, try the 7-mile **King Canyon Trail**, beginning 2 miles south of the visitor center.

The 0.5-mile informative **Desert Discovery Trail** is wheelchair accessible.

Essential Information

Tucson, a short drive from the park, sits at the junction of the I-10, I-19 and Hwy 86.

Rincon Mountain District Visitor Center
(520-733-5153; www.nps.gov/sagu; 3693 S Old Spanish Trail; 9am-5pm) Stop by this eastern visitor center for permits for backcountry camping ($8 per site per day). Camping is allowed at six hike-in campsites.

Cycling

The 8-mile **Cactus Forest Loop Drive** in the eastern district is an invigorating introduction to the park. Scenic overlooks line the ride, which begins just beyond the Rincon Mountain District Visitor Center. For off-road cycling, jump onto the **Cactus Forest Trail**, which divides Cactus Forest Loop Dr and rolls past historic lime kilns. There is no drinking water on either loop, so bring plenty with you. ∎

SWAM/SHUTTERSTOCK ©

The Narrows

Zion National Park

The soaring red-and-white cliffs of Zion Canyon, one of southern Utah's most dramatic natural wonders, rise high over the Virgin River. Lush vegetation and low elevation give these magnificent rock formations a different feel from the barren parks in the east. Get ready for an overdose of awesome.

Great For...

State
Utah

Entrance Fee
7-day pass per vehicle/motorcycle/person on foot or bicycle $35/30/20

Area
229 sq miles

❶ The Narrows

Zion's most famous backcountry route is the unforgettable Narrows, a strenuous 16-mile journey through the towering canyon along the Virgin River's north fork (p226). Plan on getting wet: most of the hike is in the river.

Overnight camping is by far and away the best experience, though you can hike from the top in one very strenuous, long day (90 minutes driving from Springdale to Chamberlain's Ranch, up to 12 hours hiking). Remember that the most difficult sections are at the end of the hike, when you'll be the most tired; we don't recommend this unless you have exceptional stamina and have done the hike before. You can also day hike the Narrows from the bottom, the most popular approach and the only one that doesn't require a permit.

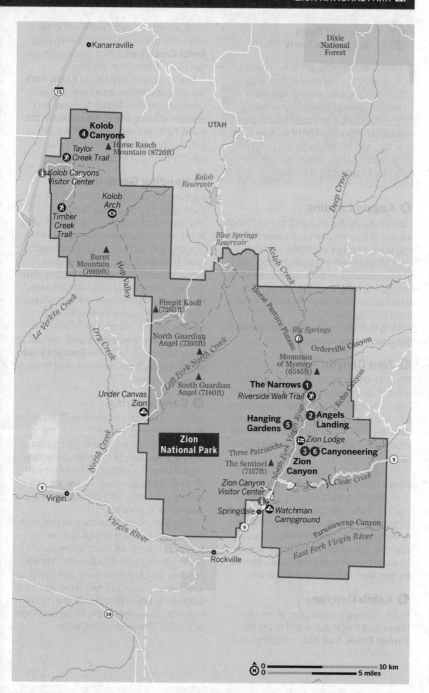

Emerald Pools & Kayenta Trails

This extremely popular sequence of trails links to a series of ponds, photogenic cascades and a surprisingly verdant desert oasis. Water seeps from sandstone and colorful pools are rimmed with life; wildflowers spring up in May and fall leaves turn in October. From Zion Lodge, cross the road and bridge to get to the trailhead.

❷ Angels Landing

Zion's 5.4-mile Angels Landing Trail (1488ft ascent) is the one everyone's heard of – and fears. At times the trail is no more than 5ft wide, with precipitous drop-offs to the canyon floor on both sides. Steel your nerves and hang on to those chains for dear life, and soon you'll be atop the park's most thrilling summit.

Note that the park is considering making this popular hike permit-only.

❸ Zion Canyon

The park encompasses roughly 229 sq miles of land, though the vast majority of visitors head straight for Zion Canyon, the park's crème de la crème: sheer sandstone cliffs, secret hanging gardens, leg-busting adventure-filled hikes and heart-stopping scenery.

Of the easy-to-moderate trails, the paved, mile-long **Riverside Walk** at the end of the road is a good place to start. When the trail ends, you can continue along in the Virgin River for 5 miles to Big Springs; this is the bottom portion of the spectacular Narrows, one of the park's most famous hikes. Yes, you'll be hiking in the water, so be prepared and rent gear if advised.

❹ Kolob Canyons

In the northwestern section of the park, the easiest trail is at the end of the road: **Timber Creek Trail** (0.5 miles) follows a 100ft ascent to a small peak with great views. The main hike is the 2.7-mile-long **Taylor Creek Trail**, which passes pioneer ruins and crisscrosses the creek.

The 7-mile one-way hike to **Kolob Arch** has a big payoff: this arch competes with Landscape Arch in Arches National Park in terms of being one of the biggest in the world. Fit hikers can manage it in a day, or continue on to make it a multiday backcountry trans-park connector.

❺ Hanging Gardens

If a mere five minutes in the Utah sun has you feeling as shriveled up as a raisin, you're going to find these lush desert oases all the more remarkable. Fed by mesa-top precipitation that has slowly percolated down through Navajo sandstone over millennia, these vertical gardens appear where dripping seeps exit shaded canyon walls, forced outward by a layer of harder Kayenta rock. Look for scarlet monkey flowers, mosses, golden columbines, maidenhair ferns and purple violets clinging marvelously to the rock face. The **Emerald Pools and Kayenta Trails** have some particularly lovely examples.

❻ Canyoneering

If there's one sport that makes Zion special, it's canyoneering. Rappelling over the lip of a sandstone bowl, swimming icy pools, tracing a slot canyon's curves...canyoneering is daring, dangerous and sublime all at once. Zion's slot canyons are the park's most sought-after backcountry experience; reserve far in advance.

Zion Canyon also has some of the most famous big-wall rock climbs in America. However, there's not much for beginners or those who like bolted routes. Permits are required for all canyoneering and climbing. You'll usually need to reserve them as far in advance as possible, but walk-in information is also available at the Wilderness Desk at the Zion Canyon Visitor Center.

Left: Angels Landing Trail; Right: Bighorn sheep

ALASKAPHOTO/SHUTTERSTOCK ©

FRANK BACH/GETTY IMAGES ©

⚠ Tortoise Crossing

A desert tortoise can live for up to 80 years, munching on wildflowers and grasses. With its canteen-like bladder, it can go up to a year without drinking. Using its strong hind legs, it burrows to escape the summer heat and freezing winter temperatures, and also to lay eggs.

Disease, predation and shrinking habitat have decimated the desert tortoise population. They like to rest in the shade, including under parked cars, so take a quick look around before driving away. They are often hit by high-speed and/or off-road drivers. If you see a tortoise in trouble, call a ranger. Do not pick it up, as a frightened tortoise may often pee on what it perceives to be an attacker, possibly leading to it dying of dehydration before the next rains come.

Drive Scenic Zion Canyon

The premier drive in the park leads between the towering red-rock cliffs of Zion's incredible main canyon and accesses all the major front-country trailheads. Note that most of the road is actually closed to private cars from March through October; you'll be traveling aboard the excellent park shuttle instead.

Duration 45 minutes

Distance 6.2 miles

Start South entrance

Finish Temple of Sinawava

Leaving from the visitor center, the first stop is the **Human History Museum** (⊙9am-7pm late May-early Sep, shorter hours rest of year) FREE. Just past the museum on Hwy 9 are a few turnouts that overlook the Streaked Wall. In spring, with binoculars, scan the rim for nesting peregrine falcons. Officially, the scenic drive begins where you turn north, and cars are restricted, at **Canyon Junction**.

Continuing up the canyon, you'll pass the **Sentinel Slide** on the left. About 7000 years ago, a big chunk of the cliff face sloughed off and blocked the water flow, turning the canyon into a big lake. The water eventually carved its way through the blockage and carried on.

Next, the **Court of the Patriarchs** stop fronts the shortest trail in the park, a 50yd, staircase of a walk uphill to a view of the namesake peaks. Named by a Methodist minister in 1916, from left to right are Abraham, Isaac and Jacob, while crouching in front of Jacob is Mt Moroni (named for a Mormon angel).

Ahead on your right, **Zion Lodge** houses the park's only cafe and restaurant. The lodge was first built in the 1920s, but burned down in 1966.

The **Grotto**, barely a half-mile north, is a large, cottonwood-shaded picnic area with plenty of tables, restrooms and drinking water. Across the road from the picnic area, the West Rim Trail leads north toward Angels Landing. Those who'd rather admire Angels Landing than climb it should stroll the first flat quarter-mile of the West Rim Trail to a stone bench for the perfect vantage.

Make sure you spend some time at **Weeping Rock**. Pause to admire Angels Landing, the Organ, Cable Mountain, the Great White Throne and looming Observation Point. A short detour up the bucolic Weeping Rock Trail to a sheltered alcove and hanging garden is worthwhile.

There are no trailheads at **Big Bend**, but rock climbers get out here on their way to some of Zion's famous walls. It's a good

place to bring binoculars and scan the skies for California condors.

If you're using the shuttle, the only way to the next two sights is to walk. As you continue north, on a ledge up to the right look for a reconstructed granary. Although ancient Native American in origin, it was rebuilt in the 1930s by the Boy Scouts. After about a half-mile, you get to **Menu Falls**, so-named because it was pictured on Zion Lodge's first menu cover. From there, it's easier to backtrack to Big Bend shuttle than to hoof it all the way up to the last stop. The canyon narrows near the cliff face that forms a natural amphi-theater known as the **Temple of Sina-wava**, at the road's end. Across the road the rock called the Pulpit does indeed look a bit like a giant lectern. From here you can take the popular Riverside Walk to the ultimate Zion experience, the Narrows.

Temple of Sinawava

ERIC URQUHART/SHUTTERSTOCK ©

Essential Information

Entrances

Arriving via the south entrance, expect traffic jams of 30 minutes or more just to pass the kiosk – arrive well before 8am (or after 4pm) to avoid the worst of it.

Arriving from the east on Hwy 9, you have to pass through the Zion–Mt Carmel Tunnel.

If your RV or trailer is 7ft 10in wide or 11ft 4in high or larger, it must be escorted through ($15).

Visitor Centers

Kolob Canyons Visitor Center (☏435-586-0895; www.nps.gov/zion; Kolob Canyons Rd; ⊙8am-6pm late May-Sep, shorter hours rest of year) Small visitor center in Kolob Canyons.

Zion Canyon Visitor Center (☏435-772-3256; www.nps.gov/zion; Hwy 9, Zion National Park; ⊙8am-7pm Jun-Aug, shorter hours rest of year) Main visitor center by the south entrance. Contains the **Wilderness Desk** (☏435-772-0170), which issues all permits.

Safety

If you plan on entering a slot canyon or the Narrows, make sure you check the daily flash-flood forecast at the visitor center or www.weather.gov. Late summer is the primary season for floods, but they can happen at any time of the year. If necessary call **National Park Rangers Emergency** (☏435-772-3322).

Sleeping

Both of the park's large, established campgrounds are near the Zion Canyon Visitor Center at the south entrance. Both sites are tops for location, but must be reserved.

Watchman Campground (☏877-444-6777; www.recreation.gov; Hwy 9; tent sites $20, RV sites with hookups $30) Towering cottonwoods provide fairly good shade for the 184 well-spaced sites at Watchman, located south of the visitor center. Sites are by reservation (six months in advance; 14-day maximum stay) and you should book as far in advance as possible. Flush toilets; no showers.

Zion Lodge (☏888-297-2757, 435-772-7700; www.zionlodge.com; Zion Canyon Scenic Dr; cabins/r $260/225; ❄@☎) We love the stunning surrounding red-rock cliffs and the location in the middle of Zion Canyon. But be warned: today's reconstructed lodge is not as grand as other national park lodges (the 1920s original burned down in 1966). Reserve months ahead.

Under Canvas Zion (☏435-359-2911; www.undercanvas.com; 3955 Kolob Terrace Rd; tents $239-549) If you love the idea of camping but are less enthused about actually sleeping on the ground, Under Canvas could be for you. Ringed by red mesas and distant sandstone peaks, these secluded luxury tents off Kolob Terrace Rd sleep up to four and come equipped with woodburning stoves and private bathrooms – some have stargazing windows, too!

Eating

Most visitors pack their own lunch. Zion Lodge has the only in-park dining; otherwise head to Springdale, just outside the park.

Red Rock Grill (☏435-772-7760; Zion Canyon Scenic Dr, Zion Lodge; breakfast & sandwiches $6-17, dinner $16.50-30; ⊙6:30-10am & 11:30am-9pm Mar-Oct, hours vary Nov-Feb) Settle into your replica log chair or relax on the big deck with magnificent canyon views. The dinner menu touts its sustainable-cuisine stance, the results are hit-or-miss. Dinner reservations recommended.

Getting Around

The **Zion Park Shuttle** makes nine stops along the canyon, from the main visitor center to the Temple of Sinawava (a 45-minute round-trip). The **Springdale Shuttle** also makes nine stops along Hwy 9 between the park's south entrance and the Majestic View Lodge in Springdale.

The propane-burning shuttle buses are wheelchair-accessible, can accommodate large backpacks and carry up to two bicycles or one baby stroller. Generally high-season shuttles (mid-May to September) operate from 6am to 9:15pm, every five to 15 minutes.

Great White Throne

CLASSIC HIKES

The Narrows: Top Down

If there's one route that's made Zion famous, it's the wade down the Virgin River through a 1000ft sheer gorge known as the Narrows. Soaring walls, scalloped alcoves and wading through chest deep pools with your backpack lifted over your head make it truly memorable.

Duration 2 days

Distance 16 miles

Difficulty Hard

Start Chamberlain's Ranch (East Zion)

Finish Temple of Sinawava

DAY 1: Chamberlain's Ranch to Kolob Creek (6 hours, 9 miles)

The trail begins at Chamberlain's Ranch, on the east side of the park, 90 minutes' drive from the south entrance. This is a one-way hike, so make reservations for a hiker shuttle, unless you have two cars and drivers. Shuttles usually leave Springdale at 6:15am; a second may leave around 9am if there are enough people. Past the ranch gate, a dirt road leads to the river, where you'll find an NPS trailhead marker.

The first day is the quietest, the flowing water and undulating walls casting a mesmerizing spell. The first 3 miles are out of the river and the least interesting – power through so you can spend more time with the fun stuff, exploring side canyons and taking photographs. Once you see

Bulloch's Cabin, an old homestead about an hour from the trailhead, you'll know that soon enough the trail becomes the river. The **First Narrows**, about 3½ hours into the hike and near the park boundary, is an early highlight and provides a taste of what's to come.

From here the hike is quite photogenic, with the canyon walls gradually coming closer together. A little over four hours from the trailhead, you'll reach a log-jam **waterfall** that appears impassable. Upon closer inspection you'll soon pick out the trail that skirts around to the left. Depending on what time you started, this could be a good lunch spot.

Deep Creek is the first major confluence, doubling the river's volume. In the subsequent 2-mile stretch, expect secretive side canyons and faster water, sometimes waist deep and involving swims. Almost six hours from the trailhead is **Kolob Creek** (generally dry), an interesting side canyon to explore. This area is the location of the 12 overnight campsites, each on a sandy outcrop far from the others.

DAY 2: Kolob Creek to Temple of Sinawava (4.5 hours, 7 miles)

On day 2 you'll pass **Big Springs**, a good place to fill water bottles. After this are the 5 miles open to day hikers and plenty of deep pools and fast-moving water. In 2 miles you'll reach well-known **Wall Street**, certainly one of the most memorable parts of all of Zion. Save some energy for **Orderville Canyon**, a narrow side canyon that is lots of fun to explore. Orderville is about three hours downstream from Big Springs; you can follow it upstream for a half-mile. From here your company will steadily increase until you're just one of the crowd on the **Riverside Walk**.

Practicalities & Permits

The Narrows permits are some of the most sought-after in the park and are attached to campsites, except for through hikers. Only 40 permits per day are issued: six campsites are available online; the other six are reserved for walk-ins at the Wilderness Desk (p224).

Permits are not issued any time the river is flowing more than 120 cubic feet per second, so this hike may be closed at times between March and June. The optimum time to hike is late June through September. Flash floods are not uncommon in late summer when, again, the park may close the route. Outside of summer, wet or dry suits are often necessary, as hypothermia is a real danger. The Wilderness Desk carefully tracks weather, and Springdale outfitters rent all the appropriate gear.

A summer-season checklist includes a walking stick or trekking poles, synthetic clothing (no cotton!), extra fleece layers and at least one dry bag, in addition to all the usual camping gear. Canyoneering shoes and neoprene socks are useful, but not necessary outside spring. Overnight hikers are required to use human-waste disposal (WAG) bags, which are given free to permit holders. ∎

CHECUBUS/SHUTTERSTOCK ©

ALASKA
& THE PACIFIC
NORTHWEST

In This Chapter

Crater Lake 232
Denali...................................242
Gates of the Arctic
& Kobuk Valley.....................254
Glacier Bay...........................260
Katmai..................................268
Kenai Fjords 274
Lake Clark 278
Mt Rainier.............................280
North Cascades....................292
Olympic 298
Wrangell-St Elias 310

Alaska & the Pacific Northwest

Lush rainforests and volcanic peaks are the hallmarks of the Pacific Northwest. Glacial snowfields emerge from a sea of clouds, and virgin stands of massive Douglas fir and red cedar serve as reminders of what the continent's ancient forests must have once looked like. Mt Rainier and Crater Lake steal the limelight in the lower 48, but over 1500 miles to the north lies wilder, remoter Alaska whose eight national parks cover 54 million acres.

Don't Miss

○ Seeing the moss-draped trees of the thick, wet Hoh Rain Forest (p298)

○ Cycling or busing Denali's long and winding Park Rd (p242)

○ Hiking among wildflower meadows by Mt Rainier (p280)

○ Taking in the North Cascades scenery of glaciers, jagged peaks and alpine lakes (p292)

○ Paddling an icy wilderness in Glacier Bay (p260)

When to Go

All of the parks enjoy a short but intense high season between early June and early September with sunny, warm days and good chances of seeing wildflowers and big fauna. High season also means more crowds and higher prices for accommodations and sights.

In shoulder season (April, May and October) crowds and prices drop off, but services are more limited. Alaska in particular can be pretty cold.

While parks technically remain open year-round, you'll need to be a hardy soul to enjoy them in the winter. Olympic National Park has a small ski station.

Previous page: Denali National Park (p242)
MICHAEL ROSEBROCK/SHUTTERSTOCK ©

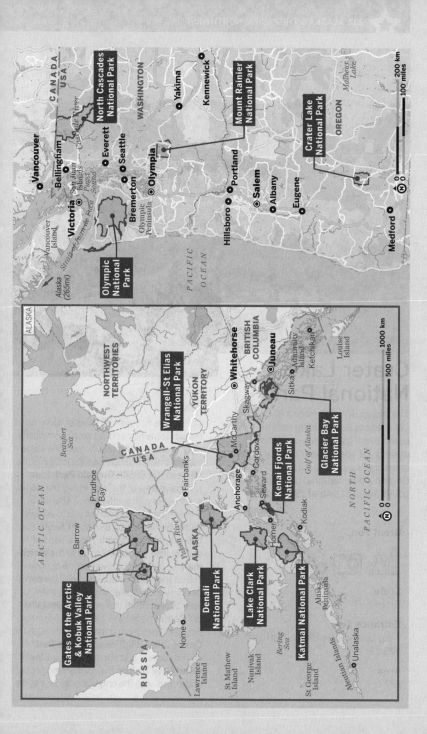

H. PETER JI PHOTOGRAPHER/SHUTTERSTOCK ©

Crater Lake National Park

The gloriously blue waters of Crater Lake reflect surrounding mountain peaks like a giant dark-blue mirror, making for spectacular photographs and breathtaking panoramas. Crater Lake is Oregon's only national park and also the USA's deepest lake at 1943ft deep.

Great For...

State
Oregon

Entrance Fee
7-day pass per vehicle/pedestrian
$25/12

Area
287 sq miles

Hiking

Crater Lake has over 90 miles of hiking trails, though some higher ones aren't completely clear of snow until late July. From the eastern edge of the Rim Village parking lot, a 1.7-mile trail leads up 8054ft **Garfield Peak** to an expansive view of the lake; in July the slopes are covered with wildflowers. A strenuous 5-mile round-trip hike takes you to an even better lake vista atop 8929ft **Mt Scott**, the highest point in the park. For a steep but shorter hike, trek up 0.7 miles to the **Watchman**, an old lookout tower on the opposite side of the lake that boasts one of the park's best views. For flower enthusiasts, there's an easy 1-mile nature trail near the **Steel Visitor Center** (☎541-594-3000; ⊗9am-5pm May-Oct, 10am-4pm Nov-Apr) that winds through the **Castle Crest Wildflower Garden Trail**.

The popular and steep mile-long **Cleetwood Cove Trail**, at the northern end of the crater, provides the only water access at the

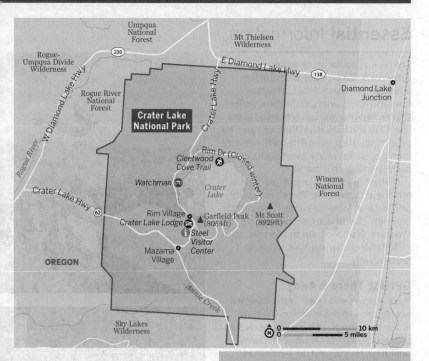

cove. Two-hour **boat tours** ([📞]888-774-2728; www.craterlakelodges.com/activities/volcano-boat-cruises; Cleetwood Cove boat dock; adult/child $42/28; ⊙late Jun-early Sep) are available; reserve, as these are popular.

Skiing & Snowshoeing

In winter, only the southern entrance road to Rim Village is kept plowed to provide access to several Nordic skiing trails. Rentals are unavailable inside the park, so bring skis with you. Only experienced skiers should attempt the dangerous, avalanche-prone loop around Crater Lake, which takes two to three days and requires a backcountry permit from park headquarters.

Snowshoes are provided for free ranger-led snowshoe walks, which are held at 1pm on weekends from Thanksgiving through March or April; call [📞]541-594-3100 for reservations.

 Mt Mazama

The ancient mountain whose remains now form Crater Lake was Mt Mazama, a roughly 12,000ft volcanic peak that was heavily glaciered and inactive for many thousands of years until it came back to life 7700 years ago. A catastrophic explosion scattered ash for hundreds of miles as flows of superheated pumice solidified into massive banks. These eruptions emptied the magma chambers at the heart of the volcano, and the summit cone collapsed to form the caldera.

Only snowfall and rain contribute to the lake water. This purity and the lake's great depth give it that famous blue color. Sparse forests can be seen growing in pumice and ash in the Pumice Desert, just north of Crater Lake along N Entrance Rd.

Essential Information

The park's popular south entrance is open year-round and provides access to Rim Village and Mazama Village, as well as the park headquarters at the Steel Visitor Center. In winter you can only go up to the lake's rim and back down the same way; no other roads are plowed. The north entrance is only open from early June to late October, depending on snowfall.

It's best to top up your gas tank before arriving at Crater Lake. There's reasonably priced gas at Mazama Village (summertime only); the closest pumps otherwise are in Prospect, Diamond Lake and Fort Klamath.

Summer is often cold and windy, so dress warmly.

Getting There & Away

You'll need a car to reach Crater Lake; it's wise to carry chains in winter. The north entrance and most of the roads inside the park are closed from November usually until June. Hwy 62 and the 4-mile road from the highway to park headquarters are plowed and open year-round. The 3-mile road from headquarters to Rim Village is kept open when possible, but heavy snowfall means it may be closed; call ahead to check (☎541-594-3100).

Sleeping

Other than **Crater Lake Lodge** (☎888-774-2728; www.craterlakelodges.com; r from $220; ☺late May–mid-Oct; ☎) which is the only lodging at the lake, and Mazama Village (7 miles from the rim), the nearest noncamping accommodations are 20 to 40 miles away. Park lodging is closed mid-October to late May, depending on snowfall. Fort Klamath has several good lodgings. Union Creek, Prospect, Diamond Lake and Lemolo Lake all have nice, woodsy places to stay, and there's lots of accommodations in Medford, Roseburg and Klamath Falls.

Top left: Hikers on Garfield Peak; Top right: Castle Crest Wildflower Garden Trail; Bottom: Garfield Peak

CLASSIC ROAD TRIPS

Crater Lake Circuit

Make it a (big) day trip or stay a week – serene, mystical Crater Lake is one of Oregon's most enticing destinations. The best route takes you on a heavily forested, waterfall-studded loop.

Duration 2–3 days

Distance 365 miles

Best Time to Go
Late May to mid-October when all the roads are open.

Essential Photo
No surprise here: Crater Lake.

Best Waterfall
Two-tiered Toketee Falls is our favorite.

❶ Ashland

A favorite base for day trips to Crater Lake, Ashland is bursting at the seams with lovely places to sleep and eat (though you'll want to book your hotel room far in advance during the busy summer months). Home of the **Oregon Shakespeare Festival** (OSF; ☑541-482-4331; www.osfashland.org; cnr Main & Pioneer Sts; tickets $30-136; ☺Tue-Sun Feb-Oct), it has more culture than most towns its size, and is just far enough off the highway to resist becoming a chain-motel mecca.

It's not just Shakespeare that makes Ashland the cultural heart of southern Oregon. If you like contemporary art, check out the **Schneider Museum of Art** (☑541-552-6245; http://sma.sou.edu; 1250 Siskiyou Blvd; suggested donation $5; ☺10am-4pm Mon-Sat).

Ashland's historic downtown and lovely **Lithia Park** (59 Winburn Way) make it a dandy place to go for a walk before or after your journey to Crater Lake.

The Drive » Medford is 13 miles north of Ashland on I-5.

❷ Medford

Southern Oregon's largest metropolis is where you hop off I-5 for your trek out to Crater Lake, and it can also serve as a suitable base of operations if you want a cheap, convenient place to bunk down for the night.

On your way out, check out the **Table Rocks**, impressive 800ft mesas that speak of the area's volcanic past and are home to unique plant and animal species. Flowery spring is the best time for hiking to the flat tops, which were revered Native American sites. After **TouVelle State Park** (Table Rock Rd), fork either left to reach the trailhead to Lower Table Rock (3.5-mile round-trip hike) or right for Upper Table Rock (2.5-mile round-trip hike).

The Drive » The drive along Hwy 62 isn't much until after Shady Cove, when urban sprawl stops and forest begins. Your next stop is 45 miles northeast in Prospect.

❸ Prospect

No wonder they changed the name of Mill Creek Falls Scenic Area – that implies you're just going to see another waterfall (not that there's anything wrong with that). But the real treat at **Prospect State Scenic Viewpoint** is hiking down to the **Avenue of Giant Boulders**, where the Rogue River crashes dramatically through huge chunks of rock and a little bit of scrambling offers the most rewarding views.

Take the trail from the southernmost of two parking lots on Mill Creek Dr. Keep left to get to the boulders or right for a short hike to two viewpoints for **Mill Creek Falls** and **Barr Creek Falls**. If you've got one more falls-sighting left in you, take the short hike from the upper parking lot to the lovely **Pearsony Falls**.

Lithia Park

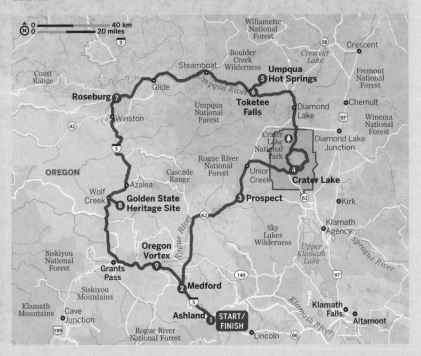

The Drive » Follow Hwy 62 for another 28 miles to get to the Crater Lake National Park turnoff at Munson Valley Rd.

❹ Crater Lake

This is it: the main highlight and reason for being of this entire trip is Oregon's most beautiful body of water, **Crater Lake** (☏541-594-3000; www.nps.gov/crla; 7-day vehicle pass $25). This amazingly blue lake is filled with some of the clearest, purest water you can imagine – you can easily peer 100ft down – and sits inside a 6-mile-wide caldera created when Mt Mazama erupted nearly 8000 years ago. Protruding from the water and adding to the drama of the landscape is **Wizard Island**, a volcanic cinder cone topped by its own mini crater called Witches Cauldron.

Get the overview with the 33-mile **Rim Drive** (⊘Jun–mid-Oct), which offers over 30 viewpoints as it winds around the edge of Crater Lake. The gloriously still waters reflect surrounding mountain peaks like a giant dark-blue mirror, making for spectacular photographs and breathtaking panoramas.

You can also camp, ski or hike in the surrounding old-growth forests. The popular and steep mile-long **Cleetwood Cove Trail**, at the north end of the crater, provides the only water access at the cove. Or get up close with a two-hour boat tour (p233).

The Drive » Head north on Hwy 138 for 41 miles and turn right on Rd 34.

❺ Umpqua Hot Springs

Set on a mountainside overlooking the North Umpqua River, Umpqua Hot Springs is one of Oregon's most splendid hot springs, with a little bit of height-induced adrenaline thanks to its position atop a rocky bluff.

Top: Table Rocks; Bottom left: Umpqua Hot Springs; Bottom right: Mill Creek Falls

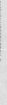

Rising Vines

A warmer, sunnier climate has helped create some of Oregon's fledgling wine regions. Grapes in the Umpqua and Applegate Valleys, and around Jacksonville, Grants Pass and Medford, are transformed into big reds and oaky whites.

Springs are known for soothing weary muscles, so earn your soak at Umpqua by starting with a hike – it is in a national forest, after all – where you'll be treated to lush, old-growth forest and waterfalls punctuating the landscape. Half a mile from the parking lot is the scenic **North Umpqua Trail**.

The Drive » The turnout for Toketee Falls is right on Hwy 138, 2 miles past the Umpqua turnoff.

❻ Toketee Falls

More than half a dozen waterfalls line this section of the Rogue-Umpqua Scenic Byway, but the one that truly demands a stop is the stunning, two-tiered **Toketee Falls** (USFS Rd 34). The falls' first tier drops 40ft into an upper pool behind a cliff of columnar basalt, then crashes another 80ft down the rock columns into yet another gorgeous, green-blue pool below. One tiny disclaimer: although the hike is just 0.4 miles, there's a staircase of 200 steps down to the viewpoint, so climbing back up to your car is a bit of a workout.

The Drive » From here, the scenery tapers back down to only moderately spectacular as you leave the Umpqua National Forest. It's just one hour to Roseburg.

❼ Roseburg

Sprawling Roseburg lies in a valley near the confluence of the South and North Umpqua Rivers. The city is mostly a cheap, modern sleepover for travelers headed elsewhere (such as Crater Lake), but it does have a cute, historic downtown area and is surrounded by award-winning wineries.

Don't miss the excellent **Douglas County Museum** (☎541-957-7007; www.umpquavalleymuseums.org; 123 Museum Dr, I-5 exit 123; adult/child $8/2; ☺10am-5pm Tue-Sat), which displays the area's cultural and natural histories. Especially interesting are the railroad derailment photos and History of Wine exhibit. Kids have an interactive area and live snakes to look at.

The Drive » Go south on I-5 for 47 miles and take the Wolf Creek exit. Follow Old State Hwy 99 to curve back under the interstate. Golden is 3.2 miles east on Coyote Creek Rd.

❽ Golden State Heritage Site

Not ready to return to civilization quite yet? Stop off in the ghost town of **Golden**, population zero. A former mining town that had over 100 residents in the mid-1800s, Golden was built on the banks of Coyote Creek when gold was discovered there.

A handful of structures remain, as well as some newfangled interpretive signs that tell the tale of a curiously devout community that eschewed drinking and dancing, all giving a fascinating glimpse of what life was like back then. The weathered wooden buildings include a residence, the general store/post office, and a classic country church. Fun fact: the town was once used as a location for the long-running American Western TV series *Gunsmoke*.

The Drive » Go south another 45 miles on I-5 and take exit 43. The Oregon Vortex is 4.2 miles north of the access road.

❾ Oregon Vortex

Just outside the town of Gold Hill lies the **Oregon Vortex** (☎541-855-1543; www.oregonvortex.com; 4303 Sardine Creek L Fork Rd, Gold Hill; adult/child $12.75/9; ☺9am-4pm Mar-Oct, to 5pm Jun-Aug), where the laws of physics don't seem to apply – or is it all just an optical illusion created by skewed buildings on steep hillsides? However you see it, the place is definitely bizarre: objects roll uphill, a person's height changes depending on where they stand, and brooms stand up on their own...or so it seems. ∎

Toketee Falls

MICHAEL ROSEBROCK/SHUTTERSTOCK ©

George Parks Hwy

Denali National Park

The joy of Denali National Park is that it's both primeval and easily accessible. Here, you can peer at a grizzly bear, moose or caribou from the comfort of a bus, or trek into 6 million acres of tundra, boreal forest and ice-capped mountains.

Great For...

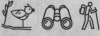

State
Alaska

Entrance Fee
7-day pass adult/under 15 $10/free

Area
9492 sq miles

Park Road

Park Road begins at **George Parks Hwy** and winds 92 miles through the heart of the park, ending at Kantishna, an old mining settlement and the site of several wilderness lodges. Early on, park officials envisaged the onset of bumper-to-bumper traffic along this road and wisely closed almost all of it to private vehicles. During the summer, motorists can only drive to a parking area along the Savage River at Mile 15. To venture further along the road you must walk, cycle, be part of a tour or, most popularly, take a park shuttle or tour bus.

If you're planning on spending the day riding the buses (it's an eight-hour round-trip to the Eielson Visitor Center (p250), the most popular day trip in the park), pack plenty of food and drink. It can be a long, dusty ride, and in the park there are only limited services at the Toklat River Contact Station (p250) and Eielson Visitor

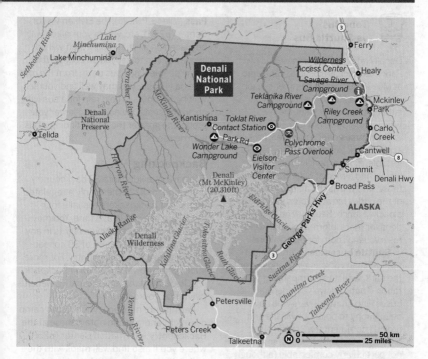

Center. Carry a park map so you know where you are and can scope out ridges or riverbeds that appeal for hiking.

Wildlife Watching

Because hunting has never been allowed in the park, professional photographers refer to animals in Denali as 'approachable wildlife.' That means bear, moose, Dall sheep and caribou aren't as skittish here as in other regions of the state. For this reason, and because Park Rd was built to maximize the chances of seeing wildlife by traversing high open ground, the park is an excellent place to view a variety of animals.

On board the park shuttle buses, your fellow passengers will be armed with binoculars and cameras to help scour the terrain for animals, most of which are so accustomed to the rambling buses that they rarely run and hide. When someone spots something and yells 'Stop!', the driver will pull over for viewing and picture taking. The best wildlife watching is on the first morning bus.

Day Hiking

Even for those who have neither the desire nor the equipment for an overnight trek, hiking is the best way to enjoy the park and see the land and its wildlife. You can hike virtually anywhere that hasn't been closed to prevent an impact on wildlife.

For a day hike (which doesn't require a permit), ride the shuttle bus and get off at any valley, riverbed or ridge that grabs your fancy. Check in at the Backcountry Information Center (p250) or Denali Bus Depot for suggestions.

Here's an important reminder for shuttle bus riders: while you can hop on any shuttle bus heading back to the park gates, those buses are often packed. It's generally easier to get yourself on a bus if you try to board at a recognized bus stop, such as Toklat River (p250), **Polychrome**

Tour Bus vs Shuttle Bus

Denali National Park is traversed by Park Rd, which is closed to car traffic at Mile 15 during the summer season. Past here, visitors must come in on either a tour bus or a shuttle bus. Which should you opt for?

Tour buses offer a narrated, prescribed park experience. They're comfortable, more expensive than shuttle buses, and aimed at older travelers and those who will not be able to hike inside of the park. Narrated tours include a packed lunch. See www.nps.gov/dena for more information and www.reservedenali.com for reservations.

Shuttle buses are ostensibly just that: a means of going into and out of the park, with no accompanying narration. That said, we've ridden shuttle buses with chatty drivers who have been happy to point out wildlife and provide commentary. Shuttle buses are converted school buses, so they're not particularly comfortable (although they're not uncomfortable either). They're cheaper than tour buses, and you can hop on and off to hike.

In general, we recommend shuttle buses for independent travelers who want to explore the park at their own pace. If you don't want to hike, a tour bus may be the better option.

If you take the shuttle bus, where should you get off? You buy your shuttle ticket to a certain destination within the park; while you can ride the bus back from anywhere, your ticket only allows you to proceed, via bus, up to a certain point within Denali. So how far in should you go?

The answer is entirely up to you, but most shuttle bus passengers disembark at the Eielson Visitor Center (p250), which is a good way inside the park. Getting off at Eielson gives you a good taste of park landscape, but also gives you some free time to hike before heading back toward the entrance.

Pass (Mile 46, Park Rd), the Eielson Visitor Center (p250), etc, where your name will be placed on a list and park staff will do what they can to get you on board. While many people flag a bus down from the road on a daily basis, you may well find yourself waiting for hours in cold rain for a bus with an empty seat. Obviously, the larger your group, the greater the risk of finding a bus with no room.

Backpacking

The park is divided into 87 backcountry units, and for 41 of these only a regulated number of backpackers (usually four to six) are allowed in at a time. You may spend a maximum of seven nights in any one unit, and a maximum of 30 consecutive nights in the backcountry. For more information download a *Denali Backpacking Guide* from the national park's website (www.nps.gov/dena).

Permits are needed if you want to camp overnight and you can obtain these at the Backcountry Information Center (p250), where you'll also find wall maps with the unit outlines and a quota board indicating the number of vacancies in each. Permits are issued only a day in advance, and the most popular units fill up fast. It pays to be flexible: decide which areas you're aiming for, and be prepared to take any zone that's open. If you're picky, you might have to wait several days.

After you've decided where to go, the next step is to watch the required backcountry orientation video, followed by a brief safety talk that covers, among other things, proper use of the bear-proof food containers you'll receive free of charge with your permit. The containers are bulky, but they work – they've reduced bear encounters dramatically since 1986. It's also worth noting that you're required to carry out dirty toilet paper (you bury your waste), so be sure to take at least a dozen ziplock bags. Finally, after receiving your permit, buy the topographic maps ($8) for your unit and head over to the Wilderness Access Center (p250) to purchase a ticket for a camper bus ($40) to take you to the starting point of your hike.

For an overview of the different units in the park, check out the park's website for the brilliant *Backcountry Camping and Hiking Guide*. Its unit-by-unit descriptions include access points, possible hiking corridors, dangers and, maybe best of all, pictures from the area.

Cycling

No special permit is needed to cycle on Park Rd, but cycling off-road is prohibited. Camper buses and some shuttle buses will carry bicycles, but only two at a time and only if you have a reservation. Many cyclists ride the bus in and cycle back out, carrying their gear and staying at campsites they've reserved along the way. It's also possible to take an early-morning bus in, ride for several hours and catch a bus back the same day. The highest point on the road is Highway Pass (3980ft). The entrance area is at 1585ft. Note that Park Rd is narrow, but buses are used to cyclists, and drivers generally do a grand job of giving riders a decent berth.

River Rafting

Thanks to Denali tourists, the Nenana River is the most popular white-water-rafting area in Alaska. The river's main white-water stretch begins near the park entrance and ends 10 miles north, near Healy. It's rated class III and IV, and involves standing waves, rapids and holes with names such as 'Coffee Grinder' in sheer-sided canyons. South of the park entrance, the river is much milder, but to many it's just as interesting as it veers away from both the highway and the railroad, increasing your chances of sighting wildlife.

Rafting companies offer similar guided trips on both stretches, in which either the guide does all the work or you help paddle. Advance reservations (no deposit) are accepted, and all trips include dry suits and shuttle pick-ups. The canyon and the easier 'wilderness' paddles go for about $99, and last around three hours.

Moose in Denali

MICHAL SARAUER/SHUTTERSTOCK ©

A Mountain by Any Other Name

The Athabascans called it Denali or the 'Great One.' Their brethren to the south in the Susitna Valley called it Doleika, the 'Big Mountain.' The Aleuts meanwhile referred to it as Traleika. The first European to spot the peak, George Vancouver, didn't bother to call it anything, while Ferdinand von Wrangell, a prominent Russian administrator in the 19th century, wrote 'Tenada' on his maps. So why was North America's highest peak called McKinley for over a century?

During the gold-rush days, the mountain was known locally as Densmore's Mountain, in honor of a local prospector. But soon it was dubbed Mt McKinley for William McKinley, an Ohioan who later became president of the United States. McKinley ran for office against a politician who wanted to use silver instead of gold as the backing standard for American currency, but McKinley was a strong defender of the gold standard. A man named William Dickey, a gold miner, named the mountain in order to flip the bird at rival silver miners.

In 1975, the state of Alaska, via its Board of Geographic Names, changed the name of the mountain to Denali, and sent an official request to Washington, DC, asking for the nation to do the same. That authority is vested in the United States Board on Geographic Names, but the agency had its hands tied by Ohio Congress members and senators (remember, William McKinley was from Ohio), who apparently thought the federal government was slacking when it came to insulting Native Americans.

This impasse continued until 2015, when then president Barack Obama ordered his Secretary of the Interior, Sally Jewell, to rename the mountain.

Scaling the Mountain

So, has gazing at lordly Mt McKinley – sorry, Denali – from the seat of an aircraft infected you with summit fever?

Denali's storied mountaineering history adds considerably to the mythic business of scaling the peak. Between 1200 and 1300 climbers attempt it each year, spending an average of three weeks on the slopes. About 80% use the West Buttress route, which involves flying in a ski plane from Talkeetna to the 7200ft Kahiltna Glacier and from there climbing for the South Peak, passing a medical/rescue camp maintained by mountaineering clubs and the National Park Service (NPS) at 14,220ft.

Top: Savage River; Bottom: Wonder Lake

In a good season (April through July), when storms are not constantly sweeping across the range, more than 50% of expeditions will be successful. In a bad year, that rate falls below 40%, and several climbers may die. Particularly grim was the annus horribilis of 1991, when 11 lives were lost.

If you're a seasoned alpinist you can mount an expedition yourself, or be among the 25% of Denali climbers who are part of guided ascents. If you're looking for a local guiding company, try **Alaska Mountaineering School** (☏907-733-1016; www.climb alaska.org), which charges $8900 to lead you up the mountain. Another acclaimed company with a high success rate is Seattle-based **Alpine Ascents** (☏206-378-1927; www.alpineascents.com). Its trips start at $8600 excluding meals, lodging and flights to Alaska. Book at least a year in advance.

Campground Programs

Rangers present 30- to 45-minute nightly talks on Denali's wildlife and natural history at the park's campgrounds – Riley Creek (p250), **Savage River** (www.nps.gov/dena; Mile 14, Park Rd; campsites $24-30) ✎, **Teklanika River** (Mile 29, Park Rd; campsites $25) ✎ and **Wonder Lake** (Mile 85, Park Rd; tent sites $16) ✎. You're welcome to show up even if you're not camping. The talks are at 7:30pm nightly; call ☏907-683-9532 or visit www.nps.gov/dena/planyourvisit for more information. Talks begin on June 8 at Wonder Lake, and in mid-May at the other campgrounds; all talks end around mid-September.

Lectures are also offered in the amphitheater at **McKinley Chalet Resort** (☏907-683-6450; www.westmarkhotels.com/destinations/denali-hotel; Mile 238.9, George Parks Hwy; ☉10am Mon, 3:30pm Tue-Sat) FREE.

Essential Information

Consider making reservations at least six months in advance for a park campsite during the height of summer, and at least three months ahead for accommodations outside the park. The park entrance fee is $10 per person, good for seven days.

There's only one road through the park: the 92-mile unpaved Park Rd, which is closed to private vehicles after Mile 15 in summer. Shuttle buses run from the middle of May until September past Mile 15. Sometimes, if the snow melts early in April, visitors will be allowed to proceed as far as Mile 30 until the shuttle buses begin operation. The park entrance area, where most visitors congregate, extends a scant 4 miles up Park Rd. It's here you'll find the park headquarters, visitor center and main campground, as well as the **Wilderness Access Center** (WAC; ☑907-683-9532; Mile 0.5, Park Rd; ⊙5am-7pm late May–mid-Sep), where you pay your park entrance fee and arrange campsites and shuttle-bus bookings to take you further into the park. Across the lot from the WAC sits the **Backcountry Information Center** (BIC; ☑907-683-9532; ⊙9am-6pm late May–mid-Sep), where backpackers get backcountry permits and bear-proof food containers.

There are few places to stay within the park, excluding campgrounds, and only one restaurant. Most visitors base themselves in the nearby communities of Cantwell, McKinley Park, Carlo Creek and Healy.

When to Come

From May 15 to June 1, park services are just starting up and access to the backcountry is limited. Visitor numbers are low but shuttle buses only run as far as **Toklat River** (Mile 53, Park Rd; ⊙9am-7pm late May–mid-Sep) ✔ **FREE**. From June 1 to 8, access increases and the shuttle buses run as far as **Eielson Visitor Center** (☑907-683-9532; www.nps.gov/dena/planyourvisit/the-eielson-visitor-center.htm; Mile 66, Park Rd; ⊙9am-5:30pm early Jun-mid Sep) **FREE**. After June 8, the park is in full swing till late August.

Shuttle buses stop running after the second Thursday after Labor Day in September. Following a few days in which lottery winners are allowed to take their private vehicles further, the road closes to all traffic until the following May.

While most area lodges close, **Riley Creek Campground** (www.nps.gov/dena; Mile 0.25, Park Rd; tent sites $24, RV sites $24-30) ✔ stays open in winter and camping is free, though the water and sewage facilities don't operate. If you have the equipment, you can use the unplowed Park Rd and the rest of the park for cross-country skiing, snowshoeing or dogsledding.

Reservations

From December 1 you can reserve campsites and shuttle buses online for the following summer tourist season through the **Denali National Park Reservation Service** (☑800-622-7275; www.reservedenali.com) operated by Aramark.

Note that sites in the Sanctuary River and Igloo Creek campgrounds can only be reserved in person at the WAC two days in advance, and backcountry permits one day in advance.

Sleeping

You should definitely reserve something in midsummer – even if it's just a campsite – before showing up. Note the Denali Borough charges a 7% accommodations tax on top of listed prices. High-end accommodations in and around the park generally feels overpriced.

Canyon is as close as the Denali area comes to a 'village.' In essence, it's a convenient service center consisting of a thin strip of wooden shops, accommodations, gas stations and stores clustered either side of the George Parks Hwy, roughly a mile north of the park entrance area (a walking path links the two). The western side of the road is dominated by two cruise-line-owned hotels. The eastern side harbors a skinny line of shops, restaurants and outdoor-adventure specialists. ∎

Top left: Wilderness Access Center; Top right: Toklat River; Bottom: Eielson Visitor Center

Alaska's Historical Monuments

Few people travel to Alaska for historical enlightenment, yet the state harbors plenty of echoes from a past clouded by battles, WWII bombings and late-19th-century gold rushes.

Chilkoot Trail

The Chilkoot Trail, the epic trek undertaken by over 30,000 gold-rush stampeders in 1897–98, is sometimes known as the 'Meanest 33 Miles in America.' Its appeal is legendary and, consequently, more than 3000 people spend three to five days following the historic route between Skagway (Alaska) and Lake Bennett (Canada) every summer.

Aleutian WWII National Historic Area, Unalaska

In 1996 Congress created this 134-acre national historic site to commemorate the bloody events of WWII that took place on the Aleutian Islands. To learn about the 'Forgotten War,' begin at the Aleutian WWII Visitor Center, near the airport, in the original air-control tower built in 1942.

Sitka National Historical Park

This mystical juxtaposition of tall trees and totems is Alaska's smallest national park and the site where the Tlingits were finally defeated by the Russians in 1804. The mile-long Totem Trail winds its way past 18 totems first displayed at the 1904 Louisiana Exposition in St Louis, MO, and then moved to the park.

Iñupiat Heritage

This 24,000-sq-ft facility houses a museum, gift shop and a large multipurpose room where short traditional dancing-and-drumming performances take place each afternoon. Local crafts-people often assemble in the lobby to sell masks, whalebone carvings and fur garments and are happy to talk about their craft and techniques.

TOM WALKER/GETTY IMAGES ©

Gates of the Arctic & Kobuk Valley National Parks

Caribou, Kobuk Valley National Park

With no roads, no cell-phone coverage and a population of precisely zero, Gates of the Arctic National Park is a wilderness virtually unchanged in four millenia. The dunes of Kobuk Valley National Park, to its southwest, have a surreal, severe beauty.

Great For...

State
Alaska

Entrance Fee
Free

Area
13,238 sq miles (Gates of the Arctic)

2805 sq miles (Kobuk Valley)

You don't come to these remote Alaskan parks to stroll along interpretive boardwalks, or even follow something as rudimentary as a trail (there aren't any). Tackled alone, this is a land for brave travelers with advanced outdoor experience, plenty of time on their hands and a flexible budget (read: it's costly). Alternatively, you can sign up with one of a handful of agencies and go on a guided backcountry or flightseeing tour.

Gates of the Arctic is the more accessible park as it starts just 5 miles west of the Dalton Hwy, meaning you can technically hike in, although charter flights out of Coldfoot and Bettles are more common. Kobuk Valley is reached via charters out of the small settlement of Kotzebue

Hiking

Most backpackers enter the parks by way of charter air-taxis, which can land on lakes, rivers or river bars. Once on the ground,

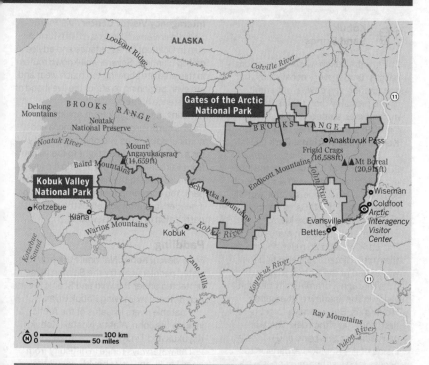

Kobuk Sand Dunes

Kobuk Sand Dunes

The great Alaskan wilderness encompasses almost every ecosystem your imagination can devise, but admit it: you probably didn't think 'sand dunes' when someone brought up the 49th state. But they're here in **Kobuk Valley National Park** (☑907-442-3890; www.nps.gov/kova) – some 20,500 acres of rolling sand, the largest collection of dunes in Arctic North America, a landscape so otherworldly it's been used by NASA as an analog for the environment on Mars.

There's not just sand dunes at this park, located 25 miles above the Arctic Circle. You'll also find the watershed of the **Kobuk River**, which runs through a dramatically beautiful valley in the shadow of the Baird Mountains. But you have to get here first, and that's the trick. There are no roads into this park, and no trails inside of it – Kobuk is expensive to access, and visitors must possess a high level of wilderness savvy.

they often follow the long, open valleys for extended treks or work their way to higher elevations where open tundra provides good hiking terrain.

While this appears to make planning an impossibly vague task, the landscape limits the areas that aircraft can land or pick you up, as well as where you can hike. Park staff suggest consulting flight and guide companies, as well as topographic maps, for possible routes and then running it by them to make sure the area is not overused. If it is, they can suggest alternatives.

The only treks that don't require chartering a plane are those in Gates of the Arctic beginning from the Dalton Hwy (near Wiseman), or from the village of Anaktuvuk Pass. For hikes from the highway, which lead into several different areas along the eastern side of the park, stop at the **Arctic**

Interagency Visitor Center (☑907-678-5209; CentralYukon@blm.gov; ☺11am-10pm Jun-Aug) in Coldfoot for assistance and advice on trip planning. Several well-known routes in this area are showing too much wear and are even beginning to affect the livelihood of subsistence hunters.

Hiking into the park from Anaktuvuk Pass is surprisingly one of the more economical options, as you only need to pay for a regular scheduled flight to the village from Fairbanks. From the airstrip it's just a few miles' hike to the northern edge of the park. You can camp for free by the airstrip if needed, but until you enter the park get permission to camp elsewhere.

Paddling

For a view of Kobuk National Park from the water, paddlers can try the Salmon River, protected under the Wild and Scenic Rivers Act, or the slow-moving Kobuk River.

Floatable rivers in Gates of the Arctic include the John, Alatna, Noatak, Kobuk, Koyukuk and Tinayguk.

The waterways range in difficulty from class I to III, and you should consult the park or guide companies about possible routes.

Canoes can be rented in Bettles at **Bettles Lodge** (☑907-692-5111; www.bettleslodge.com; tour packages incl accommodation per person s/d $890/1020, plus $250/275 each additional night) for around $270 per week.

Flightseeing

The approved air-taxi services that operate to the national parks also generally run flightseeing tours, from which you can snap excellent pictures of the Kobuk Valley watershed and caribou herds.

Guided Trips

The tour operator **Arctic Wild** (☑907-479-8203; www.arcticwild.com) can put together guided backpacking or canoeing trips of various lengths into the parks, including expeditions aimed at spotting the Western Arctic caribou herd, the largest caribou herd in the country. Trips run in August.

Arctic Interagency Visitor Center

Essential Information

Getting There & Away

Gateway towns are reached from Anchorage and Fairbanks via commercial airline.

The most common way to enter Kobuk Valley is via park-approved air taxis and tour operators. In summer, some visitors enter by boat on the Kobuk River after being dropped off at indigenous villages by bush plane.

Bettles offers meals, lodging and air transport into Gates of the Arctic backcountry. Other visitors fly in from Coldfoot on the Dalton Hwy, or hike in directly from Wiseman, just north of Coldfoot. To the north, the remote Alaska Native village of Anaktuvuk Pass is another access point if traveling by foot. Contact the Anaktuvuk Ranger Station for more information on visiting from here.

The park is accessible via snowmachine through winter.

Visitor Information

The park is open year-round. There is a visitor center in Kotzebue within the **Northwest Arctic Heritage Center** (9am-6pm Mon-Sat, Jun-Sep, Mon-Fri Oct-May). **Anaktuvuk Ranger Station** (907-661-3520; www.nps.gov/gaar; 8am-5pm Jun-Sep) can help you plan your trip from Anaktuvuk. In Bettles, **Bettles Ranger Station & Visitor Center** (907-692-5495; www.nps.gov/gaar; 8am-5pm Jun-Sep) is in a log building less than a quarter mile from the airstrip.

Summer temperatures can climb to 100°F, yet freezing conditions and snow can occur anytime. There is private land within the park; avoid areas clearly marked as such.

Independent travelers do not require permits, but organized groups do – contact the park at 907-442-3890. Independent visitors must be completely self-sufficient; there are no facilities in the park.

The **Morris Thompson Cultural & Visitors Center** (907-459-3700; www.morristhompsoncenter.org; 8am-9pm late May-early Sep, to 5pm mid-Sep–mid-May) in Fairbanks has a parks desk that dispenses good information on NPS destinations in Alaska. ∎

Kobuk River

Glacier Bay National Park

Humpback whale

Glacier Bay is the crowning jewel of the cruise-ship industry and a dreamy destination for anybody who has ever paddled a kayak. Seven tidewater glaciers spill out of the mountains and fill the sea with icebergs of all shapes, sizes and shades of blue, making this an icy wilderness renowned worldwide.

Great For...

State
Alaska

Entrance Fee
Free

Area
5220 sq miles

Apart from its high concentration of tidewater glaciers, Glacier Bay is a dynamic habitat for humpback whales. Other wildlife seen at Glacier Bay includes porpoises, sea otters, brown and black bears, wolves, moose and mountain goats.

The park is an expensive side trip, even by Alaskan standards. Plan on spending at least $400 for a trip from Juneau. Of the 500,000 annual visitors, more than 95% arrive aboard a ship and never leave it. The rest are a mixture of tour-group members, who head straight for the lodge, and backpackers, who gravitate toward the free campground.

❶ Glacier Bay

This bay offers an excellent opportunity for people who have some experience on the water but not necessarily as kayakers, because a tour boat run by Glacier Bay Lodge & Tours (p266), drops off and

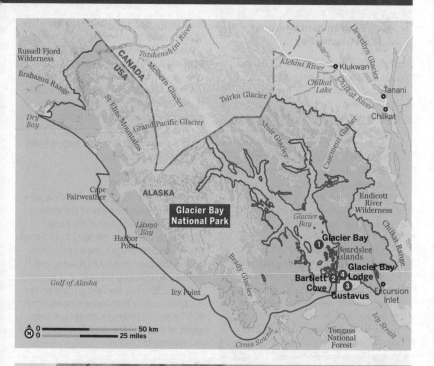

Kayaking in Glacier Bay

Environmental Issues in Glacier Bay

Glacier Bay has seen several disputes between the cruise-ship industry and environmentalists. After the number of whales seen in the park dropped dramatically in 1978, the NPS reduced ship visits during the three-month season. But the cruise-ship industry lobbied the US Congress and the NPS in 1996 to approve a 30% increase in vessels allowed in the bay. Environmentalists sued, and eventually a compromise of two large cruise ships per day was hammered out.

But the whales aren't the only area of concern here. Glacier Bay's ice, like glaciers all over Alaska, is rapidly melting. This is particularly true in Muir Inlet, or the East Arm as it's commonly called. Twenty years ago it was home to three active tidewater glaciers, but now there is only one, McBride. Only two glaciers in the park are advancing; Johns Hopkins and Margerie. The rest are receding and thinning.

picks up paddlers at two spots, usually at the entrance of the Muir Inlet (East Arm) and inside the West Arm. By using the tour boat, you can skip the long and open paddle up the bay and enjoy only the well-protected arms and inlets where the glaciers are located. The most dramatic glaciers are in the West Arm, but either one will require at least four days to paddle to glaciers if you are dropped off *and* picked up. With only a drop-off, you need a week to 10 days to paddle from either arm back to Bartlett Cove.

Paddlers who want to avoid the tour-boat fares but still long for a kayak adventure should try the **Beardslee Islands**. While there are no glaciers to view, the islands are a day's paddle from Bartlett Cove and offer calm water, protected channels and pleasant beach camping. Wildlife includes

black bears, seals and bald eagles, and the tidal pools burst with activity at low tide.

Alaska Mountain Guides & Climbing School (☎800-766-3396; www.alaskamountainguides.com) runs several guided kayak trips into Glacier Bay. A seven-day paddle to the West Arm, which includes tour transportation as well as all equipment and food, is $2950 per person, and an eight-day paddle up the East Arm that begins from Bartlett Cove is $2950.

❷ Bartlett Cove

Bartlett Cove is home to the national park headquarters and the site of the visitor center (p266) and Glacier Bay Lodge (p266). This is where the ferry from Juneau ties up, paddlers rent kayaks and visitors hop on the tour boat for a cruise to the glaciers 40 miles up the bay.

Glacier Bay has few hiking trails and in the backcountry foot travel is done along riverbanks, on ridges or across ice remnants of glaciers. The only developed trails are in Bartlett Cove.

❸ Gustavus

About 9 miles from Bartlett Cove is the small settlement of Gustavus, an interesting backcountry community. The town's 400 citizens include a mix of professional people – doctors, lawyers, former government workers and artists – who decided to drop out of the rat race and live on their own in the middle of the woods. Electricity only arrived in the early 1980s and in some homes you must pump water at the sink or build a fire before you can have a hot shower.

Gustavus has no downtown: it's little more than an airstrip left over from WWII and a road to Bartlett Cove, known to most locals as 'the Road.' Along the Road there is little to see, as most cabins and homes are tucked away behind a shield of trees.

The state ferry docks at Gustavus and Alaska Airlines jets land at the small airport nearby.

CORALIE MATHIEU/SHUTTERSTOCK ©

Bartlett Cove

Left: Glacier Bay National Park from above;
Right: Brown bear

❹ Glacier Bay Lodge

This is essentially a national park lodge (p266) and the only accommodations in the park itself. Located at Bartlett Cove, 8 miles northwest of Gustavus, the self-contained lodge has 55 rooms, a crackling fire in a huge stone fireplace and a dining room that usually hums in the evening with an interesting mixture of park employees, backpackers and locals from Gustavus.

Nightly slide presentations, ranger talks and movies held upstairs cover the park's natural history.

Packages with bed, breakfast and an eight-hour park boat tour go for around $645 for two people.

Essential Information

Sleeping

Most of the accommodations are in Gustavus, which adds a 7% bed-and-sales tax. The **Glacier Bay Lodge** (📞888-229-8687; www.visitglacierbay.com; 199 Bartlett Cove Rd; r $219-249; ⊙May-Sep) is 8 miles out of town at Bartlett Cove.

Tourist Information

Glacier Bay National Park Visitor Center

(📞907-697-2661; www.nps.gov/glba; ⊙11am-8pm) On the 2nd floor of Glacier Bay Lodge, this center has exhibits, a bookstore and an information desk. There are also daily guided walks from the lodge, park films and slide presentations.

Gustavus Visitors Association (📞907-697-2454; www.gustavusak.com) Has loads of information on its website.

Visitor Information Station (📞907-697-2627; ⊙7am-8pm May-Sep) Campers, kayakers and boaters can stop at the park's Visitor Information Station at the foot of the public dock in Bartlett Cove for backcountry and boating permits, logistical information and a 20-minute orientation video.

Getting There & Away

The cheapest way to reach Gustavus is via the **Alaska Marine Highway** (📞800-642-0066; www.ferryalaska.com). Several times a week the MV *LeConte* makes the round-trip run from Juneau to Gustavus (one way $48, 4½ hours) along a route that often features whale sightings. **TLC Taxi** (📞907-697-2239) meets most ferry arrivals and also charges $15 per person for a trip to Bartlett Cove.

Alaska Airlines (📞800-426-0333; www.alaskaair.com) Offers the only jet service, with a daily 25-minute trip from Juneau to Gustavus.

Alaska Seaplanes (📞907-789-3331; www.flyalaskaseaplanes.com) Has up to five flights per day between Gustavus and Juneau for $119 one way. ∎

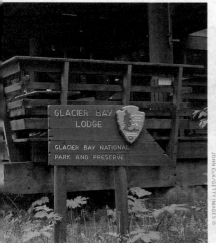

Top left: Glacier Bay Lodge; Top right: Female moose; Bottom: Alaska Marine Highway

MELISSAANN/SHUTTERSTOCK ©

Katmai National Park

A national park since 1980, Katmai is famous for its salmon-trapping brown bears, epic sport-fishing and unusual volcanic landscapes. Unconnected to the main Alaskan road network, a visit here, for most people, is a once-in-a-lifetime experience involving meticulous pre-planning and a big wad of cash.

Great For...

State
Alaska

Entrance Fee
Free

Area
6395 sq miles

Nearly all park visitors fly in via floatplane to the main tourist area of **Brooks Camp**, 35 miles east of King Salmon. Here they will stand spine-tinglingly close to formidable 1000lb brown bears pawing giant salmon out of the river (some bears even catch the fish clean in their chops). It's the most heavily visited section of the park, equipped with a rustic lodge plus a couple of short trails.

Brooks Falls

Every year, hundreds of brown bears emerge from hibernation and make their way to Brooks Falls, a small but important waterfall in Katmai National Park. Around the same time, salmon begin their journey up Brooks River to spawn in Brooks Lake upstream. At this crossroads, salmon can be seen leaping into waiting bears' jaws. Brown bear concentrations are at their highest in July, when dozens can often be spotted at or around the falls.

Brooks Falls

Bear Viewing

Katmai supports a healthy population of 2200 brown bears. Many of the bears arrive with instinctual punctuality at Brooks Falls on July 1 for the annual salmon spawning, which lasts until the end of the month. The bears return in September for a second showing to feed on the dead salmon carcasses.

Brooks Camp has three established bear-watching areas. From the lodge, a dirt road leads to a floating bridge over the river and the first observation deck. From here you can see the bears feeding in the mouth of the river or swimming in the bay.

Continue on the road to the Valley of Ten Thousand Smokes, and in half a mile a marked trail winds to Brooks Falls. Two more viewing platforms lie along this half-mile trail. The first sits above some shallows that occasionally draw sows trying to keep their cubs away from aggressive males at the falls.

The last deck at the falls is the prime viewing area, where you can photograph the salmon making spectacular leaps or a big brownie at the top of the cascade waiting with open jaws to catch a fish. At the peak of the salmon run, there might be eight to 12 bears here, two or three of them atop the falls themselves. The observation deck holds 40 people, and in early to mid-July it will be crammed with photographers, forcing rangers to rotate people on and off.

Brooks Camps' bear season is relatively short, but more adventurous visitors can charter floatplanes and guides to take them out to other bear-viewing areas on the coast between June and October.

Despite Katmai's dense bear population (two bears per sq mile in places) only two serious human–bear incidents have been recorded in 100 years – a testament to fine park management.

Valley of Ten Thousand Smokes

A scar in the earth left behind by the massive 1912 Novarupta volcanic eruption, the Valley of Ten Thousand Smokes is a stark landscape of deep gorges, volcanic ash and lava flows. In 1916 Robert Griggs led an expedition into the region to examine the eruption's aftermath. He found a valley of thousands of fumaroles (steam and gas vents) emitting clouds of vapor into the sky, hence the valley's name.

The post-apocalyptic spectacle served as Katmai's original raison d'être and led to the area being declared a national monument in 1918.

Visitors can access the valley by reserving a tour (from $88) through Katmailand (p272).

Hiking

Hiking and backpacking are the best ways to see the park's unusual backcountry. Like Denali National Park in Alaska's Interior, Katmai has few formal trails; backpackers follow river bars, lakeshores, gravel ridges and other natural routes. Many hiking trips begin with a ride on the park bus along the dirt road to Three Forks Overlook, in the Valley of Ten Thousand Smokes. The bus will also drop off and pick up hikers and backpackers along the road – or you can walk its full 23-mile length.

The only developed trail from Brooks Camp is a half-day trek to the top of **Dumpling Mountain** (2440ft). The trail leaves the ranger station and heads north past the campground, climbing 1.5 miles to a scenic overlook. It then continues another 2.5 miles to the mountain's summit, where there are superb views of the surrounding lakes.

Paddling

The area has some excellent paddling, including the **Savonoski Loop**, a five- to seven-day adventure. Other popular trips include a 30-mile paddle from Brooks Camp to the Bay of Islands and a 10-mile paddle to Margot Creek, which has good fishing and lots of bears.

Kayaks are the overwhelming choice for most paddlers due to high winds blowing across big lakes, and possible rough water. Accomplished paddlers should have no problem, but the conditions can sometimes get dicey for novices.

Fishing

Fishing trips are popular and rainbow trout are plentiful in the park's large lakes. In fact, most park facilities were first built to accommodate anglers. Fishing populations are carefully managed by Katmai National Park and Alaska Department of Fish and Game. Sport fishing licenses are required for nonresidents aged 16 and older and most residents 16 to 59. Further regulations exist depending on where anglers cast their reels.

Because fishers and brown bears are often attracted to the same catch, anglers must be careful when fishing in Katmai and follow safe bear country practices such as maintaining bear awareness, cutting the line if a bear approaches and safe catch storage.

Valley of Ten Thousand Smokes

Essential Information

Package Tours

Because of the logistics of getting there and the need to plan and reserve so much in advance, many visitors arrive in Katmai as part of a one-call-does-it-all package tour. A shockingly large number are part of a one-day visit, spending large sums of money for what is basically an hour or two of bear watching.

Getting There & Away

Most visitors to Katmai fly from Anchorage into King Salmon on Alaska Airlines (☎800-252-7522; ww.alaskaair.com) for between $450 and $600 round-trip. Once you're in King Salmon, a number of air-taxi companies offer the 20-minute floatplane flight out to Brooks Camp. **Katmai Air** (☎800-544-0551, 907-243-5448; www.katmaiair.com), the Katmailand-affiliated company, charges $228 for a round-trip.

Companies like **Regal Air** (☎907-243-8535; www.regal-air.com; 4506 Lakeshore Dr) and **Rust's Flying Service** (☎907-243-1595; www.flyrusts.com; 4525 Enstrom Circle) offer day trips straight from Anchorage, but the 2½-hour flight aboard a cramped floatplane, plus limited time with the bears, make this a less-ideal option.

Sleeping

If you plan to stay at Brooks Camp, either at the lodge or in the campground, you must make a reservation. Otherwise, you're limited to staying in King Salmon and visiting the park on day trips.

Grosvenor Lodge, Kulik Lodge and Brooks Lodge are all operated by concessionaire **Katmailand** (☎907-243-5448, 877-771-1849; www.katmailand.com). Two-night stays start at $1602 per person (double occupancy) and include round-trip flights from Anchorage.

Independent options like **Katmai Wilderness Lodge** (www.katmai-wilderness.com) provide alternatives. ∎

Top left: Brooks Camp; Top right: Fishing near Brooks Falls; Bottom: Dumpling Mountain

PATRICK CIVELLO/SHUTTERSTOCK ©

Exit Glacier

Kenai Fjords National Park

Kenai Fjords National Park was created in 1980 to protect 587,000 acres of Alaska's most awesome, impenetrable wilderness. Crowning the park is the massive Harding Ice Field; from it, countless tidewater glaciers pour down, carving the coast into dizzying fjords. Road-accessible Exit Glacier is its highlight attraction.

Great For...

State
Alaska

Entrance Fee
Free

Area
917 sq miles

With such a glaciated landscape – and an abundance of marine wildlife – the park is a major tourist attraction. Unfortunately, it's also an expensive one. That is why road-accessible Exit Glacier is its highlight attraction. Hardier souls can ascend to the Harding Ice Field from the same trailhead, but only experienced mountaineers equipped with skis, ice axes and crampons can investigate the 900 sq miles of ice.

The majority of visitors either take a quick trip to Exit Glacier's face or splurge on a tour-boat cruise along the coast. For those who want to spend more time in the park, the coastal fjords are a blue-water kayaker's dream.

Exit Glacier

The marquee attraction of Kenai Fjords National Park is Exit Glacier, named by explorers crossing the Harding Ice Field who found the glacier a suitable way to 'exit' the ice and mountains.

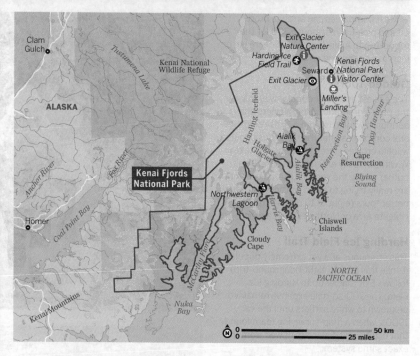

From the Exit Glacier Nature Center (p277), the **Outwash Plain Trail** is an easy three-quarter-mile walk to the glacier's alluvial plain – a flat expanse of pulverized silt and gravel, cut through by braids of gray meltwater. The **Edge of the Glacier Trail** leaves the first loop and climbs steeply to an overlook at the side of the glacier before returning. Both trails make for a short hike that will take one or two hours; you can return along the half-mile **nature trail** through cottonwood forest, alder thickets and old glacial moraines before emerging at the ranger station. Note how the land becomes more vegetated the further you get from the ice, the result of having had more time to recover from its glacial scouring. Signs indicate how far the glacier extended.

If you have the time and legs for it, the hike up to the **Harding Ice Field** (p276) is well worth it; where else can you see a large remnant of the Pleistocene Ice Age?

Paddling

Blue-water paddles out of Resurrection Bay along the coastline of the park are for experienced kayakers only; others should invest in a drop-off service. You'll be rewarded, however, with wildlife encounters and close-up views of the glaciers from a unique perspective.

With several glaciers to visit, **Aialik Bay** is a popular arm for kayakers. Many people hire water-taxis to drop them near Aialik Glacier, then take three or four days to paddle south past Pedersen Glacier and into Holgate Arm, where they're picked up. The high point of the trip is Holgate Glacier, an active tidewater glacier that's the main feature of all the boat tours.

Northwestern Lagoon is more expensive to reach but much more isolated, with not nearly as many tour boats. The wildlife is excellent, especially the seabirds and sea otters, and more than a half-dozen glaciers can be seen. Plan on three to four days if you're being dropped inside the lagoon.

Most companies can arrange drop-off and pick-up; it's about $300 for the round-trip to Aialik Bay; prices decrease or increase depending on distance.

Guided Tours

The easiest and most popular way to view the park's dramatic fjords, glaciers and abundant wildlife is from a cruise ship. Several companies offer the same basic tours: wildlife cruises (three to five hours) take in W without really entering the park. Don't bother taking the short cruise, unless you are really trying to avoid seasickness. Much better tours (eight to 10 hours) explore Holgate Arm or Northwestern Lagoon.

Harding Ice Field Trail

This strenuous and yet extremely popular 4-mile trail (six- to eight-hour round-trip) follows Exit Glacier up to Harding Ice Field. The 700-sq-mile expanse remained unknown to white settlers until the early 1900s, when a map-surveying team found that eight coastal glaciers flowed from the exact same system.

Today you can rediscover it via a steep, roughly cut and sometimes slippery ascent to 3500ft. Beware of bears; they're common here. Only experienced glacier-travelers should head onto the ice field proper.

The trek is well worth it for those with the stamina, as it provides spectacular views of not only the ice field but Exit Glacier and the valley below. The upper section of the route is snow-covered for much of the year; bring a jacket and watch for ice-bridges above creeks. Camping up here is a great idea, but the free, tiny public-use cabin at the top is for emergencies only. ∎

Top left: Hiking the Harding Ice Field Trail;
Top right: Kayaking Aialik Bay; Bottom: Harding Ice Field

Essential Information

Getting There & Away
To reach the coastal fjords, you'll need
to take a tour or catch a water-taxi with
Miller's Landing (📞907-331-3113; www.
millerslandingak.com). Getting to Exit
Glacier is a bit easier. If you don't have a
car, the **Exit Glacier Shuttle** (📞907-
224-5569; www.exitglaciershuttle.com;
round-trip $15; ⊕9:30am-5pm Mon-Thu, from
8:30am Fri-Sun) runs an hourly shuttle to
the glacier. The van scoops passengers
up in downtown Seward and at the
small-boat harbor. **Resurrection Taxi**
(📞907-224-5678; www.resurrectiontaxi.com)
charges $80 (round-trip) from Seward.

Sleeping
A few lovely options exist in the park,
but for all except Exit Glacier Campground you'll need a water-taxi.

Tourist Information
Exit Glacier Nature Center (⊕9am-8pm)
At the Exit Glacier trailhead; has interpretive
displays, sells field guides, and is the starting point for ranger-guided hikes.

Kenai Fjords National Park Visitor Center
(📞907-224-3175; ⊕9am-7pm) Located in
Seward's small-boat harbor; has info on hikes
and paddles in the park.

CARL JOHNSON/DESIGN PICS/GETTY IMAGES ©

Twin Lakes

Lake Clark National Park

Only 100 miles southwest of Anchorage, Lake Clark National Park features spectacular scenery that is a composite of Alaska: an awesome array of tundra-covered hills, mountains, glaciers, coastline, the largest lakes in the state and two active volcanoes.

Great For...

State
Alaska

Entrance Fee
Free

Area
6296 sq miles

The centerpiece of the park is a 45-mile shimmering body of turquoise water fringed by the snowy summits of glacier-tipped peaks. The park is also where the Alaska Range merges into the Aleutian Range to form the Chigmit Mountains, and is home to two volcanoes: Mt Iliamna and Mt Redoubt. Despite its overwhelming scenery and close proximity to Alaska's largest city, fewer than 5000 visitors a year make it to this 6296-sq-mile preserve.

Water Activities

Kayaking and canoeing are popular ways to explore the lake itself, the shores of which range from craggy horizons to low tundra. In the park's main town, Port Alsworth, **Tulchina Adventures** (www.tulchinaadventures.com) will rent kayaks (per day single/double $65/100) or set up an unguided kayak/camping trip ($475 for two people for one night).

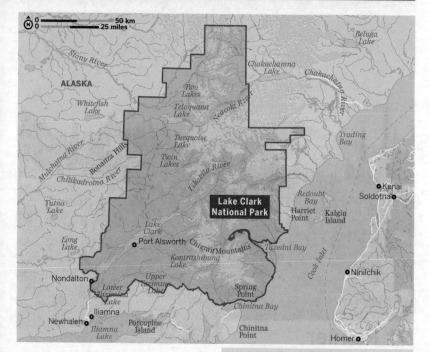

Hiking

The hiking is phenomenal, but Lake Clark is best suited to the experienced backpacker. For any pre-trip planning, visit the park website, which has the latest guidance on traveling in the backcountry.

Port Alsworth has a **visitor center** (☑907-781-2218; 1 Park Pl; ☺8am-5pm Mon-Fri, 9am-6pm Sat & Sun) with displays and videos on the park. There you'll find information on both the **Telaquana Trail Route**, a historic Dena'ina Athabascan route running from Telaquana Lake to Kijik Village, and **Twin Lakes**, where dry tundra slopes provide easy travel to ridges and great views.

Float Trips

Float trips down any of the three designated wild rivers (the **Chilikadrotna**, **Tlikakila** and **Mulchatna**) are spectacular and exciting, with waterways rated from class III to class IV. The best way to

Essential Information

To reach the park, you will need to arrange with an Anchorage charter pilot for drop-off at the start of your adventure (around $490 round-trip).

organize a boat rental is through **Alaska Raft & Kayak** (www.tulchinaadventures. com), which rents out inflatable sea kayaks and canoes (per day $65) and 14ft rafts (per day $100) in Anchorage. The shop will also deliver the boat to **Lake Clark Air** (☑907-781-2208, 888-440-2281; www. lakeclarkair.com) in Anchorage for your flight into the national park and pick it up when you return. ■

NICHIMAR/SHUTTERSTOCK ©

Mt Rainier National Park

Emblazoned on every Washington license plate and visible throughout much of the western state, Mt Rainier is the contiguous USA's fifth-highest peak and, in the eyes of many, its most awe-inspiring.

Great For...

State
Washington

Entrance Fee
7-day pass per vehicle/pedestrian $30/15

Area
368 sq miles

The mountain's snowcapped summit and forest-covered foothills boast numerous hiking trails, swaths of flower-carpeted meadows and an alluring peak that presents a formidable challenge for aspiring climbers. The park website includes downloadable maps and descriptions of 50 park trails.

❶ Paradise

Aside from hiding numerous trailheads and being the starting point for most summit hikes, Paradise guards the iconic Paradise Inn (built in 1916) and the large, informative **Henry M Jackson Visitor Center** (☏360-569-6571; ☉10am-5pm daily May-Oct, Sat & Sun Nov-Apr), which holds a cutting-edge museum with hands-on exhibits on everything from flora to glacier formation and shows a must-see 21-minute film entitled *Mount Rainier: Restless Giant*.

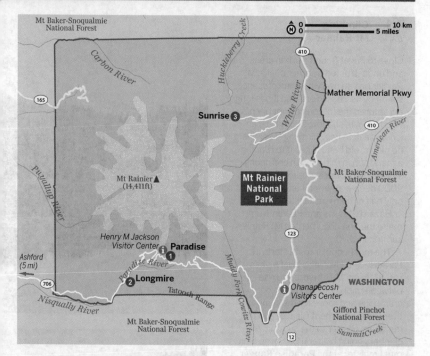

Park naturalists lead free interpretive hikes from the visitor center daily in summer, and snowshoe walks on winter weekends.

The daughter of park pioneer James Longmire unintentionally named this high mountain nirvana, when she exclaimed what a paradise it was on visiting this spot for the first time in the 1880s. Suddenly, the high-mountain nirvana had a name, and a very apt one at that. One of the snowiest places on earth, 5400ft-high Paradise remains the park's most popular draw, with its famous flower meadows backed by dramatic Rainier views on the days (a clear minority annually) when the mountain decides to take off its cloudy hat.

The Paradise area is crisscrossed with trails, of all types and standards, some good for a short stroll (with the kids), others the realm of more serious hikers. For a medium-pacer, hike the 5-mile **Skyline Trail**, starting behind the Paradise Inn and climbing approximately 1600ft to Panorama Point, with good views of Mt Rainier and the neighboring Tatoosh Range.

❷ Longmire

The **National Park Inn** (☑360-569-2275; Hwy 706; r with shared/private bath from $132/187; ❄) – built in classic 'parkitecture' style – has stood here since 1917. It's complemented by park offices, the tiny, free **Longmire Museum** (☑360-569-6575; Hwy 706; ⊙9am-4:30pm May-Jul) and a number of important trailheads. James Longmire first came here in 1883 and noticed the hot mineral springs that bubbled up in a lovely meadow opposite the present-day National Park Inn. The next year he established Longmire's Medicinal Springs, and in 1890 he built the Longmire Springs Hotel.

❸ Sunrise

Mt Rainier's main eastern entrance is the gateway to Sunrise, which at 6400ft

Climbing Mt Rainier

Close to Puget Sound's urban areas and unobstructed by other peaks, Mt Rainier has an overwhelming presence, set off by its 26 glaciers, and it has long enraptured the millions of inhabitants who live in its shadow. Though it's an iconic peak to bag, climbing Rainier is no picnic; old hands liken it to running a marathon in thin air with crampons stuck to your shoes. Approximately 9000 people attempt it annually, but only half of them make it to the top.

Hazard Stevens and PB Van Trump made the first documented Mt Rainier summit in 1870.

The most popular route starts at Paradise and involves a brief night's rest at Camp Muir before you rise between midnight and 2am to don crampons and ropes for the climb over Disappointment Cleaver and the Ingraham Glacier to the summit. All climbers going higher than Camp Muir must register at the **Paradise Ranger Station** next to the Henry M Jackson Visitor Center (p280). Excellent four-day guided ascents are led by **Rainier Mountaineering Inc** (☎888-892-5462; www.rmiguides.com; 30027 Hwy 706 E, Ashford; 4-day climb $1163).

marks the park's highest road. Thanks to the superior elevation here, the summer season is particularly short and snow can linger well into July. The area is also noticeably drier than Paradise, resulting in an interesting variety of subalpine vegetation, including masses of wildflowers.

The views from Sunrise are famously spectacular and – aside from stunning close-ups of Mt Rainier itself – you can also, quite literally, watch the weather roll in over the distant peaks of Mts Baker and Adams. Similarly impressive is the glistening Emmons Glacier, which, at 4 sq miles in size, is the largest glacier in the contiguous USA.

Top left: Mount Rainier; Top right: National Park Inn;
Bottom: Fall in the park

Essential Information

Getting There & Away

For the most part, you're better off
driving yourself, but there are also tour
options out of Seattle.

Nisqually Entrance

This southwestern corner of Mt Rainier
National Park is its most developed
(and hence most visited) corner. Here
you'll find the only year-round road and
the gateway settlements of Ashford
and Copper Creek, which offer plenty
of useful park-related facilities.

Hwy 706 enters the park about 1½
hours' drive southeast of Seattle. After
the entry tollbooth, a well-paved road
continues east, offering the first good
views of Mt Rainier – weather permit-
ting. At the 7-mile mark you'll pass
Longmire (p281). From here the road
climbs steeply for 12 miles, passing
numerous hairpin turns and viewpoints
until it emerges at the elevated alpine
meadows of Paradise (p280).

Sleeping

There are camping and lodge options
in the park and plenty of other types
of lodging outside, mostly along the
Longmire entrance route.

CLASSIC ROAD TRIPS

Mt Rainier Scenic Byways

Wrapped in a 368-sq-mile national park, and standing 2000ft higher than anything else in the Pacific Northwest, Rainier is a mountain of biblical proportions.

Duration 2–3 days

Distance 454 miles

Best Time to Go
June to October when alpine flowers bloom.

Essential Photo
Rainier's snow-topped summit reflected in Reflection Lakes.

Best Alpine Meadows
A toss-up between Paradise and Sunrise.

❶ Seattle

Seattle is an appropriate place to start this epic circuit around what locals refer to reverently as 'the Mountain.' Before heading off, take some time to walk around, seeking out the soul of the city at **Pike Place Market** (www.pikeplacemarket.org; 85 Pike St; ⊘9am-6pm Mon-Sat, to 5pm Sun; ⏴Westlake) ✐ – for that's where it hides. On the rare days when Rainier reveals itself from the cloudy heavens, you can also wander down to the waterfront for a glimpse of the high-altitude glories to come.

The Drive » There is little to delay you out of Seattle until the tiny town of Elbe, 72 miles away. Drive south on I-5 to exit

154A, then east on I-405, and south again on SR-167 and SR-161. Just southwest of Eatonville, SR-161 merges with SR-7; follow this road into Elbe on the cusp of the national park.

❷ Elbe

The pinprick settlement of Elbe (population 29) has two claims to fame: its tiny white Lutheran **church** built by German immigrants in 1906 (and positively ancient by Pacific Northwest standards), and the heritage **Mt Rainier Scenic Railroad** (☎360-492-5588; www.mtrainierrailroad.com; 54124 Mountain Hwy E; adult/child $41/21) that runs summer steam trains between Elbe and Mineral (7 miles south). Trips depart three times daily from May to September. Aping the railway theme is the **Hobo Inn & Diner** (www.rrdiner.com; 54106 Mountain Hwy E; r from $115), whose restaurant, bar and rooms all inhabit vintage, but lovingly tended, cabooses (train carriages).

The Drive » From Elbe take SR-706 (the National Park Hwy) due east to Ashford.

❸ Ashford

Situated a couple of miles outside the busy Nisqually entrance, Ashford is the national park's main service center with some medium-ranking accommodations, an info center and **Whittaker's Motel & Bunkhouse** (☎360-569-2439; www.whittakersbunkhouse.com; 30205 SR 706 E; dm $40, d $90-145; 🛜), a hostel-cafe conceived by legendary local mountaineer Lou Whittaker in the early 1990s. It would be heresy to leave town without popping inside for an espresso before grabbing brunch (or lunch) down the road at the **Copper Creek Inn** (☎360-569-2326; www.coppercreekinn.com; 35707 SR 706 E; breakfast from $8, burgers $10, dinner mains $12-29; ⊘11am-8pm Mon-Fri, 8am-9pm Sat, 8am-8pm Sun, opens earlier in summer), where the wild blackberry pies have fueled many a successful summit attempt.

The Drive » Just east of Ashford on SR-706 you'll see the park entrance gate.

④ Nisqually Entrance

The southwestern Nisqually entrance (named for the nearby river, which in turn is named after a local Native American tribe) is the busiest in **Mt Rainier National Park** and the only year-round entry gate. The simple entrance arch was built in 1922. Pay your park fee at the ticket window. As you drive through the entrance, you'll notice how, almost immediately, the trees appear denser and older. Many of these moss-covered behemoths date back over 700 years and measure up to 200ft in height.

The Drive » Follow the road alongside the Nisqually River for a couple of miles to Kautz Creek, where the summit of Rainier appears like a ghostly apparition.

⑤ Longmire

Worth a stop to stretch your legs or gain an early glimpse of Rainier's mossy old-growth forest, Longmire was the brainchild of a certain James Longmire who first came here in 1883 during a climbing trip when he noticed the hot mineral springs that bubbled up in a lovely meadow opposite the present-day National Park Inn (p281). He and his family returned the following year and established Longmire's Medicinal Springs, and in 1890 he built the Longmire Springs Hotel. Since 1917 the National Park Inn has stood on this site and is complemented by a small store, the tiny Longmire Information Center & Museum (p281) and a number of important trailheads. For a laid-back look at some old-growth forest and pastoral meadows, try the **Trail of the Shadows Loop**, a 0.8-mile circuit that begins across the road from the museum.

The Drive » After Longmire the road slowly starts to climb, passing the Cougar Rock Campground and Christine Falls, both on the left. A couple of miles after the falls, bear right onto a short stretch of summer-only one-way road (signposted 'Viewpoint') for a view stop at Ricksecker Point.

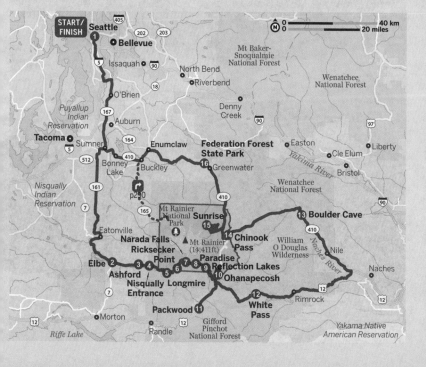

❻ Ricksecker Point

One of the park's premier viewpoints beloved by photographers, professional or otherwise, Ricksecker Point is a fine place to study five of Rainier's 26 glaciers – Nisqually, Pyramid, Success, Kautz and Wilson. The summit you see here is actually a false one (Point Success); the obscured *true* summit is 257ft higher. Equally majestic to the southeast is the saw-toothed Tatoosh Range.

The Drive ⟩⟩ Rejoin the main road and continue uphill.

❼ Narada Falls

Eight miles east of Longmire, a parking area marks the starting point for a steep 0.2-mile trail that leads down through flowers and ferns to the misty 168ft Narada Falls. The falls, often embellished by brilliant rainbows, carry the Paradise River over a basalt cliff. In high season, expect to get a face-full of water spray and an earful of oohing and ahhing as this is the park's most popular waterfall. In winter the falls freeze over and attract daring ice-climbers.

The Drive ⟩⟩ Soon after the falls, the road forks; stay left for Paradise. Follow the winding asphalt for another 2 miles to the Upper Parking Lot.

❽ Paradise

In the elevated alpine meadows of Paradise (p280) you'll find the area's biggest and best information center–museum, the Henry M Jackson Visitor Center (p280), which was completely rebuilt and reopened in 2008.

It's also home of the iconic **Paradise Inn** (☏360-569-2275; r with shared/private bath from $123/182; ⊙May-Oct; 🛜), which was built in 1916 and also refurbished in

GERARDO MARTINEZ CONS/GETTY IMAGES ©

Top: Pike Place Market, Seattle; Bottom left: View from Ricksecker Point; Bottom right: Narada Falls

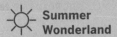

Summer Wonderland

You've circumnavigated it in a car; now how about walking it? Rainier is not only encircled by a road; you can also walk around it on foot via the long-distance Wonderland Trail. Laid out in 1915, the 93-mile-long precipitous path initially served as a patrol beat for park rangers and in the 1930s it was briefly earmarked as a paved ring road for cars. Fortunately, the plan never reached fruition and today the unbroken trail (which gains 21,000ft in cumulative elevation) is one of the most challenging and iconic hikes in the Pacific Northwest. You'll need food, camping gear, eight to 12 free days and a permit from the Longmire Information Center & Museum (p281) to do Wonderland. Longmire is a popular start point. There are 18 backcountry campgrounds en route; reservations ($20) are advisable in peak season (July and August). The official park page (www.nps.gov/mora) has more information.

2008. Designed to blend in with the environment and constructed almost entirely of local materials, including the exposed cedar logs in the Great Room, the inn was an early blueprint for National Park–rustic architecture. Following the two-year, $30-million, earthquake-withstanding revamp, the smallish rooms retain their close-to-the-wilderness essence, while the communal areas are nothing short of regal.

The Drive » Drive out of the east end of the Paradise Upper Parking Lot, cross the Paradise River (looking out for marmots) and descend the one-way road for 2 miles to a junction. Turn left and rejoin the main two-way road heading toward Reflection Lakes and Steven's Canyon.

❾ Reflection Lake

Rainier eyes itself in the mirror on calm cloudless days at Reflection Lake, formed during a violent volcanic eruption nearly 6000 years ago. You can pull over for double-vision photos of the mountain framed by tufts of precious wildflowers. The main lake used to have a boat concession, but now it's deliciously tranquil bar the odd passing tour bus.

The Drive » Avalanche chutes plague the U-shaped Steven's Canyon Rd in the winter, ensuring it remains closed outside peak season (unlike Paradise on the western side). Seen from above, the canyon is rather spectacular. Stop for a bird's-eye view a mile or so after Reflection Lakes before the trees close in. From here it's downhill all the way to Ohanapecosh.

❿ Ohanapecosh

Ohanapecosh (o-*ha*-nuh-peh-*kosh*) – the name means 'at the edge' – in the park's southeastern corner is usually accessed by the small settlement of Packwood, 12 miles to the southwest on US 12, which harbors a small number of eating and sleeping options. Shoehorned between Mt Rainier and its two southern neighbors, Mt St Helens and Mt Adams, this is a good base for travelers wanting to visit two or more of the mountains.

Just inside the Steven's Canyon gate, you'll find the 1.5-mile **Grove of the Patriarchs Trail**, one of the park's most popular short hikes. The trail explores a small island in the Ohanapecosh River replete with craning Douglas fir, cedar and hemlock trees, some of which are over 1000 years old. To reach the **Ohanapecosh Visitor Center** (⊘9am-5pm May–mid-Oct), turn right at the Steven's Canyon entrance onto SR-123 and drive 1.5 miles south. Alternatively, you can hike down from the Grove of the Patriarchs.

The Drive » Go right at the Steven's Canyon entrance and follow SR-123 south past the visitor center to the intersection with US 12. For Packwood, bear right.

⓫ Packwood

A service center for Mt St Helens, Mt Rainier and the nearby ski area of White Pass, Packwood is what in the Old West they called a 'one-horse town.' A few low- to mid-ranking eating joints and accommodations glued to US 12 provide a good excuse to pull over and mingle with other road-trippers. Chin-waggers congregate at **Mountain Goat Coffee** (📞360-494-5600; https://facebook.com/MountainGoatCoffeeCo/; 105 E Main St; pastries from $2; ⏰7am-5pm), where you may run into a park ranger or two.

The Drive » Retrace your route to the intersection of US 12 and SR-123. The climb to White Pass begins here. Stop at a pullover soon after the intersection to appreciate the indelible sight of Mt Rainier as it appears briefly above the trees.

⑫ White Pass

Higher than Snoqualmie and Stevens Passes to the north, White Pass carries a quieter, open-year-round road that, at various points, offers glimpses of three Cascadian volcanoes: Mt Rainier, Mt Adams and Mt St Helens. The pass itself, perched at 4500ft, is home to an understated **ski area** (www.skiwhitepass.com; day passes adult/child $62/43), which has one condo complex for overnighters. Otherwise, people stay in nearby Packwood or drive up for the day from Yakima.

The Drive » A classic east–west Washington scenery shift kicks in soon after White Pass as you follow US 12 amid

Grove of the Patriarchs Trail

JON MARC LYTTLE/SHUTTERSTOCK ©

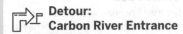

Detour: Carbon River Entrance

Start: 16 Federation Forest State Park

The park's northwest entrance is its most isolated and undeveloped corner, with two unpaved (and unconnected) roads and little in the way of facilities, save a lone ranger station and the very basic **Ipsut Creek Campground** (☑360-829-5127). But while the tourist traffic might be thin on the ground, the landscape lacks nothing in magnificence.

Named for its coal deposits, Carbon River is the park's wettest region and protects one of the few remaining examples of inland temperate rain forest in the contiguous USA. Dense, green and cloaked in moss, this verdant wilderness can be penetrated by a handful of interpretive trails that fan off the Carbon River Rd.

Getting here takes you part of the way back to Seattle. Take Hwy 410 W to 116 S (Carbon River Rd) then turn left. After about 15.5 miles you'll come to the Carbon River ranger station just before the entrance.

increasingly scattered trees and bald, steep-sided river coulees. At the intersection with SR-410, swing north on the Chinook Scenic Byway just west of the town of Naches to reach Boulder Cave, 65 miles from White Pass.

13 Boulder Cave

Among the many excuses to pull over on this stretch of the Chinook Scenic Byway is **Boulder Cave** (⊙May-Oct), a rarity in the relatively cave-free terrain of the Pacific Northwest and doubly unique due to its formation through a combination of volcanic and erosive processes. A 2-mile round-trip trail built by the Civilian Conservation Corp in 1935 leads into the cave's murky interior, formed when Devil's Creek cut a tunnel through soft sedimentary rock, leaving hard volcanic basalt on top. Up to 50 rare big-eared bats hibernate in

the cave each winter, when it is closed to the public. Bring a flashlight.

The Drive » Continue west and uphill toward Chinook Pass, 25 miles from Boulder Cave, as the air cools and the snowdrifts pile up roadside.

14 Chinook Pass

Closed until May and infested with lingering snowdrifts well into July, Chinook Pass towers 5430ft on Rainier's eastern flank. The long-distance **Pacific Crest Trail** crosses the highway here on a pretty stone bridge, while nearby **Crystal Mountain** (☑360-663-2265; www.crystalmountainresort.com; 33914 Crystal Mountain Blvd, Hwy 410) comprises Washington's largest ski area and only bona fide overnight 'resort.' Rather than stop at the pass, cruise a few hundred yards further west to **Tipsoo Lake**, another reflective photographer's dream where a paved trail will return the blood to your legs.

The Drive » From Tipsoo Lake the road winds down to relatively 'low' Cayuse Pass (4694ft). Turn north here and descend a further 1000ft in 3 miles to the turning for Mt Rainier's White River entrance. This is the gateway to Sunrise, 16 miles uphill via a series of switchbacks.

15 Sunrise

The highest point you can drive to within the park, Sunrise (p281) is known for its spectacular views. If you want to go for a walk, a trailhead directly across the parking lot from the **Sunrise Lodge Cafeteria** (snacks $6-9; ⊙10am-7pm Jul & Aug) provides access to **Emmons Vista**, with good views of Mt Rainier, Little Tahoma and the Emmons Glacier. Nearby, the 1-mile **Sourdough Ridge Trail** leads to pristine subalpine meadows for stunning views over other volcanic giants.

The **Sunrise Visitors Center** (⊙10am-6pm daily, early Jul–early Sep) is a helpful spot, where you can check out the exhibits or take part in an interpretive hike.

The Drive » Coast downhill to the White River entrance and turn north onto the

Mather Memorial Pkwy in order to exit the park. In the small community of Greenwater on SR-410 you can load up with gas and food.

⑯ Federation Forest State Park

Just when you thought you'd left ancient nature behind, up springs Federation Forest State Park, created by a foresighted women's group in the 1940s in order to preserve a rapidly diminishing stock of local old-growth forest from logging interests. Today its fir, spruce, hemlock and cedar trees cluster around the lackadaisical White River, while the **Catherine Montgomery Interpretive Center** (⊘8am-dusk) offers a rundown of the contrasting ecosystems of east–west Washington state. There's also a bookstore and 12 miles of trails, most of them family friendly. ∎

Sourdough Ridge Trail

PHILIP KRAMER/ALAMY STOCK PHOT ©

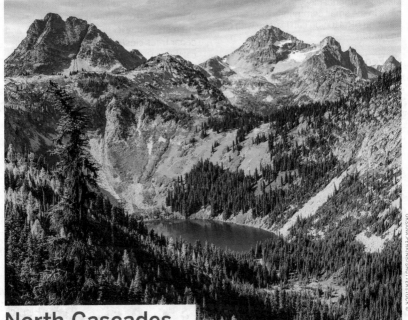

OKSANA.PERKINS/SHUTTERSTOCK ©

North Cascades National Park

Inaugurated in 1968, North Cascades National Park is Alaska transplanted into the lower 48, half a million acres of dramatic, daunting wild country strafed with mountains, lakes, glaciers (over 300 of them) and wildlife, but with almost no trace of civilization.

Great For...

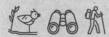

State
Washington

Entrance Fee
Free

Area
789 sq miles

Erratic weather, massive precipitation, thick rainforest and vertiginous cliffs have long ensured the remoteness of the park's mountains: steep, alpine behemoths furnished with names like Mt Terror, Mt Fury, Mt Despair and Forbidden Peak. Aspiring bushwhackers and free-climbers love the unique challenges offered by this eerie wilderness. The less adrenaline-hungry stick close to arterial Hwy 20 and prepare for the drive of a lifetime.

Hiking
It's possible to get a basic overview of this vast alpine wilderness by motoring through in a car on US 20, making use of the numerous pullouts and short interpretive hikes that are scattered along the route. But in order to taste the park's real gritty essence you'll need a tent, a decent ruck-sack and a gung-ho sense of adventure.

Cascade Pass Trail

PATRICK TR/SHUTTERSTOCK ©

Three-piece Park

For administrative reasons, the park is split into two sections – north and south – separated in the middle by the Ross Lake National Recreation Area, which encases a spectacular 20-mile section of the North Cascades Hwy (US 20). Along the park's southern border around Stehekin lies a third region, the Lake Chelan National Recreation Area, a 62,000-acre protected park that surrounds the fjord-like Lake Chelan. To avoid confusion, the three zones are managed as one contiguous area and overlaid by the Stephen Mather Wilderness, created in 1988.

Free permits are required for backcountry camping in the park and must be obtained in person from the Wilderness Information Center (p296) or at a park ranger station.

One of the park's most challenging but rewarding day hikes is the strenuous **Sourdough Mountain Trail**, which gains a mile in height for the 5.5 miles (one way) travelled on the ground. Most say that the effort is worth it; the views of Cascadian peaks and turquoise Diablo Lake 5000-plus feet below are some of the best in the park.

The 3.7-mile hike to 5384ft **Cascade Pass** is the best loved in these mountains, and gets you very quickly up into a flower-carpeted, glacier-surrounded paradise that will leave you struggling for superlatives.

From the southern end of the Colonial Creek Campground (Mile 130, Hwy 20), the long **Thunder Creek Trail** leads along a powerful glacier-fed river through old-growth forest and clumps of wildflowers flourishing in the dank forest. After 2.5 miles the **Fourth of July Trail** branches left to a pass of the same name and makes a good early-season hike (10 miles round-trip from the campground). Alternatively, you

can continue along Thunder Creek to Park Creek Pass and, ultimately, Stehekin.

Just past the Ross Dam trailhead at Mile 134.5, the easy and wheelchair-accessible **Happy Creek Forest Walk** (0.5 miles) gives you an up-close look at the forest on a raised boardwalk.

Ross Lake

Ross Lake (Hwy 20, Mile 134) stretches north for 23 miles, across the Canadian border, but – in keeping with the wild terrain – is accessible only by trail or water. Incorporated into the Ross Lake National Recreation Area, the lake was formed by the building of the Ross Dam, an ambitious hydroelectric project, from 1937, designed to generate electricity for the fast-growing Seattle area.

You can hike down to the Ross Dam from a trailhead on Hwy 20. The trail descends for 1 mile and crosses over the dam. For an extra leg-stretch you can follow the west bank of Ross Lake another mile to Ross Lake Resort (p296).

Rafting

Although it doesn't offer the heart-in-the-mouth white-water runs of less tamed waterways, the dam-controlled Upper Skagit makes for a good class II or III family trip through old-growth forest, offering plenty of opportunities for wildlife-watching. A number of companies offer excursions here, including **Alpine Adventures** (www.alpineadventures.com; day trips per person from $79).

Diablo Lake

Just below Ross Lake, **Diablo Lake** (supply ferries adult/child one way $10/5) is held back by the similarly huge 389ft **Diablo Dam**. A pullout off Hwy 20 known as the **Diablo Dam Overlook** provides incredible views of the turquoise-green lake framed by glacier-capped peaks.

Diablo was the world's highest arch-type dam at the time of its completion in 1930, and building it in such a hostile region with no road access was one of the greatest engineering feats of the interwar period.

Diablo Lake is popular with kayakers and canoeists (there's a launch site at Colonial Creek Campground). The water's turquoise hue is a result of powdered rock ground down by glaciers.

North Cascades Environmental Learning Center (www.ncascades.org) 🍃, on the lake's northern banks, is operated by the North Cascades Institute in partnership with the National Park Service.

Diablo Dam

ZACK FRANK/SHUTTERSTOCK ©

Essential Information

Getting There & Away

You'll need your own wheels to get into and around the national park.

Taking the Supply Boat

If you're heading to the **Ross Lake Resort** (📞206-386-4437; www.rosslakeresort.com; 503 Diablo St, Rockport; cabins $205-385; 🕐mid-Jun–late Oct) you can access it by hiking or taking one of the twice-daily boat and supply truck combos (round-trip $20). The resort has a car park and ferry dock situated on the right just after you cross the Diablo Dam. The first boat leaves at 8:30am and turns around at the Ross Powerhouse dock at 9am. The second leaves Diablo at 3pm and turns around at 3:30pm. Visitors can take the ferry one way and hike back to the Diablo Dam on the moderate 3.8-mile Diablo Lake Trail.

Tourist Information

North Cascades Visitors Center (📞206-386-4495, ext 11; 502 Newhalem St, Newhalem; 🕐9am-5pm daily Jun-Sep, Sat & Sun May & Oct) 🌿 A walk-through exhibit mixes informative placards about the park's ecosystems with nature videos. Expert rangers will enlighten you on everything from melting glaciers to the fickleness of the weather. Various short trails track the Skagit River and Newhalem Creek, the longest of which is the 1.8-mile River Loop Trail. Rangers give interpretive talks in the vicinity in summer.

Wilderness Information Center (7280 Ranger Station Rd, Marblemount; 🕐8am-5pm early May-Jun & Sep, 7am-6pm Jul-early Sep, closed Oct-early May) Pick up backcountry permits here. ■

Diablo Lake

SEAN PAVONE/SHUTTERSTOCK ©

Hall of Moss Trail

Olympic National Park

Olympic NP shelters a rainforest, copious glaciated mountain peaks and a 57-mile strip of coast. One of North America's great wilderness areas, most of it remains relatively untouched by humans, with 1000-year-old cedar trees juxtaposed by pristine alpine meadows, clear glacial lakes and a roadless interior.

Great For...

State
Washington

Entrance Fee
7-day pass per vehicle/pedestrian
$30/15

Area
1406 sq miles

❶ Hoh Rain Forest

The most famous section of the Olympic rain forest, the Hoh River area offers lots of hikes and an interpretive center. If you can only make one stop on the western side, this should be it. The paved Upper Hoh Rd winds 19 miles from US 101 to the visitor center, passing a **giant Sitka spruce tree** along the way. This lord of the forest is 270ft high and over 500 years old.

At the end of Hoh River Rd, the **Hoh Rain Forest Visitor Center** (☏360-374-6925; ⏲9am-4:30pm Sep-Jun, to 6pm Jul & Aug) offers displays on the ecology of the rain forest and the plants and animals that inhabit it, as well as a bookstore. Rangers lead free guided walks twice a day during summer.

Leading from the visitor center are several excellent day hikes into virgin rain forest, the most popular of which is the 0.8-mile **Hall of Moss Trail**. The 1.25-mile **Spruce Nature Trail**, another short interpretative loop, also starts at the visitor

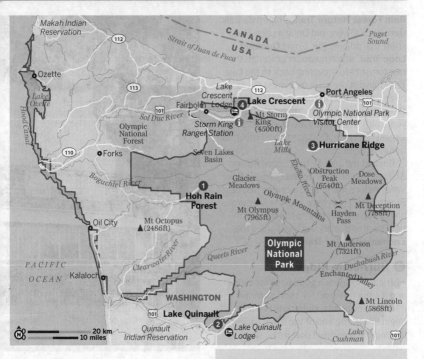

center. There is also a short wheelchair-accessible nature trail through a rain-forest marsh.

The **Hoh River Trail** is the major entry trail into the Hoh River Valley and the principal access route to Mt Olympus.

② Lake Quinault

The enchanting Quinault River Valley is one of the park's least crowded corners. Clustered around the lake's deep-blue waters lie forested peaks, a historic lodge and some of the oldest Sitka spruce, Douglas fir and western red cedar trees in the world. The lake itself offers plenty of activities such as fishing, boating and swimming, while upstream both the north and south branches of the Quinault River harbor a couple of important trans-park trails.

A number of short hiking trails begin just below **Lake Quinault Lodge**; pick up a free map from the US Forest Service (USFS) office. The shortest of these is the **Quinault**

Essential Information

You'll need your own car here.

You can choose to stay in one of the handful of historic park lodges, in campgrounds or in backcountry campgrounds.

The **Olympic National Park Visitor Center** (☑360-565-3100; www.nps.gov/olym; 3002 Mt Angeles Rd; ⊗8am-6pm Jul & Aug, to 4pm Sep-Jun) is about a mile south of Port Angeles and is the park's most comprehensive information center. Aside from giving out excellent free maps and leaflets, the center offers children's exhibits, a bookstore, a replica of a prehistoric Makah seal-hunting canoe and a 25-minute film. Pick up a (free) detailed park map along with an even more detailed 'Wilderness Trip Planner' with backcountry trails and campgrounds marked.

Rain Forest Nature Trail, a half-mile walk through 500-year-old Douglas firs. This short trail adjoins the 3-mile **Quinault Loop Trail**, which meanders through the rain forest before circling back to the lake. The Quinault region is renowned for its huge trees. Close to the village is a 191ft Sitka spruce (purported to be up to 1000 years old), and nearby are the world's largest red cedar, Douglas fir and mountain hemlock trees.

Beyond the lake, both N Shore Rd and S Shore Rd continue up the Quinault River Valley before merging at a bridge just past Bunch Falls. From here, more adventurous hikers can sally forth into the backcountry. The area's sparkling highlight is the **Enchanted Valley Trail**.

❸ Hurricane Ridge

Hurricane Ridge is a good base for skiing, and it's the trailhead for short summer hikes to viewpoints. Hurricane Hill Trail, beginning at the end of the road leading up, and the Meadow Loop Trails, starting

Top: Lake Quinault Lodge; Bottom: Quinault Rain Forest Nature Trail

at the **visitor center** (◷9:30am-5pm daily summer, Fri-Sun winter), are moderately easy hikes. The first half-mile of these trails is wheelchair accessible. Note that the ridge is renowned for its fickle weather.

From Hurricane Ridge, you can drive a rough, white-knuckle 8-mile road to Obstruction Peak, laid out by the Civilian Conservation Corps (CCC) in the 1930s. Here, hikers looking for long-distance treks can pick up either the Grand Ridge Trail, which leads 7.5 miles to Deer Park, much of the way above the timberline, or the Wolf Creek Trail, an 8-mile downhill jaunt to Whiskey Bend, where it picks up the Elwha Trail.

❹ Lake Crescent

If you're heading anticlockwise on the Olympic loop from Port Angeles toward Forks, one of the first scenic surprises is luminous Lake Crescent, a popular boating and fishing area and a departure point for a number of short national park hikes.

The area is also the site of **Lake Crescent Lodge** (☏888-896-3818; www.olympicnationalparks.com; 416 Lake Crescent Rd; lodge r from $139, cabins from $309; ◷May-Dec, limited availability winter; ❋☏), the oldest of the park's trio of celebrated lodges – it first opened in 1916.

The best stop-off point is in a parking lot to the right of US 101 near the **Storm King Ranger Station** (☏360-928-3380; 343 Barnes Point Rd; ◷May-Sep). A number of short hikes leave from here, including the Marymere Falls Trail, a 2-mile round-trip to a 90ft cascade that drops over a basalt cliff. For a more energetic hike, climb the side of Mt Storm King, the peak that rises to the east of Lake Crescent. The steep, 1.7-mile ascent splits off the Barnes Creek Trail.

Trout fishing is good here – the lake is deep with steep shorelines – though only artificial lures are allowed. Rowboat rentals ($15/40 per hour/half day) are available at Lake Crescent Lodge in the summer months.

Hiking

There is so much beautiful wilderness to see in the park – and the best way to see it is on foot. Many visitors keep to the park's well-trodden edges on easily accessible 'touch the wilderness' hikes. Far fewer plunge into the Olympic's mossy, foggy, roadless interior.

Hikers should always take stock of weather conditions, rules and regulations, and necessary equipment. Stop in at the visitor center (p299).

Seattle Press Expedition Hike
One of the most popular cross-park treks follows the pioneering route taken by James H Christie. A former Arctic explorer, he answered the call of the *Seattle Press* newspaper in 1889 to 'acquire fame by unveiling the mystery which wraps the land encircled by the snow-capped Olympic range.' Starting at the Whiskey Bend trailhead on the Elwha River, the route tracks south and then southwest through the Elwha and Quinault River valleys to Lake Quinault, covering 44 moderately strenuous miles. It commonly takes walkers five days to complete.

Pacific Coastal Hike (North)
There are two long-distance beach hikes along the isolated coast. The more northerly is the 32.7-mile stretch between the Makah Shi Shi trailhead near Cape Flattery and Rialto Beach near La Push, which commonly makes up a moderate five-day, four-night trek. This hike stays close to the shoreline, meaning that a good understanding of tidal charts is imperative. There are 14 campgrounds en route, eight of which take reservations.

If you are contemplating a trek along the coast, request information from the National Park Service (www.nps.gov/olym), buy good maps, learn how to read tide tables and be prepared for bad weather year-round.

Top left: Hurricane Ridge; Top right: Lake Crescent Lodge; Bottom: Lake Crescent

CLASSIC ROAD TRIPS

Olympic Peninsula Loop

Freakishly wet, fantastically green and chillingly remote, the Olympic Peninsula looks like it has been resurrected from a wilder, pre-civilized era.

Duration 4 days

Distance 435 miles

Best Time to Go
June to September when deluges are slightly less likely.

Essential Photo
Hoh Rain Forest to see greens you've never imagined.

Best Wildlife
Roosevelt elk at the Hoh Rain Forest.

❶ Olympia

Welcome to Olympia, city of weird contrasts, where streetside buskers belt out acoustic grunge, and stiff bureaucrats answer their ringtones on the lawns of the expansive state legislature. A quick circuit of the **Washington State Capitol** (☑360-902-8880; 416 Sid Snyder Ave SW; ⏰7am-5:30pm Mon-Fri, 11am-4pm Sat & Sun) **FREE**, a huge Grecian temple of a building, will give you a last taste of civilization before you depart. Then load up the car and head swiftly for the exits.

The Drive » Your basic route is due west, initially on Hwy 101, then (briefly) on SR-8 before joining US-12 in Elma. In Grays Harbor, enter the twin cities of Aberdeen and Hoquiam, famous for producing William

Boeing and the grunge group Nirvana. Here, you swing north on Hwy 101 (again!) to leafier climes at Lake Quinault, 88 miles from Olympia.

❷ Lake Quinault

Situated in the extreme southwest of the **Olympic National Park**, the thickly forested Quinault River Valley is one of the park's least-crowded corners. Clustered on the south shore of deep-blue glacial Lake Quinault is the tiny village of **Quinault**, complete with the luscious **Lake Quinault Lodge** (☑360-288-2900; www.olympicnational parks.com; 345 S Shore Rd; r $219-450; ❄🐾🍽), a USFS office and a couple of stores.

A number of short **hiking trails** begin just below Lake Quinault Lodge; pick up a free map from the USFS office. The shortest of these is the **Quinault Rain Forest Nature Trail**, a half-mile walk through 500-year-old Douglas firs. This brief trail adjoins the 3-mile Quinault Loop Trail, which meanders through the rain forests before circling back to the lake. The Quinault region is renowned for its huge trees. Close to the village is a 191ft Sitka spruce (supposedly over 1000 years old), and nearby are the world's largest red cedar, Douglas fir and mountain hemlock trees.

The Drive » West from Lake Quinault, Hwy 101 continues through the Quinault Indian Reservation before entering a thin strip of national park territory that protects the beaches around Kalaloch (*klay*-lock). This is some of the wildest coastal scenery in the US accessible by road; various pullovers allow beach forays. After a total of 40 miles you'll reach Ruby Beach.

❸ Ruby Beach

Inhabiting a thin coastal strip that was added to the national park in 1953, Ruby Beach is accessed via a short 0.2-mile path that leads down to a large expanse of windswept coast embellished with polished black stones and wantonly strewn tree trunks. To the south toward Kalaloch, other accessible beaches include unimaginatively named Beach One through to Beach Six, all of which are popular with beachcombers.

Lake Quinault

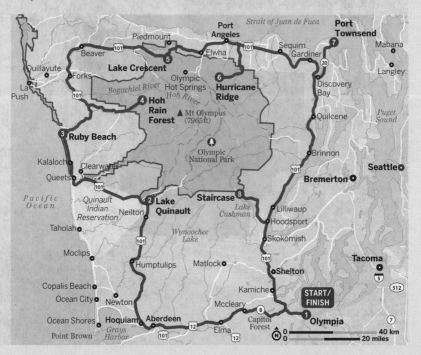

At low tide, rangers give talks on tidal-pool life at **Beach Four** and on the ecosystems of the Olympic coastal strip.

The Drive » North of Ruby Beach, Hwy 101 swings sharply northeast and inland, tracking the Hoh River. Turn right off 101 onto the Hoh River Rd to explore one of the national park's most popular inner sanctums, the Hoh Rain Forest. Suspend your excitement as the trees eerily close in as you (re)enter the park.

❹ Hoh Rain Forest

Count yourself lucky if you arrive on a day when it isn't raining! The most popular detour off Hwy 101 is the 19-mile paved road to the Hoh Valley, the densest, wettest, greenest and most intensely surreal temperate rain forest on earth. The essential hike here is the short but fascinating

Hall of Moss Trail, an easy 0.8-mile loop through the kind of weird, ethereal scenery that even JRR Tolkien couldn't have invented. Old-man's beard drips from branches above you like corduroy fringe, while trailside licorice ferns and lettuce lichens overwhelm the massive fallen trunks of maple and Sitka spruce. Rangers lead interesting free guided walks here twice a day during summer and can help you spot some of the park's 5000-strong herd of **Roosevelt elk**.

The Drive » Rejoining Hwy 101, motor north to the small and relatively nondescript but handy settlement of Forks. Press on through as Hwy 101 bends north then east through a large logging area before plunging back into the national park on the shores of wondrous Lake Crescent, which is 66 miles from the Hoh Rain Forest.

ANTON FOLTIN/SHUTTERSTOCK ©

Top: Ruby Beach; Bottom left: Hall of Moss Trail; Bottom right: Roosevelt elk

JOHN T GALLERY/SHUTTERSTOCK ©

DAVID MAKI/SHUTTERSTOCK ©

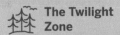

The Twilight Zone

It would have been impossible to envisage 15 years ago: diminutive Forks, a depressed lumber town full of hard-nosed loggers, reborn as a pilgrimage site for 'tweenage' girls following in the ghostly footsteps of two fictional sweethearts named Bella and Edward. The reason for this weird metamorphosis was, of course, the *Twilight* saga, a four-part book series by US author Stephenie Meyer about love and vampires on the foggy Olympic Peninsula that in just a few years has shifted more than 100 million books and spawned five Hollywood movies. With Forks acting as the book's main setting, the town was catapulted to international stardom, and the cachet has yet to wear off. Daily **Twilight Tours** (360-374-5634; 130 S Spartan Ave, Forks; www.forkswa.com) visit most of the places mentioned in Meyer's books.

❺ Lake Crescent

Before you've even had time to erase the horror of teenage vampires from your head, the scenery shifts again as the road winds along the glittering pine-scented shores of glacial-carved Lake Crescent. The lake looks best from water level, on a rental kayak, or from high above at its eastern edge on the **Storm King Mountain Trail** (named after the peak's wrathful spirit), accessible via a steep, 1.7-mile ascent that splits off the Barnes Creek Trail. For the less athletic, the **Marymere Falls Trail** is a 2-mile round-trip to a 90ft cascade that drops down over a basalt cliff. Both hikes leave from a parking lot to the right of SR 101 near the Storm King Ranger Station (p301). The area is also the site of the Lake Crescent Lodge (p301), the oldest of the park's trio of celebrated lodges, which first opened in 1916.

The Drive » From Lake Crescent take Hwy 101 22 miles east to the town of Port Angeles, a gateway to Victoria, Canada, which is reachable by ferry to the north. Starting in Race St, the 18-mile Hurricane Ridge Rd climbs up 5300ft toward extensive wildflower meadows and expansive mountain vistas often visible above the clouds.

❻ Hurricane Ridge

Up above the clouds, stormy Hurricane Ridge lives up to its name with fickle weather and biting winds made slightly more bearable by the park's best high-altitude views. Its proximity to Port Angeles is another bonus; if you're heading up here be sure to call into the museum-like Olympic National Park Visitor Center (p299) first. The smaller Hurricane Ridge Visitor Center (p300) has a snack bar, gift shop, toilets and is the starting point of various hikes. **Hurricane Hill Trail** (which begins at the end of the road) and the **Meadow Loop Trails** network are popular and moderately easy. The first half-mile of these trails is wheelchair accessible.

The Drive » Wind back down the Hurricane Ridge Rd, kiss the suburbs of Port Angeles and press east through the retirement community of Sequim (pronounced 'squwim'). Turn north on SR-20 to reach another, more attractive port, that of Port Townsend.

❼ Port Townsend

Leaving the park momentarily behind, ease back into civilization with the cultured Victorian comforts of Port Townsend, whose period charm dates from the railroad boom of the 1890s, when the town was earmarked to become the 'New York of the West.' That never happened, but you can pick up a historic walking tour map from the **visitor center** (360-385-2722; www. ptchamber.org; 2409 Jefferson St; 9am-5pm Mon-Fri) and wander the waterfront's collection of shops, galleries and antique malls. Don't miss the old-time **Belmont Saloon** (925 Water St; mains lunch $10-14, dinner $15-32; 10:30am-2am Mon-Fri, 9am-2am Sat & Sun), the **Rose Theatre** (235 Taylor St), a gorgeously renovated theater that's been showing movies since 1908, and the fine Victorian mansions on the bluff above town, where several charming residences have been turned into B&Bs.

The Drive » From Port Townsend, head back to the junction of Hwy 101, but this time head south passing Quilcene, Brinnon, with its great diner, and the Dosewallips park entrance. You get more unbroken water views here on the park's eastern side courtesy of the Hood Canal. Track the watery beauty to Hoodsport where signs point west off Hwy 101 to Staircase, 67 miles from Port Townsend.

⑧ Staircase

It's drier on the park's eastern side and the mountains are closer. The Staircase park nexus, accessible via Hoodsport, has a ranger station, campground and a decent trail system that follows the drainage of the North Fork Skokomish River and is flanked by some of the most rugged peaks in the Olympics. Nearby **Lake Cushman** has a campground and water-sports opportunities. ∎

SNC ART AND MORE/SHUTTERSTOCK ©

Lake Cushman

MINT IMAGES – FRANS LANTING/GETTY IMAGES ©

Wrangell-St Elias National Park

Imagine an area the size of Switzer-land. Now strip away its road network, eradicate its cities and take away all but 40 of its eight million people. The result would be something approximating Wrangell-St Elias National Park, a feast of brawny ice-encrusted mountains that make up the second-largest national park in the world.

Great For...

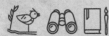

State
Alaska

Entrance Fee
Free

Area
20,625 sq miles

One more time: this park is *big*. If Wrangell-St Elias were a country it would be larger than 70 of the world's independent nations. Its biggest glacier covers an area larger than the US state of Rhode Island. Plenty of its mountain peaks have never been climbed. And that's even before you've started counting the bears, beavers, porcupines and moose.

❶ McCarthy

Alaska doesn't lack isolated frontier towns that act as magnets for a colorful cast of folk who want to live away from everything, and nor does it suffer a paucity of tourist destinations. But it's a rare place that manages to bridge the gap between these two identities – a spot that is authentically on the edge of civilization, yet welcomes those curious folk who want to peep in on the raw, wild pulse of the Alaskan bush.

Enter McCarthy. Once the red-light district and drinking strip for bored miners

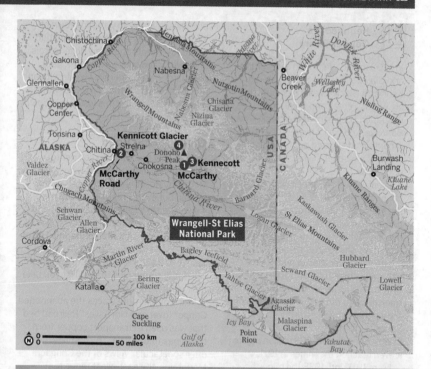

McCarthy

Kennecott's Copper Boom

In 1900 miners 'Tarantula Jack' Smith and Clarence Warner reconnoitered Kennicott Glacier's east side until they arrived at a creek and found traces of copper. They named the creek Bonanza, and was it ever – the entire mountainside turned out to hold some of the richest copper deposits ever uncovered.

Eventually, a group of investors bought the existing stakes and formed the Kennecott Copper Corporation, named when a clerical worker misspelled Kennicott (which is why, nowadays, the town is spelled with an 'e' while the river, glacier and other natural features have an 'i'). First the syndicate built its railroad: 196 miles of track through the wilderness, including the leg that's now McCarthy Rd and Cordova's famous Million Dollar Bridge. The line cost $23 million before it even reached the mines in 1911.

From 1911 until 1938 the mines operated around the clock and reported a net profit of more than $100 million. By 1938 most of the rich ore had been exhausted, and in November that year the mine was closed permanently. With the exception of a steam turbine and two large diesel engines, everything was left behind, and Kennecott became a perfectly preserved slice of US mining history.

Unfortunately, when the railroad bed was converted to a road in 1974, Kennecott also became the country's biggest help-yourself hardware store. Locals were taking windows, doors and wiring, while tourists were picking the town clean of tools, railroad spikes and anything else they could haul away as souvenirs.

In 1998 the NPS purchased the mill, power plant and many of the buildings from private owners as the first step to restoring them.

bivouacked at the 'dry' mining town of Kennecott, today this is an intersection of muddy streets and a few dozen locals and seasonal workers, who work hard, play harder, and generally live life with an unvarnished gusto that's a joy to witness. It helps that they live in a valley that could give Eden a fit of jealousy.

❷ McCarthy Road

There's only one way you can get to McCarthy by land: the bumpy, unpaved McCarthy Rd. This dirt route is a rump-shaker, but even a regular car can make it if you go slow (35mph maximum) and stay in the center to avoid running over old rail spikes – contact **Ma Johnson's Hotel** (📞907-554-5402; www.mccarthylodge.com; Main St; d/tr $229/299) in McCarthy about car-rental companies that will let you take their vehicles on the road.

Much of the route traces the abandoned Copper River and Northwest Railroad bed that was used to transport copper from the mines to Cordova. The first few miles offer spectacular views of the Chugach Mountains, the east–west range that separates the Chitina Valley lowlands from the Gulf of Alaska. Peaks average 7000ft to 8000ft. Below is the mighty Copper River, one of the world's great waterways for king and red salmon.

❸ Kennecott

Between 1911 and 1938, the mining outpost of Kennecott was the serious 'dry' working town to free-living, hard-drinking McCarthy. These days it is effectively an open-air museum on mining history, as well as the jump-off point for several excellent hikes.

Old mill town constitutes pretty much all of present-day Kennecott. Dozens of old wood and log buildings have been restored, stabilized or purposely left in a state of decrepitude. You're welcome to wander around the outside of the buildings at will, or you can join daily tours.

Concentration Mill & Leaching Plant

Like a rickety fantasy hatched out of a lunatic's dream, this 14-story **building** (tour $28) in Kennecott once processed the copper mined out of the surrounding mountains. You can only enter via two-hour tours led by **St Elias Alpine Guides** (☏907-554-4445; www.steliasguides.com), but this is highly recommended for a chance to peek into a truly surreal tableau of 20th-century mining equipment.

There are three tours daily. St Elias Alpine Guides has a small kiosk at the entrance to Kennecott, where the shuttle drops off passengers.

Root Glacier Trail

Beginning at the far edge of town past the Concentration Mill, the Root Glacier Trail is an easy 4- or 8-mile round-trip route out to the sparkling white-and-blue ice. Signposts mark the route and the path itself is clear and well used as far as the primitive Jumbo Creek campsites.

From here you can head left to the glacier or continue straight another 2 miles along a rougher track. At the end, the Erie Mine Bunkhouse will be visible on the slopes above you. Check at the visitor center for the latest on the trail conditions. Most of this trail can also be ridden on a mountain bike.

Bonanza Mine Trail

This excellent hike from Kennecott follows an alpine trail – a round-trip of almost 9 miles. Begin on the Root Glacier Trail and turn off to the right at the clearly marked junction. This is a steep uphill walk with 3800ft of elevation gain. Once above the tree line, the view of the confluence of the Root and Kennicott Glaciers is stunning.

Expect three to five hours for this hike up if the weather is good and half that time to return. Water is available at the top, but carry at least a quart if the day is hot. Snow lingers higher up until early June.

The former Kennecott Copper Mine

MICHAEL HEFFERNAN/LONELY PLANET ©

Left: Root Glacier Trail;
Right: Ma Johnson's Hotel, McCarthy

❹ Kennicott Glacier

'Oh no, they destroyed this valley!' If you're like 99% of visitors, that's exactly what you'll think as you reach Kennecott and look across the valley at a rolling landscape of dirt and rubble. But no, that isn't a dump of mine tailings from the copper-boom days, but the Kennicott Glacier moraine. The ice is buried underneath.

The glacier is thinning terribly and has dropped 175ft in height over the past eight decades. To put that statistic in perspective, back in the 1930s some locals didn't even realize they lived in a valley, as the ice field was so high.

Essential Information

Be honest: had you heard about Wrangell-St Elias before you cracked open this book? If so, we nod our heads in respect. For every eight tourists who track north to Denali, only one intrepid traveler tackles the little-known wilderness of Wrangell. Why? Good question. Granted, most of the park is desolate and doesn't have the infrastructure or satellite towns of Denali, though it did have its improbable copper-mining history, preserved for posterity by the NPS.

So, how do you tackle such an immense place? Most visitors enter the park via the tiny, off-the-grid settlements of McCarthy and Kennecott, accessible by bush plane or a single unpaved road that branches off the Richardson Hwy near Copper Center. Between them, these hamlets have several eating establishments, a store and a hardy year-round population of around 40 people who hunt and grow their own vegetables. Popular activities in the area include glacier hiking, ice climbing and historical tours of Kennecott's mine buildings.

You don't need a backcountry permit for overnight hikes, but you are encouraged to leave an itinerary at any of the ranger stations, where you can also get advice and a bear-proof canister for your trip. There's a refundable deposit required for the canister.

You can also drop by the visitor center in Kennecott for maps and ideas for both day and overnight hikes. There are literally two full folders of options. Popular overnight hikes include Donoho Peak, Erie Lake and McCarthy Creek.

Sleeping

There are numerous privately owned and operated campsites, B&Bs and roadhouses all around the borders of the park, as well as lodges and hotels within areas like McCarthy and along the Nabesna Rd. Wrangell-St Elias is also home to 14 *very* basic public-use backcountry cabins. Most are first-come, first-served, but three can be reserved on the park website (www.nps.gov/wrst). No permit is required for backcountry camping; use bear-proof food containers. ∎

Lake on Kennicott Glacier

ROCKY
MOUNTAINS

In This Chapter

Black Canyon
of the Gunnison 322

Glacier 324

Grand Teton.................................... 336

Great Sand Dunes 348

Rocky Mountain.............................. 354

Yellowstone 362

Rocky Mountains

The Rockies continue to embody the spirit of the American frontier, and the range's parks remain among the country's most prized. Yellowstone, the world's first national park, is the superstar, with primordial geysers and mega wildlife sightings at every turn. Grand Teton, Glacier and Rocky Mountain reward those in search of top-of-the-world vistas and alpine adventure, while far to the south of Colorado is the region's most curious sight – the mirage-like Great Sand Dunes.

Don't Miss

● Spotting bears, bison and geysers at Yellowstone (p362)

● Climbing the craggy wild trails of Grand Teton (p336)

● Roaming the Great Sand Dunes desertscapes (p348)

● Driving the spectacularly scenic Going-to-the-Sun Rd (p333)

● Scaling Longs Peak or just ogling its glaciated slopes from below (p356)

When to Go

With the bulk of the Rockies located at altitude with significant winter snow-cover, most visitors arrive in the summer. Full park facilities are usually open from Memorial Day (late May) to Labor Day (early September). This is when most trails are accessible, but also when the parks are busiest.

September and October bring fall foliage, some terrific lodging deals and far fewer crowds.

Many services close in the winter, although the parks remain open to avid skiers.

Previous page: Grand Teton mountains (p336)

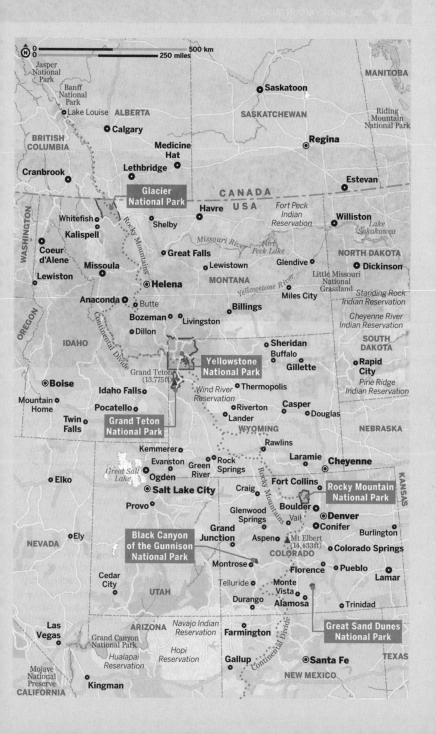

PATRICK LIENIN/GETTY IMAGES ©

Black Canyon of the Gunnison National Park

The Black Canyon is the inverse geographic feature of the Rockies – a yawning chasm etched out over millions of years by the Gunnison River and volcanic uplift. Here a dark, narrow gash above the Gunnison leads down a 2000ft chasm as eerie as it is spectacular.

No other canyon in America combines the narrow openings, sheer walls and dizzying depths of the Black Canyon, and a peek over the edge evokes a sense of awe (or vertigo). In just 48 canyon miles, the Gunnison River loses more elevation than the entire 1500-mile Mississippi. This fast-moving water, carrying rock and debris, is powerfully erosive.

Hiking

Short rim trails branch out from the **South Rim Visitor Center**, which has maps and information on additional hiking trails. See rangers here for a backcountry permit if you want to descend one of the South Rim's three demanding unmarked routes to the infrequently visited riverside campsites.

Great For...

State
Colorado

Entrance Fee
7-day pass per vehicle/pedestrian
$20/10

Area
48 sq miles

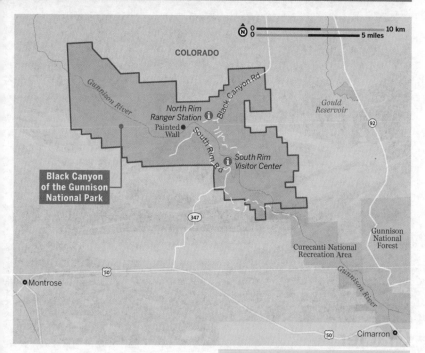

Fishing

A Colorado fishing license is required and bait fishing is not allowed – only lures and flies. If caught, all rainbow trout must be released, and a limit of four brown trout per person per day (with a bag limit of eight) applies. Fishing within 200 yards of the Crystal Dam is prohibited.

A free backcountry permit must be obtained from the South Rim Visitor Center or the North Rim Ranger Station.

South Rim Road

This 6-mile road visits 11 overlooks at the edge of the canyon, some reached via short trails up to 1.5 miles long (round-trip). At the narrowest part of Black Canyon, Chasm View is 1100ft across yet 1800ft deep. Rock climbers are frequently seen on the opposing North Wall. Colorado's highest cliff face is the 2300ft Painted Wall. ■

Essential Information

The **South Rim Visitor Center** (☑970-249-1915, 800-873-0244; www.nps.gov/blca; South Rim Dr; ☺8am-6pm late May-early Sep, 8:30am-4pm late Sep-early May) is located 2 miles past the park entrance on South Rim Dr. The more remote **North Rim Ranger Station** (North Rim; ☺8:30am-4pm, closed mid-Nov–mid-Apr) is accessed via Hwy 92 from Delta.

Access the park with a private vehicle. The park is 12 miles east of the US 550 junction with US 50. Exit at Hwy 347 and head north for 7 miles.

Glacier National Park

Few places on earth are as magnificent and pristine as Glacier. Protected in 1910 during the first flowering of the American conservationist movement, Glacier ranks with Yellowstone, Yosemite and the Grand Canyon among the United States' most astounding natural wonders.

Great For...

State
Montana

Entrance Fee
7-day pass per vehicle $35

Area
1489 sq miles

The glacially carved remnants of an ancient thrust fault have left a brilliant landscape of towering snowcapped pinnacles laced with plunging waterfalls and glassy turquoise lakes. The mountains are surrounded by dense forests, which host a virtually intact pre-Columbian ecosystem. Grizzly bears still roam in abundance and smart park management has kept the place accessible and authentically wild.

Glacier is renowned for its historic 'parkitecture' lodges, the spectacular Going-to-the-Sun Rd and 740 miles of hiking trails. These all put visitors within easy reach of the wild and astonishing landscapes found at the crown of the continent.

❶ Logan Pass

Perched above the tree line, atop the wind-lashed Continental Divide, and blocked by snow for most of the year, 6646ft (2026m) Logan Pass – named for William R Logan,

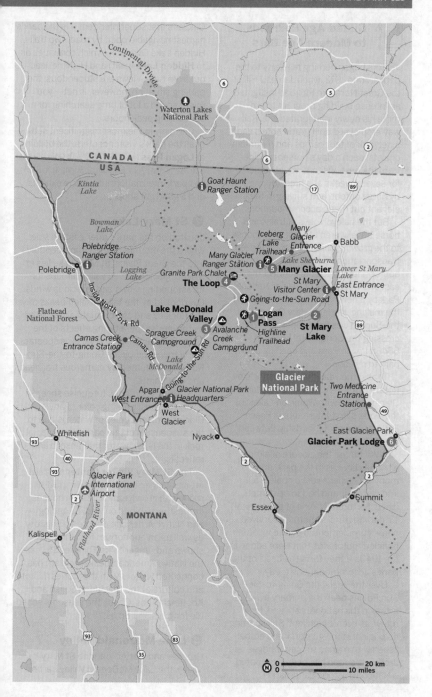

Gilded-Age Railroads to Modern Age Cars

Visitors began coming regularly to the park around 1912, when James J Hill of the Great Northern Railroad instigated an intense building program to promote his newly inaugurated line. Railway employees built grand hotels and a network of tent camps and mountain chalets, each a day's horseback ride from the next. Visitors would come for several weeks at a time, touring by horse or foot, and staying in these elegant but rustic accommodations.

But the halcyon days of trains and horse travel weren't to last. In response to the growing popularity of motorized transportation, federal funds were appropriated in 1921 to connect the east and west sides of Glacier National Park by a new road. Over a decade in the making, the legendary Going-to-the-Sun Rd was finally opened in 1932, crossing the Continental Divide at 6646ft Logan Pass and opening up the park to millions.

That same year, thanks to efforts by Rotary clubs in Alberta and Montana, Glacier joined with Waterton Lakes in the world's first International Peace Park, a symbol of friendship between the USA and Canada.

WWII forced the closure of almost all hotel services in the park, and many of Glacier's rustic chalets fell into disrepair and had to be demolished. Fortunately, nine of the original 13 'parkitecture' structures survived and – complemented by two wood-paneled motor inns that were added in the 1940s – they form the basis of the park's accommodations today.

Over the years, the Going-to-the-Sun Rd has been the primary travel artery in the national park and, for many, its scenic highlight. Still sporting its original stone guardrail and embellished with myriad tunnels, bridges and arches, the road has been designated a National Historic Landmark.

Glacier's first superintendent – is the park's highest navigable point by road. Two trails, Hidden Lake Overlook (which continues on to **Hidden Lake** itself) and Highline, lead out from here. Views are stupendous; the parking situation, however, is not – you might spend a lot of time searching for a spot during peak hours.

Certainly in the most magnificent setting of all the park's visitor centers, the building at **Logan Pass** (☏406-888-7800; Going-to-the-Sun Rd; ◷9am-7pm Jun-Aug, 9:30am-4pm Sep) has park information, interactive exhibits and a good gift shop.

❷ St Mary Lake

Located on the park's drier eastern side, where the mountains melt imperceptibly into the Great Plains, St Mary Lake lies in a deep, glacier-carved valley famous for its astounding views and ferocious winds. Overlooked by the tall, chiseled peaks of the Rockies and still dramatically scarred by the landscape-altering effects of the 2006 Red Eagle Fire, the valley is spectacularly traversed by the Going-to-the-Sun Rd and punctuated by numerous trailheads and viewpoints.

St Mary's gorgeous turquoise sheen, easily the most striking color of any of Glacier's major bodies of water, is due to the suspension of tiny particles of glacial rock in the lake's water that absorb and reflect light.

The **St Mary Visitor Center** (east end of Going-to-the-Sun Rd; ◷8am-6pm mid-Jun–mid-Aug, 8am-5pm early Jun & Sep) houses interesting exhibits on wildlife, geology and Native American culture and history, as well as an auditorium featuring slide shows and ranger talks. For over 35 years, the Native America Speaksprogram has connected visitors with the stories, history and culture of the Blackfeet, Salish and Kootenai tribes. Check the seasonal schedule for days and times.

❸ Lake McDonald Valley

Greener and wetter than the St Mary Valley, the Lake McDonald Valley harbors the park's largest lake and some of its densest and oldest temperate rainforest. Crisscrossed by a number of popular trails, including the wheelchair-accessible, 0.8-mile Trail of the Cedars, the area is popular with drive-in campers, who frequent the Sprague Creek and Avalanche Creek campgrounds, as well as winter cross-country skiers who use McDonald Creek and the Going-to-the-Sun Rd as seasonal skiing trails.

❹ The Loop

This sharp hairpin bend acts as a popular trailhead for hikers descending from the Granite Park Chalet and the Highline Trail. Consequently, it's normally chock-a-block with cars. The slopes nearby were badly scarred by the 2003 Trapper Fire, but nature and small shrubs are beginning to reappear.

❺ Many Glacier

Anchored by the historic 1915 Many Glacier Lodge and sprinkled with more lakes than glaciers, this picturesque valley on the park's east side has some tremendous

Red Bus Tours

Glacier's stylish red 'Jammer' buses (so-called because drivers had to 'jam' hard on the gears) are iconic park symbols. Guided tours take visitors along a dozen routes, from 3-hour trips to 8-hour journeys.

The open-roof buses were introduced on the Going-to-the-Sun Rd between 1936 and 1939. They have thus been serving the park loyally for nearly 80 years, save for a two-year sabbatical in 1999 when the fleet was reconfigured by the Ford Motor Company. After an extensive makeover, they are safer, sturdier and 93% more environmentally friendly (now running off propane gas). In 2015, the company introduced a bus outfitted to serve passengers with disabilities.

The drivers provide excellent information about what you are seeing during the drive, though the four-person seats can be cramped and you may not have the best views from the middle.

Hidden Lake

COLE STECYK/SHUTTERSTOCK ©

hikes, some of which link to the Going-to-the-Sun Rd. A favorite is the 9.4-mile (return) **Iceberg Lake Trail**, a steep but rewarding jaunt through flower meadows and pine forest to an iceberg-infested lake.

⑥ Glacier Park Lodge

Set in attractive, perfectly manicured flower-filled grounds overlooking Montana's oldest golf course, this historic 1914 **lodge** (⌕406-226-5600; www.glacierparkinc. com; r $169-256; ⊙Jun-Sep; 🛜🏊) 🐾 was built in the classic national park tradition with a splendid open-plan lobby supported by lofty 900-year-old Douglas fir timbers (imported from Washington state). Eye-catching Native American artwork adorns the communal areas, and a full-sized tipi is wedged incongruously onto a 2nd-floor balcony.

Top left: 'Jammer' bus; Top right: View along Going-to-the-Sun Road; Bottom: St Mary Lake

Traffic-Free
Going-to-the-Sun Road

Imagine traveling up the mind-blowingly beautiful **Going-to-the-Sun Road** (www.nps.gov/glac/planyourvisit/goingtothesunroad.htm; ⊘mid-Jun–late Sep) with not a single car in sight. You can, but you have to work for it. While crews are plowing the pass in the spring, hikers and bicyclists can ride from Avalanche Creek toward Logan Pass as far as the road has been cleared. It's an excellent adventure that is becoming increasingly popular – but somehow we don't see too many bicycles ever being a problem.

Hike Hidden Lake Overlook Trail

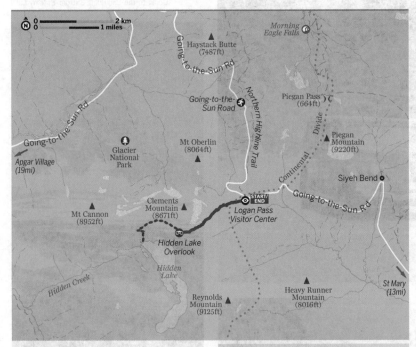

For many Glacier visitors this relatively straightforward hike is the one occasion when they step out of their cars and take a sniff of the sweet-scented alpine air for which the area is famous.

Starting at Logan Pass Visitor Center, the hike ascends gradually along a raised boardwalk (with steps) through expansive alpine meadows replete with monkeyflower and pink laurel. Slippery melting snowfields might add a challenge, but, rain or shine, this trail is a hit with everyone.

After about 0.6 miles, the boardwalk gives way to a gravel-dirt path. If the snow has melted, the diversity of grasses and wildflowers in the meadows around you is breathtaking. Resident trees include Engelmann spruce, subalpine fir and whitebark pine. Hoary marmots, ground squirrels and mountain goats are not shy along this trail. The elusive ptarmigan, whose brown feathers turn white in winter, also lives nearby.

Duration 2 hours round-trip

Distance 3 miles

Difficulty Easy–moderate

Elevation Change 494ft

Start & Finish Logan Pass Visitor Center

Nearest Town/Junction Logan Pass

Up-close mountain views include Clements Mountain to the north and Reynolds Mountain in the southeast.

About 300yd before the overlook, you will cross the Continental Divide – probably without realizing it – before your first stunning glimpse of the otherwordly, deep-blue **Hidden Lake**, bordered by mountain peaks and rocky cliffs. Look out for glistening Sperry Glacier visible to the south.

Hearty souls can continue on to Hidden Lake via a 1.5-mile trail from the overlook, steeply descending 765ft.

Hike Highline Trail

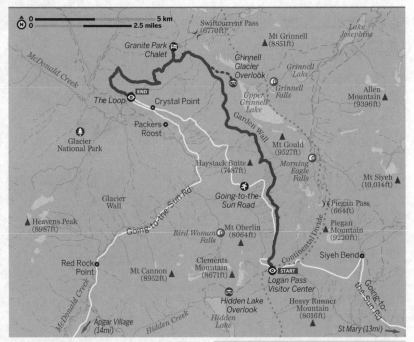

A Glacier classic, the Highline Trail cuts across the famous Garden Wall, a sharp, glacier-carved ridge that forms part of the Continental Divide.

Cutting immediately into the side of the mountain (a garden-hose-like rope is tethered to the rockwall for those with vertigo), the trail presents stunning early views of the Going-to-the-Sun Rd and snowcapped Heavens Peak. Look out for the toy-sized red 'jammer' buses motoring up the valley below and the white foaming waters of 500ft **Bird Woman Falls** opposite.

After its vertiginous start, the trail is flat for 1.8 miles before gently ascending to a ridge that connects Haystack Butte with Mt Gould at the 3.5-mile mark. From here it's fairly flat as you bisect the mountainside on your way toward the Granite Park Chalet. After approximately 6.8 miles, with the chalet in sight, a spur path (on your right) offers the option of climbing up less than

Duration 7 hours one-way

Distance 11.6 miles

Difficulty Moderate

Elevation Change 830ft

Start Logan Pass Visitor Center

Finish The Loop

Nearest Town/Junction Logan Pass

1 mile to the **Grinnell Glacier Overlook** for a peek over the Continental Divide. The Granite Park Chalet appears at around 7.6 miles, providing a welcome haven for parched throats and tired feet.

From here you have three options: retrace your steps back to Logan Pass; head for Swiftcurrent Pass and the Many Glacier Valley; or descend 4 miles to the Loop, where you can pick up a shuttle bus to all points on the Going-to-the-Sun Rd.

Hike Sun Point to Virginia Falls

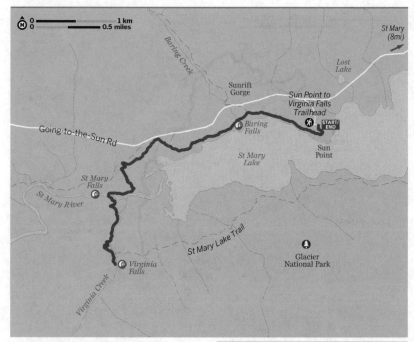

Handily served by the free park shuttle, the myriad trailheads along the eastern side of the Going-to-the-Sun Rd offer plenty of short interlinking hikes, a number of which can be pooled together to make up a decent ramble.

Starting at the Sun Point shuttle stop, track down a 0.25-mile trail to a rocky (and often windy) **overlook** perched above St Mary Lake.

Take the path west through sun-flecked forest along the lake toward shady **Baring Falls**, at the 0.6-mile mark, for respite from the sun and/or wind. Cross the river and continue on the opposite bank to link up with the busy St Mary Falls Trail that joins from the right. Undemanding switchbacks lead up through the trees to the valley's

Duration 4 hours round-trip

Distance 7 miles

Difficulty Easy

Elevation Change 300ft

Start & Finish Sun Point shuttle stop

Nearest Town/Junction St Mary

most picturesque falls, set amid colorful foliage on St Mary River. Beyond, the trail branches along Virginia Creek, past a narrow gorge, to mist-shrouded **Virginia Falls** at the foot of a hanging valley.

Retrace your steps to Sun Point for the full-length hike or shortcut to St Mary Falls or Sunrift Gorge shuttle stops.

Drive Going-to-the-Sun Road

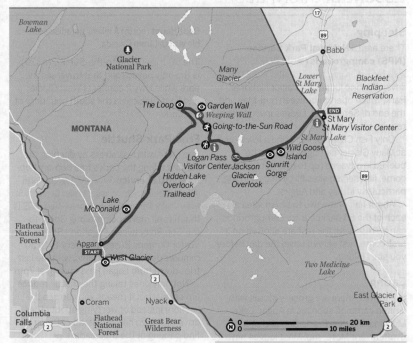

This is one of the most spectacular drives in the US. The road starts at Glacier NP's western entrance before tracking northeast along **Lake McDonald**. The valley here is lush, though a quick glance through the trees will show evidence of the 2003 Robert Fire on the opposite side of the water.

After following McDonald Creek for about 10 miles, the road begins its long, slow ascent to Logan Pass with a sharp turn to the southeast at the **Loop**, a famous hiking trailhead and the start of an increasingly precipitous climb toward the summit. Views here are unfailingly sublime as the road cuts precariously into the **Garden Wall**, an 8999ft granite ridge that delineates the west and east regions of the park along the Continental Divide. Look out for Bird Woman Falls, stunning even from a distance, and the more in-your-face **Weeping Wall**, as the gaping chasm to your right grows ever deeper.

Duration 3 hours (with stops)

Distance 53 miles

Start West Entrance, Apgar Village

Finish St Mary Visitor Center

Nearest Town/Junction West Glacier

Stop at lofty **Logan Pass** to browse the visitor center or to stretch your legs amid alpine meadows on the popular Hidden Lake Overlook Trail.

Descending eastwards, keep an eye out for majestic Going-to-the-Sun Mountain, to the north. At the 36-mile mark, you can pull over to spy one of only 25 remaining park glaciers at **Jackson Glacier Overlook**, while a few clicks further on, you can sample narrow **Sunrift Gorge** near the shores of St Mary Lake. **Wild Goose Island**, a photogenic stub of land, is situated in the center of the lake.

Essential Information

Sleeping

There are 13 **National Park Service (NPS) campgrounds** (📞518-885-3639; www.recreation.gov; tent & RV sites $10-23) and seven historic lodges in Glacier National Park, which operate between mid-May and the end of September. Lodges invariably require reservations.

Only Fish Creek, St Mary and a few sites at Many Glacier campgrounds can be booked in advance (up to five months). First-come, first served sites fill by mid-morning, particularly in July and August.

About half of the two to seven sites at each of the 65 backcountry campgrounds can be reserved; the rest are allotted on a first-come, first served basis the day before you start hiking.

Eating

In summer, there are grocery stores with limited camping supplies in Apgar, Lake McDonald Lodge, Rising Sun and at the Swiftcurrent Motor Inn. Most lodges have on-site restaurants. Dining options in West Glacier and St Mary offer mainly hearty hiking fare.

If cooking at a campground or picnic area, be sure to take appropriate bear-safety precautions and do not leave food unattended.

Orientation

Glacier's 1489 sq miles are divided into several regions, with distinct characters:

North Fork (northwest) A seldom-visited area with the isolated settlement of Polebridge.

Lake McDonald Valley (west) The park's largest lake has Apgar Village, Lake McDonald Lodge, and the west end of Going-to-the-Sun Rd.

Two Medicine (southeast) A less-visited lake area that was once the center of east-side activity.

St Mary (east) The eastern end of Going-to-the-Sun Rd has multiple hiking trails.

Many Glacier (northeast) Towering peaks box in a lake and the park's most dramatic lodge location.

Goat Haunt (north) A hikers' paradise accessible via boat from Canada.

The 50-mile Going-to-the-Sun Rd (p329) is the only paved road that traverses the park while Hwy 2 connects West Glacier and East Glacier via the south boundary of the park.

Free Park Shuttle

See more with less stress by ditching the car and taking the park's free hop-on, hop-off **shuttle service** (www.nps.gov/glac/plan yourvisit/shuttles.htm; Apgar Visitor Center to St Mary Visitor Center; ⊙9am-7pm Jul-Aug) 🏷️ FREE that hits all major points along Going-to-the-Sun Rd between Apgar and St Mary Visitor Centers. Buses run every 15 to 30 minutes depending on traffic, with the last trips down from Logan Pass leaving at 7pm.

Not only does taking the shuttle reduce emissions, but it means you can see the scenery instead of worrying about other drivers, and go hiking instead of trying to find parking at the trailheads.

Getting There & Away

Glacier Park International Airport (FCA; 📞406-257-5994; www.iflyglacier.com; 4170 Hwy 2 East) in Kalispell has year-round service to Salt Lake, Minneapolis, Denver, Seattle and Las Vegas, and seasonal service to Atlanta, Oakland, LA, Chicago and Portland.

The **Glacier Park Express** (📞406-253-9192; www.bigmtncommercial.org; Whitefish Library; adult/child round-trip $10/5; ⊙Jul-early Sep) shuttle connects Whitefish to West Glacier.

Amtrak's *Empire Builder* stops daily at **West Glacier** (www.amtrak.com; ⊙year-round) and **East Glacier Park** (⊙Apr-Oct). Xanterra provides a shuttle ($10, 10 to 20 minutes) from West Glacier to its lodges on the west end, and Glacier Park, Inc. shuttles (from $15, one hour) connect East Glacier Park to St Mary. ∎

Top left: Lake McDonald; Top right: Black bear; Bottom: Overlooking Hidden Lake

RIFE STOCK/SHUTTERSTOCK ©

Grand Teton National Park

Snake River

Awesome in their grandeur, the Tetons have captivated the imagination from the moment humans laid eyes on them. This wilderness is home to bear, moose and elk in number, and played a fundamental role in the history of American alpine climbing.

Great For...

State
Wyoming

Entrance Fee
7-day pass per vehicle/pedestrian
$35/20

Area
484 sq miles

❶ Climbing Grand Teton

The crowning glory of the park, dagger-edged Grand Teton (13,770ft) has taunted many a would-be mountaineer. The first white people to claim to have summited were James Stevenson and Nathanial Langford, part of the 1872 Hayden Geological Survey. However, when William Owen, Franklin Spalding and two others arrived at the top in 1898, they found no evidence of a prior expedition. So they chiseled their names in a boulder, claimed the first ascent, and ignited a dispute that persists today.

Today, climbers speckle the mountain's multiple routes throughout the summer season, and even very fit nonclimbers can reach the summit with a little training and a competent guide. The most popular route requires a combination of scrambling, easy 5th-class climbing and a few rappels, but should not be taken lightly. The park rescues 15 to 20 people a year, and fatalities are not uncommon.

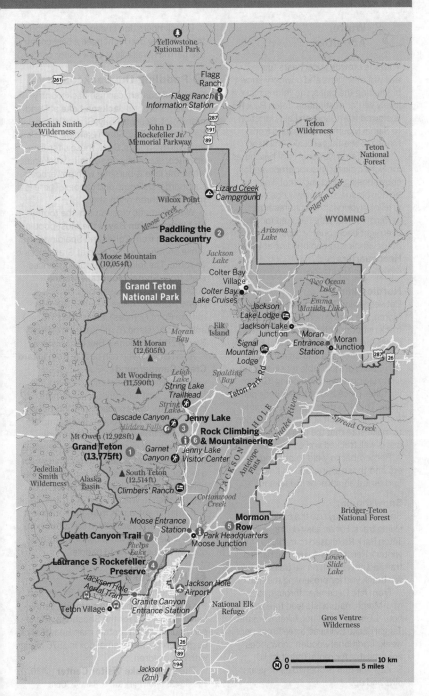

Yellowstone
National Park

Flagg
Ranch

261

Flagg Ranch
Information Station

Jedediah Smith
Wilderness

John D
Rockefeller Jr
Memorial Parkway

287

191

89

Teton
Wilderness

Teton
National
Forest

Wilcox Point

Moose Creek

Lizard Creek
Campground

Arizona
Lake

WYOMING

Pilgrim Creek

Paddling the
Backcountry 2

Jackson
Lake

Moose Mountain
(10,054ft)

Grand Teton
National Park

Colter Bay
Village

Colter Bay
Lake Cruises

Moran
Bay

Elk
Island

Two Ocean
Lake

Emma
Matilda Lake

Mt Moran
(12,605ft)

Jackson
Lake Lodge

Jackson Lake
Junction

Moran
Entrance
Station

Moran
Junction

Mt Woodring
(11,590ft)

Leigh
Lake

String Lake
Trailhead

Spalding
Bay

Signal
Mountain
Lodge

Teton Park Rd

287

26

Cascade Canyon

Midden Falls

String
Lake

Jenny Lake

Rock Climbing
& Mountaineering 6

Mt Owen (12,928ft)

Grand Teton
(13,775ft) 1

Garnet
Canyon

Jenny Lake
Visitor Center

JACKSON HOLE

Snake River

Spread Creek

Jedediah
Smith
Wilderness

Alaska
Basin

South Teton
(12,514ft)

Climbers' Ranch

Cottonwood
Creek

Antelope Flats

Mormon
Row 5

Bridger-Teton
National Forest

Death Canyon Trail 7

Moose Entrance
Station

Park Headquarters
Moose Junction

Laurance S Rockefeller
Preserve 4

Phelps
Lake

Lower
Slide
Lake

Jackson Hole
Aerial Tram

Teton Village

Granite Canyon
Entrance Station

Jackson Hole
Airport

National Elk
Refuge

Gros Ventre
Wilderness

26

89

194

Jackson
(2mi)

N

0   10 km
0   5 miles

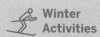

Winter Activities

With the crowds gone, bears tucked away in their dens and powdery snow blanketing the pines, the Tetons make a lovely winter destination. Teton Park Rd is plowed from Jackson Lake Junction to Signal Mountain Lodge and from Moose to the Taggart Lake Trailhead.

Grand Teton National Park brochures for Nordic skiing (also appropriate for snowshoeing) and snowmobiling can be downloaded from www.nps.gov/grte/planyourvisit/brochures.htm.

Permits (free) are required for all overnight backcountry trips. Get one at the administration building at **Park Headquarters** (☎307-739-3300; ⊙9am-4:30pm Mon-Fri) in Moose.

Nordic Skiing
Between mid- December and mid-March, the park grooms 15 miles of track right under the Tetons' highest peaks, between the Taggart and Bradley Lakes parking area and Signal Mountain. Lanes are available for ski touring, skate skiing and snowshoeing. Grooming takes place two or three times per week. The NPS does not always mark every trail: consult at the ranger station to make sure that the trail you plan to use is well tracked and easy to follow.

Remember to yield to passing skiers and those skiing downhill. You can find rental equipment in Jackson.

Snowshoeing
Snowshoers may use the park's Nordic skiing trails. For an easy outing, try Teton Park Rd (closed to traffic in winter). Remember to use the hardpack trail and never walk on ski trails – skiers will thank you for preserving the track!

From late December through to mid-March, naturalists lead free two-hour, 1.5-mile snowshoe hikes from the Taggart Lake trailhead three times per week. Traditional wooden snowshoes are available for rental (adult/child $5/2). The tour is open to eight-year-olds and up.

Day climbers don't need to register, but those staying overnight need a backcountry-use permit (available at park visitor centers).

❷ Paddling the Backcountry
Overnight boaters can use backcountry campsites around **Jackson Lake** at Deadman Point, Bearpaw Bay, Grassy Island, Little Mackinaw Bay, South Landing, Elk Island and Warm Springs. Book these sites in advance, especially on summer weekends, when the lake is bursting with powerboats, sailboards, sailboats and canoes. There is a maximum three-night stay.

With dramatic close-ups of the toothy Mt Moran, **Moran Bay** is the most popular destination from Colter and Spalding Bays. While boating you can stop at Grassy Island en route. The following sample distances start from **Signal Mountain Marina** (☎307-543-2831; www.signalmountainlodge.com; ⊙7am-7:30pm mid-May–mid-Sep): Hermitage Point (2 miles), Elk Island (3 miles) and Grassy Island (6 miles); from Colter Bay to Little Mackinaw Bay it's 1.5 miles.

Alternatively, you can paddle from **Lizard Creek Campground** (☎800-672-6012; www.signalmountainlodge.com; off N Park Rd; sites $30; ⊙mid-Jun–early Sep) to remote backcountry trails on Jackson's northwest shore. Wilcox Point backcountry campsite (1.25 miles from Lizard Creek) provides backcountry access to Webb Canyon along the Moose Basin Divide Trail (20 miles). For a longer intermediate-level trip, paddle the twists and turns of the **Snake River** from Flagg Ranch to Wilcox Point or Lizard Creek.

Predominant winds from the southwest can be strong, especially in the afternoon, when waves can swamp canoes. Morning is usually the best time to paddle.

❸ Jenny Lake
The scenic heart of the Grand Tetons and the epicenter of the area's crowds, Jenny Lake was named for the Shoshone wife of early guide and mountain man Beaver Dick Leigh. Jenny died of smallpox in 1876 along with her children.

The **Jenny Lake Visitor Center** (☎307-739-3343; Teton Park Rd; ⊙8am-4:30pm

Sep-May, to 7pm Jun-Aug) is worth a visit for its geological displays and 3D map of Jackson Hole. The cabin was once in a different location as the Crandall photo studio.

The Jenny Lake area is finishing a massive $19 million restoration to trails and infrastructure. The five-year project unveils in 2019.

From the visitor center, a network of trails leads clockwise around the lake for 2.5 miles to **Hidden Falls** and then continues for a short uphill run to fine views at **Inspiration Point**. Once you're here, it's worth continuing up **Cascade Canyon** with a good supply of water for more excellent views. From here, you can return the way you came or continue clockwise 1.5 miles to the **String Lake Trailhead** to make a 3.8-mile circle around the lake. If you're walking the Jenny Lake Trail in the early morning or late afternoon, detour approximately 15 minutes (about 0.5 miles) from the visitor center to **Moose Ponds** for a good chance of spotting moose.

Alternatively, **Jenny Lake Boating** (%307-734-9227; www.jennylakeboating.com; round-trip shuttle adult/child 2-11yr $15/8, scenic cruise $19/11; h7am-7pm Jun-late Sep) runs shuttles across Jenny Lake between the east-shore boat dock near Jenny Lake Visitor Center and the west-shore dock near Hidden Falls, offering quick (12-minute) access to Inspiration Point and the Cascade Canyon Trail. Shuttles run every 15 minutes, but expect long waits for return shuttles between 4pm and 6pm.

❹ Laurance S Rockefeller Preserve

For solitude coupled with the most stunning views that don't include the Grand, visitors should check out this newer section of Grand Teton National Park. Once the JY Ranch, an exclusive Rockefeller family retreat, these 3100 acres around Phelps Lake were donated in full by Laurance S Rockefeller in 2001. His grandfather, John D Rockefeller, had been an early park advocate, purchasing the first tracts of land to donate in 1927. Despite strong local opposition, by 1949 he had donated some 33,000 acres of former ranchland to Grand Teton National Park.

Jenny Lake

KRISHNA WU/SHUTTERSTOCK ©

With this sector, Laurance Rockefeller's vision was to create a space of refuge and renewal. In contrast to other visitor centers, the beautiful **Laurance S Rockefeller Preserve Center** (☎307-739-3654; www.nps.gov/grte/planyourvisit/lsrpvc.htm; Moose–Wilson Rd; ◷9am-5pm Jun-Sep) ✔ is a meditative experience. Sparely furnished and certified by LEED (Leadership in Energy and Environmental Design), the green building features quotes from naturalists and writers etched into walls, giant picture windows to admire the views, and a library with leather armchairs and books on conservation and nature to browse. The center also hosts a full menu of ranger programs.

❺ Mormon Row

This is possibly the most photographed spot in the park – and for good reason. The aged wooden barns and fence rails make a quintessential pastoral scene, perfectly framed by the imposing bulk of the Tetons. The barns and houses were built in the 1890s by Mormon settlers, who farmed the fertile alluvial soil irrigated by miles of hand-dug ditches.

Top: Hikers in Grand Teton; Bottom: Death Canyon

Just north of Moose Junction, head east on Antelope Flats Rd for 1.5 miles to a three-way intersection and parking area. Landmark buildings are north and south of the intersection.

⑥ Rock Climbing & Mountaineering

The Tetons are known for excellent short-route rock climbs, as well as classic longer routes to summits such as Grant Teton, Mt Moran and Mt Owen (12,928ft), all best attempted with an experienced guide.

Jenny Lake Ranger Station (☑307-739-3343; off Teton Park Rd, South Jenny Lake Junction; ☺8am-6pm Jun-Aug) is the go-to office for climbing information. It sells climbing guidebooks, provides information and has a board showing campsite availability in **Garnet Canyon**, the gateway to climbs including the technical ascent of Grand Teton.

An excellent resource and the spot to meet outdoor partners in crime, the member-supported American Alpine Club's **Climbers' Ranch** (☑307-733-7271; www.americanalpineclub.org/grand-teton-climbers-ranch; End Highlands Rd; dm $27; ☺Jun-Sep) has been a climbing institution since 1970. It also offers lodging.

⑦ Death Canyon Trail

Death Canyon is one of our favorite hikes – both for the challenge and the astounding scenery. The trail ascends a mile to the Phelps Lake overlook before dropping down into the valley bottom and following Death Canyon.

For a tougher add-on with impossibly beautiful views, turn right at the historic ranger cabin onto the Alaska Basin Trail and climb another 3000ft to Static Peak Divide (10,792ft) – the highest trail in Grand Teton National Park.

Drive Hole-in-One

PAUL BRADY PHOTOGRAPHY/SHUTTERSTOCK ©

*A scenic drive through sagebrush flats
and forest with picturesque barns and
Teton panoramas.*

You could say Gros Ventre Butte ruined it
for Jackson – there are no Teton views from
the park's main hub due to the blockage
created by this hump. But this driving tour,
not suitable for RVs or other oversize vehicles, is just the remedy.

Head out of Jackson on Hwy 191. First
stop: the **National Museum of Wildlife
Art** (☑307-733-5771; www.wildlifeart.org; 2820
Rungius Road; adult/child $14/6; ☺9am-5pm
daily May-Oct, reduced hours rest of year). You
may ask, why do this when you have the
real thing? Just look. The way these masters envisioned this landscape will change
the way you see it yourself.

Continue north on Hwy 191. At the Gros
Ventre Junction, take a right and drive

Duration 1 hour plus stops

Distance 40-mile loop

Start & Finish Jackson

along Gros Ventre Rd, skirting the **Gros
Ventre River**, lined with cottonwoods,
juniper, spruce and willows. The river ecology contrasts sharply with the dry sagebrush flats to its north, where pronghorn
can often be seen, bounding at speeds
up to 60mph. At the next junction, take a
left onto Antelope Flats Rd to drive north
on **Mormon Row**, a picturesque strip that
includes a much-photographed rambling
barn (pictured). At the end of the row, loop
left on **Antelope Flats Road**, where bison
and pronghorn roam the grasslands. It
soon meets Hwy 191: go left, then right at
Moose Junction.

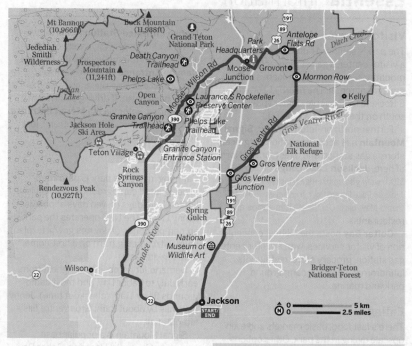

Before the park entrance gate, take a left onto narrow **Moose–Wilson Road**. You will need to squeeze onto the shoulder for oncoming traffic: this is why oversize vehicles are explicitly banned. Mind the blind curves, twisting through dense foliage. You will pass turnoffs for Death Canyon trailhead, Phelps Lake trailhead (near the Laurance S Rockefeller Preserve Center) and Granite Canyon trailhead. If you're keen on a swim, these trails will take you to **Phelps Lake**; it's a 30- to 45-minute walk along the Woodland Trail from Phelps Lake trailhead. This short section of the road is unpaved but even.

The road spills out near **Teton Village**, where you can take a gondola (p347) to the top for views or grab lunch. Follow the Moose–Wilson Rd south to Hwy 22. Go left to return to Jackson.

🚲 Cycle Hole-in-One

Duration 5 hours

Distance 33-mile loop

Difficulty Moderate

Elevation Change 340ft

Start in Jackson and head north on Hwy 191 to **Moose Junction**. Go left here and left again onto the narrow and winding Moose–Wilson Rd. While it is paved, there are some deep potholes, so stay alert. Horned owls nest along this section.

Approaching **Teton Village**, the road becomes smooth and stays that way. Continue on the flats of Moose–Wilson Rd until you hit a junction with Hwy 22; turn left here for Jackson. There will be a lot of car traffic on Hwy 22.

An early start will help you avoid traffic on the narrows of Moose–Wilson Rd.

Essential Information

Visitor Service Hubs

The park's southern hub is **Moose**, with a visitor center, a gas station, accommodations, restaurants, groceries and equipment rental. The nearby Laurance S Rockefeller Preserve Center (p340) is south on the Moose–Wilson Rd.

Further north on Teton Park Rd, **Signal Mountain** has accommodations, a grocery store, a gas station and a restaurant. North of here, **Jackson Lake Lodge** (☑307-543-3100; www.gtlc.com/lodges/jackson-lake-lodge; Jackson Lake Lodge Rd; r & cottages $330-449; ☺mid-May–early Oct; ☎☀) has shops and restaurants.

Colter Bay hosts the highest concentration of visitor services, with a visitor center, gas station, grocery store, restaurants, laundromat, showers, campground, RV park and marina.

Eating

There's fast food, basic markets and even upscale dining in the park. Other options include taking a Jackson Lake dinner or breakfast **cruise** (☑307-543-2811; www.gtlc.com/activities/jackson-lake-boat-cruises; Colter Bay Marina; cruise adult/child 3-11yr $34/14; ☺late May-late Sep) or packing a picnic basket. **Dornan's Trading Post** (☑307-733-2415; www.dornans.com; ☺8am-8pm) in Moose offers an impressive selection of wines. Campground diners must store food in bear-proof boxes or cars – never leave it unattended and always dispose of food properly.

Getting There & Away

Jackson Hole Airport (JAC; ☑307-733-7682; www.jacksonholeairport.com; 1250 E Airport Rd) lies inside the park's boundaries and sees a steady stream of traffic. Currently, there is no regular shuttle service through the park, though several companies in Jackson provide guided tours.

The park begins 4.5 miles north of Jackson. There are three entrance stations. The easiest to access from Jackson is the

Moose Entrance Station (South Entrance; Teton Park Rd; ☺hours vary), west of Moose Junction. From Teton Village, the **Granite Canyon Entrance Station** (Southwest Entrance; Moose-Wilson Rd; ☺hours vary) is a mile or so north. If driving south from Yellowstone, enter via the **Moran Entrance** (North Entrance; Hwy 287; ☺hours vary), just north of Moran Junction.

Sleeping

Camping inside the park is permitted in designated campgrounds only and is limited to 14 days (seven days at popular Jenny Lake). The NPS operates the park's six campgrounds (www.nps.gov/grte/planyourvisit/camping.htm) on a first-come, first-served basis.

Demand for campsites is highest from early July to Labor Day, and most campgrounds fill by 11am (checkout time). Jenny Lake fills by about 8am; Gros Ventre fills later, if at all.

Signal Mountain is a popular base because of its central location. Colter Bay, Jenny Lake, Lizard Creek and Signal Mountain have tent-only sites reserved for walk-in hikers and ride-in cyclists ($11 to $12).

Lodging should be reserved as far in advance as possible, especially for peak-season dates. Grand Teton Lodge Company accepts reservations for the following season starting November 1. Most campgrounds are first-come, first-served but some allow a limited number of reservations. See websites for details.

The park's concessionaires:

Grand Teton Lodge Company (GTLC; ☑307-543-3100; www.gtlc.com)

Spur Ranch Log Cabins (☑307-733-2522; www.dornans.com; Moose; cabins $250-350; ☺closed Nov & Apr)

Signal Mountain Lodge (☑307-543-2831; www.signalmtnlodge.com; Teton Park Rd; r $262-368, cabins $218-278, ste $367-408; ☺early May–mid-Oct; ☎)

Top left: Antelope Flats; Top right: Bald eagle; Bottom: Signal Mountain Lodge

CLASSIC HIKES

Teton Crest Trail

This classic route is one to remember. Dipping in and out of the neighboring Jedediah Smith Wilderness, the trail has numerous routes out – namely the canyons and passes that access it on either side. Hikers must arrange for a shuttle or have two cars to leave at the start and end points.

Duration 4 or 5 days

Distance 31.4 or 39.9 miles

Difficulty Moderate–difficult

Start String Lake trailhead

Finish Granite Canyon trailhead or Teton Village

Nearest Town/Junction North Jenny Lake Junction

DAY 1: String Lake trailhead to Holly Lake (5 hours, 6.2 miles)

From the String Lake parking lot, take the trail that curves south around String Lake. It climbs gently until the left-hand junction with Paintbrush Canyon, 1.6 miles in. This steep but moderate trail borders a stream flowing over granite boulders, passing through the Lower Paintbrush Camping Zone and some stock campsites. It climbs ever higher to reach an upper basin surrounded by snowy peaks. The first lake is unnamed; continue right of it to reach

Holly Lake (9424ft). There are two good shady designated campsites at the lake's southeast corner. If these sites are booked, camp in the Upper Paintbrush Canyon Camping Zone. For a great day hike, you can return via the same route (12.4 miles, 7 hours total), enjoying the lake views framed by the valley above.

DAY 2: Holly Lake to South Fork Cascade Camping Zone (time varies with conditions, 6.6 miles)

Day two takes you over a scree field to Paintbrush Divide. This section with loose boulders can be sketchy, so take it very slowly. Ice tools may be necessary, so check with rangers on conditions before heading out. Follow the divide down switchbacks to Lake Solitude (9035ft), until the Forks junction between the North and South Forks of Cascade Canyon. Here the trail branches up the South Fork to the South Fork Cascade Camping Zone (19 campsites).

Alternatively, you can start the hike from Jenny Lake, catching a boat shuttle across the lake to Inspiration Point and hiking up Cascade Creek Trail to spend the first night at the South Fork Cascade Camping Zone. With the boat shuttle, this 10.4-mile hike (2050ft elevation gain) shaves off a day. The hike may be longer, depending on your assigned campsite. Allow a minimum of seven hours.

DAY 3: South Fork Cascade Camping Zone to Alaska Basin (3–3½ hours, 6.1 miles)

The trail climbs up to **Avalanche Divide** junction: head right (southwest) to **Hurricane Pass** (10,372ft), which has unsurpassed views of the Grand, South and Middle Tetons. (An excursion from the Avalanche Divide junction leads 1.6 miles to the divide, a scenic overlook above Snowdrift Lake.) From the pass, the trail descends into the Jedediah Smith Wilderness, past

Sunset Lake, into the **Basin Lakes** of the Alaska Basin, where you'll find several popular campsites. No permits are needed here since you're outside the park, but you must camp at least 200ft from lakes and 150ft from streams.

DAY 4: Alaska Basin to Marion Lake (4½ hours, 8.2 miles)

The trail crosses South Fork Teton Creek on stepping stones and switchbacks up the Sheep Steps to the wide saddle of **Mt Meek Pass** (9718ft) to reenter the park. For the next 3 miles, the trail dips into the stunning plateau of **Death Canyon Shelf** and the camping zone. Past the turnoff to Death Canyon, it climbs to **Fox Creek Pass** (9560ft) and continues southwest over a vague saddle to **Marion Lake** and its designated campsites.

DAY 5: Marion Lake to Teton Village via Tram (5 hours, 6.5 miles to tram top)

The trail descends into the Upper Granite Canyon Camping Zone and continues past the Upper Granite Canyon patrol cabin to the junction with the Valley Trail. From here, head southeast to Teton Village, ascending the back side of the resort to take the **Jackson Hole Aerial Tram** (307-733-2292; adult/child $43/28, mountain-biking pass $37, descent free; 9am-5pm mid-May–early Oct), or continue east to the Granite Canyon trailhead (10.3 miles total). ∎

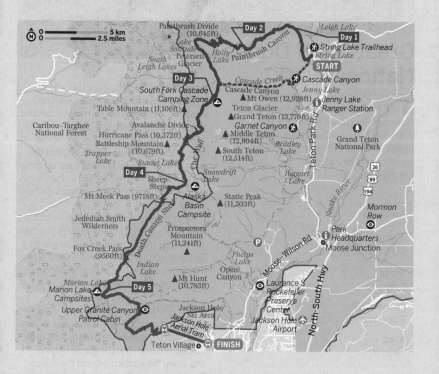

GALYNA ANDRUSHKO/SHUTTERSTOCK ©

Great Sand Dunes National Park

For all of Colorado's striking natural sights, the surreal Great Sand Dunes National Park, a veritable sea of sand bounded by jagged peaks and scrubby plains, is a place of stirring optical illusions where nature's magic is on full display.

Great For...

State
Colorado

Entrance Fee
7-day pass per vehicle $20

Area
55 sq miles

From the approach up Hwy 150, watch as the angles of sunlight make shifting shadows on the dunes; the most dramatic time is the day's end, when the hills come into high contrast as the sun drops low on the horizon. Hike past the edge of the dune field to see the shifting sand up close; the ceaseless wind works like a disconsolate sculptor, constantly amending the landscape.

Most visitors limit their activities to the area where Medano Creek divides the main dune mass from the towering Sangre de Cristo Mountains. The remaining 85% of the park's area is designated wilderness: not for the unfit or fainthearted.

Inner Tubing

One of the most curious spectacles in the entire park, the snowmelt **Medano Creek** flows down from the Sangre de Cristos and along the eastern edge of the dunes. Peak flow is usually in late May or early

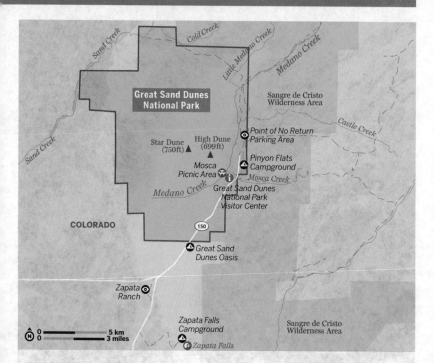

June, and the rippling water over the sand creates a temporary beach of sorts, which is extremely popular with families. In years when the water is high enough (check the park website for daily water-level reports; the level of late has been very low), children can even float down the creek on an inner tube, right along the dunes. The combination of the creek's appeal and the end of the school year means that this is the park's peak season.

Hiking

There are no trails through this expansive field of sand, but it's the star attraction for hikers. Two informal hikes afford excellent panoramic views of the dunes. The first is a hike to **High Dune** (699ft; strangely, not the highest dune in the park), which departs from a parking area just beyond the visitor center. It's about 2.5 miles out to the peak and back, but be warned: it's not easy. As you trudge along up the hills of sand, it feels like you're taking a half-step

back for every one forward. If you're up for it, try pushing on to the second worthy goal: just west of High Dune is **Star Dune** (755ft), the tallest in the park.

From the Great Sand Dunes National Park Visitor Center (p352), a short trail leads to the **Mosca Picnic Area** next to ankle-deep Medano Creek, which you must ford (when the creek is running) to reach the dunes. Across the road from the visitor center, the **Mosca Pass Trail** climbs up into the Sangre de Cristo Wilderness.

The area beyond the Point of No Return parking lot is a good spot to get further out into the backcountry on backpacking trips; a road theoretically leads up to Medano Pass (9982ft) at the top of the Sangres, but because of the sand it's not recommended unless you have a suitable off-road vehicle.

In the middle of summer, hikers should hit the hills during the early morning, as the sand can reach 140°F (60°C) during the heat of the day. Although you might think sandals would be the footwear of choice,

Zapata Falls

closed-toe shoes provide better protection against the heat. Those with limited mobility can borrow a dunes-accessible wheelchair from the visitor center. If you are hiking with children, don't let them out of your sight. It is very easy to become separated once you've entered the dunes.

Dune Sandboarding & Sledding

The heavy wooden sled may seem like a bad idea when you're trudging out to the dunes, but the gleeful rush down the slopes is worth every footstep. There's a bit of a trick to making this work. Sand conditions are best after a recent precipitation; when it's too dry you'll simply sink. Also, the best rides are had by those who are relatively light, so if you've bulked up on microbrews and steaks, don't expect to zip down the hill.

During the winter days when snow covers the dunes, the sledding is excellent. To rent a board, visit **Kristi Mountain Sports** (☑719-589-9759; www.slvoutdoor.com; 3323 Main St; sandboard/bike rental per day $18/20; ☺9am-6pm Mon-Sat) in Alamosa or the **Great Sand Dunes Oasis** (☑719-378-2222; www.greatdunes.com; 5400 Hwy 150; tent/RV sites $25/38, cabins $55, r $100; ☺Apr-Oct; 🐾) at the edge of the park.

Mountain Biking

Off-road cyclists should plan for a real slog. The unimproved roads of the park get washed over in sand and are very difficult until the road climbs the beautiful narrow valley to **Medano Pass**. The pass is 11 miles from the Point of No Return parking area at the north end of the paved road. A detailed mileage log for the Medano Pass Primitive Rd is available at the visitor center.

For a shorter fat-tire ride, visit the spectacular area around **Zapata Falls**, south of the park, which also offers outstanding views of the valley. A consortium of 13 agencies has opened 4 miles of trail in the Zapata Falls Special Recreation Area on the west flank of Blanca Peak.

Why All the Sand?

Upon your first glimpse of the dunes, you can't help but wonder: where did all this sand come from, and why does it stay here? Has it got something to do with the aliens you might spy from the **UFO Watchtower** (☑805-886-6959; www.ufowatchtower.com; Hwy 17; per person/car $2/5)?

The answer lies in the unique geography and weather patterns of the San Luis Valley. Streams, snowmelt and flash floods have been carrying eroded sand and silt out of the San Juan Mountains (about 60 miles to the west) to the valley floor for millions of years.

There, prevailing winds from the southwest gradually blow the sand into the natural hollow at the southern end of the Sangre de Cristo range. At the same time, streams and stronger prevailing winds from the eastern mountains push back in the other direction, causing the sand to pile up into what are now the highest dunes in North America.

If you look closely at the sand (the visitor center has a magnifying glass) you'll see a spectrum of shapes and colors: 29 different rock and mineral types – from obsidian and sulfur to amethyst and turquoise – are represented in the sand's makeup.

Guided Tours

Throughout summer NPS rangers lead interpretive nature walks from the visitor center and hold evening programs at the amphitheater. This is an excellent way to learn more about the unseen world of the dunes – surprising thickets of sunflowers, burrowing owls and even tiger salamanders! Inquire at the visitor center about specific programs and times.

Essential Information

Sleeping

For beauty at its spookiest, plan your visit during a full or new moon. Stock up on supplies, get your backcountry camping permit and hike into the surreal landscape to set up camp: bring plenty of shade and water.

There are also half-a-dozen backcountry sites that can be accessed from the Point of No Return parking lot, north of Pinyon Flats. These sites vary in terrain, from alpine and woodland to desert.

Tourist Information

Stop by the informative **Great Sand Dunes National Park Visitor Center** (☎719-378-6399; www.nps.gov/grsa; 11999 Hwy 150; ☺8:30am-5pm Jun-Aug, 9am-4:30pm Sep-May) before venturing out, to learn about the geology and history of the dunes or to chat with a ranger about hiking or backcountry-camping options. A free backcountry permit is required if you're planning on being adventurous, and it pays to let the ranger know where you're going.

Be sure to ask about scheduled nature walks and nightly programs held at the amphitheater near Pinyon Flats.

Getting There & Away

Great Sand Dunes National Park is 33 miles northeast of Alamosa. To get here, travel east on US 160 for 14 miles toward prominent Blanca Peak, turn left (north) on Hwy 150 and follow the road for 19 miles to the visitor center, 3 miles north of the park entrance. You can also get here from the north, turning west off Hwy 17 onto County Lane 6 N. ∎

Top left: Visitor Center entrance; Top right: Sandboarding; Bottom: Medano Creek

CARL FINOCCHIARO/500PX ©

Rocky Mountain National Park

This is a place of natural spectacle on every scale: from hulking granite formations, many taller than 12,000ft, some over 130 million years old, to the delicate yellow burst of the glacier lily, one of the dozen alpine wildflowers that explode in short, colorful life at the edge of receding snowfields every spring.

Wonders of the natural world are the main attractions here: huge herds of elk and scattered bighorn sheep, pine-dotted granite slopes and blindingly white alpine tundra. However, there are a few museums and historic sites within the park's borders that are worthy of a glance and good for families.

Rocky Mountain National Park is surrounded by some of the most pristine wild area in the west: Comanche Peak and Neota Wilderness Areas in the Roosevelt National Forest to the north and Indian Peaks Wilderness to the south. The jagged spine of the Continental Divide intersects the park through its middle.

Great For...

State
Colorado

Entrance Fee
7-day pass per vehicle/person $35/20

Area
415 sq miles

❶ Moraine Park Discovery Center

Built by the Civilian Conservation Corps in 1923 and once the park's proud visitors lodge, this **building** (☎970-586-1206; Bear Lake Rd; ⏰9am-4:30pm Jun-Oct) **FREE** has

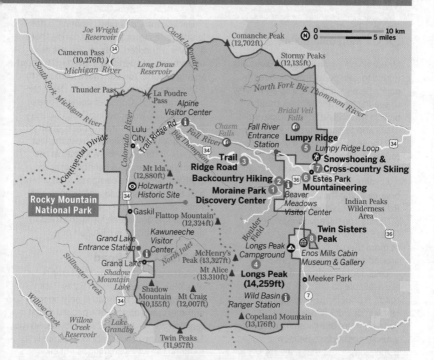

ANN MOORE/SHUTTERSTOCK ©

Holzwarth Historic Site

When Prohibition was enacted in 1916, John Holzwarth Sr, a Denver saloonkeeper, started a new life as a subsistence rancher. This **site** (Never Summer Ranch; park headquarters 970-586-1206; Trail Ridge Rd/US 34; ⏰10am-4pm Jun-Oct) houses several buildings kept in their original condition, including the 'Mama cabin' and cabins that were part of a dude ranch, which the Holzwarths rented out for $2 a day.

Historical reenactments and ranger-led programs are now held at the site. The **Heritage Days** celebration happens in late July.

Holzwarth lies at the end of a graded half-mile path, easily accessible with strollers.

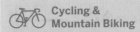

Cycling & Mountain Biking

Mountain biking and cycling have continued to gain popularity despite the park's heavy traffic. It's a splendid way to see the park and wildlife, though bicycle travel is restricted to paved roads and to one dirt road, Fall River Rd. Those looking to ride technical routes on a mountain bike should go to Roosevelt National Forest.

On either a road bike or a mountain bike, climbing the paved **Trail Ridge Rd** (www.nps.gov/romo; ☺summer only) **FREE** has one big advantage over Fall River Rd (a 9-mile one-way climb of more than 3000ft): you can turn around should problems arise.

Less daunting climbs and climes are available on the park's lower paved roads. A popular 16-mile circuit is the Horseshoe Park/Estes Park Loop. For a bit more of a climbing challenge you can continue to Bear Lake Rd, an 8-mile-long route that rises 1500ft to the high mountain basin with a decent shoulder.

To avoid hypothermia and dehydration, bring a set of dry, long-sleeved clothes, plus plenty of water.

been renovated in recent years to host exhibits on geology, glaciers and wildlife. Kids will like the interactive exhibits and half-mile nature trail out the door.

❷ Backcountry Hiking

Most people never leave the road and major trails in Rocky Mountain National Park – and it's a damned shame. Luckily for you, this means the backcountry is a desolate paradise where you can find solitude, amazing views, wild hikes and serious mountain ascents. You'll need to get permits through the **Wilderness Offices** (☏970-586-1242; www.nps.gov/romo; 1000 W Hwy 36, Estes Park, CO 80517) before heading out.

Backcountry camping happens in designated sites throughout the park – there are over a hundred. This means the real opportunity of spending a few days without seeing anyone. You can move from site to site, or stay in one site for a few days, taking on day trips. Consider going to one of the Technical Orienteering Cross Country Zones to really get into the backcountry and enjoy trailless hiking across the lost corners of the park. You will need at the minimum: a permit, a bear bin, proper clothing, a map and compass, food, a tent, a sleeping bag and pad, good shoes and water filtration. Remember to keep bear-safe camps and watch for falling trees in areas where blight is killing off pines.

❸ Trail Ridge Road

Travel through the sky on this remarkable 48-mile road between Estes Park and Grand Lake. The road is only open summers, and can be jam-packed. But it is really worth it – by car, RV or bicycle. About 11 miles of the road sit above the tree line.

Along the way, you might sight elk, moose, marmots and plenty of birds and plant species.

❹ Longs Peak

You need not worry about getting lonesome on the 15-mile (full-day) round-trip to Longs Peak (14,259ft) summit, as it's the centerpiece of many a hiker's itinerary. During summer, you're likely to find a line of more than 100 parked cars snaking down the road from the Longs Peak trailhead.

This is a serious climb, and you should be prepared before taking it on. After the initial 6 miles of moderate trail to the Boulder Field (12,760ft), the path steepens at the start of the **Keyhole Route** to the summit, which is marked with yellow-and-red bull's-eyes painted on the rock (while there are dozens of ways up, this is the easiest). Even superhuman athletes who are used to the thin air will be slowed by the route's ledge system, which resembles a narrow cliffside stairway without a handrail. After this, hikers scramble the final homestretch to the summit boulders. The view from the top – snow-kissed granite stretching out to the curved horizon – is incredible. The round-trip hike takes anywhere from 10 to 15 hours. The rule in Colorado is you need to hit the summit before noon to avoid lightning storms, so expect to make an early alpine start.

For a shorter hike, head south just above the tree line to make it to **Chasm Lake**, a high-alpine wonder that sits below the jagged face of Longs Peak's signature **Diamond**, where heavy-duty rock gods and goddesses test their mettle.

Overnighting at **Longs Peak Campground** (☏970-586-1206; Longs Peak Rd, off State Hwy 7; tent sites $26; ⊗closed winter) is a good idea.

❺ Lumpy Ridge

Easily accessed from the north side of Estes Park, Lumpy Ridge offers some great hikes to places like Bridal Veil Falls and Gem Lake, plus some of the best rock climbing in the area. The **Lumpy Ridge Loop** circles around the granite crag in an 11-mile loop. Check in about raptor nesting before going here.

Rock climbing here is focused on traditional crack climbing. Expect solid granite, great views and accessional crowds.

❻ Mountaineering

Rocky Mountain National Park has a total 124 named peaks. While Longs is the only one over 14,000ft, another 20 sit above 13,000ft, making this a top mountaineering spot. Before departing check in at wilderness offices (p356) for raptor closings as well as beta on climbing and bivouac permits.

Routes range from easy hikes up to day-long affairs on vertical cliffs, plus steep snow, ice and rock routes. Take classes at the **Colorado Mountain School** (☏720-387-8944; https://coloradomountainschool.com; 341 Moraine Ave; half-day guided climbs per person from $150).

MARGARET.W/SHUTTERSTOCK ©

View from Trail Ridge Road

❼ Snowshoeing & Cross-country Skiing

From December into May, the high valleys and alpine tundra offer cross-country skiers unique opportunities to view wildlife and the winter scenery undisturbed by crowds. January and February are the best months for dry, powdery snowpack; spring snows tend to be heavy and wet. Most routes follow summer hiking trails, but valley bottoms and frozen streambeds typically have more snow cover and are less challenging. Ask about avalanche hazards before heading out – Colorado has one of the most dangerous snowpacks in the world with people dying in slides most years – and avoid steep, open slopes.

Novices should consider hiring a guide or traveling with experienced leaders. Rangers lead weekend snowshoe hikes in the east side of the park from January to April, depending on snow conditions. Trailhead locations and times are available from the park visitor centers.

Overnight trips require permits, and the US Forest Service (USFS) and NPS will have a list of closed trails.

You can gear up at the **Estes Park Mountain Shop** (☏970-586-6548; www. estesparkmountainshop.com; 2050 Big Thompson Ave; 2-person tents $12-16, bear boxes per night $3; ⊙8am-9pm).

❽ Twin Sisters Peak

This up-and-back hike provides an excellent warm-up to climbing Longs Peak. In addition, the 11,428ft summit of Twin Sisters Peak offers unequaled views of Longs Peak. It's an arduous walk, gaining 2300ft in just 3.7 miles.

Erosion-resistant quartz rock caps the oddly deformed rock at the summit and delicate alpine flowers (plenty of mountain harebell) fill the rock spaces near the summit's stone hut. The trailhead is near Mills Cabin, 10 miles south of Estes Park on Hwy 7.

Essential Information

Camping

The park's formal campgrounds provide campfire programs, have public telephones and a seven-day limit during summer months; all except Longs Peak (p356) take RVs (no hookups). The water supply is turned off during winter.

You will need a **backcountry permit** (www.nps.gov/romo/planyourvisit/wilderness -camping.htm; permit for up to 7 people $26) to stay outside developed park campgrounds. None of the campgrounds have showers, but they do have flush toilets in summer and outhouse facilities in winter. Sites include a fire ring, a picnic table and one parking spot. Most have bear boxes for food storage.

Getting There & Around

Trail Ridge Rd (US 34) is the only east–west route through the park; the US 34 eastern approach from I-25 and Loveland follows the Big Thompson River Canyon. The most direct route from Boulder follows US 36 through Lyons to the east entrances. Another approach from the south, mountainous Hwy 7, passes by **Enos Mills Cabin** (970-586-4706; www.enosmills.com; 6760 Hwy 7; $20; 11am-4pm Tue & Wed summer, by appointment only) and provides access to campsites and trailheads on the east side of the divide. Winter closure of US 34 through the park makes access to the park's west side dependent on US 40 at Granby.

A majority of visitors enter the park in their own cars, using the long and winding Trail Ridge Rd (US 34) to cross the Continental Divide. There are options for those without wheels, however. In summer a free shuttle bus operates from the **Estes Park Visitor Center** (970-577-9900; www.visit estespark.com; 500 Big Thompson Ave; 9am-8pm daily Jun-Aug, 8am-5pm Mon-Fri, 9am-5pm Sat, 10am-4pm Sun Sep-May) multiple times daily, bringing hikers to a park-and-ride location where they can pick up other shuttles. The year-round option leaves the

Glacier Basin parking area and heads to Bear Lake, in the park's lower elevations. During the summer peak, a second shuttle operates between Moraine Park campground and the Glacier Basin parking area. The second shuttle runs on weekends only from mid-August through September.

Information

The park has three full-service visitor centers – one on the east side, one on the west and one in the middle. Though they all have different displays and programs, this is where you can study maps and speak with rangers about permits and weather conditions.

Alpine Visitor Center (www.nps.gov/romo; Fall River Pass; 10:30am-4:30pm late May–mid-Jun, 9am-5pm late Jun-early Sep, 10:30am-4:30pm early Sep–mid-Oct) The views from this popular visitor center and souvenir store at 11,796ft, and right in the middle of the park, are extraordinary. You can see elk, deer and sometimes moose grazing on the hillside on the drive up Old Fall River Rd. Much of the traffic that clogs Trail Ridge Rd all summer pulls into Alpine Visitor Center, so the place is a zoo. Rangers here give programs and advice about trails. You can also shop for knickknacks or eat in the cafeteria-style dining room.

Beaver Meadows Visitor Center (970-586-1206; www.nps.gov/romo; US Hwy 36; 8am-9pm late Jun-late Aug, to 4:30pm or 5pm rest of year) The primary visitor center and best stop for park information if you're approaching from Estes Park. You can see a film about the park, browse a small gift shop and reserve backcountry camping sites.

Kawuneeche Visitor Center (970-627-3471; 16018 US Hwy 34; 8am-6pm last week May–Labor Day, to 5pm Labor Day–Sep, to 4:30pm Oct-May) This visitor center is on the west side of the park, and offers a film about the park, ranger-led walks and discussions, backcountry permits and family activities. ∎

Top left: Mule deer; Top right: Cross-country skiing; Bottom: Waterfall

Bison in the Lamar Valley

Yellowstone National Park

Yellowstone National Park is the wild, free-flowing, beating heart of the Greater Yellowstone Ecosystem. Its real showstoppers are the geysers and hot springs – nature's crowd-pleasers – but at every turn this land of fire and brimstone breathes, belches and bubbles like a giant kettle on the boil.

Great For...

State
Wyoming

Entrance Fee
7-day pass per vehicle/pedestrian
$35/20

Area
3472 sq miles

Yellowstone is split into five distinct regions – Canyon Country, Geyser Country, Lake Country, Mammoth Country and Tower-Roosevelt Country – each with unique attractions. Upon entering the park you'll be given a basic map and the park newspaper, *Yellowstone Today*, detailing the excellent ranger-led talks and walks (p366; well worth attending). All the visitor centers have information desks staffed by park rangers who can help you tailor a hike to your tastes, from great photo locations to the best chance of spotting a bear.

❶ Old Faithful

Though it's neither the tallest nor even the most predictable geyser in the park, Old Faithful is the poster child for Yellowstone and a consistent crowd-pleaser. Every 90 minutes or so the geyser spouts some 8000 gallons (150 bathtubs) of water up to 180ft in the air. It's worth viewing the eruption from several locations – the

MARK READ/LONELY PLANET ©

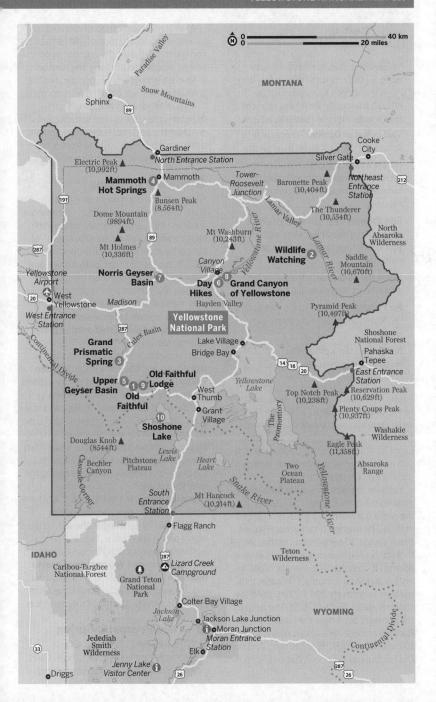

0 40 km
0 20 miles

MONTANA

Paradise Valley

Snow Mountains

Sphinx
89

Gardiner
North Entrance Station

Cooke City

Silver Gate

Electric Peak
(10,992ft)

Mammoth
Hot Springs **4** Mammoth

Tower-
Roosevelt
Junction

Baronette Peak
(10,404ft)

Northeast
Entrance
Station

212

191

Bunsen Peak
(8,564ft)

The Thunderer
(10,554ft)

Dome Mountain
(9894ft)

89

Lamar Valley

North
Absaroka
Wilderness

287

Mt Holmes
(10,336ft)

Mt Washburn
(10,243ft)

Yellowstone River

Saddle
Mountain
(10,670ft)

Yellowstone
Airport

Canyon
Village

Wildlife
Watching **2**

Lamar River

Norris Geyser
Basin **7**

Day **6**
Hikes

8 Grand Canyon
of Yellowstone

West
Yellowstone

20

West Entrance
Station

Madison

Hayden Valley

Pyramid Peak
(10,497ft)

Yellowstone
National Park

287

Calex Basin

Lake Village

Shoshone
National
Forest

Grand
Prismatic
Spring **3**

Bridge Bay

14 16

20

Pahaska
Tepee

East Entrance
Station

Upper **5**
Geyser Basin **1 9**
Old
Faithful

Old Faithful
Lodge

West
Thumb

Yellowstone
Lake

Top Notch Peak
(10,238ft)

Reservation Peak
(10,629ft)

Plenty Coups Peak
(10,937ft)

10
Shoshone
Lake

Grant
Village

The Promontory

Washakie
Wilderness

Douglas Knob
(8544ft)

Lewis
Lake

Heart
Lake

Two
Ocean
Plateau

Eagle Peak
(11,358ft)

Absaroka
Range

Bechler
Canyon

Pitchstone
Plateau

Cascade Corner

South
Entrance
Station

Mt Hancock
(10,214ft)

Snake River

Yellowstone River

Continental Divide

Flagg Ranch

IDAHO

Caribou-Targhee
National Forest

287

Lizard Creek
Campground

Grand Teton
National
Park

Teton
Wilderness

33

Jedediah
Smith
Wilderness

Jackson
Lake

Colter Bay Village

Jackson Lake Junction

i Moran Junction
Moran Entrance
Station

WYOMING

Continental Divide

Driggs

Jenny Lake **i**
Visitor Center

26

Elk

287

26

Continental Divide

Beating the Crowds

Yellowstone's wonderland attracts up to 30,000 visitors daily in July and August and tops four million gate-crashers annually. Avoid the worst of the crowds with the following advice:

Visit in May or October Services may be limited, but there will be far fewer people.

Hit the trail Most (95%) of visitors never set foot on a backcountry trail; only 1% camp at a backcountry site (permit required).

Bike the park Most campgrounds have underutilized hiker/biker sites, and your skinny tires can slip through any traffic jam.

Mimic the wildlife Be active during the golden hours after dawn and before dusk.

Pack a lunch Eat at one of the park's many overlooked and often lovely scenic picnic areas.

Bundle up Enjoy a private Old Faithful eruption during the winter months.

geyser-side seats, the upper-floor balcony of the **Old Faithful Inn** (☑307-344-7311; www.yellowstonenationalparklodges.com; Old Faithful; Old House d with shared/private bath from $160/260, r $320-390; ☺early May-early Oct) and (highly recommended) from a distance on Observation Hill.

For over 75 years the geyser faithfully erupted every hour or so – one reason for the name the Washburn expedition gave it in 1870. The average time between shows these days is 90 minutes and getting longer, though this has historically varied between 45 and 110 minutes. The average eruption lasts around four minutes. The water temperature is normally 204°F (95°C) and the steam is about 350°F (176°C). The longer the eruption, the longer the recovery time. Rangers correctly predict eruptions to within 10 minutes about 90% of the time. And no, Old Faithful has never erupted on the hour.

A fairly reliable method of calculating exactly when an eruption of Old Faithful is imminent is to count the number of people seated around the geyser – the number of tourists is inversely proportional to the amount of time left until the next eruption.

If you find yourself twiddling your thumbs waiting for the old salt, pause to consider the power of recycling – you are sitting on a boardwalk made from around three million recycled plastic water jugs.

❷ Wildlife Watching

Along with the big mammals – grizzly, black bear, moose and bison – Yellowstone is home to elk, pronghorn antelope and bighorn sheep. Wolves have been part of the national park since reintroduction in 1996. Native to the area, both wolves and bison nearly met extinction because of hunting and human encroachment. While their numbers have resurged, taking them off the endangered species list means they can now be legally hunted outside park boundaries.

In Yellowstone's heart between Yellowstone Lake and Canyon Village, **Hayden Valley** is your best all-round bet for wildlife viewing. For the best chances of seeing wildlife, head out at dawn or dusk and stake out a turnout anywhere off the Grand Loop Rd. Bring patience and binoculars – a grizzly just might wander into your viewfinder, or perhaps you'll spy a rutting elk or hear the bugle of a solitary moose reaching the river for a drink.

Lamar Valley, in the northeast, is where wolves were first reintroduced and is ground zero for spotting them. Ask rangers where packs are most active or attend a wolf-watching (or other) excursion with the recommended **Yellowstone Forever Institute** (☑406-848-2400; www.yellowstone.org). Hearing howls echo across the valley at dusk is a magical, primeval experience.

❸ Grand Prismatic Spring

At 370ft wide and 121ft deep, Grand Prismatic Spring is the park's largest and deepest hot spring. It's also considered by many to be the most beautiful thermal feature in the park. Boardwalks lead around the multicolored mist of the gorgeous pool and its spectacularly colored rainbow rings of algae. From above, the spring looks like a giant blue eye weeping exquisite multi-colored tears.

➍ Mammoth Hot Springs

The imposing **Lower** and **Upper Terraces** of Mammoth Hot Springs are the highlight of the Mammoth region. An hour's worth of boardwalks wind their way between ornate and graceful limestone pools, ledges and plateaus. **Palette Springs** (accessed from the lower parking lot) and sulfur-yellow **Canary Springs** (accessed from the upper loop, 1km south) are the most beautiful sites, but thermal activity is constantly in flux, so check the current state of play at the visitor center.

➎ Upper Geyser Basin

While Old Faithful gets the most attention, there's lots to explore in Upper Geyser Basin, which has the densest collection of geysers in Yellowstone. On Geyser Hill

you'll find charismatic **Anemone** and fickle **Beehive Geysers**. If you see a group of backpack- and radio-wielding Geyser Gazers huddled near the latter, stick around for an impressive show. Below, fantastic **Castle Geyser** is one of the largest formations of its kind in the world, and the view from **Daisy Geyser** is excellent.

➏ Day Hikes

Even if you drive every road in Yellowstone you'll still see only 2% of the park. Easily the best way to get a close-up taste of Yellowstone's unique combination of rolling landscape, wildlife and thermal activity is on foot, along the 900-plus miles of maintained trails.

Hiking is also the best way to escape the summer crowds. Only 10% of visitors step off the road or boardwalks, only half of those venture further than a mile and just 1% overnight in the backcountry. It's one thing to photograph a bison from your car; it's quite another to hike gingerly past a snorting herd out on their turf. So pick up a map, pack some granola bars and work at least a couple of great hikes into your Yellowstone itinerary.

Grand Prismatic Spring

Where you hike depends on when you visit the park. Early in summer (May, June) you'll likely have to focus on the north of the park around the Mammoth and Tower-Roosevelt regions. Snowfall and bear restrictions close many higher-altitude hikes and regions around Yellowstone Lake until the middle of July. Many hikes in the centre and south of the park are muddy or snowy until July, so bring appropriate footwear.

If you're a novice hiker consider joining a **ranger hike**. These change from year to year, subject to budget and staffing constraints, but at present rangers lead summertime hikes to Mystic Falls, along the south rim of the Canyon region and to Storm Point, as well as several boardwalk strolls at places like Mud Volcano. Check the park newspaper for details.

Note that the park uses a three-character code (eg 2K7) to identify both trailheads and specific backcountry campsites.

❼ Norris Geyser Basin

Norris Geyser Basin comprises **Porcelain Basin** and **Back Basin**, accessed through two connecting loops. If the world's tallest geyser, **Steamboat Geyser**, isn't erupting (it probably isn't), continue around to the explosive remains of **Porkchop Geyser** and the appropriately named **Vixen Geyser**, whose random machine-gun eruptions will beguile you.

❽ Grand Canyon of Yellowstone

Near Canyon Village, this is one of the park's true blockbuster sights. After its placid meanderings north from Yellowstone Lake, the Yellowstone River suddenly plummets over Upper Falls and then the much larger Lower Falls before raging through the 1000ft-deep canyon. Scenic overlooks and a network of trails along the canyon's rims highlight its multicolored beauty from a dozen angles – South Rim Dr leads to the most spectacular overlook, at **Artist Point**.

❾ Old Faithful Inn

Designed by Seattle architect Robert C Reamer and built in 1904, this is the only building in the park that looks as though it actually belongs here. The log rafters of its

Lower Falls

seven-story lobby rise nearly 80ft, and the chimney of the central fireplace (actually eight fireplaces combined) contains more than 500 tons of rhyolite rock. It's definitely a worthwhile visit, even for nonguests.

The Crow's Nest, a top-floor balcony where musicians once played for dancers in the lobby below, is wonderful (but unused since 1959). Look also for the huge popcorn popper and fire tools at the back of the fireplace. The 2nd-floor **observation deck** offers the chance to enjoy fine views of **Old Faithful geyser** over a drink, and the lobby hosts local artists and authors. Free 45-minute Historic Inn tours depart from the fireplace at 9:30am, 11am, 2pm and 3:30pm.

The inn's biggest secret? If you make a request when you book your room a year in advance, you just might be one of half a dozen people allowed up on the rooftop to watch the flags being lowered at around 6pm. The geyser-basin views are unparalleled.

⑩ Shoshone Lake

The largest backcountry lake in the lower 48, Shoshone Lake spells paradise for canoeists and kayakers. The serene lake is closed to motorized vessels and is lined with a dozen secluded boater-only campsites. On its far western edge, Shoshone Geyser Basin's pools, thermals and mud pots make up the largest backcountry thermal area in the park. One-third of all of Yellowstone's backcountry use takes place along its shores, which are accessible only to hikers and hand-propelled boats.

Boaters must access the lake up the channel from Lewis Lake. From mid-July to August the channel requires portage of a few hundred yards in cold water (bring appropriate footwear), though in spring you can often paddle through.

Of 20 lakeshore campsites, 13 are reserved for boaters, four for hikers and three are shared. All have pit toilets. Rangers claim the nicest campsites are 8Q4, 8R4 and 8R1. Wood fires are not allowed along the lakeshore.

 Overnight Hikes

There's no better way to experience the raw wildness of Yellowstone than on an overnight backpacking trip. Some experience of backcountry camping is important before heading out into the wild, particularly in bear awareness, hanging food and leave-no-trace practices. That said, there's a huge range of challenges available, from easy strolls, to easy backcountry overnights an hour from the road, to multiday expedition-style traverses of the Thorofare corner or Gallatin Range through some of the remotest terrain south of Alaska. Choose the right trip at the right time of year and arrive prepared, and there's no better way to experience the park.

If you don't fancy organizing a multiday trek yourself, consider a company like **Trail Guides Yellowstone** (☑406-595-1823; www.trailguides yellowstone.com; 2149 Durston Rd, Unit 35, Bozeman) or **Wildland Trekking Company** (☑800-715-4453; www.wildland trekking.com; 2304 N 7th Ave, Unit K, Bozeman), both based in Bozeman, MT, whose backpacking trips cost $255 to $270 per person per day, including meals, guide and transportation from Bozeman. Wildland Trekking Company even offers llama treks.

Most boaters make their first camp on the southern shore (campsites nearest to the channel are reserved for first- and last-night use only). If you need to cross the lake, do so early in the morning and at the half-mile-wide Narrows in the center of the lake. Prevailing winds are from the southwest and pick up after noon. The lake is icebound until mid-June, when flooding is possible at shoreline campsites. Backcountry boating campsites at Shoshone Lake cannot be reserved before July 1 or 15, depending on the site.

Hike Mt Washburn

MATT_TRAIN/SHUTTERSTOCK ©

This popular return hike climbs gradually to the fire lookout tower on the summit of 10,243ft Mt Washburn for some of the park's best views. Over 10,000 hikers tackle this trail annually, so leave early to get trailhead parking. Older teenagers should be able to do the hike.

Mt Washburn is all that remains of a volcano that erupted around 640,000 years ago, forming the vast Yellowstone caldera. Interpretive displays in the lookout tower point out the caldera extents, making this a memorable place to get a sense of the awesome scale of the Yellowstone supervolcano. The peak is named after Montana surveyor-general Henry Washburn, who rode up the peak to see the view during the Washburn, Langford and Doane expedition of 1870.

The route described here starts from Dunraven Pass (8859ft) on the Grand Loop

Duration 4 hours

Distance 6.4 miles round-trip

Difficulty Moderate

Elevation Change 1400ft

Start & Finish Dunraven Pass trailhead

Nearest Town/Junction
Canyon Village

Rd, 4.8 miles north of Canyon and 14.2 miles south of Tower. An alternative route begins from the larger Chittenden parking area (5 miles north of the pass) for a marginally shorter but less interesting hike (but good bike trail) to the summit. Use Trails Illustrated's 1:63,360 map No 304 *Tower/Canyon*.

Snow often obstructs the Dunraven Pass approach through the end of June. Wildflower displays in July and August are legendary. Frequent afternoon thunderstorms

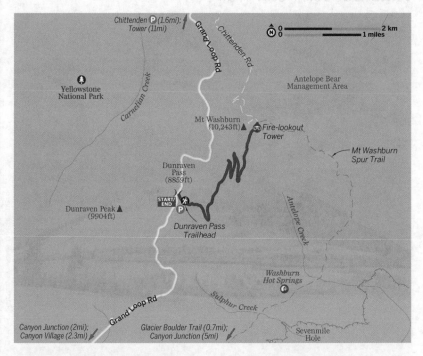

Chittenden P (1.6mi); Tower (11mi)

Grand Loop Rd

Chittenden Rd

N 0 ___ 2 km
0 ___ 1 miles

Yellowstone National Park

Antelope Bear Management Area

Carnelian Creek

Mt Washburn (10,243ft) ▲

Fire-lookout Tower

Mt Washburn Spur Trail

Dunraven Pass (8859ft)

Dunraven Peak ▲ (9904ft)

START/END P

Antelope Creek

Dunraven Pass Trailhead

Washburn Hot Springs

Grand Loop Rd

Sulphur Creek

Sevenmile Hole

Canyon Junction (2mi); Canyon Village (2.3mi)

Glacier Boulder Trail (0.7mi); Canyon Junction (5mi)

bring fierce winds and lightning, so pack a windbreaker even if the weather looks clear and be ready to make a quick descent if a storm rolls in.

Keep in mind that grizzlies flock to Mt Washburn's eastern slopes in large numbers during August and September in search of ripening whitebark pine nuts.

The wide trail follows a rough, disused road (dating from 1905) and so makes for a comfortable, steady ascent, following a series of long, ribbon-like loops through a forest of subalpine firs. After 20 minutes the views start to open up. The fire tower appears dauntingly distant, but the climb really isn't as painful as it looks. Continue northeast up broad switchbacks to a viewpoint, then follow a narrow ridge past a few stunted whitebark pines (look out for bears) to the gravel **Chittenden Rd** at the Mt Washburn Trail junction. At the junction the road curves up to the three-story

fire-lookout tower, about two hours from the trailhead. The side trail right at the junction leads down the Mt Washburn Spur Trail to Canyon Junction.

The viewing platform and ground-level public observation room has restrooms (but no water), a public 20x Zeiss telescope, displays on the Yellowstone caldera and graphics to help you identify the surrounding peaks and valleys. The fire tower was built in the 1930s and is one of three in the park still staffed from June to October. The majestic panoramas (when the weather is clear) stretch over three-quarters of the park, across the Yellowstone caldera south to Yellowstone Lake, Canyon, the Hayden Valley and even the Tetons, and north to the Beartooth and Absaroka Ranges. Below you are the smoking Washburn Hot Springs. Keep your eyes peeled for bighorn sheep basking near the summit.

Hike Bunsen Peak Trail

NATURAL HISTORY LIBRARY/ALAMY STOCK PHOTO ©

Bunsen Peak (8564ft) is a popular half-day hike, and you can extend it to a more demanding day hike by continuing down the mountain's gentler eastern slope to the Bunsen Peak Rd and then waaay down (800ft) to the base of seldom-visited Osprey Falls.

The initial Bunsen Peak Trail climbs east out of Gardner's Hole to the exposed summit of Bunsen Peak, offering outstanding panoramas of Mammoth, the Gallatin Range, Swan Lake Flat and the Blacktail Deer Plateau. Even if you just make it halfway up the hill you'll be rewarded with superb views.

Bunsen Peak was named by the 1872 Hayden Survey for German scientist Robert Wilhelm Eberhard von Bunsen (after whom the Bunsen burner was also named), whose pioneering theories about the inner workings of Icelandic geysers influenced early Yellowstone hydrothermal research. The mountain is actually an ancient lava plug,

Duration	2½ hours
Distance	4.2-mile round-trip
Difficulty	Moderate
Elevation Change	1300ft
Start & Finish	Bunsen Peak trailhead
Nearest Town/Junction	Mammoth

the surrounding volcanic walls of which have partly eroded away. So, yes, you are climbing the inside of a former volcano!

From the Mammoth Visitor Center, drive 4.5 miles south on Grand Loop Rd, cross the light-colored rock defile of the **Golden Gate** and turn left into the unpaved parking area on the eastern side of the road, just beyond the Rustic Falls turnout. The parking lot is small and fills up quickly, so either get here early, try the Glen Creek trailhead across the road or continue a little further to Swan Lake Flat.

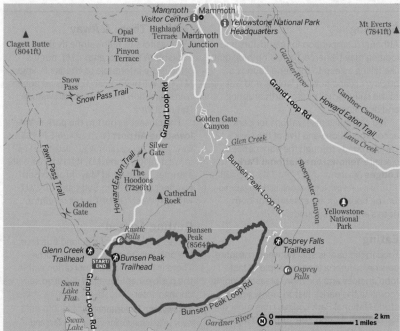

From 7250ft, the well-trodden single-track dirt trail branches left (north) just beyond a barricade on the left (north) side of unpaved **Bunsen Peak Rd**. The trail climbs immediately through sagebrush interspersed with wildflowers, then enters a young Douglas fir and lodgepole pine mosaic. You'll get early views of the Golden Gate pass below and to the left, and the ash-colored jumble of the limestone Hoodoos to the north. About half an hour from the trailhead a series of meadows offers fabulous views southwest to Swan Lake Flat, Antler Peak (10,023ft), Mt Holmes (10,336ft), Terraced Mountain and Electric Peak (10,992ft).

Five minutes later, at one of the many switchbacks, you'll gain a great view of the eroded sandstone cliffs and spires of **Cathedral Rock**, with vistas down to the red roofs and bleached travertine mounds of Mammoth. The layered sandstone-and-shale mountain of Mt Everts (7841ft), to

the north, offers proof that the area was underwater 70 to 140 million years ago.

Beyond the Cathedral Rock outcrop, the switchbacks get steeper on the north side of the mountain and the exposed dome-shaped peak comes into view. Keep your eyes peeled for bighorn sheep.

The trail passes under electricity wires before a small cabin and communications equipment marks the first of three small summits, 2.1 miles from the trailhead. Continue east along the loose talus ridge, past the cairns of the middle summit, to the exposed easternmost summit for the best southern panoramas. Electric Peak, one of the highest in the Gallatin Range, looms largest to the northwest, marking the park's northern boundary, with the Absaroka Range to the northeast.

Either retrace your steps down the western slope or wind around the peak to descend the unsigned eastern slope to the Osprey Falls Trail.

Essential Information

Sleeping

Although competition for campsites and lodging may be fierce, there's nothing quite like falling asleep to the eerie sounds of bugling elk and howling wolves and waking to the sulfur smell of the earth erupting and bubbling.

You can make reservations for park accommodations and five of the park's 12 campgrounds through the park concessionaire **Yellowstone National Park Lodges** (Xanterra; ☎307-344-7311, 866-439-7375; www.yellowstonenationalparklodges.com). Online bookings are essential for both hotels and campgrounds.

Eating

Food in the park is split between campfire cuisine, cafeteria food, a couple of fast-food choices and the more pleasant dining rooms of the park's historic inns. Yellowstone National Park Lodges runs most dining options, so don't be surprised if you get a serious dose of déjà vu every time you open a menu. That said, most places are pretty good value considering the prime real estate and there have been significant moves in recent years to add a range of healthy, gluten-free and locally sourced options. You can preview park menus at www.yellowstonenationalparklodges.com.

The park's cafeterias are bland but convenient, and reasonably economical for families. All places serve breakfast and most offer an all-you-can-eat buffet that can quickly wipe out even the best-laid hiking plans. Kids' menus are available almost everywhere. Almost all offer sandwiches for lunch and heavier, pricier and more interesting fare for dinner.

There's also fast food at major junctions, plus snack shops and grocery supplies in the Yellowstone General Stores. The Grant Village, Old Faithful Inn and Lake Yellowstone Hotel dining rooms all require dinner reservations.

Getting There & Away

Most visitors to Yellowstone fly into Jackson, WY, or Bozeman, MT, but it's often more affordable to choose Billings, MT. You will need a car; there is no public transportation to or within Yellowstone National Park.

The closest airport to the park is **Yellowstone Airport** (WYS; ☎406-646-7631; www.yellowstoneairport.org; ☉late May-Sep), in West Yellowstone, MT. It has three daily summer flights (end May through September) to and from Salt Lake City, UT, with SkyWest/Delta. Closes in winter.

Getting Around

Unless you're part of a guided bus tour, the only way to get around is to drive. There is no public transportation within the park, except for a few ski-drop services during winter.

Yellowstone Roadrunner (☎406-640-0631; www.yellowstoneroadrunner.com) Taxi and charter service in West Yellowstone that offers one-way drops and shuttles for backpacking trips, though it's not cheap.

Park Entrances

Park entrances are open to vehicles 24 hours a day during open months. The **North Entrance** is at Gardiner, MT, and the **Northeast Entrance** is near Cooke City; both are open year-round. The **East Entrance** is on US 14/16/20, from Cody, WY, and the **South Entrance** is on US 89/191/287, north of Grand Teton National Park; both are open early May to early November. The **West Entrance** is on US 20/191/287 near West Yellowstone, MT, and is open mid- or late April to early November. ■

Old Faithful

Yellowstone's Thermal Features

Fueled by its underground furnace, Yellowstone is a bubbling cauldron of more than 10,000 geothermal features – more than all other geothermal areas on the planet combined. The average heat flow from the region is 40 times the global average.

Geysers

Only a handful of Yellowstone's thermal features are active geysers (from the Icelandic *geysir*, meaning 'to gush or rage'), but these still comprise about 50% of the global total, making the park a globally significant resource.

Yellowstone Lake

One of the world's largest alpine lakes, Yellowstone Lake was formed by the collapse of the Yellowstone caldera and shaped by glacial erosion. Hydrothermal explosions have further shaped the shoreline.

Travertine Terraces

The limestone rock of the Mammoth region contrasts with the silica-rich rhyolite found elsewhere in the park. Here, carbon dioxide in the hot water forms carbonic acid, which then dissolves the surrounding limestone (calcium carbonate). As this watery solution breaks the surface, some carbon dioxide escapes from the solution and limestone is deposited as travertine, forming beautiful terraces.

Mud Pots

Are Yellowstone's mud pots really boiling? No, the bubbling is actually the release of steam and gas. Sulfur and iron content give rise to the nickname 'paint pots.'

Fumaroles

Essentially dry geysers, fumaroles' water boils away before reaching the surface, where they burst with heat. These steam vents also give off carbon dioxide and some hydrogen sulfide (that nice 'rotten egg' smell) with a hiss or roaring sound.

GREAT LAKES & GREAT PLAINS

In This Chapter

Badlands 380
Cuyahoga Valley 382
Gateway Arch 384
Isle Royale 386
Theodore Roosevelt 388
Voyageurs 392
Wind Cave 394

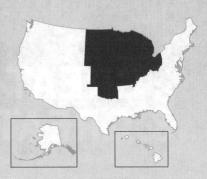

Great Lakes & Great Plains

With howling wolves, shaggy bison and sweeping prairies, the Great Lakes and Great Plains are truly wild. The lakes, carved out by glaciers and filled with melting snow and ice, seem like boundless inland seas. Get a sense of perspective on Lake Superior's largest island, Isle Royale, or experience an epic canoe trip in Voyageurs. Further west are the prairies of the Dakotas where rolling grasslands and striated, eroding buttes make up a quintessentially American landscape.

Don't Miss

○ Spotting wildlife along trails in Theodore Roosevelt (p388)

○ Cycling Cuyahoga Valley's Scenic Railroad (p383)

○ Marveling at Badlands' vivid colors and stark shapes (p380)

○ Touring the stony labyrinths of Wind Cave (p394)

○ Finding solitude in watery Isle Royale (p386)

○ Gazing up at the hulking Gateway Arch (p384)

When to Go

Thunderstorms and even tornadoes blast the Great Plains from June to August, though days are sultry with blooming wildflowers.

September and October see fair weather, bountiful farm and orchard harvests, and shoulder-season bargains. Like April and May, these are uncrowded months to visit.

From November to March attractions cut back hours or close. Blizzards can shut down roads for days in some areas, while skiers and snowmobilers hit the trails in others.

Previous page: Badlands National Park (p380)

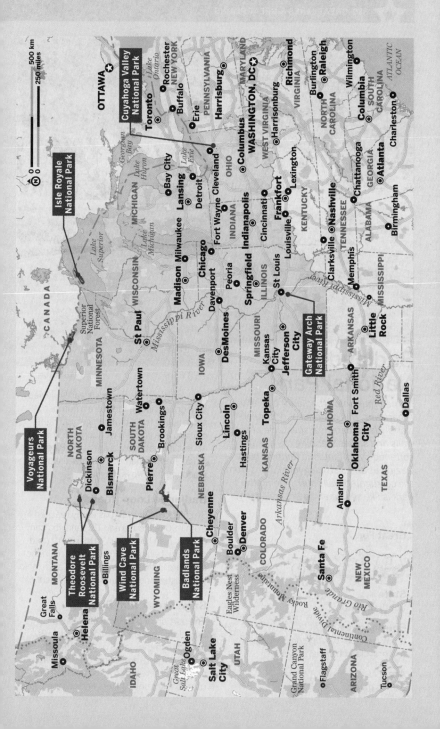

Badlands Loop Road

Badlands National Park

Named mako sica (badland) by Native Americans, this national park's other-worldly landscape is a spectacle of sheer walls and spikes stabbing the dry air, softened by its fantastic rainbow hues. Gazing upon its striking formations from the corrugated walls surrounding the park is like seeing an ocean boiled dry.

Great For...

State
South Dakota

Entrance Fee
7-day pass per car/person on foot, motorcycle or bicycle $20/10

Area
379 sq miles

The north unit of the park is easily viewed on a drive, though there are a number of short hiking trails that can get you right out into this earthen wonderland. The less-accessible south units are in the Pine Ridge Indian Reservation and see few visitors. Bisecting the two is Hwy 44.

Badlands Loop Road

Stunning Highway 240 is easily reached from I-90 (exits 110 and 131) and you can drive it in an hour if you're in a hurry (and not stuck behind an RV). It is the main thoroughfare in the park's north unit, with lookouts, vistas and animal sightings aplenty.

Sage Creek Rim Road

The portion of the Badlands west of Hwy 240 along this gravel road is much less visited than the sights of the Badlands Loop Rd. There are scenic overlooks and stops at prairie-dog towns; this is where most backcountry hikers and campers go

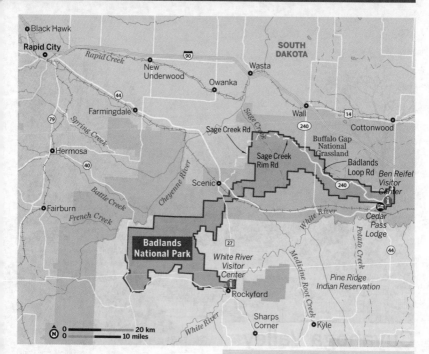

to escape the crowds. As there is almost no water or shade here, don't strike out into the wilderness unprepared.

Buffalo Gap National Grassland

The Badlands, along with the surrounding Buffalo Gap National Grassland, protects the country's largest prairie grasslands, several species of Great Plains mammal (including bison and black-footed ferret), prairie falcons and lots of snakes. Rangers can map out back-road routes that will let you do looping tours of Badlands National Park and the grasslands without ever touching I-90.

Sleeping & Eating

The park has two campgrounds and a seasonal lodge. Hotels can be found on I-90 in Kadoka and Wall. There are also campgrounds and inns near the southern entrance at Interior. There are restaurants of varying quality in Wall and Interior.

Essential Information

The park is 60 miles east of Rapid City, exiting I-90 at Wall. There's no public transportation to (or within) the park.

Ben Reifel Visitor Center (📞605-433-5361; www.nps.gov/badl; Hwy 240; ⊙7am-7pm Jun-Aug, 8am-5pm Apr, May, Sep & Oct, 8am-4pm Nov-Mar) The main visitor center. Don't miss the on-site paleontology lab.

National Grasslands Visitor Center (📞605-279-2125; www.fs.fed.us/grasslands; 708 Main St, Wall; ⊙8am-4:30pm Mon-Fri) Has good displays on the wealth of life in this complex ecosystem.

White River Visitor Center (Hwy 27; ⊙9am-4pm Jun-Aug) Small information outlet in the little-visited south unit.

Stay at a cozy cabin inside the park at **Cedar Pass Lodge** (📞605-433-5460; www.cedarpasslodge.com; Hwy 240; d $176; ⊙mid-Apr-mid-Oct; ❄@). There is a restaurant and shops. ∎

KENNETH SPONSLER/SHUTTERSTOCK ©

Ohio & Erie Canal

Cuyahoga Valley National Park

Ohio's only national park has a mystical beauty, especially on a cold morning when the mists thread the woods and all you hear is the sound of a great blue heron flapping over its hunting grounds. Its Native American name is 'crooked river' or possibly 'place of the jawbone.'

Great For...

State
Ohio

Entrance Fee
Free

Area
51 sq miles

Brandywine Falls

This pretty spill of ice-cold water sits nestled in a wooden idyll, and can be accessed via a 1.5-mile round-trip hike that features some light-elevation (160ft) gain. A small bridge and a boardwalk lookout make this a visitor favorite.

Hiking & Cycling

The park's main trail follows the old **Ohio & Erie Canal**. Boats pulled by mules once ran adjacent to this trail, now an ideal thoroughfare for hikers and cyclists. Information about the canal and towpath is available at the **Canal Exploration Center** (☏216-524-3537; www.nps.gov/cuva; 7104 Canal Rd; ⊙10am-4pm Jun-Aug, limited hours rest of year).

The most photographed place is probably **The Ledges** overlook. There's a moderately difficult loop trail nearby, a little over 2 miles in length.

The 5.3-mile **Old Carriage Trail**, past forested ledges, streams and a 500-foot

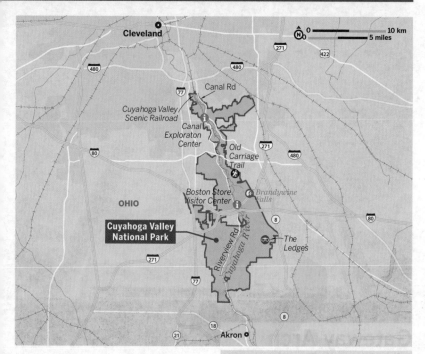

ravine, is one of the longer loop trails, but it's not particularly difficult.

Scenic Railroad

An old-school iron carriage chugs along the pleasant **Cuyahoga Valley Scenic Railroad** (CVSR; ☑800-468-4070; www.cvsr. com; adult $16-29, child $11-24) course from Akron to Independence, OH, through the heart of the park. The most expensive tickets score seating in the glass-topped 'dome.' A full round-trip takes around 3½ hours. You can take a bicycle on board ($5; April to October).

Camping & Lodging

There are five primitive campsites within the park, available for booking from late May through October ($25; www. reserveamerica.com). Bring water. The park is close enough to Cleveland or Akron for a day trip, and there are some more posh lodging options in Peninsula.

Essential Information

The park is easily accessible by car from Cleveland (20 miles) or Akron (18 miles), and lies just off of I-77.

Boston Store Visitor Center (☑330-657-2752; www.nps.gov/cuva/planyourvisit/boston-store; 1550 Boston Mills Rd; ⏰9:30am-5pm Sep-May, 8am-6pm Jun-Aug) A historic warehouse-cum-information depot, this center serves as the main visitor hub for the park. You can get updated information on any trail closures here, as well as detailed maps. If there is a lecture, ranger walk or visiting expert or artist at the park, all of the above will be based out of this building.

The Inn at Brandywine Falls (☑330-467-1812; www.innatbrandywinefalls.com; 8230 Brandywine Rd, Northfield; d $149-229, ste $239-349; ❄☎), an 1848 Greek Revival country home, has six individually differentiated rooms and delicious breakfasts. ∎

FLIPHOTO/SHUTTERSTOCK ©

Gateway Arch National Park

Officially dedicated as a national park in 2018, the park's footprint is small, fitting snugly into downtown St Louis along the Mississippi River. But its main attraction, the Gateway Arch, dominates the city's skyline and pays tribute to the Lewis and Clark expedition and westward expansion of the US.

Great For...

State
Missouri

Entrance Fee
Free

Area
0.14 sq miles

Gateway Arch

As a symbol for St Louis, the Gateway Arch has soared above any expectations its backers could have had in 1965 when it opened. The **Arch** (☑877-982-1410; www. gatewayarch.com; tram ride adult/child $13/10; ⊘8am-10pm Jun-Aug, 9am-6pm Sep-May, last tram 1hr before closing), designed by Eero Saarinen, serves as both a monument to the country's old western frontier and as an unmistakable icon for the city. At 630ft tall, it's the largest manmade monument in the US (more than twice as tall as the Statue of Liberty). A short tram ride to the top lets you take in the view, but tram cars can be a tight squeeze as they clank their way skyward.

Back on the ground, you can walk right up and touch the Arch's base, and kids will swear they can see the structure swaying in the wind as they look up (it is designed to do so, but only actually does in severe weather).

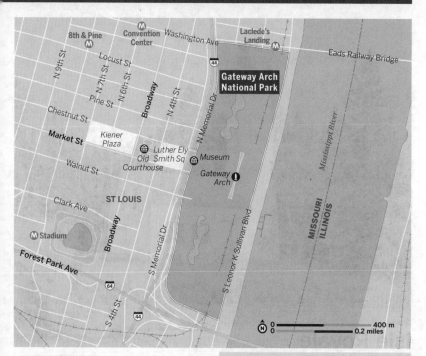

Old Courthouse

Free to enter, this **historic structure** (11 North 4th St; ⊘8am-4:30pm) was the site of two trials in the Dred Scott case, now considered among the very worst US Supreme Court decisions. Scott, an enslaved man who attempted to sue for his freedom, was denied standing to bring the suit. Now a museum, the courthouse's galleries deal with the ignominious history of slavery and the fight for emancipation.

Historical Museum

After receiving a facelift along with the rest of the park and reopening in summer 2018, this museum not only offers more high-tech interactive exhibits but an updated historical view of westward expansion, with displays acknowledging that the West was either 'won' or stolen, depending on your perspective. Visitors can also learn about the innovative engineering behind the Arch monument. ■

Essential Information

If you're in downtown St Louis, just look up and walk towards the giant silver arch. Can't miss it.

A greenway now seamlessly covers the highway that used to divide the arch grounds from the courthouse and rest of downtown.

Those further afield can take I-64, I-44 or I-55 into the city. There's no dedicated parking directly on-site, so look for a spot in the nearby Laclede's Landing bar district or in one of the garages around Busch Stadium (just not on a gameday). Public transportation options include the Metrolink light rail, which stops at Laclede's Landing, or city buses 99 and 40.

The park grounds are open daily from 5am to 11pm.

STEVE LAGRECA/SHUTTERSTOCK ©

Rock Harbor Lighthouse

Isle Royale National Park

Totally free of vehicles and roads, Isle Royale National Park in Lake Superior is the place to go for peace and quiet. It gets fewer visitors in a year than Yellowstone National Park gets in a day, which means the 1600 moose creeping through the forest are all yours.

Great For...

State
Michigan

Entrance Fee
1-day pass per person $7

Area
210 sq miles

The island is laced with 165 miles of hiking trails that connect dozens of campgrounds along Superior and inland lakes. You must be totally prepared for this wilderness adventure, with a tent, camping stove, sleeping bags, food and water filter. The park is open from mid-April through October, then it closes due to extreme weather.

Sleeping & Eating

Isle Royale offers two options: snooze with lake views at **Rock Harbor Lodge** (☏906-337-4993; www.rockharborlodge.com; r/cottage from $260/504; ☺late May-early Sep) or hike to the rustic campgrounds with outhouses that dot the island. There's no extra fee for camping – it's covered in the $7 per day park entrance fee.

The lodge has two eateries: a dining room serving American fare and a more casual cafe. The Dockside Store at Rock

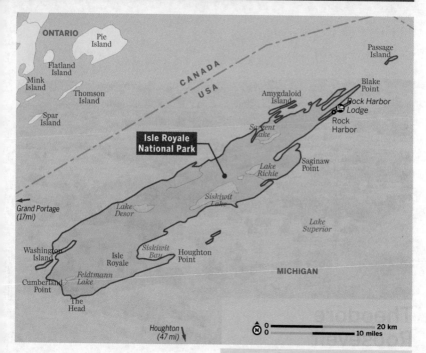

Harbor stocks a small array of groceries and there's another small store in Windigo. Prices are steep.

Getting There & Around

Reserve transportation well in advance. From the dock outside the park headquarters in Houghton, the **Ranger III** (⊘late May-early Sep) departs at 9am on Tuesday and Friday for the six-hour boat trip (one way adult/child $70/35) to Rock Harbor, at the east end of the island.

Isle Royale Seaplanes (☑906-483-4991; www.isleroyaleseaplanes.com; 21125 Royce Rd, Hancock) is quicker, flying from the Portage Canal Seaplane Base in Hancock to Rock Harbor or to Windigo (the island's west end) in 35 minutes (round-trip $320).

Or head 50 miles up the Keweenaw Peninsula to Copper Harbor and jump on the **Isle Royale Queen IV** (☑906-289-4437;

Essential Information

Isle Royale Park Headquarters (☑906-482-0984; www.nps.gov/isro; 800 E Lakeshore Dr, Houghton; ⊙8am-6pm Mon-Fri, from 10am Sat Jun-mid-Sep, 8am-4pm Mon-Fri mid-Sep-May) The park headquarters in Houghton provides information on entrance fees, ferries, camping etc.

www.isleroyale.com; 14 Waterfront Landing, Copper Harbor), an 8am 3½-hour crossing (round-trip adult/child $136/100), running daily from late July through August. Bringing a kayak or canoe on the ferries costs an additional $50 round-trip.

You can also access Isle Royale from Grand Portage, MN on the **Voyageur II** and **Seahunter III** (☑218-600-0765; www.isleroyaleboats.com; 402 Upper Road, Grand Portage). ∎

ZAKZEINERT/SHUTTERSTOCK ©

Theodore Roosevelt National Park

Wildlife abounds in these surreal mounds of striated earth, from mule deer to wild horses, bison, bighorn sheep and elk. Sunrise is your best time for animal encounters, while sunset is particularly evocative as shadows dance across the lonely buttes, painting them in an array of earth tones before they fade to black.

Great For...

State
North Dakota

Entrance Fee
7-day pass per car/motorcycle/person on foot or bicycle $30/25/15

Area
110 sq miles

The park is divided into North and South Units, 70 miles apart. South Unit, near Medora, houses the main visitor center and is closer to the interstate highway (I-94). The more remote North Unit is 15 miles south of Watford City.

Hiking

In the South Unit, the 0.4-mile **Wind Canyon Trail** leads to a dramatic viewpoint over the Little Missouri River. The slightly more strenuous 0.6-mile **Coal Vein Trail** traces the history of a coal vein that caught fire and burned for 26 years in the mid-20th century.

In the less visited North Unit, the 1.5-mile **Buckhorn Trail** leads to Prairie Dog Town, a favorite spot for observing these animated little critters. The challenging but spectacular 18-mile **Achenbach Trail** crosses the Little Missouri River twice and dips through American bison habitat: you'll see where bison roll on their backs for a dust bath.

Essential Information

South Unit Visitor Center (www.nps.gov/thro; off I-94 exits 24 & 27, Medora; ⏱8am-5pm Jun-Sep, to 4:30pm Oct-May) Bookstore, museum and information on ranger-led activities.

Teddy Roosevelt's Cabin

Future president Theodore Roosevelt retreated from New York to this remote spot after losing both his wife and mother in a matter of hours. The 25-year-old future president spent the winter of 1883–84 here, and it's said that his time in the Dakota badlands inspired him to become an avid conservationist – he set aside 230 million acres of federal land while in office.

Behind the South Unit Visitor Center, the cabin is faithfully reconstructed using its original Ponderosa pine logs. It houses a few artifacts belonging to Roosevelt, including a writing desk and a traveling trunk.

Horseback Riding

History buffs and adventurous spirits will find it hard to resist seeing these landscapes as Roosevelt himself did, on horseback. The 144-mile **Maah Daah Hey Trail**, which links the park's North and South Units, passes through a dauntingly rugged, scenic stretch of badlands.

Sleeping & Eating

The resort town of Medora makes a great base with comfortable lodgings across all budgets. The park itself has two campgrounds, including the more popular Cottonwood Campground in the South Unit. Wild camping is permitted in the backcountry for up to 14 consecutive nights; get a free permit at either visitor center. Pets, bicycles and motorized vehicles are strictly prohibited in the backcountry. Hazards to watch out for include ticks, poison ivy, scorpions, snakes and fast-moving bison.

Medora is the only place to eat near the South Unit Visitor Center, while less-attractive Watford City is closer to the less-visited North Unit. ∎

Great Plains Wildlife

Great Plains national parks protect large swaths of forest and grassland where bison, elk and wild horses roam. There are also hundreds of bird species, and innumerable prairie dogs in sprawling subterranean towns.

Mule Deer

Somewhere along your journey you're likely to encounter mule deer, named for their large mule-like ears, as they browse on leaves and twigs from shrubs. Look for them around dusk, grazing in herds.

Bison

Bison nearly met extinction because of hunting and human encroachment; by the 20th century, only a few hundred remained. Overcoming near extinction, new herds arose from these last survivors, so that one of America's noblest animals can again be admired in its gruff majesty – among other places, in Badlands, Theodore Roosevelt and Wind Cave National Parks.

Pronghorn Antelope

Curious-looking deer-like animals with two single black horns instead of antlers, pronghorns belong to a unique antelope family. They are only found in the American West, but they are more famous for being able to run up to 60mph for long stretches; they're the second-fastest land animal in the world.

Elk

Seeing a herd of North American elk, or *wapiti* (a Native American name meaning 'white rump,' a description of the animal's rear), grazing in their natural setting is unforgettable. Full-grown males may reach 1100lb and carry 5ft racks of antlers.

Prairie Dogs

The prairie dog is neither a prairie-dweller nor a dog: related to the squirrel, it lives in sprawling burrows known as prairie dog 'towns.'

Voyageurs National Park

It's all about water up in Voyageurs National Park, most of which is accessible only by hiking or motorboat. In the 17th century, French-Canadian fur traders began exploring the Great Lakes and northern rivers by canoe. The park covers part of their customary waterway, which became the border between the USA and Canada.

Great For...

State
Minnesota

Entrance Fee
Free

Area
341 sq miles

Boat Tours & Houseboats

The park operates **boat tours** (☏218-286-5258; www.recreation.gov; 2½hr tours adult/child $30/15; ⊙2pm Wed & Fri-Mon mid-Jun–early Sep, 2pm Mon & Wed mid-Sep) to see eagles, an 1890s gold-mining camp and more. It's best to reserve in advance. The park also offers free, 1½-hour jaunts in mighty voyageur canoes from late June to mid-August.

Novice boaters are welcome at family-run **Ebel's Voyageur Houseboats** (☏218-374-3 571; www.ebels.com; 10326 Ash River Trail; per day from $335; ⊙early May–early Oct). The pricier houseboats have air-conditioning, DVD players and hot tubs.

Winter Sports

When the boats get put away for the winter, the snowmobiles come out. Voyageurs is a hot spot for the sport, with 110 miles of staked and groomed trails slicing through the pines. Rainy Lake Visitor Center

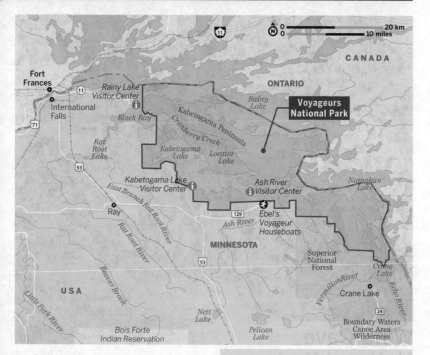

provides maps and advice. It also lends out snowshoes and cross-country skis for local trails, including a couple that depart outside the center. To the south, an ice road for cars spans the boat launches of the Ash River and Kabetogama Lake Visitor Centers. A fun sledding hill also plunges near the Kabetogama center.

Sleeping & Eating

Far-flung resorts and camping are the choices, aside from sleeping on your own houseboat.

Restaurants are few and usually connected to lodges. The communities of Kabetogama, Crane Lake, Ash River and International Falls hold the majority of places to eat.

Destination Voyageurs National Park (www.dvnpmn.com) has lodging and activity details for the park's gateway communities. ∎

Essential Information

Hwy 53 is the main highway to the region. It's about a five-hour drive from the Twin Cities (or a three-hour drive from Duluth) to Crane Lake, Ash River or Lake Kabetogama. International Falls, near the park's northwest edge, holds the closest airport.

Rainy Lake Visitor Center (☎218-286-5258; www.nps.gov/voya; Hwy 11; ⊗9am-5pm daily Jun-Aug, 9am-5pm Sat-Wed Sep, 10am-4pm Thu-Sun Oct-May) Eleven miles east of International Falls on Hwy 11, this is the main park office. Ranger-guided walks and boat tours are available here in summer, and equipment rentals in winter.

Ash River (☎218-374-3221; Mead Wood Rd; ⊗9am-5pm late May–late Sep) and **Kabetogama Lake** (☎218-875-2111; off Hwy 53; ⊗9am-5pm late May–late Sep) Seasonal visitor centers, both of which offer ranger-led programs.

Boxwork formations

Wind Cave National Park

Above ground, Wind Cave National Park protects forests and grasslands where bison, elk and prairie dogs roam. But the central draw is below ground: Wind Cave, containing 148 miles of mapped passages, is one of the world's longest underground realms. Strong gusts at the entrance give the cave its name.

Great For...

State
South Dakota

Entrance Fee
Free

Area
44 sq miles

Cave Tours

Several **tours** ($10 to $30) plunge you into the scene. The easiest is the hour-long **Garden of Eden Tour**, a 0.33-mile walk. The most strenuous is the four-hour **Wild Cave Tour**, where you crawl and climb through further-flung passages. The moderate **Natural Entrance Tour** is the most popular, while the romantic **Candlelight Tour** dips into less-developed sections of the cave, lit only by – that's right – candles.

Hiking

Back at the surface, hikers reap big rewards on 30 miles of unspoiled trails that ramble through rolling prairie and pine forest. **Rankin Ridge** is an easy walk where you amble up a one-mile path to an old fire tower, the park's highest point. The **Cold Brook Canyon Trail** is a moderate 2.8-mile hike that takes in meadows, a prairie dog town and falcon-laden cliffs. The **Centennial Trail** is a bit more difficult, meandering

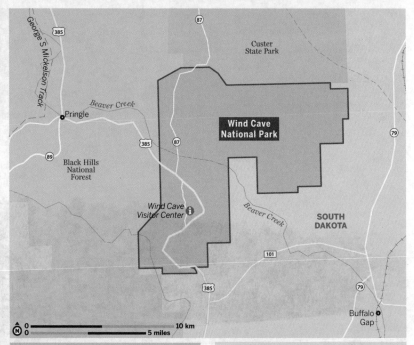

Rock Formations

The cave's foremost feature is its 'boxwork' calcite formations, which look like honeycomb and date back 60 to 100 million years. Wind Cave is one of the few places where you can see boxwork, along with strange formations such as popcorn, moon milk, frostwork and gypsum flowers.

six miles one way through patches of prairie and along Beaver Creek.

Wildlife Spotting

Wildlife watchers get an eyeful driving the park's rustic roads. Keep an eye out for large herds of bison, elk and pronghorn antelope that wander the plains munching fresh grass. Prairie dog towns see lots of action, and not just from the cute main characters, but also from sneaky coyotes

Essential Information

The nearest airport is 60 miles away in Rapid City. There's no public transport.

Wind Cave Visitor Center (☏605-745-4600; www.nps.gov/wica; off US 385; ☺8am-4:30pm daily, expanded hours Jun-Aug) Has exhibits, maps and books and is the place to go for tour details and bookings, and camping permits.

and slithering black-footed ferrets. The town at the intersection of Hwys 385 and 87 provides a good peek at the scene.

Sleeping

The park (www.nps.gov/wica) has one campground with flush toilets (no showers or electricity). The 62 campsites (per night $18) are available first-come, first-served. Backcountry camping is allowed in certain areas; get a free permit from the visitor center. ■

NEW ENGLAND
& THE
MID-ATLANTIC

In This Chapter

Acadia 402
Shenandoah 412

New England & the Mid-Atlantic

New England undulates with the rolling hills and rocky peaks of the ancient Appalachian Mountains. By the coast, views of thrashing surf inspire; inland, the rugged landscape begs to be explored on leisurely scenic drives.

Near the country's northeasternmost tip is Acadia, a parcel of untamed New England coastline. Southeast in Virginia is Shenandoah, often visited in combination with the Great Smoky Mountains and linked via the scenic Blue Ridge Pkwy and the Appalachian Trail.

Don't Miss

○ Driving the spectacular Acadia National Park road trip (p408)

○ Mountain vistas along Skyline Drive (p412)

○ Cycling Acadia's fabled carriage roads (p403)

○ The bird's-eye view from Precipice Trail (p408)

○ Tremendous hikes to Old Rag Mountain and Hawksbill Summit (p413)

When to Go

During high season (May to October) accommodation prices increase by 50% to 100%; book in advance. In spring, the weather's temperate and fruit trees bloom. It's hot and humid by July and August, except in mountain areas. Cooler weather arrives with harvest season in September and October, with peak foliage in October.

There's less demand for accommodations during the shoulder season (March to April), and there are significantly lower price tags from November to February, although some sights in seasonal destinations close.

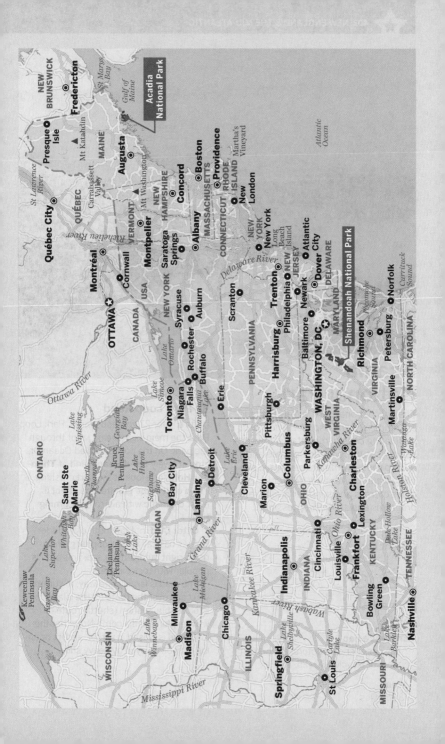

SKYLER EWING/SHUTTERSTOCK ©

Acadia National Park

The only national park in New England encompasses an unspoiled wilderness of undulating coastal mountains, towering sea cliffs, surf-pounded beaches and quiet ponds. Swimmers can brave the chilly waters, hikers will delight in 125 miles of trails and summer brings ranger programs and stargazing sessions.

Great For...

State
Maine

Entrance Fee
7-day pass per car/motorcycle/person on foot or bicycle $30/25/15

Area
73 sq miles

❶ Park Loop Road

Unfurling for 27 gorgeous miles, Park Loop Rd is the main sightseeing jaunt through the park. On the portion called Ocean Dr, stop at lovely **Sand Beach**, and at **Thunder Hole** for a look at the surf crashing into a cleft in the granite. The effect is most dramatic with a strong incoming tide.

Otter Cliff, not far south of Thunder Hole, is basically a wall of pink granite rising right out from the sea. This area is popular with rock climbers.

The road is largely one-way; in summer you can cover the route on the Island Explorer bus system (shuttle route 4; www.exploreacadia.com). Note that the loop road is closed in winter, and its opening may be delayed by heavy snow.

❷ Cadillac Mountain

Don't leave the park without driving – or hiking – to the 1530ft summit of Cadillac Mountain. For panoramic views of Frenchman Bay, walk the paved 0.5-mile **Cadillac Mountain Summit Loop**. The summit is a popular place in the early morning because it's long been touted as the first spot in the US to see the sunrise. The truth? It is, but only between October 7 and March 6. The crown is passed to northern coastal towns the rest of the year because of the tilt of the earth. But, hey, the sunset is always a good bet.

❸ Cycling the Carriage Roads

John D Rockefeller Jr, a lover of old-fashioned horse carriages, gifted Acadia with some 45 miles of crisscrossing carriage roads. Made from crushed stone, the roads are free from cars and are popular with cyclists, hikers and equestrians. Several of them fan out from Jordan Pond House, but if the lot is too crowded continue north to the parking area at **Eagle Lake** on US 233 to link to the carriage road network.

The Bicycle Express Shuttle runs to Eagle Lake from the Bar Harbor Village Green from late June through September. Pick up a *Carriage Road User's Map* at the visitor center.

❹ Hiking & Swimming

Acadia has more than 125 miles of trails. Some are easy enough to stroll with a small child, while others require sturdy boots, full water bottles and plenty of lung power. The Cadillac Mountain Summit Loop is an easy choice, and a good moderate pick is the forested 2.2-mile trail to the summit of **Champlain Mountain**. A little further south, the **Beehive Trail**, at less than a mile, involves clinging to iron rings bolted to the cliff face and is for the fit.

Near the Beehive trailhead, swimmers can brave the icy (55°F, even in midsummer!) waters of **Sand Beach** or take a dip in the marginally warmer **Echo Lake**, west of Somes Sound. Both areas have lifeguard patrols in summer.

❺ Jordan Pond

On clear days, the glassy waters of this 176-acre pond reflect the image of Penobscot Mountain like a mirror. A stroll around the pond and its surrounding forests and flower meadows is one of Acadia's most popular and family-friendly activities. (Sorry, no swimming allowed.) Follow the 3-mile self-guided nature trail around the pond before stopping for a cuppa at the Jordan Pond House (p406).

Essential Information

Sleeping

Most of the hotels, B&Bs and private campgrounds are in Bar Harbor. There are two great rustic campgrounds in the Mt Desert Island section of the park, with around 500 tent sites between them. Both are densely wooded but only a few minutes' walk to the ocean.

Note that reservations for the park campgrounds are handled by Recreation. gov, not the park itself.

Seawall Campground (☑877-444-6767; www. recreation.gov; 668 Seawall Rd; tent sites $22-30, RV sites $30; ☺late May-Sep) Four miles south of Southwest Harbor, Seawall has 200 sites (no electric hookups). There are flush toilets, running water, a dump station, picnic tables and fire rings. Paid showers and a campers store are 1 mile away. Reservations are essential.

Eating

Picnickers will find plenty of areas to enjoy alfresco dining – bring supplies from Bar Harbor.

Jordan Pond House (☑207-276-3316; https:// jordanpondhouse.com; Park Loop Rd; tea & popovers $11, mains $11-33; ☺11am-9pm mid-May–mid-Oct) Afternoon tea at this lodge-like teahouse has been an Acadia tradition since the late 1800s. Steaming pots of Earl Grey come with hot popovers (hollow rolls made with egg batter) and strawberry jam. The large lunch menu ranges from lobster quiche to meatloaf sandwich.

Visitor Center

The informative **Hulls Cove Visitor Center** (☑207-288-8832; www.nps.gov/acad; ME 3; ☺8:30am-4:30pm mid-Apr–Jun, Sep & Oct, 8am-6pm Jul & Aug) anchors the park's main Hulls Cove entrance, 3 miles northwest of Bar Harbor via ME 3. Buy your park pass and pick up maps and info. The 27-mile-long Park Loop Rd, which circumnavigates the eastern section of Mt Desert Island, starts near here.

When the visitor center is closed (November to mid-April), head to park headquarters, 3 miles west of Bar Harbor on ME 233, for information.

Getting Around

Hiring a bike in nearby Bar Harbor is a breeze, and a good way to avoid traffic snarls and parking problems.

The free shuttle system, the Island Explorer (www.exploreacadia.com), features nine routes that link hotels, inns and campgrounds to destinations within Acadia National Park. Route maps are available at local establishments and online. Most of the routes converge on the Village Green in Bar Harbor. The shuttle runs from late June to mid-October.

Top left: Sunrise from Cadillac Mountain; Top right: Hikers on Champlain Mountain; Bottom: Jordan Pond

CLASSIC ROAD TRIPS

Acadia National Park

John D Rockefeller Jr and other wealthy landowners gave Acadia its bridges, overlooks and stone steps. Travelers can put Rockefeller's planning to good use by touring the wonderful Park Loop Rd by car.

Duration 3 days

Distance 112 miles

Best Time to Go
May through October for good weather and open facilities.

Essential Photo
Capture that sea-and-sunrise panorama from atop Cadillac Mountain.

Best for Outdoors
Hike a 'ladder trail' up a challenging cliff.

❶ Hulls Cove Visitor Center

Whoa, whoa, whoa. Before zooming into Bar Harbor on ME 3, stop at the park visitor center (p406) to get the lay of the land and pay the admission fee. Inside, head directly to the large diorama, which provides a helpful overview of Mt Desert Island (MDI). As you'll see, Acadia National Park shares the island with several nonpark communities, which are tucked here and there beside Acadia's borders.

From the visitor center, the best initiation to the park is to drive the 27-mile **Park Loop Road**, which links the park's highlights in the eastern section of MDI. It's one way (traveling clockwise) for most of its length.

The Drive ›› From the visitor center, turn right onto the Park Loop Rd, not ME 3 (which leads into Bar Harbor). Take in a nice view of Frenchman Bay on your left before passing the spur to ME 233. A short distance ahead, turn left to begin the one-way loop on Park Loop Rd.

❷ Sieur de Monts Spring

Nature lovers and history buffs will enjoy a stop at the Sieur de Monts Spring area at the intersection of ME 3 and the Park Loop Rd. Here you'll find a nature center and the summer-only branch of the **Abbe Museum** (📞207-288-3519; www.abbemuseum.org; ME 3 & Park Loop Rd; adult/child $3/1; ⏲10am-5pm late May-Oct), which sits in a lush, nature-like setting and hosts a fascinating collection of natural artifacts related to Maine's Native American heritage. Twelve of Acadia's biospheres are displayed in miniature at the **Wild Gardens of Acadia** FREE, from bog to coniferous woods to meadow. Botany enthusiasts will appreciate the plant labels. There are also some amazing stone-step trails here, appearing out of the talus as if by magic.

The Drive ›› If you wish to avoid driving the full park loop, you can follow ME 3 from here into Bar Harbor. Push on for the full experience – you won't regret it.

❸ Precipice Trail

What's the most exciting way to get a bird's-eye view of the park? By climbing up to where the birds are. Two 'ladder trails' cling to the sides of exposed cliffs on the northeastern section of Park Loop Rd, dubbed Ocean Dr. If you're fit and the season's right, tackle the first of the ladder trails, the steep, challenging 1.6-mile Precipice Trail, which climbs the east face of Champlain Mountain on iron rungs and ladders. (Note that the trail is typically closed late spring to mid-August because it's a nesting area for peregrine falcons. If it is closed, you might find volunteers and staff monitoring the birds through scopes from the trailhead parking lot.) Skip the trail on rainy days.

The Drive » Continue south on Park Loop Rd. The Beehive Trail starts 100ft north of the Sand Beach parking area.

❹ Beehive Trail & Sand Beach

Another good ladder trail is the Beehive Trail. The 0.8-mile climb includes ladders, rungs, narrow wooden bridges and scrambling – with steep drop-offs. As with the Precipice Trail, it's recommended that you descend via a nearby walking route, rather than climbing down.

Don't let the crowds keep you away from Sand Beach. It's home to one of the few sandy shorelines in the park, and it's a don't-miss spot. But you don't have to visit in the middle of the day to appreciate its charms. Beat the crowds early in the morning, or visit at night, especially for the **Stars over Sand Beach** program. During these free one-hour talks, lie on the beach, look up at the sky and listen to rangers share

stories and science about the stars. Even if you miss the talk, the eastern coastline along Ocean Dr is worth checking out at night, when you can watch the Milky Way slip right into the ocean.

The Drive » Swoop south past the crashing waves of Thunder Hole. If you want to exit the loop road, turn right onto Otter Cliff Rd, which hooks up to ME 3 north into Bar Harbor. Otherwise, pass Otter Point then follow the road inland past Wildwood Stables.

❺ Jordan Pond House

Share hiking stories with other nature-lovers at the lodge-like Jordan Pond House (p406) over a traditional afternoon tea. If you catch clear weather, Mt Penobscot's mirror image is visible in the waters of Jordan Pond.

The Drive » Look up for the rock precariously perched atop South Bubble from the pull-off almost 2 miles north. Continue north to access Cadillac Mountain Rd.

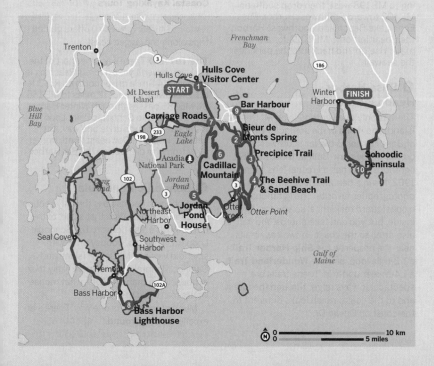

❻ Cadillac Mountain

The summit of Cadillac Mountain is the first spot in the US to see the sunrise (well, between October 7 and March 6). Drink in the views of Frenchman Bay, whether or not you arise to greet the dawn.

The Drive » You could complete the loop road and exit the park, heading for your accommodations or next destination. But consider finding a parking lot and tackling walking trails, heading to Bar Harbor to hire bikes, or continuing on with your drive.

❼ Carriage Roads

One of John D Rockefeller Jr's gifts to the park was 45 miles of carriage roads. Car-free and popular among cyclists, several such roads branch out from Jordan Pond House, or you can meet them a bit further north, here by Eagle Lake.

The Drive » Still in the mood for cruising? Before you head for the bright lights of Bar Harbor, take a detour: drive ME 233 toward the western part of MDI, connecting to ME 198 west, then drop south on ME 102 toward Southwest Harbor. Pass Echo Lake Beach and Southwest Harbor, then bear left onto ME 102A for a dramatic rise up and back into the park near the seawall.

❽ Bass Harbor Head Lighthouse

There is only one lighthouse on Mt Desert Island, and it sits in the somnolent village of Bass Harbor in the far southwest corner of the park. Built in 1858, the 36ft lighthouse still has a Fresnel lens from 1902. It's in a beautiful location that's a photographer favorite. The lighthouse is a coastguard residence, so you can't go inside, but you can take photos. You can also stroll to the coast on two easy trails near the property: the **Ship Harbor Trail**, a 1.2-mile loop, and the **Wonderland Trail**, a 1.4-mile round-trip. These trails are spectacular ways to get through the forest and to the coast, which looks different to the coast on Ocean Dr.

The Drive » For a lollipop loop, return on ME 102A to ME 102 through the village of Bass Harbor. Follow ME 102 then ME 233 all the way to Bar Harbor.

❾ Bar Harbor

Tucked on the rugged coast in the shadows of Acadia's mountains, Bar Harbor is a busy gateway town with a J Crew joie de vivre. Restaurants, taverns and boutiques are scattered along Main St, Mt Desert St and Cottage St. Shops sell everything from books to camping gear to handicrafts and art. Visit this large branch of the **Abbe Museum** (26 Mt Desert St; adult/child $8/4; ⊙10am-5pm May-Oct, 10am-4pm Thu-Sat Nov-Apr). The collection holds more than 50,000 objects, such as pottery, tools, combs and fishing instruments spanning the last 2000 years, including contemporary pieces.

Done browsing? Spend the rest of the afternoon, or early evening, exploring the area by water. Sign up in Bar Harbor for a half-day or sunset sea-kayaking trip. **Coastal Kayaking Tours** (☑207-288-9605; www.acadiafun.com; 48 Cottage St; 2½hr/half-day tours $46/56; ⊙May-Oct) offers guided trips along the jagged coast.

The Drive » There's another part of the park you haven't yet explored. Reaching it involves a 44-mile drive (north on Rte 3 to US 1, following it about 17 miles to ME 186 S). ME 186 passes through Winter Harbor and then links to Schoodic Point Loop Rd. It's about an hour's drive one way. Alternatively, hop on a Downeast Windjammer ferry from the pier beside the Bar Harbor Inn.

❿ Schoodic Peninsula

The Schoodic Peninsula is the only section of Acadia National Park that's part of the mainland. It's also home to the Schoodic Loop Rd, a rugged, woodsy drive with splendid views of Mt Desert Island and Cadillac Mountain. You're more likely to see a moose here than on MDI – what moose wants to cross a bridge?

Much of the drive is one way. There's an excellent **campground** (☑877-444-6777; www.recreation.gov; campsites $22-30; ⊙late

May–mid-Oct) near the entrance, then a picnic area at **Frazer Point**. Further along the loop, turn right for a short ride to **Schoodic Point**, a 440ft-high promontory with ocean views.

The full loop from Winter Harbor is 11.5 miles and covers park, town and state roads. If you're planning to come by ferry, you could rent a bike beforehand at **Bar Harbor Bicycle Shop** (☏207-288-3886; www.barharborbike.com; 141 Cottage St; rental per day $25-50; ⊗8am-6pm) – the loop road's smooth surface and easy hills make it ideal for cycling.

In July and August, the Island Explorer Schoodic shuttle bus runs from Winter Harbor to the peninsula ferry terminal and around the Park Loop Rd. It does not link to Bar Harbor. ■

Top: Wild Gardens of Acadia; Bottom: Bass Harbor Head Lighthouse

Skyline Drive

Shenandoah National Park

Shenandoah is a showcase of natural color and beauty: in spring and summer the wildflowers explode, in fall the leaves burn red and orange, and in winter a starkly beautiful hibernation period sets in. White-tailed deer are common and, with luck, you might spot a black bear, bobcat or wild turkey.

Great For...

State
Virginia

Entrance Fee
7-day pass per car/motorcycle/person on foot or bicycle $30/25/15

Area
310 sq miles

With the famous 105-mile Skyline Dr and more than 500 miles of hiking trails, including 101 miles of the Appalachian Trail, there is plenty to do and see.

Skyline Drive

A 105-mile-long road running down the spine of the Blue Ridge Mountains, Shenandoah National Park's Skyline Dr redefines the definition of 'Scenic Route.' You're constantly treated to an impressive view, but keep in mind the road is bendy and slow-going (35mph limit), and is congested in peak season.

It's best to start this drive just south of Front Royal, VA; from here you'll snake over Virginia wine and hill country. Numbered mileposts mark the way; there are lots of pull-offs. Our favorite is around Mile 51.2, where you can take a moderately difficult 3.6-mile-loop hike to **Lewis Spring Falls**.

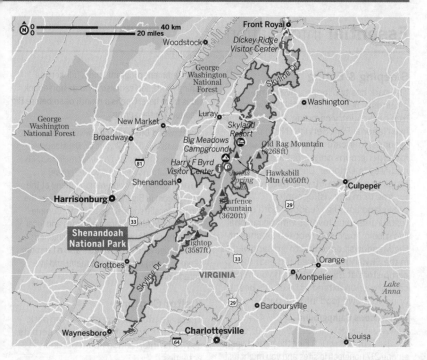

Hiking

The hike to the rocky summit of **Old Rag Mountain** is one of the best in the state. This extremely tough, full-day 9.2-mile circuit trail culminates in an adventurous rocky scramble – one that's suitable only for the physically fit. Your reward is the summit of Old Rag Mountain, not to mention the fantastic views along the way.

Hawksbill Summit is another breath-taking hiking destination (literally). The tremendous climb to the park's highest peak offers an unforgettable picture of the mountain landscape. There are two options: either a 2.9-mile loop or 1.7-mile up-and-back. For the shorter route, start at the Hawksbill Gap parking area (Mile 45.6) and look for the Lower Hawksbill Trail, which leads into the woods. The steep ascent is lined with mountain ash and red spruce – beware of small, frequent rock-slides along the jumbled path.

At **Bearfence Mountain** a short trail leads to a spectacular 360-degree view-point. The circuit hike is only 1.2 miles, but one section involves an adventurous scramble over rocks.

Cycling

The park holds occasional 'Ride the Drive' car-free days when Skyline Dr is closed to motorized vehicles from Mile 0 south to Mile 31.5 in the northern district, leaving it open for cyclists. Check the park website to see when the next car-free day is scheduled.

Essential Information

Sleeping & Eating

The park has two lodges, five camp-grounds, a number of rental cabins and free backcountry camping. Camping is at five National Park Service (NPS) camp-grounds; four cater to individuals, one is for larger groups only. Most are open from mid-May to October. Camping elsewhere requires a backcountry permit, available for free from any visitor center.

Skyland and Big Meadows both have restaurants, plus taverns with occasional live music. You can buy boxed lunches at Big Meadows Lodge and to-go sandwiches in the Skyland lobby area and near the camp store at Big Meadows. If you're going camping or on extended hikes, it's best to bring your own food into the park.

Big Meadows Campground (☎877-444-6777; www.recreation.gov; Mile 51.3, Skyline Dr; tent & RV sites $20; ☺May-Oct) Find the perfect spot among 217 nonelectric sites and you might just snap a quick photo of a resident bear lumbering past your campfire. This campground tends to be crowded, especially during fall, but it's smack in the middle of Skyline Dr, has good facilities (flush toilets, showers, store, laundry) and is a convenient base for all exploration.

Skyland Resort (☎855-470-6005; www. goshenandoah.com; Mile 41.7, Skyline Dr; r $141-265, cabins $130-281; ☺late Mar–mid-Nov; ❄🛜) Founded in 1888, this spectacu-larly located resort commands views over the countryside. You'll find a variety of room types, including recently renovated premium rooms; rustic but comfy cabins; a taproom with a live

entertainment program; and a full-service dining room. You can also arrange horseback rides from here. Opens a month or so before Big Meadows in the spring.

Spottswood Dining Room (www.visitshenan doah.com; Mile 51.3, Skyline Dr, Big Meadows Lodge; lunch mains $8-17, dinner mains $12-28; ☺7:30-10am, noon-2pm & 5:30-9pm early May-early Nov) The wide-ranging menu at the dining room in Big Meadows Lodge makes the most of locally sourced ingredients. Comple-ment your food with Virginian wines and local microbrews, all enjoyed in an old-fashioned rustic-lodge ambience. There's also a taproom (2pm to 11pm) with a limited menu and live entertainment.

Visitor Centers

There are two visitor centers in the park. Both have maps and backcountry permits, as well as information about outdoor activities.

Dickey Ridge (www.nps.gov/shen; Mile 4.6, Sky-line Dr; ☺9am-5pm Mon-Fri, to 6pm Sat & Sun, closed late Nov-early Apr) In the north.

Harry F Byrd (www.nps.gov/shen; Mile 51, Skyline Dr; ☺9am-5pm late Mar-late Nov, 9:30am-4pm Fri-Sun late Nov-late Mar) In the south.

Getting There & Around

The park lies just 75 miles west of Washing-ton, DC, and can be easily accessed from several exits off I-81. ∎

Top left: Blue Ridge; Top right: On Bearfence Mountain; Bottom: Old Rag Mountain

THE SOUTH

In This Chapter

Congaree 420
Great Smoky Mountains 422
Hot Springs 436
Mammoth Cave 438

The South

Mighty mountains, meandering waterways, yawning caves...all are gathered in the South. Here you'll find America's most-visited national park, the Great Smoky Mountains, replete with sparkling waterfalls and foggy peaks to conquer. Meanwhile, Mammoth Caves beckons travelers to stroll, scramble or spelunk through a subterranean wonderland.

More leisurely pursuits await at the piping-hot waters of Hot Springs and Congaree, where days are spent canoeing through high-rise hardwood forests.

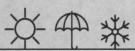

Don't Miss

● Drinking in panoramic views on the Charlies Bunion & Kephart Loop (p434)

● Gawping at grottoes in Mammoth Cave (p438)

● Canoeing among cypresses in Congaree (p420)

● Being kissed by mist in Laurel Falls (p429)

● A historic spa experience in Hot Springs (p436)

When to Go

Springtime (April to June) is mild and abloom with flowers. It's a good time to beat the crowds if you don't mind nights that can dip below freezing.

Summer gets steamy, often unpleasantly so. The Smoky Mountains can be frustratingly crowded from June to August but this is prime time for water sports, higher-elevation trails and ranger-led activities. In October, fall foliage is a sight to melt the heart.

The snowy months of December through February draw only hardy, well-prepared souls.

Previous page: Great Smoky Mountains National Park (p422)

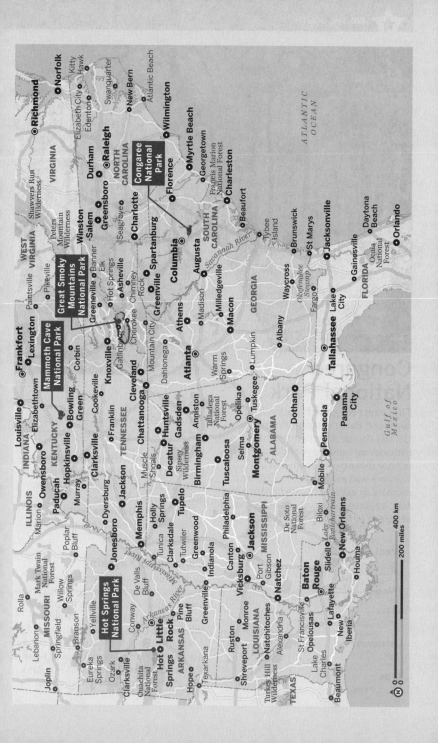

JASON YODER/SHUTTERSTOCK ©

Congaree National Park

The largest old-growth, bottomland hardwood forest in the southeastern US, this floodplain ecosystem has meandering waterways and a sky-high canopy replete with champion trees. The park was established in 1976 and remains an excellent place to canoe and hike, as you occasionally glance skyward at upland pines and bald cypresses.

Great For...

State
South Carolina

Entrance Fee
Free

Area
35 sq miles

Hiking

There are 10 walking trails serving all ages and levels of athleticism, ranging from half a mile to nearly 12 miles.

The popular 2.4-mile **boardwalk**, which begins at the visitor center, takes about an hour to complete. Wheelchairs, strollers and dogs are all welcomed.

The 6.6-mile **Oakridge Trail** is among the best hikes in the state, with its lofty oaks and scenic creeks.

Canoeing & Kayaking

Cedar Creek's ink-black waters wind through 27 miles of wilderness, and canoeing is an ideal way to explore the park, particularly on the seasonal, ranger-led **Wilderness Canoe Tour**.

Another option is to rent a canoe or take a guided tour with Columbia-based **River Runner Outdoor Center** (☏803-771-0353; www.shopriverrunner.com; 905 Gervais St).

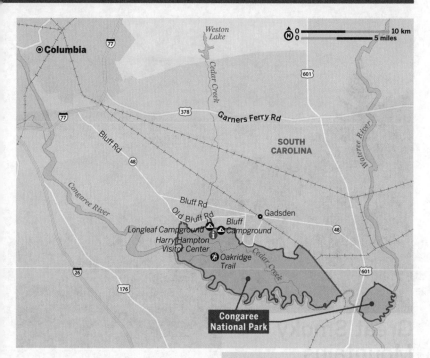

Sleeping & Eating

Tent camping is the only overnight option in Congaree National Park. **Longleaf Campground** (📞877-444-6777; www.recreation.gov; campsites for up to 8/24 people $10/20) is easily accessible by car along the entrance road, and the further-flung **Bluff Campground** (📞877-444-6777; www.recreation.gov; tent sites for up to 8 people $5) requires a mile's hike. Backcountry camping is also available and free; guests must register with the the visitor center.

For those who prefer a bed and walls, Columbia (a 30-minute drive away) has good hotels, including lovely historic inns. Southern kitchen **JD's Place** (📞803-353-0061; 7727 Bluff Rd, Gadsen; mains $9.25-11.25; ⊘8am-7:30pm) is a great stop after a hike or a paddle. ∎

Essential Information

Harry Hampton Visitor Center (📞803-776-4396; www.nps.gov/cong; 100 National Park Rd, Hopkins; ⊘9am-5pm) has an auditorium showing an 18-minute film on the park, a museum and a bookstore selling field guides, snacks, souvenirs and other items.

Mosquito Meter

Be sure to check the 'mosquito meter' at the visitor center so you know what you're getting into. It will let you know on a scale of 1 to 6 how buggy the park will be.

DAVE ALLEN PHOTOGRAPHY/SHUTTERSTOCK ©

Great Smoky Mountains National Park

Part of the vast Appalachian chain, among the oldest mountains on the planet, this is a forested, four-season wonderland. Get back to nature among mist-shrouded peaks, shimmering waterfalls and lush forests in this great American wilderness.

Great For...

State
North Carolina & Tennessee

Entrance Fee
Free

Area
816 sq miles

Great Smoky Mountains National Park straddles the North Carolina and Tennessee border, which runs diagonally through the heart of the park, shadowed by the Appalachian Trail.

Cades Cove

In Appalachian parlance, a cove means a valley, but Cades Cove is far more than that. Many consider this special place to be a national treasure, thanks to its poignant cultural legacy, telling pioneer architecture and plentiful wildlife. Then there's the landscape itself: lush green fields enveloped by an unbroken expanse of mountains. It's no wonder so many families return year after year. The best wildlife viewing is in the very early morning and late afternoon.

Because of bumper-to-bumper traffic during peak season, it can take five hours to drive the 11-mile one-way loop road – longer than it would take to walk! The loop road is open to car traffic from dawn to dusk, except on Wednesdays and Saturdays from early May through late September, when bicycles and hikers rule the road until 10am. Pick up the self-guiding *Cades Cove Tour* booklet ($1) from any visitor center.

Mt LeConte

The park's third-highest peak and one of its most familiar sights, Mt LeConte (6593ft) is visible from practically every viewpoint. The only way to the top is on foot. It is accessible on five trails, which range from 5 to 8.9 miles in length.

Reaching the summit (located 0.2 miles above the lodge) is a challenging goal, and it's well worth the effort. Aside from great views, you can stop in the office and lounge at **LeConte Lodge** to check out photos of cabin life dating back to the 1930s and browse the small shop.

Hiking Trails

Even if you're only here for a short visit, be sure to include at least one hike in your itinerary. Trails range from flat, easy and short paths to longer, more strenuous endeavors.

The trail to **Ramsey Cascades** travels through old-growth forest dotted with massive tulip trees to one spectacular waterfall. The hike's start is deceptively easy, along a wide, packed trail but you'll need to work hard to make it all the way – it's tough going, with an elevation gain of 2280ft. Also a slog is the **Rainbow Falls Trail**, which involves ascending 1600ft in a scant 2.7 miles. But oh, is it worth it when you see misty Rainbow Falls, one of the park's prettiest and most delicate waterfalls.

Near the start of the Roaring Fork Motor Nature Trail, the **Baskins Creek Trail** is a fascinating 5.6-mile (round-trip) out-and-back hike, drawing a fraction of the

Ancient Mountains

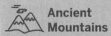

The story of the Smoky Mountains began in primordial times when clashing supersized continents created a chain of mountains that are today among the oldest on the planet. Humans have also left their mark on these ancient Appalachian landscapes. Nomadic tribes were the first to the area, followed by early settlers. In the 1900s lumber companies arrived, nearly wiping out the forests. Luckily, in the 1920s a few visionary locals fought for the park's creation, which finally became a reality in 1934.

On November 23, 2016 tragedy struck Great Smoky Mountains National Park when fire was reported on Chimney Tops, one of the park's most popular trails. The combination of exceptional drought conditions, low humidity and wind gusts that topped 80 miles an hour caused the fire to spread quickly in what would soon become the the deadliest wildfire in the eastern USA since the Great Fires of 1947. There were 14 deaths, 175 injuries, more than 2400 structures damaged or destroyed, and the forced evacuation of 14,000 residents.

TOP: PAT CANOVA/ALAMY STOCK PHOTO ©; BOTTOM RIGHT: ANTON FOLTIN/SHUTTERSTOCK ©; BOTTOM LEFT: KELLY VANDELLEN/SHUTTERSTOCK ©

Top: Baskins Creek Trail; Bottom right: Ramsey
Cascades; Bottom left: LeConte Lodge

number of visitors to more popular nearby
sites. Along the way, you'll spy white vein
quartz, see fire-blackened tree trunks
from the 2016 fires and make a few creek
crossings.

Cycling

Bicycles are welcome on most park roads,
with the exception of the Roaring Fork
Motor Nature Trail. However, it is important
that you choose your road wisely. Because
of steep terrain, narrow byways and heavy
car traffic, many park roads are not well
suited to safe or enjoyable riding. Great
Smoky has no mountain-biking trails.
Bicycles are allowed only on the Gatlinburg
Trail, the Oconaluftee River Trail and the
Lower Deep Creek Trail. They are prohibited on all other park trails.

By far the best place for a carefree
cycling tour is Cades Cove, particularly
when the road is closed to cars (Wednes-
day and Sunday before 10am from
mid-May to late September). In summer
and fall, rent cycles from **Cades Cove
Campground Store** (☐865-448-9034; www.
cadescovetrading.com; 10035 Campground Dr;
☺9am-9pm late May-Oct, to 5pm Mar-May, Nov
& late Dec).

Rafting

Many winding creeks and crystal-clear
streams rushing through the Smokies find
their way into the Big Pigeon River. When
they converge, they create a fantastic setting for **white-water adventures** (☐800-
776-7238; www.raftinginthesmokies.com; rafting
trip $35-42) on churning rapids amid a
gorgeous forest backdrop. Families with
small kids can enjoy a peaceful paddle on
the Lower Pigeon, while those seeking a bit
more adventure should opt for the Upper
Pigeon with its class III and IV rapids. It all
makes for a fun day's outing with some of
the best rafting in the southeast.

Horseback Riding

A staggering – or should we say galloping – 550 miles of the park's hiking trails are open to horses and their humans. Assuming you're not towing your own horse, sign on for a trail ride at one of the park's three stables (www.nps.gov/grsm/planyourvisit/horseriding.htm), all open between mid-March and mid-November. It's best to call ahead to make reservations.

One-hour trail rides cost about $35 per person. Those who want a bit more saddle time can sign up for longer rides, ranging from 2½ to four hours. Unfortunately, the park no longer offers overnight trips.

Top left: Alum Cave Bluffs; Top right: Rainbow Falls;
Bottom: Cades Cove

Plan Your Trip

The park is open year-round, but summer and fall are the most popular seasons. Some facilities are closed late fall through early spring, and roads may be closed in winter due to inclement weather.

Newfound Gap Rd/Hwy 441 is the only thoroughfare that crosses Great Smoky Mountains National Park, winding through the mountains from Gatlinburg, TN, to the town of Cherokee, NC, passing en route the busy Oconaluftee Visitor Center in the park's southeast.

Hike Alum Cave Bluffs

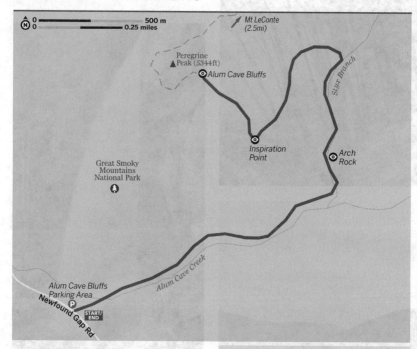

Try to be on the trail before 9am to avoid crowds. From the trailhead along Newfound Gap Rd, you quickly leave the sounds of traffic behind as you cross a stout bridge over a gurgling mountain stream and enter a wilderness of rosebay rhododendrons and thick ferns, with American beech and yellow birch trees soaring overhead.

Soon you'll be following along the rushing waters of **Alum Cave Creek**. Enjoy this fairly flat, scenic stretch as the climbing begins after Mile 1.1.

At that point you'll cross the **Styx Branch**. From here it's about 600yd to **Arch Rock**, a picturesque natural tunnel, which you'll pass through along carved stone steps leading up the steep slope.

The tough ascent continues, leading past old-growth hardwoods as it winds up **Peregrine Peak**. Around Mile 1.8 you'll reach a heath bald where the views begin to open up. A bit further (around Mile 2), you'll reach the aptly named **Inspiration Point**, offering

Duration 2½–3½ hours round-trip

Distance 4.6 miles

Difficulty Hard

Elevation Change 2200ft

Start & Finish Alum Cave Bluffs parking area

even more impressive views of the forested valley below. Stop here to catch your breath before pressing on the final 600yd to **Alum Cave Bluffs**. Despite the name, this is not a cave but rather an 80ft-high concave cliff.

Though most people turn around here, you can press on to **Mt LeConte**, another 2.7 miles uphill, if you still have plenty of energy left. The terrain on this stretch is particularly challenging, as the trail passes over narrow rock ledges – steel cables bolted into the mountain provide useful handholds. Otherwise, it's an easy downhill descent back to your starting point.

Hike Laurel Falls

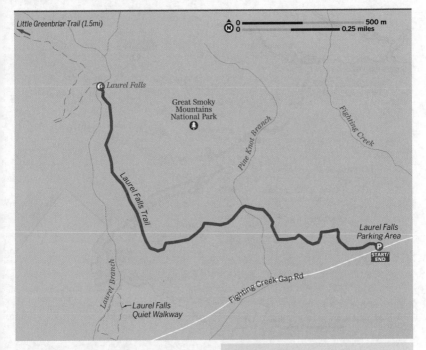

This is one of the most popular waterfall trails in the park. Come very early or late in the day to beat the worst of the crowds. The park service has paved the entire length of the trail. Although it's smooth going, the trail is a little too steep for strollers and wheelchairs, though we have spotted both on the trail.

From the parking area, the trail starts out with a short steep section, then continues along a steady uphill rise past small shrub-like mountain laurels (which turn the hills pink and white in early summer) and stands of rhododendrons. Continuing uphill, you'll soon pass pines, maples and dogwoods before the view opens up to your left and reveals a fine outlook over the valley. Further ahead, you'll pass rocks on your left, which the Civilian Conservation Corps had to partially blast their way through to create the trail back in the 1930s.

The trail continues uphill, at times growing narrower. If in a group, you'll want

Duration 1½–2 hours round trip

Distance 2.6 miles

Difficulty Easy–moderate

Elevation Change 310ft

Start & Finish Laurel Falls parking area

to go single file, and watch your step in cold weather as it can be icy (a sign reminds hikers that falls have resulted in deaths here).

At Mile 1.3 you have arrived. Powered by annual rainfall of 55in, the 75ft-high waterfall is a refreshing sight, though it's nearly always packed. After taking in the view, you can either make the return descent or leave the crowds behind and continue along the trail, which intersects with the Little Greenbrier Trail at Mile 3.1.

Look for the trailhead (and many, many cars parked along the road) on the north side of Fighting Creek Gap Rd, about 3.8 miles west of the Sugarlands Visitor Center.

Drive Newfound Gap Road

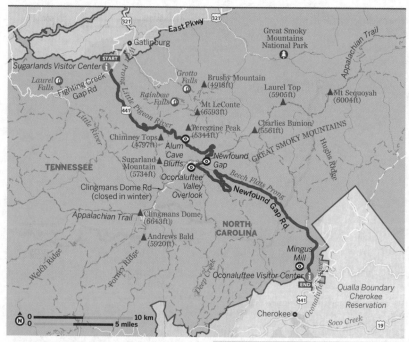

The park's main artery, Newfound Gap Rd/ Hwy 441, begins just outside Gatlinburg and heads 33 winding miles to Cherokee, NC, passing many turnouts, picnic areas, nature trails and overlooks along the way.

Between Mile 5.6 and Mile 7.1, you'll have several opportunities to pull over and admire one of the park's best-known geologic features, **Chimney Tops**. The Cherokee called these twin stony outcroppings high on the ridge 'Duniskwalgunyi' as they resembled a pair of antlers, while white settlers characterized them as a pair of stone chimneys.

The trailhead and parking area for one of the park's most popular hikes, **Alum Cave Bluffs**, is at Mile 8.8. At Mile 12.2 you'll know you've entered the cooler upper elevations of the Smokies as you come to the spruce fir forest that dominates the high mountain slopes.

At **Newfound Gap** travelers pass from Tennessee into North Carolina and the Appalachian Trail crosses the road. Straddling

| **Duration** 1–3 hours |
| **Distance** 33 miles |
| **Start** Sugarlands Visitor Center |
| **Finish** Oconaluftee Visitor Center |

the state line is the Rockefeller Memorial, marking the spot where Franklin D Roosevelt formally dedicated the park in 1940.

The turnoff for Clingmans Dome Rd is at Mile 13.4. Shortly thereafter, at Mile 13.9, is a large parking area for the impressive **Oconaluftee Valley Overlook**.

At Mile 28.7, **Mingus Mill** still grinds corn into meal just as it has done for more than a century. The mill operates from early spring through fall, though visitors are welcome any time. It's just a half-mile from the Oconaluftee Visitor Center (p432), signaling the end of the driving tour.

Drive Roaring Forks Motor Nature Trail

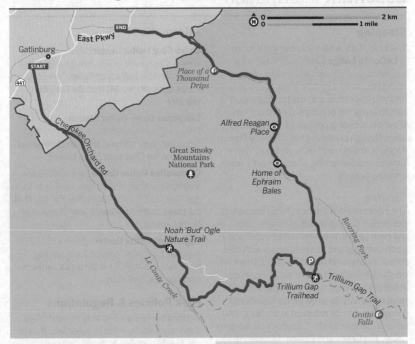

Duration 1–2 hours

Distance 8.5 miles

Start Historic Nature Trail Rd, Gatlinburg

Finish Roaring Fork Rd, Gatlinburg

If you happen to be in the park during a thunderstorm, don't let it ruin your day – this quick drive is at its best after a particularly hard rain. Keep in mind: the Roaring Trail is closed in winter – it's accessible only from late April to November.

From Hwy 441 in Gatlinburg, turn onto Airport Rd, which becomes Cherokee Orchard Rd. The Roaring Fork Motor Nature Trail begins 3 miles later.

The first stop on Cherokee Orchard Rd is the **Noah 'Bud' Ogle Nature Trail**, providing an enjoyable jaunt into a mountain farmstead with a streamside tub mill (for grinding the family corn) and an ingenious wooden-flume plumbing apparatus.

From the Trillium Gap Trailhead the delicate **Grotto Falls** can be reached via a short hike through a virgin hemlock forest.

Roaring Fork Rd is a narrow, twisting road that follows **Roaring Fork**, one of the park's most tempestuous and beautiful streams. It passes through an impressive stand of

old-growth eastern hemlocks, some of which reach heights of more than 100ft and have trunks stretching as much as 5ft across.

Of considerable historical interest is the hardscrabble cabin at the **Home of Ephraim Bales** and also the more comfortable 'saddlebag' house at the **Alfred Reagan Place** (painted with 'all three colors that Sears and Roebuck had'). Reagan was a jack-of-all-trades who served his community as a carpenter, blacksmith and storekeeper.

A wet-weather waterfall called **Place of a Thousand Drips** provides a wonderful conclusion to your explorations before returning to Gatlinburg.

Essential Information

Sleeping

The only place where you can get a room is **LeConte Lodge** (☑865-429-5704; www. lecontelodge.com; cabins incl breakfast & dinner adult $148, child 4-12yr $85; ☺mid-Mar–mid-Nov) and you have to hike to the top of a mountain to enjoy the privilege. Gatlinburg has the most sleeping options of any gateway town, though prices are high. Nearby Pigeon Forge, 10 miles north of Sugarlands Visitor Center, and Sevierville, 17 miles north, have cheaper options.

Camping

The National Park Service (NPS) maintains developed campgrounds at nine locations in the park (a 10th remains closed indefinitely). Each campground has restrooms with cold running water and flush toilets, but there are no showers or electrical or water hookups in the park (though some campgrounds do have electricity for emergency situations). Many sites can be reserved in advance, and several campgrounds (Cataloochee, Abrams Creek, Big Creek and Balsam Mountain) require advance reservations. Reserve through www.recreation.gov.

Plan ahead in the busy summer season. Cades Cove and Smokemont campgrounds are open year-round; others are open March to October.

Backcountry camping is only chargeable up to five nights ($4 per night; after that, it's free). A permit is required. You can make reservations online at http:// smokiespermits.nps.gov, and get permits at the ranger stations or visitor centers.

Eating

Bring a cooler and load up on groceries. There are lovely spots for a picnic, and it's a waste of time driving out of the park to lunch spots during the day.

Find vending machines at Sugarlands Visitor Center and some meager offerings sold at the Cades Cove Campground store. If you make the hike up to LeConte Lodge, you can purchase cookies, drinks and sack lunches.

Information

Cades Cove Visitor Center (☑865-436-7318; www.nps.gov/grsm; ☺9am-7pm Apr-Aug, closes earlier Sep-Mar) Halfway up Cades Cove Loop Rd, 24 miles off Hwy 441 from the Gatlinburg entrance.

Clingmans Dome Visitor Station (☑865-436-1200; ☺10am-6pm Apr-Oct, 9:30am-5pm Nov) Small, very busy center at the start of the paved path up to the Clingmans Dome lookout.

Oconaluftee Visitor Center (☑828-497-1904; www.nps.gov/grsm; ☺8am-7pm Jun-Aug, to 6pm Apr, May, Sep & Oct, to 4:30pm Nov-Mar; ☜) ⚲ At the park's southern entrance near Cherokee in North Carolina.

Sugarlands Visitor Center (☑865-436-1291; www.nps.gov/grsm; ☺8am-7:30pm Jun-Aug, hours vary Sep-May; ☜) At the park's northern entrance near Gatlinburg.

Park Policies & Regulations

Visitors are required to stay at least 50yd from any wildlife – this is especially true of elk. Feeding wildlife is prohibited (with a fine of up to $5000).

Travelers with Disabilities

The park has one excellent trail that is accessible: the smooth, half-mile Sugarlands Valley Nature Trail. Other places worth exploring include historic sites in Cades Cove, which has hard-packed gravel paths running around the area. Buildings can be viewed only from the exterior, though the Cable Mill and the Becky Cable House are both accessible via a ramp.

Getting There & Around

The closest airports to the national park are McGhee Tyson Airport near Knoxville (40 miles northwest of the Sugarlands Visitor Center) and Asheville Regional Airport, 58 miles east of the Oconaluftee Visitor Center.

There's no public transportation to the park. There's a wide variety of car-rental outfits at each of the airports.

Top left: Alfred Reagan Place; Top right: Roaring Fork Creek; Bottom: Newfound Gap Road

CLASSIC HIKES

Charlies Bunion & Kephart Loop

The rocky outcropping known as Charlies Bunion offers one of the most memorable panoramas in the park. Most visitors do Charlies Bunion as an out-and-back day hike (8 miles return), but you can leave the day-trippers behind and overnight in a lush valley near the Kephart Prong.

Duration 2 days

Distance 14 miles

Difficulty Moderate

Start & Finish Newfound Gap

Elevation Change 4185ft

Nearest Town/Junction Gatlinburg

DAY 1: Newfound Gap to Kephart Prong (4 hours, 8.5 miles)

The hike starts near the **Rockefeller Memorial**, which straddles two states at Newfound Gap, around 13 miles south of the Sugarlands Visitor Center. Check out the views into Tennessee and North Carolina, then find the sign indicating the Appalachian Trail just below. Hit the trail early if you want the scenery to yourself.

The first 2 miles of the hike follow a fairly steady elevation gain along cool, mixed forest before passing through Fraser fir forest, the bare limbs of the trees evidence of the balsam woolly adelgid wreaking havoc. You'll also see plenty of wildflowers in spring and blackberries in late summer.

Around Mile 1.7, you'll pass the junction with the Sweat Heifer Creek Trail, which you'll be going up the next day. A little further along, around Mile 2.7, you'll pass the turnoff to the Boulevard Trail, which leads up to Mt LeConte. A little further along, the Icewater Spring shelter is a popular overnight stop for through hikers. The piped spring just beyond does indeed have ice-cold water, though as elsewhere in the park, you'll need to treat it before drinking. From here the path descends through a cool spruce and fir forest before leveling out amid secondary forest of American beech and yellow birch. After a short ascent, you'll see the big rock face just ahead. Then at Mile 4.0, a well-weathered signpost announces your arrival at **Charlies Bunion**.

As you take the narrow spur out to the overlook, keep in mind that careless travelers have fallen to their death out on the rocks, so it's best not to scramble around on these ledges. The curious name, incidentally, comes from Horace Kephart, who was out exploring this section of the Smokies in 1929 with his friend Charlie Connor and photographer George Masa. After spotting the bulbous rock face, he paid homage to his hiking companion (or at least his companion's foot ailment), saying, jovially, that it looked just like Charlie's bunion. Somehow the farcical name stuck – it helped that Kephart was later involved in choosing place names within the park boundaries. If you haven't eaten already, this is a fine place for a long break. With dizzying 1000ft drop-offs, the sweeping panorama spreads from Mt LeConte eastward to the the jagged peaks of the Sawteeth Range.

From Charlies Bunion, you'll continue along the Appalachian Trail for another half-mile before making the right (southward) turn onto the Dry Sluice Gap Trail. You'll likely have this quiet, little-used track all to yourself as you descend through stands of Catawba rhododendrons – at times so thick, they form an enclosed Gothic arch overhead. Around Mile 5.8, you'll see the signpost for the Grassy Branch Trail leading off to your right. Take this trail, which keeps descending. You'll pass wind-whipped oak and birch trees, and cross a few small streams, including an offshoot of the Icewater Spring that you traversed far above.

After the long, steady descent, you'll soon hear the rush of the **Kephart Prong**. Then around Mile 8.4, you'll reach a forest of rich secondary growth and arrive at the **Kephart Shelter**. After dropping your pack (and hoisting up your food items with the bear-proof cable system), you can explore a bit of this former lumber site. Try to get plenty of rest, because you'll have lots of climbing on day two.

DAY 2: Sweat Heifer Creek Trail to Newfound Gap (2.5 hours, 5.5 miles, 2500ft ascent)

The day begins along the Sweat Heifer Creek Trail, which starts a few paces from the shelter. Cross a log bridge over the rushing stream and mossy boulders, then make the slow, steady ascent. Plan a rest stop around Mile 1.6 (from the shelter), beside the cooling multi-stage falls of **Sweat Heifer Cascades**. At Mile 3.8 you'll meet back up with the Appalachian Trail. Turn left and continue another 1.7 miles to return to your original starting point. ∎

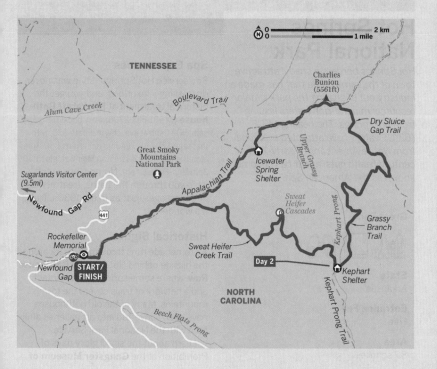

ZACK FRANK/SHUTTERSTOCK ©

Hot Springs National Park

Hot Springs borders a shady, attractive town of the same name that has made an industry out of sharing the park's major resource: mineral-rich waters issuing from hot springs. The healing 143°F (62°C) waters have attracted everyone from Native Americans to early-20th-century health nuts, and it has become known as the 'American Spa.'

Great For...

State
Arkansas

Entrance Fee
Free

Area
8.7 sq miles

Spa Experiences

Spa service Hot Springs–style was never distressingly luxurious, and you get the historical treatment at **Buckstaff Bathhouse** (☏501-623-2308; www.buckstaffbaths. com; 509 Central Ave; thermal bath $33, with massage $71; ⊗8-11:45am daily, plus 1:30-3pm Mon-Sat Mar-Nov, 8-11:45am Mon-Sat, plus 1:30-3pm Mon-Fri Dec-Feb). No-nonsense staff whip you through the baths, treatments and massages, just as in the 1930s. Truly, it's wonderful.

Historical Sights

A promenade runs through the park around the hillside behind Hot Springs' **Bathhouse Row**, where some springs survive intact, and a network of trails covers the town's mountains. Many of the old bathhouses have been converted into art galleries affiliated with the National Park Service.

Learn about the sinful glory days of Prohibition at the **Gangster Museum of**

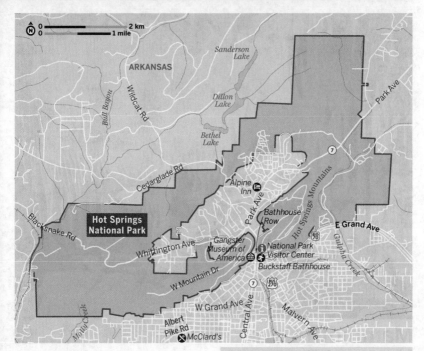

America (📱501-318-1717; www.tgmoa.com; 510 Central Ave; adult/child $15/6; ⏱10am-5pm Sun-Thu, to 6pm Fri & Sat). This small town in the middle of nowhere turned into a hotbed of lavish wealth thanks to Chicago bootleggers like Capone and his NYC counterparts.

Sleeping & Eating

While the heyday of the Hot Springs spa craze may have passed, there are still some gorgeous old hotels here.

The friendly Scottish owners of the **Alpine Inn** (📱501-624-9164; www.alpine -inn-hot-springs.com; 741 Park Ave; r $69-99; ❄🛜🏊), located less than a mile from Bathhouse Row, have spent a few years upgrading an old motel to remarkable ends. The rooms are impeccable, comfortable and include new flat-screen TVs and sumptuous beds.

Restaurants congregate along the Central Ave tourist strip in Hot Springs. The **Colonial**

Essential Information

On Bathhouse Row in the 1915 Fordyce bathhouse, the **NPS visitor center** (📱501-620-6715; www.nps.gov/hosp; 369 Central Ave; ⏱9am-5pm) **FREE** has exhibits about park history.

Buses head from Hot Springs to Little Rock with **Greyhound** (📱501-623-5574; www.greyhound.com; 100 Broadway Tce; 1½ hours, from $13, around three daily). The town is off I-30, about 60 miles southwest of Little Rock.

Pancake House (📱501-624-9273; 111 Central Ave; mains $6-10; ⏱7am-3pm) is a Hot Springs classic, with turquoise booths and homey touches like quilts and doilies on the walls, almost like your grandma's kitchen.

On the outskirts of downtown Hot Springs, Bill Clinton's favorite boyhood barbecue, **McClard's** (📱501-623-9665; www. mcclards.com; 505 Albert Pike; mains $4-15; ⏱11am-8pm Tue-Sat), is still popular. ∎

ZACK FRANK/SHUTTERSTOCK ©

Mammoth Cave National Park

Home to the longest cave system on earth, Mammoth Cave National Park has more than 400 miles of surveyed passageways. Mammoth is at least three times longer than any other known cave, with vast interior cathedrals, bottomless pits and undulating rock formations. Guided tours delve into its spookily beautiful underworld.

Great For...

State
Kentucky

Entrance Fee
Free; cave tours $6–60

Area
83 sq miles

Cave Tours

The caves have been used for prehistoric mineral gathering, as a source of saltpeter for gunpowder and as a tuberculosis hospital.

The only way to see them is on a ranger-guided tour. Options range from hour-long subterranean strolls to strenuous, day-long spelunking adventures. The **Frozen Niagara Tour** is the easiest, offering glimpses of groovy formations in large caverns. The popular **Domes and Dripstones Tour** takes in several dramatic deposits, though you must go up and down 500 stairs and squeeze through tight areas. The magical **Violet City Tour** takes place by lantern light. There's a specialty accessible tour option too.

Book tours online at www.recreation. gov; advance tickets are wise in summer. It's always chilly in the caves, so bring a sweater.

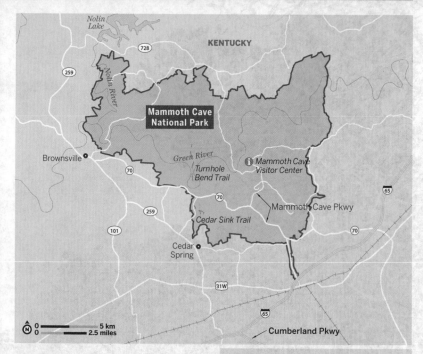

Hiking

Eighty-five miles of trails stripe the park's forested hills. The 3.5-mile **Turnhole Bend Trail** winds through old-growth stands of oaks and hickories and past secluded bluffs. The 2-mile **Cedar Sink Trail** offers the requisite cliffs and trees, plus wildflowers and odd-looking sinkholes. Most trails make for fairly easy trekking.

Canoeing & Kayaking

The Green River moseys through the park for 25 miles, as does the Nolin River for 6 miles. They're prime for paddling, carrying visitors on a slow-moving current past dramatic cliffs, towering trees and wildlife such as beavers, foxes and wild turkeys. Several outfitters rent canoes and kayaks and can set up excursions ranging from three hours to three days (with camping on river islands). The park's website has contact details.

Essential Information

The **visitor center** (☏270-758-2180; www.nps.gov/maca; 1 Mammoth Cave Pkwy; ◷8.30am-4.30pm) has trail maps and cave tour tickets.

The park lies a short distance west of I-65, halfway between Louisville, KY and Nashville, TN.

Camping

For overnight stays, there are three basic campgrounds with restrooms (sites from $20; reserve at www.recreation. gov); 13 free backcountry campsites (get a permit at the park visitor center); and a hotel and cottages (reserve at www. mammothcavelodge.com). ∎

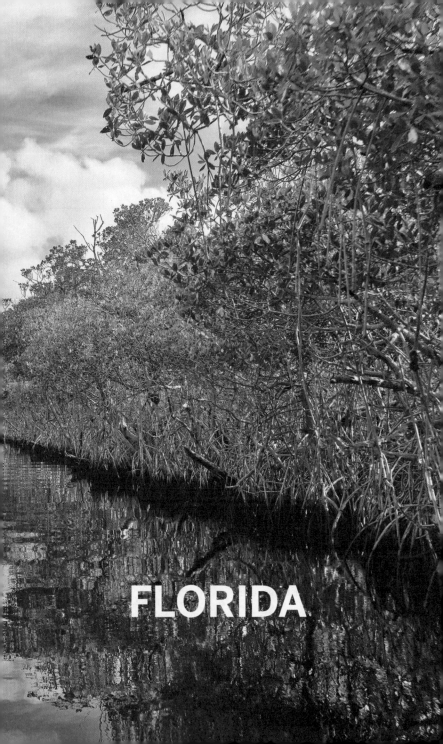

FLORIDA

442

In This Chapter

Biscayne 444
Dry Tortugas 446
Everglades 448

Florida

The only tropical state in the contiguous US is the domain of alligators, manatees, panthers and flamingos, as well as an abundance of well-protected coral reefs teeming with marine life. Three national parks inhabit America's beloved 'sunshine state': the mangrove-covered Everglades, the largely subaqueous Biscayne and the splayed keys of Dry Tortugas, which – unusually for a US national park – are guarded by a huge 19th-century military complex.

Don't Miss

● Diving to sunken ships on Biscayne's Maritime Heritage Trail (p445)

● Flying or sailing out to the remote key of Fort Jefferson (p446)

● Going on a self-guided paddle through the famously vast Everglades (p448)

● Finding an isolated island spot in Biscayne to pitch your tent (p445)

● Reptile-spotting on the short, paved Anhinga Trail (p448)

When to Go

In contrast to most other US national parks, Florida's trio of parks are best visited during the winter dry season (December to March) when there's top wildlife viewing along the watercourses of the Everglades (although some kayaking routes will be difficult).

Between April and June the weather gets pretty hot, but there's a good mix of water and wildlife. From July to November the heat increases, bringing with it lots of bugs and chances of hurricanes.

Previous page: Everglades National Park (p448)
LIGA CERINA/SHUTTERSTOCK ©

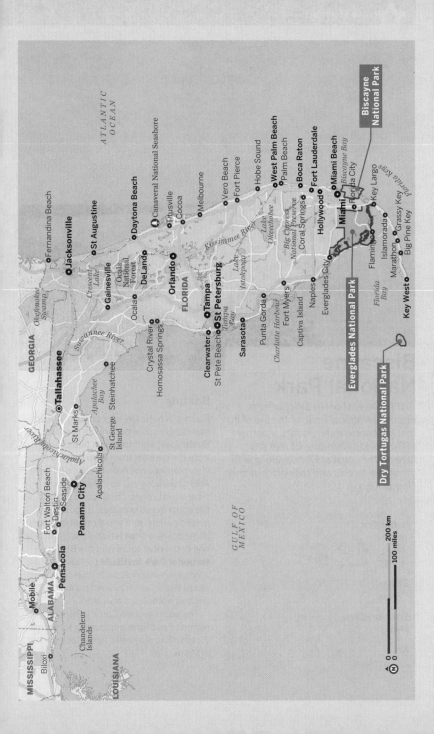

PIXELPOD / ALAMY STOCK PHOTO ©

Biscayne National Park

Just to the east of the Everglades is Biscayne National Park, or the 5% of it that isn't underwater. In fact, a portion of the world's third-largest reef sits here off the coast of Florida, along with mangrove forests and the northernmost Florida Keys.

Great For...

State
Florida

Entrance Fee
Free

Area
270 sq miles

Boating

Boating is naturally very popular, but you'll need to get some paperwork in order. Boaters will want to obtain tide charts from the park (or from www.nps.gov/bisc/planyourvisit/tide-predictions.htm). Also make sure you comply with local slow-speed zones, designed to protect the endangered manatee. If you'd like a guided paddle, or if you'd rather be taking in the scenery than tending the helm, take one of the boat tours with the **Biscayne National Park Institute** (☏786-335-3644; www.biscaynenationalparkinstitute.org; Dante Fascell Visitor Center; ☺9am-5pm Wed-Sun) or another authorised operator.

The water around Convoy Point is regarded as prime windsurfing territory. Windsurfers may want to contact outfits in Miami.

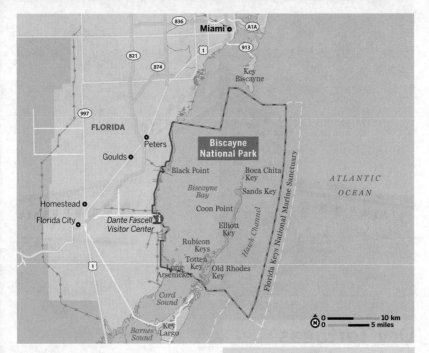

Diving

The **Maritime Heritage Trail** takes divers through one of the only trails of its kind in the USA. If you've ever wanted to explore a sunken ship, this may well be the best opportunity in the country. Six are located within the park grounds; the trail experience involves taking visitors out, by boat, to the site of the wrecks where they can swim and explore among derelict vessels and clouds of fish.

There are even waterproof information site cards placed among the ships. Three of the vessels are suited for scuba divers, but the others – particularly the *Mandalay*, a lovely two-masted schooner that sank in 1966 – can be accessed by snorkelers.

Camping

Biscayne National Park's two **campgrounds** (site per night $25, May-Sep free) are

Essential Information

Dante Fascell Visitor Center (✆305-230-1144; www.nps.gov/bisc; 9700 SW 328th St, Homestead; ☻9am-5pm) Located at Convoy Point, this center shows a great introductory film for an overview of the park, and has maps, information and excellent ranger activities.

To get to the park, you'll have to drive about 9 miles east of Homestead on SW 328th St (North Canal Dr).

both located on islands – Elliott Key and Boca Chita Key. These are lovely settings, but you need transportation (a boat) to get there. You pay on a trust system with exact change on the harbor (rangers cruise the Keys to check your receipt). Bring all supplies, including water, and carry everything out. ■

Fort Jefferson

Dry Tortugas National Park

Dry Tortugas National Park is America's most inaccessible national park. Reachable only by boat or seaplane, it rewards you for your effort in getting there with amazing snorkeling amid coral reefs full of marine life. You'll also get to tour a beautifully preserved 19th-century brick fort, one of the largest in the USA.

Great For...

State
Florida

Entrance Fee
7-day pass per person $15

Area
100 sq miles

Fort Jefferson

Explorer Ponce de León named this seven-island chain Las Tortugas (The Turtles) for the sea turtles spotted in its waters. Thirsty mariners who passed through and found no water later affixed 'dry' to the name. In subsequent years, the US Navy set an outpost here as a strategic position into the Gulf of Mexico. But by the Civil War, Fort Jefferson, the main structure on the islands, had become a prison for Union deserters and at least four other people, among them Dr Samuel Mudd, who had been arrested for complicity in the assassination of Abraham Lincoln. Hence a new nickname: Devil's Island. The name was prophetic: in 1867 a yellow-fever outbreak killed 38 people, and after an 1873 hurricane the fort was abandoned. It reopened in 1886 as a quarantine station for smallpox and cholera victims, was declared a national monument in 1935 by President Franklin D Roosevelt, and was

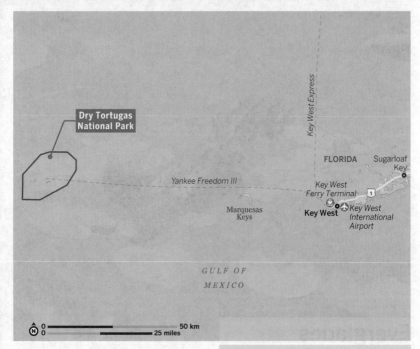

Dry Tortugas
National Park

Key West Express

FLORIDA   Sugarloaf
Key

Yankee Freedom III

Key West
Ferry Terminal

Marquesas   **Key West**   Key West
Keys   International
                             Airport

GULF OF

MEXICO

0   50 km
0   25 miles

upped to national park status in 1992 by
George Bush Sr.

Other Activities

The sparkling waters offer excellent snorkeling and diving opportunities. A visitor
center is located within fascinating Fort
Jefferson.

In March and April, there is stupendous
bird-watching, including aerial fighting.
Stargazing is mind-blowing at any time of
the year.

Camping

You can come for the day or overnight
if you want to camp. Garden Key has 10
campsites ($15 per person, per night),
which are given out on a first-come,
first-served basis. You'll need to reserve
months ahead through the ferry *Yankee
Freedom III*, which takes passengers to
and from the island. There are toilets, but
no freshwater showers or drinking water;

Essential Information

The **Yankee Freedom III** (☎800-634-
0939; www.drytortugas.com; 100 Grinell
St; adult/child/senior $180/125/170) runs
between the Key West Ferry Terminal
and Fort Jefferson. Round-trip fares
cost $180/125 per adult/child and the
journey takes just over two hours.

Key West Seaplanes (☎305-293-
9300; www.keywestseaplanecharters.com;
half-day trip adult/child $342/273, full-day
trip $600/480) can take up to 10 passen-
gers (flight time 40 minutes each way)
and departs frome near the Key West
International Airport. The half-day tour
is four hours, allowing 2½ hours on the
island. The eight-hour full-day excursion
gives you six hours on the island.

bring everything you'll need. You can stay
up to four nights. ■

ALKHUTOV DMITRY/SHUTTERSTOCK ©

Everglades National Park

This vast wilderness, encompassing 1.5 million acres, is one of America's great natural treasures. Spy alligators basking in the noonday sun as herons stalk patiently through nearby waters in search of prey, or go kayaking amid tangled mangrove canals and on peaceful lakes,

Great For...

State
Florida

Entrance Fee
7-day pass per vehicle/pedestrian
$25/8

Area
2344 sq miles

Anhinga Trail

If you do just one walk in the Everglades, make sure it's on the Anhinga Trail. Gators sun on the shoreline, anhinga spear their prey and wading birds stalk haughtily through the reeds. You'll get a close-up view of wildlife on this short (0.8-mile) trail at the Royal Palm Visitor Center, four miles from the main park entrance and the **Ernest Coe Visitor Center** (✆305-242-7700; www.nps.gov/ever; ⊙8am-7pm mid-December to mid-April, from 9am rest of year). There are various overlooks, where you can sometimes see dozens of alligators piled together in the day.

Canoes, Kayaks & Bicycles

You need a car to properly enter the Everglades and once you're in, wearing a good pair of walking boots is essential to penetrate the interior. Having a canoe or kayak helps as well; these can be rented

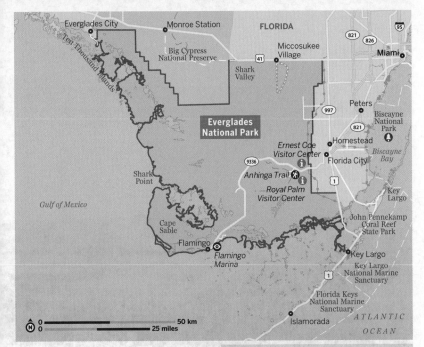

from outfits inside and outside the park, or else you can seek out guided canoe and kayak tours. Bicycles are well suited to the flat roads here, particularly in the area between Ernest Coe and Flamingo Point.

The most isolated portion of the park is squat **Flamingo Marina** (☏855-798-2207; www.flamingoeverglades.com; tours per adult/child $38/18, canoe rental 2/4/8hr $20/28/38, kayak rental half/full day $35/45; ⏰marina 7am-7pm, from 6am Sat & Sun) where you can go on a backcountry boat tour or rent boats. You can rent kayaks and canoes here; if you do, you're largely left to explore the channels and islands of Florida Bay on your own.

Southern Everglades

Head south of Miami to drive into the heart of the park and the best horizons of the Everglades. Plus there are plenty of side paths and canoe creeks for memorable

Essential Information

The largest subtropical wilderness in the continental USA is easily accessible from Miami. The Glades, which comprise the 80 southernmost miles of Florida, are bound by the Atlantic Ocean to the east and the Gulf of Mexico to the west. The Tamiami Trail (Hwy 41) goes east–west, parallel to the more northern (and less interesting) Alligator Alley (I-75).

detours. You'll see some of the most quietly exhilarating scenery the park has to offer on this route, and you'll have better access to an interior network of trails for those wanting to push off the beaten track into the buggy, muggy solar plexus of the wetlands. ■

HAWAII

In This Chapter

Haleakalā.........................456
Hawai'i Volcanoes...................466

Hawaii

Hawaii may evoke visions of surfboards, palm-fringed beaches, hulas and lei, but the state's national parks reveal a very different side. On Hawaii's Big Island, you can observe creation itself at Hawai'i Volcanoes National Park, home to the world's longest continuous volcanic eruption and a landscape that's being constantly re-sculpted by dramatic forces. On Maui's Haleakalā, a giant shield volcano, you can sleep inside the crater and swim in stream-fed pools in subtropical forest.

Don't Miss

● Motoring through Chain of Craters Rd's ever-changing tropical scenery (p469)

● Getting up early to watch the Haleakalā sun rise (p459)

● Hiking across a volcanic crater on the Kilauea Iki Trail (p469)

● Entering the unearthly world of Sliding Sands' stark lava sights and ever-changing clouds (p462)

● Admiring extensive views from Pu'u'ula'ula (p459)

When to Go

High season in Hawaii is December to April and June to August. Winter is rainier, summer is slightly hotter.

In Hawai'i Volcanoes National Park, August and September tend to have more clear days on average. Bear in mind, volcanoes don't follow schedules; try to keep yours flexible.

In Haleakalā, temperatures at the summit can be extreme, and may fluctuate rapidly. Year-round temperatures range from below freezing to 60°F. Visitor numbers remain fairly consistent year-round.

Previous page: Haleakalā volcano (p456)
IVVV1975/SHUTTERSTOCK ©

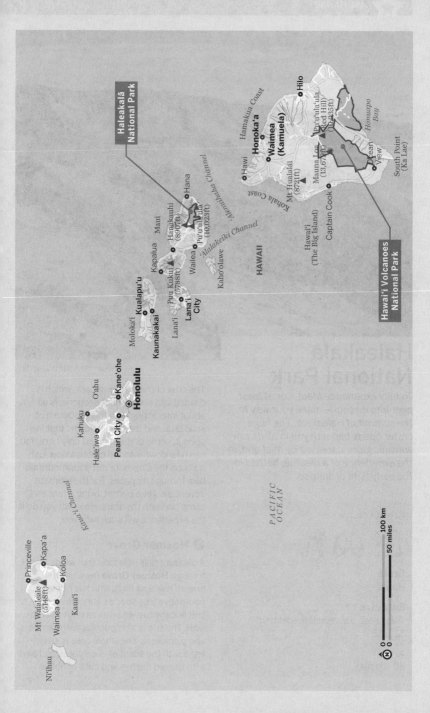

PIERRE LECLERC/SHUTTERSTOCK ©

View from Kalahaku Overlook

Haleakalā National Park

To fully experience Maui – or at least peer into its soul – make your way to the summit of Haleakalā. The huge crater opens beneath you in all its raw volcanic glory, caressed by mist and, in the experience of a lifetime, bathed in the early light of sunrise.

Great For...

State
Hawaii

Entrance Fee
7-day pass per vehicle/pedestrian
$25/12

Area
60 sq miles

The crux of this amazing park, which is divided into two distinct sections, is all about interacting with this mountain of solid lava, and the rare lifeforms that live upon it, some of them found only here. You can hike down into the crater, follow lush trails on the slopes, or put your mountain bike through its paces. For the ultimate adventure, get a permit, bring a tent and camp beneath the stars. However you do it, the experience will stick with you.

❶ Hosmer Grove

A pleasant half-mile loop trail winds through **Hosmer Grove** (www.nps.gov/hale; off Haleakalā Hwy), which is home to non-native tree species – including pine, fir and eucalyptus – as well as native scrubland. The site is also popular with campers and picnickers. The whole area is sweetened with the scent of eucalyptus and alive with the red flashes and calls of native

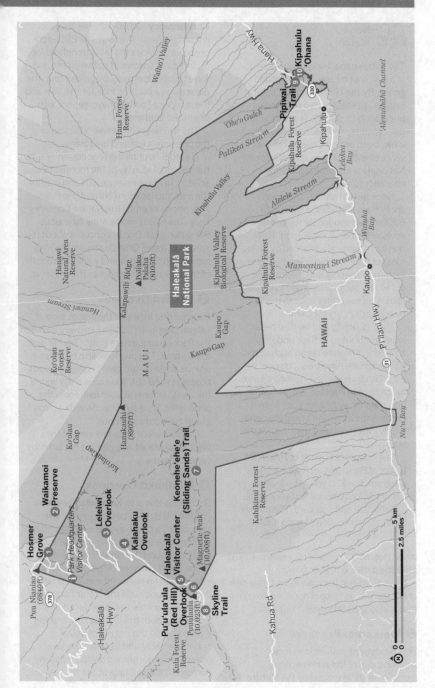

Nene Watch

The native nene, Hawaii's state bird, is a long-lost cousin of the Canada goose. By the 1950s hunting, habitat loss and predators had reduced its population to just 30. Thanks to captive breeding and release programs, it has been brought back from the verge of extinction and the Haleakalā National Park's nene population is now about 200.

Nene nest in shrubs and grassy areas from altitudes of 6000ft to 8000ft, surrounded by rugged lava flows with sparse vegetation. Their feet have gradually adapted by losing most of their webbing. The birds are extremely friendly and love to hang out where people do, anywhere from cabins on the crater floor to the Park Headquarters Visitor Center.

Their curiosity and fearlessness have contributed to their undoing. Nene don't fare well in an asphalt habitat and many have been run over by cars. Others have been tamed by too much human contact; so, no matter how much they beg for your peanut butter sandwich, don't feed the nene. It only interferes with their successful return to the wild.

The nonprofit Friends of Haleakalā National Park runs an Adopt-a-Nene program. For $30 you get adoption papers, information about your nene, a certificate and postcard. The money funds the protection of nene habitat.

birds. Hosmer Grove sits on a side road just after the park's entrance booth.

Drive slowly on the road in, as this is one of the top places to spot nene, a rare goose that is also the state bird.

❷ Waikamoi Preserve

This windswept native cloud forest supports one of the rarest ecosystems on earth. Managed by the **Nature Conservancy** (☏808-572-7849; www.nature. org; hike_waikamoi@tnc.org), the 8951-acre preserve provides the last stronghold for hundreds of species of native plants and forest birds. Open only by guided tour, the preserve is a place to look for the 'i'iwi and the 'apapane (both honeycreepers with bright red feathers).

The yellow-green 'amakihi flies among the preserve's koa and ohia trees.

A 4- to 5-hour hiking tour currently runs the second Saturday of the month starting at 8am. To make reservations and confirm the meet-up location (currently in Pukalani), phone or email the Nature Conservancy. The hike is moderately strenuous. Bring rain gear. Due to concerns about the spread of Rapid Ohia Death, no one who has visited the Big Island within six months of the tour date may access the preserve.

❸ Leleiwi Overlook

For your first look into the crater, stop at Leleiwi Overlook (8840ft), midway between the Park Headquarters Visitor Center and the summit. The overlook also provides a unique angle on the ever-changing clouds floating in and out. You can literally watch the weather form at your feet. From the parking lot, it's a five-minute walk across a gravel trail to the overlook.

En route you'll get a fine view of the West Maui Mountains and the flat isthmus connecting the two sides of Maui.

❹ Kalahaku Overlook

Don't miss this one. **Kalahaku Overlook** (9324ft), 0.8 miles beyond Leleiwi Overlook, offers a bird's-eye view of the crater floor and the ant-size hikers on the trails snaking around the cinder cones below. At the observation deck, plaques provide information on each of the volcanic formations that punctuate the crater floor. From the deck you'll also get a perfect angle for viewing both the Ko'olau Gap and the Kaupo Gap on the rim of Haleakalā.

Between May and October the 'ua'u (Hawaiian dark-rumped petrel) nests in burrows in the cliff face at the left side of the observation deck. Even if you don't spot the birds, you can often hear the parents and chicks making their unique clucking sounds. Of about 20,000 *'ua'u* remaining today, most nest right here at Haleakalā, where they lay just one egg a year. These seabirds were thought to be extinct until sighted in the crater during the 1970s.

A short trail below the parking lot leads to a field of native *'ahinahina* (silversword), ranging from seedlings to mature plants.

This overlook is only accessible on the way down the mountain.

❺ Haleakalā Visitor Center

Perched on the rim of the crater at 9745ft, this **visitor center** (⊙sunrise-noon) is the park's main viewing spot. And what a magical sight awaits. The ever-changing interplay of sun, shadow and clouds reflecting on the crater floor creates a mesmerizing dance of light and color. The center has displays on Haleakalā's volcanic origins and details on what you're seeing on the crater floor 3000ft below.

Nature talks are given, books on Hawaiian culture and the environment are for sale, and there are drinking fountains and restrooms here. Hikers, note that it may be easier to fill a thermos at the water filling station at the Park Headquarters Visitor Center.

By dawn the parking lot fills with people coming to see the sunrise show, and it pretty much stays packed all day. Leave the crowds behind by taking the 10-minute hike up **Pa Ka'oao (White Hill)**, which begins at the eastern side of the visitor center and provides stunning crater views.

❻ Pu'u'ula'ula (Red Hill) Overlook

You may find yourself standing above the clouds while exploring **Pu'u'ula'ula** (10,023ft), Maui's highest point. The **summit building** provides a top-of-the-world panorama from its wraparound windows. On a clear day you can see Hawai'i (Big Island), Lana'i, Moloka'i and even O'ahu.

Haleakalā Visitor Center

STEVE SMITH / ALAMY STOCK PHOTO ©

Left: Keonehe'ehe'e (Sliding Sands) Trail;
Right: 'Āhinahina (silversword)

STEVEN MALTBY/SHUTTERSTOCK ©

Stargazing

On clear nights, stargazing is phenomenal on the mountain. You can see celestial objects up to the seventh magnitude, free of light interference, making Haleakalā one of the best places on the planet for a sky view.

The park no longer offers star talks. These are now run by concessionaires. You can also pick up a free star map at the Park Headquarters Visitor Center and have your own cosmic experience.

When the light's right, the colors of the crater are nothing short of spectacular, with grays, greens, reds and browns.

An 'ahinahina garden has been planted at the overlook, making this the best place to see these luminous silver-leafed plants in various stages of growth.

⑦ Keonehe'ehe'e (Sliding Sands) Trail

Make time for this stunner, which starts at the southern side of the Haleakalā Visitor Center at 9740ft and winds down to the crater floor. If you take this hike after catching the sunrise, you'll walk directly into a gentle warmish wind and rays of sunshine. There is no shade, so bring water and a hat.

The path descends gently into an unearthly world of stark lava sights and ever-changing clouds. The first thing you'll notice is how quiet everything is. The only sound is the crunching of volcanic cinders beneath your feet. If you're pressed for time, just walking down for 20 minutes will reward you with an into-the-crater experience and fabulous photo opportunities. Keep in mind that the climb out takes nearly twice as long.

The full trail leads 9.2 miles to the Paliku Cabin & Campground, passing the Kapalaoa cabin at 5.6 miles after roughly four hours. The first 6 miles follow the southern wall. There are great views, but virtually no vegetation. Four miles down, after an elevation drop of 2500ft, Keonehe'ehe'e Trail intersects with a spur that leads north into the cinder desert, where it connects with the Halemau'u Trail after 1.5 miles.

Continuing on Keonehe'ehe'e, you head across the crater floor for 2 miles to Kapalaoa. Verdant ridges rise on your right, giving way to ropy pahoehoe (smooth-flowing lava). From Kapalaoa cabin to Paliku, the descent is gentle and the vegetation gradually increases. Paliku (6380ft) is beneath a sheer cliff at the eastern end of the crater. In contrast to the crater's barren western end, this area receives heavy rainfall, with ohia forests climbing the slopes.

⑧ Skyline Trail

This otherworldly trail, which rides the precipitous spine of Haleakalā, begins just beyond the summit at a lofty elevation (9750ft) and leads down to the campground at Polipoli Spring State Recreation Area (6200ft). It covers a distance of 8.5 miles and takes about four hours to walk. Get an early start to enjoy the views before clouds take over.

To get to the trailhead, go past Pu'u'ula'ula (Red Hill) Overlook and take the road to the left just before Science City. The road, which passes over a cattle grate, is signposted not for public use, but continue and you'll soon find a Na Ala Hele sign marking the trailhead.

The Skyline Trail starts in barren open terrain of volcanic cinder, a moon walk that passes more than a dozen cinder cones and craters. The first mile is rough lava rock. After three crunchy miles, it reaches the tree line (8500ft) and enters native māmane forest. In winter māmane is heavy with flowers that look like yellow sweet-pea blossoms. There's solitude on this walk. If the clouds treat you kindly, you'll have broad views all the way between the barren summit and the dense cloud forest. Eventually the trail meets the Polipoli access road, where you can either walk to the paved road in about 4 miles, or continue via the Haleakalā Ridge Trail and Polipoli Trail to the campground. If you prefer treads to hiking boots, the Skyline Trail is also an exhilarating adventure on a mountain bike. Just look out for hikers!

⑨ Pipiwai Trail

Ready for an adventure? This fun **trail** (www.nps.gov/hale; Kipahulu Area, Haleakalā National Park) ascends alongside the 'Ohe'o streambed, rewarding hikers with picture-perfect views of waterfalls and an otherworldly trip through a bamboo grove. The trail starts on the mauka (inland) side of the visitor center and leads up to Makahiku Falls (0.5 miles) and Waimoku Falls (2 miles). To see both falls, allow about two hours return. Can be muddy!

Along the path, you'll pass large mango trees and patches of guava before coming to an overlook after about 10 minutes. Makahiku Falls, a long bridal-veil waterfall that drops into a deep gorge, is just off to the right. Thick green ferns cover the sides of 200ft basalt cliffs where the water cascades – a very rewarding scene for such a short walk.

Continuing along the main trail, you'll walk beneath old banyan trees, cross Palikea Stream (killer mosquitoes thrive here) and enter the wonderland of the Bamboo Forest, where thick groves of bamboo bang together musically in the wind. The upper section is muddy, but boardwalks cover some of the worst bits. Beyond the bamboo forest is Waimoku Falls, a thin, lacy 400ft waterfall dropping down a sheer rock face. When you come out of the first grove, you'll see the waterfall in the distance. Forget swimming under Waimoku Falls – its pool is shallow and there's a danger of falling rocks.

Wear your grippy water shoes for this one. The hike is 4 miles round-trip.

⑩ Kipahulu 'Ohana

Kipahulu was once a breadbasket, or more accurately a poi bowl, for the entire region. For fascinating insights into the area's past, join the ethnobotanical tour led by **Kipahulu 'Ohana** (📞808-248-8558; www.kipahulu.org; per person $49; ⏱tours 10am & 2pm), a collective of Native Hawaiian farmers who have restored ancient taro patches. The tour includes a sampling of Hawaiian foods and intriguing details about the native plants and ancient ruins along the way.

The two-hour outing includes about 3 miles of hiking and concentrates on farm activities. The tour meets outside the Kipahulu Visitor Center; advance reservations required.

Skyline Trail

SAMURAIGIRLY/SHUTTERSTOCK ©

Essential Information

Camping

There are basic campsites and cabins in the Summit Area. One campsite is first-come, first-served. Campsites and cabins in the crater must be reserved. The campground in Kipahulu is first-come, first-served.

All of the backcountry camping options are primitive. None have electricity or showers. You will find pit toilets and limited nonpotable water supplies that are shared with the crater cabins. Water needs to be filtered or chemically treated before drinking; conserve it, as water tanks occasionally run dry. Fires are allowed only in grills and in times of drought are prohibited entirely. You must pack in all your food and supplies, and pack out all your trash. Also be aware that during periods of drought you'll be required to carry in your own water.

Permits are required for backcountry camping in the crater. They are free and issued at the Park Headquarters Visitor Center on a first-come, first-served basis between 8am and 3pm up to one day in advance. Photo identification and a 10-minute orientation video are required. Camping is limited to three nights in the crater each month, with no more than two consecutive nights at either campground.

Safety

This park can be a seriously dangerous place to drive, due to a combination of sheer drops with no guardrails, daily doses of thick mist, and strong wind. Exercise extra caution on winter afternoons, when a sudden rainstorm can add ice to the list.

Obey warning signs. They often mark a spot where a visitor has been hurt or killed by a fall, a flash flood or falling rocks.

The weather can change suddenly from dry, hot conditions to cold, windswept rain. Although the general rule is sunny in the morning and cloudy in the afternoon, fog and clouds can blow in at any time, and the windchill can quickly drop below freezing. Dress in layers and bring extra clothing.

At 10,000ft the air is relatively thin, so expect to tire more quickly, particularly if you're hiking. The higher elevation also means that sunburn is more likely.

Visitors rarely experience altitude sickness at the summit. An exception is those who have been scuba diving in the past 24 hours, so plan your trip accordingly. Children, pregnant women and those in generally poor health are also susceptible. If you experience difficulty breathing, sudden headaches and dizziness, or more serious symptoms such as confusion and lack of motor coordination, descend immediately. Sometimes driving down the crater road just a few hundred feet will alleviate the problem. Panicking or hyperventilating only makes things worse.

Getting There & Away

To explore the park in depth and on your own schedule, you will need to rent a car. There is no public bus service to either district of the park. The summit is 40 miles from Kahului, just over an hour's drive. Kipahulu is 55 miles from Kahului via the Road to Hana. Expect the drive to take at least two hours. Guided tours also stop at both sections of the park.

Information

Park Headquarters Visitor Center (☑808-572-4459; www.nps.gov/hale; ☺8am-3:45pm) Less than a mile beyond the entrance, this visitor center is the place to pick up brochures, a trail map and a map of the night sky for stargazing. You can also buy a nature book, get camping permits and find information about ranger talks and other activities offered during your visit. If you're going hiking, you'll want to make sure your water bottles are filled before leaving here. Keep an eye out for nene wandering around the grounds; many nene deaths are the result of being hit by cars. The water filling station is beside the restrooms. ■

Pipiwai Trail

Halema'uma'u Crater, July 2018

Hawai'i Volcanoes National Park

Transformed by the massive eruption of Kilauea in 2018, this park testifies to the devastating power of nature. Its rivers of lava may have disappeared for now, but this rugged land remains a micro-continent of thriving rainforests, volcanic deserts, mountain meadows and plenty of geological marvels in between.

Great For...

State
Hawaii

Entrance Fee
7-day pass per vehicle/pedestrian
$25/12

Area
505 sq miles

This vast and varied **park** (☏808-985-6000; www.nps.gov/havo) can fill as many days as you give it, particularly if you enjoy hiking. Or you can drive it all in one long 45-mile round-trip journey that takes you down the Chain of Craters Road to the ocean by the Holei Sea Arch before retracing your route. Even less time? Stick to Crater Rim Dr (partially open after the 2018 eruption), where many of the key sites are located. In any case, start at the informative Kilauea Visitor Center, just past the entrance, on your right.

❶ Kilauea Visitor Center & Museum

Make this **Visitor Center** (☏808-985-6000; www.nps.gov/havo; Crater Rim Dr; ⊙9am-5pm, film screenings hourly 9am-4pm) 🖉 your first stop in the park. Extraordinarily helpful (and remarkably patient) rangers and volunteers can advise you about volcanic activity, air quality, road closures,

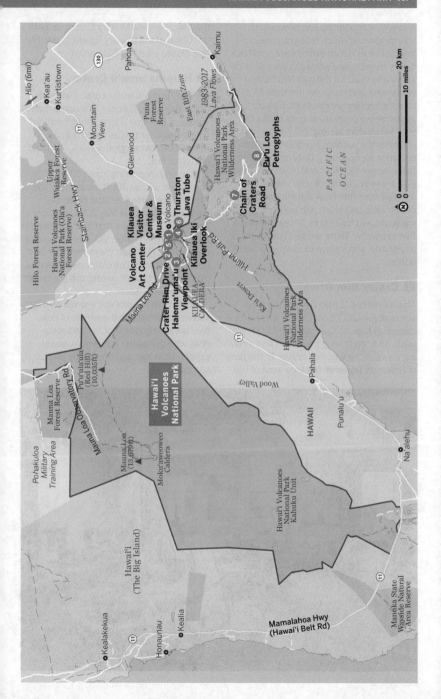

hiking-trail conditions and how best to spend however much time you have. Interactive museum exhibits are small but family friendly, and will teach even science-savvy adults about the park's delicate ecosystem and Hawaiian heritage. All of the rotating movies are excellent. Pick up fun junior ranger program activity books for your kids before leaving.

Check the outdoor signboards by the entrance for upcoming daily and evening talks, ranger-led hikes and other activities guaranteed to enhance your visit. A well-stocked nonprofit bookstore inside the center sells souvenirs, rain ponchos, walking sticks and flashlights. Wheelchairs are free to borrow. There are also restrooms, a pay phone, and a place to fill up your water bottles.

❷ Crater Rim Drive

This incredible 11-mile paved loop road starts at Kilauea Visitor Center and skirts the rim of Kilauea Caldera, passing steam vents and rifts, hiking trailheads and amazing views of the smoking crater. At the time of research, however, the loop west of the the KMC (Kilauea Military Camp) up until the Chain of the Craters Road intersection was closed after the 2018 eruption.

❸ Halema'uma'u Crater

Halema'uma'u is really a crater within the crater of Kilauea Caldera. The name means 'house of the *'ama'u* fern,' though ancient songs also refer to it as Halemaumau without the 'okina (glottal stops), or 'house of eternal fire.'

Formerly measuring about 3000ft across and almost 300ft deep, the crater almost doubled in size after collapses sustained during the May 2018 eruption. As a result, a lava lake that first appeared in a vent during an earlier 2008 eruption and once spilled lava onto the crater floor, has now disappeared. The crater overlook was closed at the time of writing and unlikely to reopen anytime soon.

How active Kilauea Volcano will be when you visit is subject to the whims of Pele, the Hawaiian goddess of fire and volcanoes who makes her home here, so set expectations low, and hope to be pleasantly surprised.

Volcano Art Center

❹ Kilauea Iki Overlook

When 'Little Kilauea' burst open in a fiery inferno in November 1959, it filled the crater with a roiling lake of molten rock fed by a 1900ft fountain that lit up the night sky with 2 million gushing tons of lava per hour at its peak. The lake took over 30 years to completely solidify.

From the **overlook** (Crater Rim Dr), you can view the mile-wide crater and wonder whether the trail traversing the middle is as astonishing as it looks. (It is.)

❺ Volcano Art Center

Near the visitor center, this sharp local **art gallery** (☎808-967-7565; www.volcanoartcenter.org; Crater Rim Dr; ⏰9am-5pm) ✎ spotlights museum-quality pottery, paintings, woodwork, sculpture, jewelry, quilts and more in a series of rotating exhibits. The nonprofit shop, housed in the historic 1877 Volcano House hotel, is worth a visit just to admire its construction. Ask about upcoming art classes and cultural workshops, including the **Aloha Fridays** weekly immersive experiences (11am to 1pm Friday).

❻ Thurston Lava Tube

On Kilauea's eastern side, Crater Rim Dr passes through a rainforest thick with tree ferns and ohia trees to the overflowing parking lot for ever-popular **Thurston Lava Tube** (Nahuku; off Crater Rim Dr). A 0.3-mile loop walk starts in an ohia forest filled with birdsong before heading underground through a gigantic (but short) artificially lit lava tube. It's a favorite with tour groups, so come early or late to avoid the crowd. For a more memorable experience, visit the glowing maw after dark.

Lava tubes form when the outer crust of a lava river hardens while the liquid beneath the surface continues to flow through. When the eruption stops, the flow drains out leaving only that hard shell behind. Nahuku, as this tube is called in Hawaiian, was 'discovered' by controversial figure Lorrin Thurston, the newspaper baron (and patron of famed vulcanogist Dr Jaggar)

 Kilauea and the 2018 Closure

By its very nature, Hawai'i Volcanoes National Park is a fickle and rapidly changing beast. Following strong volcanic and seismic activity in the Kilauea volcano in May 2018, part of the park was closed to visitors for four months, opening again in late September 2018. At the time of writing, the full extent of damage was still being assessed. Certain trails and sights, including the Jaggar Museum, have had to close and may never reopen, while sinkholes on and around Crater Rim Drive (which remains partially open) may take years to fully repair. It is also important to recognize that post-eruption, the volcano is completely quiet. There is no active lava in the park and no molten lava flowing tumultuously to the sea. The lava lake in the crater has also disappeared.

If you are planning on visiting the park, bear in mind that much of the information in this chapter is liable to change. Visit www.nps.gov/havo for regular updates.

who was instrumental in overthrowing the Kingdom of Hawaii.

At the time of writing, the lava tube was being reassessed after the 2018 eruption. It will probably reopen, but check ahead before traveling.

❼ Chain of Craters Road

This is it: possibly the most scenic road trip on an island packed with really scenic road trips. Heading south from Crater Rim Dr, paved Chain of Craters Road winds almost 19 miles and 3700ft down the southern slopes of Kilauea, ending ending by the Holei Sea Arch on the coast where a short trail leads to the ocean.

Drive slowly, especially in foggy or rainy conditions, and watch out for endangered nene (Hawaiian goose).

Left: Thurston Lava Tube;
Right: Entering the lava tube

❽ Pu'u Loa Petroglyphs

The gentle, 1.3-mile round-trip to Pu'u Loa
(roughly, 'hill of long life') leads to one of
Hawai'i's largest concentrations of ancient
petroglyphs (Mile 16.4, Chain of Craters Rd),
some over 800 years old. Here Hawaiians
chiseled more than 23,000 drawings into
pahoehoe (smooth-flowing lava) with adz
tools quarried from Keanakako'i. Stay on
the boardwalk – not all petroglyphs are
obvious, and you might damage some
if you walk over the rocks. The trailhead
parking is signed between Miles 16 and 17
on Chain of Craters Road.

There are abstract designs, animal
and human figures, as well as thousands
of dimpled depressions (or cupules)
that were receptacles for *piko* (umbili-
cal cords). Placing a baby's *piko* inside
a cupule and covering it with stones
bestowed health and longevity on the
child. Archaeologists believe a dot with a
circle around it was for a first born, while
two circles were reserved for the first born
of an *ali'i* (chief).

Hiking

Although staring into Kilauea crater after a 200ft walk from your car is monster bang for your buck, the real magic of Hawai'i Volcanoes National Park can only be found while exploring its 150 miles of trails. It is entirely possible to hike from a lonely beach to the sometimes snowy summit of Mauna Loa – passing grasslands, rainforest oases, lava deserts and steaming craters – with only a brief stint on pavement. While that feat is best reserved for a few extraordinary souls, many shorter journeys will reveal complex and magnificent details impossible to see from behind a windshield.

Be prepared for rapidly changing weather: a hot sunny stroll can turn cold and wet in an instant. Yet, despite being bordered by rainforest, this is a surprisingly dry area and dehydration comes easily. No drinking water is available, except possibly at primitive campgrounds (where it must be treated before drinking), so pack at least three quarts of water per person per day. Campfires are prohibited. A compass and binoculars are handy, because mist or vog can impede navigation.

All overnight hikes require a $10 permit, available in person only one day in advance from the **Backcountry Office** (☎808-985-6178; Crater Rim Dr, Visitor Emergency Operations Center (VEOC); ◷8am-4pm). One permit covers up to 12 people for seven nights. Be sure to download the park's backcountry trip planner covering potential hazards with safety tips and advice for protecting wildlife and archaeological sites.

If you prefer to join a group, the non-profit **Friends of Hawai'i Volcanoes National Park** (☎808-985-7373; www.fhvnp.org; annual membership adult/student/family $30/15/45) leads weekend hikes and field trips, and organizes volunteer activities including native forest restoration.

Top left: Pu'u Loa petroglyphs; Top right: Kilauea steam plume; Bottom: Chain of Craters Road

Essential Information

Sleeping & Eating

The park's two vehicle-accessible campgrounds are relatively uncrowded outside of summer months. Nights can be crisp and cool and wet. Campsites are first-come, first-served (with a seven-night limit). Nearby Volcano Village has the most variety for those who prefer a roof over their heads.

Volcano House is the most obvious eating option in the park, and it's no slouch. Volcano Village has several restaurants. Those cooking at their tent would do well to stock up in Hilo or Kona.

Safety

Although few people have died due to violently explosive eruptions at Kilauea, come prepared if you plan to walk or hike: bring sturdy shoes or boots, long pants, a hat, sunscreen, water (and snacks), and a flashlight with extra batteries. For more information see the Visitor Center's excellent safety film.

Lava

Even cooled hard lava can be dangerous. Uneven and brittle surfaces made of glass-sharp rocks can give way over unseen hollows and lava tubes while the edges of craters and rifts crumble easily. Deep earth cracks may be hidden by plants. When hiking, abrasions, deep cuts and broken limbs are all possible. In short, it's critical that you stay on marked trails and heed warning signs. Blazing paths into unknown terrain can damage fragile areas, lead to injuries and leave tracks that encourage others to follow.

Vog & Sulfuric Fumes

Another major, constant concern is air quality. Halema'uma'u and Pu'u 'O'o belch thousands of tons of deadly sulfur dioxide daily. If lava runs into the sea it creates a 'steam plume,' as sulfuric and hydrochloric acid mixes with airborne silica. All this combines to create 'vog' which, depending on the winds, can settle over the park. People with respiratory and heart conditions, pregnant women, infants and young children should take care.

Dehydration

Vast areas of the park qualify as desert, and dehydration is common. Carrying three quarts of water per person is the standard advice, but bring more and keep a gallon in the trunk: you'll drink it.

Getting There & Around

The park is 30 miles (45 minutes) from Hilo and 95 miles (2¾ hours) from Kailua-Kona via Hwy 11. The turnoffs for Volcano Village are a couple of miles east of the main park entrance. Hwy 11 is prone to flooding, washouts and closures during rainstorms. Periods of drought may close Mauna Loa Rd and Hilina Pali Rd due to wildfire hazards.

The public **Hele-On Bus** (808-961-8744; www.heleonbus.org; adult one-way $2) departs Monday through Saturday (no service Sunday) from Hilo, arriving at the park visitor center ($5 surcharge) about 1¼ hours later. One bus continues to Ka'u. There is no public transportation once you get inside the park, and hitchhiking is illegal in all national parks.

Cyclists are permitted on paved roads, and a handful of dirt ones, including Escape Rd but not on any trails – pavement or no.

Information

The park is open 24 hours a day, except when eruption activity and volcanic gases necessitate temporary closures. Post the 2018 eruption, it is strongly advised that visitors check ahead for up-to-date trail, road and campground information, along with news about the park's recovery

The park's main entrance sits at almost 4000ft, with varying elevation and climates inside the park boundaries. Chilly rain, wind, fog and vog (volcanic fog) typify the fickle weather, which can go from hot and dry to a soaking downpour in a flash. Near Kilauea Caldera, temperatures average 15°F cooler than in Kona, so be sure to bring a rain jacket and pants, especially if visiting at night. ■

Kilauea Iki

Hawaii's Other Protected Areas

In addition to its two national parks, Hawaii also has seven national historical parks, sites, trails and memorials, most of which help to preserve Hawaiian culture. Hawaii also has nine national wildlife refuges (www.fws.gov/pacific/refuges) on the main islands that protect endangered waterbirds and plants.

Pu'uhonua o Honaunau National Historical Park

Standing at the end of a long semi-desert of thorny scrub and lava plains, the park fronting Honaunau Bay provides one of the state's most evocative experiences of ancient Hawai'i, and easy access to some of the best snorkeling anywhere.

Kaloko-Honokohau National Historical Park

Though it may appear to be desolate lava rock, this national park is worth exploring. It covers 1160 acres of oceanfront and includes fishponds, ancient heiau (stone temples) and house sites, burial caves, petroglyphs, *holua* (sled courses), and a restored 1-mile segment of the ancient King's Trail footpath.

WWII Valor in the Pacific National Monument

One of the USA's most significant WWII sites, this National Park Service monument narrates the history of the Pearl Harbor attack and commemorates fallen service members. The monument is entirely wheelchair accessible. The Pearl Harbor Visitor Center also leads to other parks and museums, like the USS *Bowfin* Submarine Museum and Park (pictured).

Kalaupapa National Historical Park

The spectacularly beautiful Kalaupapa Peninsula is the most remote part of Hawaii's most isolated island. The only way to reach this lush green peninsula edged with long, white-sand beaches is on a twisting trail down the steep *pali,* the world's highest sea cliffs, or by plane. This remoteness is the reason it was, for more than a century, where Hansen's disease patients were forced into isolation.

In Focus

The Parks Today 480
One hundred years old and counting, the National Park Service still faces an ongoing battle with outside threats.

History 482
With Yellowstone the world's first national park, the foresight of a few indivduals has created a legacy for millions to enjoy.

Outdoor Activities 488
There's more to the national parks than spectacular hiking. Wildly diverse landscapes offer activities to suit every taste.

Wildlife Watching 494
National parks have helped some of America's most iconic animals – grizzly bears, mountain lions, bison – back from the brink of extinction.

Conservation 499
Safeguarding the parks' treasures has always been a struggle, and today conservationists are facing new challenges.

Landscapes & Geology 502
Glaciers and lava flows, fossils and hot springs: America's parks are a testament to its violent and spectacular geological history.

Gateway Arch National Park (p384)

The Parks Today

A 2016 anniversary celebrated a century in which the US National Park Service grew from 12 parks to almost 60. But 2017 brought new challenges to the USA's protected areas. The Trump administration's downsizing of several national monuments left many reflecting on the precarious nature of America's great natural landscapes and our unending duty to protect them for future generations.

Cutbacks in Utah

When President Trump took office in January 2017 the National Parks System protected 417 areas comprising 84 million acres across every state of the continental US, DC, Hawaii, American Samoa, Guam, Puerto Rico and the US Virgin Islands. Between 2009 and 2016, President Obama had been particularly proactive in expanding the park network overseeing the creation of one new national park (Pinnacles) and establishing or expanding 34 equally spectacular national monuments. However, following a wide-ranging Interior Department review of more recent monument designations, the Trump administration committed to reducing several of the protected areas significantly. In December 2017 Utah's Bears Ears National Monument was reduced by around 85% from 2031 sq miles to 315 sq miles, and 1996-designated Grand Staircase-Escalante National

Monument was almost halved in size. The move is unprecedented. While presidents have shrunk national monuments in the past, most recently in the early 1960s, it has never been undertaken on such a significant scale.

At the time of research the details of these restructures were being finalized by Congress. When it likely goes through, millions of formerly protected acres will be available for commercial use, potentially generating billions of dollars of revenue through extraction leases of natural resources, including copper, oil and gas. And though the projected revenues are considerable, the cost is likewise significant: the activity is likely to cause irreversible damage to these pristine, culturally significant lands, prompting large-scale protests from Native American and environmental advocacy groups.

Paring Back & Other Threats

It was also in 2017 that a number of federally enforced environmental regulations were pared back, including laws concerning air and water pollution (emissions control), toxic waste management, infrastructure, public safety and wildlife protection.

Despite record-breaking park visitor numbers in 2016, the 2018 federal budget contained cuts of around $300 million to the NPS's operating budget, prompting the NPS to warn of possible staff cuts and reduced services in up to 90% of its parks. Campground closures and reduced operating hours may also be implemented in some parks. For the lowdown on the NPS and the most up-to-date information, visit www.nps.gov.

Climate change is another existential threat to the parks in both the near and long-term future, whether it be in the form of more intense and frequent wildfires in the West or devastating hurricanes in the Southeast. The most obvious consequences can already be seen in Glacier National Park, where rapidly melting glaciers may render a name-change by 2030. It has also been suggested that rising summer temperatures in California might make Joshua Tree National Park too hot for its famous trees before the end of the century.

Welcome to Gateway Arch

Fortunately, it's not all shrinkage. In February 2018, President Trump signed a new law creating Gateway Arch, the country's 60th national park and the fourth new addition since the beginning of the 21st century. While Gateway Arch is relatively small (indeed, at 0.14 sq miles it is the smallest national park in the US network) and its designation, in the eyes of many, was little more than a renaming of an existing national memorial, the move was an important symbolic victory for a network not impervious to outside threats.

Mariposa Grove (p120), Yosemite National Park

FERENC CEGLEDI/SHUTTERSTOCK ©

History

Few things are as quintessentially American as national parks. Their genesis, implementation and growth since 1872 is a work of genius second only to the US constitution. A handful of people once had the foresight to pull the reins in on rampant hunting, logging, mining and tourist development, so that some magnificent treasures might be saved for future generations – their actions constitute one of the greatest chapters in US history.

1864
President Lincoln designates Yosemite Valley and the Mariposa Grove a protected state park.

1872
President Ulysses S Grant designates Yellowstone the world's first national park.

1890
Yosemite National Park is established, but the state of California retains control of Yosemite Valley and Mariposa Grove.

Mesa Verde National Park (p204)

ZACK FRANK/SHUTTERSTOCK ©

A Magnificent Park

American portrait artist George Catlin (1796–1872) is credited with being the first person to conceptualize a 'nation's park.' He envisioned a 'magnificent park' to protect the country's remaining indigenous people, buffalo and wilderness from the onslaught of western expansion. But over three decades would pass before anything remotely resembling that vision existed.

In 1851 members of an armed militia accidentally rode into a massive granite valley in the Sierra Nevada and decided to call it 'Yosemity,' possibly a corruption of the Miwok word *Oo-hoo'-ma-te* or *uzumatel*, meaning 'grizzly bear.' The name stuck, and soon word of the valley and its waterfalls got out. Within no time, entrepreneurs were divvying up the land in hopes of profiting from tourists.

Thanks to a handful of outspoken writers, artists, naturalists and – most importantly – the efforts of the great landscape architect Frederick Law Olmstead, Yosemite Valley was spared privatization. In 1864 President Abraham Lincoln signed a bill into law that put

1894
After a poacher is caught killing bison in Yellowstone, Congress grants the park the power to enforce conservation laws.

1906
Mesa Verde becomes the seventh national park and the first dedicated to protecting cultural heritage.

1916
Stephen Mather convinces the Department of the Interior to create the National Park Service.

The Father of National Parks

Often considered the 'father of the US national park system,' Scottish-born John Muir (1838–1914) was an eloquent writer, naturalist and arguably the greatest defender of wilderness areas in the late-19th century. His writings were pivotal in the creation not just of Yosemite, but of Sequoia, Mt Rainier, Petrified Forest, and Grand Canyon National Parks. Famously – but unsuccessfully – Muir fought to save Yosemite's Hetch Hetchy Valley, which he believed rivaled Yosemite Valley in beauty and grandeur. Although he couldn't stop the damming of the river, his writings on the issue cemented the now widely held belief that our national parks should remain as close as possible to their natural state.

Yosemite Valley, and the nearby Mariposa Grove of giant sequoias, under the control of California. Although it wasn't a national park, it was the first time *any* government had mandated the protection of a natural area for public use.

Birth of a National Park

Four years later, a group of men bankrolled by Northern Pacific Railroad headed into the Wyoming wilderness to investigate reports of thermal pools and geysers. Among their discoveries were the Great Fountain Geyser and another geyser they would name Old Faithful. Soon, lobbyists at Northern Pacific, with their eyes on tourist dollars, rallied alongside conservationists for a public park like Yosemite. In 1872 Ulysses S Grant signed the landmark Yellowstone National Park Act, creating the country's first national park.

Meanwhile, in Yosemite, the famed naturalist John Muir lamented the destruction that logging companies, miners and sheep – which he famously deemed 'hoofed locusts' – were wreaking upon the park. In 1890 Yosemite became the country's second national park, but it wasn't until 1905 that Muir convinced Congress to expand the boundaries to include all of Yosemite Valley and the Mariposa Grove.

Over the next 25 years, presidents signed off on six more national parks, including Mt Rainier (1899), Crater Lake (1902), Mesa Verde (1906) and Glacier (1910).

In 1908 Theodore Roosevelt declared the Grand Canyon a national monument. The act was met with utter outrage from Arizona politicians, mining claim holders and ranchers, who believed he overstepped his bounds as president – a theme that continues to this day concerning the designation of federal lands.

Mather & the National Park Service

Still, there existed no effective protection or management of the new parks until the creation of the National Park Service (NPS) in 1916. The NPS was the brainchild of an industrialist and conservationist named Stephen Mather, who convinced the Department

1923
Yosemite's Hetch Hetchy Valley is dammed, the first shot in a continuing battle between conservationists and developers.

1926
Yellowstone's last wolves are killed in the federal predator control program, which also targeted mountain lions, bears and coyotes.

1933
FDR creates the Civilian Conservation Corps; CCC workers improve infrastructure in national parks and plant over 3 billion trees.

of the Interior that a single governing body was precisely what the parks needed. When President Woodrow Wilson signed the National Park Service Act into law, Mather became the first director.

Mather believed that the best way to promote and improve the parks was to get people into them. A public relations guru, Mather encouraged park superintendents to run publicity campaigns, created the park ranger system, initiated campfire talks and opened the first park museums. His efforts – always coupled with media outreach – were so successful that by 1928 he had tripled the number of park visitors to three million.

While Mather was extremely successful in developing the parks, some felt he'd gone too far. Conservation groups such as the National Parks Association and the Sierra Club felt that Mather's emphasis on development came at the expense of the parks themselves. Mather's successor and protégé, Horace Albright, partially addressed these concerns by creating a national wildlife division within the NPS.

FDR & the CCC

With the Great Depression, the parks went through significant changes. President Franklin Delano Roosevelt (FDR) created the Civilian Conservation Corps (CCC) and put thousands of young men to work improving national park roads, visitors shelters, campsites and trails. During his presidency, FDR also created Joshua Tree, Capitol Reef, and Channel Islands National Monuments (all of which would become national parks), and Olympic and Kings Canyon National Parks.

With the beginning of WWII, the country's greatest public relief program came to an end, CCC workers went off to war, and the national park budget was slashed. Simultaneously, postwar prosperity allowed more Americans to travel – and hordes of them headed to the parks. By 1950 some 32 million people visited America's national parks. Within five years the number topped 60 million.

Theodore Roosevelt: The Conservation President

As part of a 1903 campaign tour, President Theodore Roosevelt spent two weeks exploring Yellowstone and three nights camping out with John Muir in Yosemite. But the greatest legacy of that trip arose from time spent at the Grand Canyon. Upon seeing the canyon for the first time, Roosevelt famously opined that the mystical natural wonder could not be improved by any human intervention – it should be left exactly as it was. A nascent conservationist movement had just gained an influential new member.

Muir may have provided the philosophical underpinnings of the national parks, but it was Roosevelt who transformed the vision into reality. An avid hunter, birder, far-sighted thinker and lover of the outdoors, Roosevelt's time out West – before he became president – profoundly shaped his life and legacy. By the time he left office in 1909, he had signed off on five national parks, 18 national monuments, 51 federal bird sanctuaries and 100 million acres of national forest.

1941–49	**1956–66**	**1980**
Ansel Adams photographs every national park in the US, bar the Everglades, for the NPS.	Mission 66 improves park facilities and creates the first national park visitor centers.	The Alaska National Interest Lands Conservation Act doubles the amount of land under NPS control.

The Antiquities Act, National Monuments & other NPS Sites

In 1906 Congress passed the Antiquities Act, which gives the president the authority to protect public land by designating it a National Monument. Originally designed to protect Native American archaeological sites out West, Theodore Roosevelt quickly realized that he could use the Act to protect any tract of land for any reason – and without opposition from lobbyists or political opponents in Congress. The Grand Canyon was the most famous example of Roosevelt's decisive stroke.

In 2015 there were 117 national monuments. More are designated every year, while others change status. Other sites that come under NPS jurisdiction include historic sites, memorials, parkways, seashores, recreation areas and preserves, which are like parks, except that fossil fuel extraction and sport hunting are permitted. In total the NPS currently administers over 400 natural and historic sites, including 60 national parks.

Mission 66

The number of travelers descending on the parks put tremendous pressure on them. In 1956 NPS Director Conrad Wirth created Mission 66, a 10-year plan to improve park infrastructure and dramatically increase visitor services. The plan established the first park visitor centers, more staff and improved facilities. Over the course of Mission 66, Congress also added more than 50 new protected areas to the National Park System.

In 1964 George Hartzog succeeded Wirth as director of the NPS and continued to add new acquisitions. During his tenure nearly 70 new parks would come under the jurisdiction of the NPS. In 1972 President Nixon replaced Hartzog with his own appointee, and expansions to the park service were halted.

Doubling Down

Little was added to the national parks system until 1980, when President Carter signed the Alaska National Interest Lands Conservation Act into law. The landmark legislation instantly protected over 80 million acres and doubled the amount of land under control of the NPS. Ten new national parks and monuments were created in the process. Although controversial in Alaska, the move has been widely heralded as one of the greatest conservation measures in US history.

The Parks Today

Since Yellowstone was created in 1872, the National Park System has grown to encompass over 400 sites and 84 million acres. The parks today protect many of the continent's most sensitive ecosystems, some of the world's most remarkable landscapes and

1995	2011	2013
Fourteen grey wolves are reintroduced to Yellowstone nearly seventy years after they disappeared from the park ecosystem.	A proposed ban on the sale of plastic bottles in the Grand Canyon is blocked after Coca-Cola, an NPS donor, expresses displeasure.	Congressional gridlock shuts down the federal government; all national parks are forced to close for a 16-day period.

America's most important historical and cultural landmarks. Over the years, more than 11 billion people from the US and around the world have visited them. They are the country's greatest treasure.

Despite a steady increase in visitation, however, the parks still face a variety of threats and obstacles, including loss of biodiversity, declining air and water quality, climate disruption and insufficient funding. In 2011, the NPS released a Call to Action: an initiative to help the service prepare for its second century, with aims such as reducing greenhouse gas emissions by 20%, increasing community involvement and continuing to raise awareness for the parks among all Americans.

Want to join the 221,000 people already volunteering in the national parks? To date, more than 97 million volunteer hours have been logged to make these places better. To learn more about opportunities, visit www.volunteer.gov.

NPS Logo

The National Park Service adopted its official logo in 1951. Shaped like an arrowhead, it features a bison and sequoia tree set against a snow-capped peak in the background with a body of water nearby – representing values of culture and history, wildlife and vegetation conservation and scenic beauty.

Hot Topics

While conservationists, policy makers and the NPS debate how to best protect the parks, nearly everyone agrees the parks need money – except, it seems, for Congress. With budget cuts and obstructionist gridlock becoming increasingly the norm in Washington, the NPS has begun to turn to private donors and corporate sponsorships in order to make up for the federal shortfall. With the suggestion of sponsors' 'naming rights to any unit of the National Park System or a National Park System facility' in the 2015 National Defense Authorization Act, the future of NPS funding is on a slippery slope indeed.

System-wide challenges are not the only matters garnering national attention. Congestion, crowds and cars remain a constant source of concern, and more and more parks are introducing free shuttles to combat traffic and reduce air pollution. In Yellowstone, snowmobile has started to be carefully regulated. And with, for example, the concern about melting glaciers in Glacier National Park, there are plenty of other park-specific issues fueling debate beyond the doors of local diners.

2014
Park visitation reaches an all-time high with 292.8 million visitors over the course of the year.

2016
The National Park System celebrates the 100th anniversary of its founding.

2018
Gateway Arch in St Louis, Missouri becomes the US's 60th and – to date – smallest national park measuring just 0.14 sq miles.

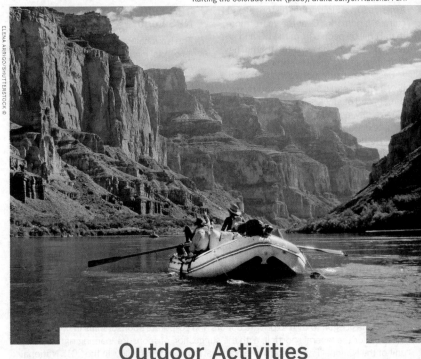

ELENA ARRIGO/SHUTTERSTOCK ©

Outdoor Activities

No one visits a national park so they can hang around indoors. Getting out and about and breathing in big bursts of fresh air is what the parks are all about, and that often means getting active. With environments ranging from the subtropics of the Everglades to the Alaskan tundra, the possibilities are endless.

Hiking

Nothing encapsulates the spirit of the national parks like hiking. Thousands of miles of trails crisscross the parks, offering access to their most scenic mountain passes, highest waterfalls, deepest canyons and quietest corners. Trails run the gamut of accessibility, from the flat, paved paths of Yosemite's **Loop Trails** to the thrilling exposed ascent of **Longs Peak** in Rocky Mountain.

Regardless of the style of the trail, you'll find that exploring on foot generally offers the best park experience. The relatively slow pace of walking brings you into closer contact with the wildlife, and allows you to appreciate the way different perspectives and the day's shifting light can alter the scenery. The satisfaction gained from completing a hike is also a worthy reward; it's one thing to look over the rim of the Grand Canyon, it's another to work up a sweat hiking back up from the canyon floor.

Each park chapter in this guide has its own Hiking or Activities section with descriptions of the park's top hikes. We've done our best to cover a variety of trails, not just our favorites. Our goal with descriptions is less about navigation than it is about helping you choose which hikes to squeeze into your trip. Detailed trail descriptions and maps are readily available at visitor centers in every park, and they will complement this guide well. Know your limitations, know the route you plan to take and pace yourself.

Backpacking

There are hundreds of amazing day hikes to choose from in the National Park System, but if you want the full experience, head out into the wilderness on an overnight trip. The claim that 99% of park visitors never make it into the backcountry may not be true everywhere, but you will unquestionably see far fewer people and witness exponentially more magic the farther from a road you go. Backcountry campsites are also much more likely to have openings than park lodges and car campsites (which fill up months in advance), making accommodations less of a headache.

Even if you have no backpacking experience, don't consider it out of reach. Most national parks have at least a few backcountry campsites within a couple of hours' walk of a trailhead, making them excellent options for first-time backpackers. You will need gear, however: an appropriate backpack, tent, sleeping bag and pad, stove, headlamp and food are all essential.

Familiarize yourself with the park rules and backcountry ethics before heading out. You will need a permit; if you have your heart set on a famous excursion, apply well in advance online. Most park visitor centers have a backcountry desk, where you can apply for walk-in permits, get trail information, learn about wildlife (bear canisters are generally required in bear country) and check conditions. Before hitting the trail, learn about low-impact camping principles at Leave No Trace (Int.org).

Preparation & Safety

Walks can be as short or long as you like, but remember this when planning: be prepared. The wilderness may be unlike anything you have ever experienced, and designating certain parcels as 'national parks' has not tamed it.

The weather, particularly out West, can be extraordinary in its unpredictability and sheer force. The summer sun is blazing hot, sudden thunderstorms can drop enough water in 10 minutes to create deadly flash floods, snow can fall at any time of year above the tree line, while ferocious wind storms can rip or blow away your poorly staked tent.

No matter where you are, water should be the number one item on your packing checklist – always carry more than you think you'll need. If you're doing any backpacking, make sure you have a way to purify water, and check with rangers ahead of time about the availability of water along the trail.

If your trip involves any elevation change, take the time to acclimatize before tackling a long hike to avoid altitude sickness. Sunblock, a hat, ibuprofen and warm wind- and waterproof layers are all non-negotiable at high altitudes. Snow cover can last through the end of June above 11,000ft; check with rangers to see if you'll need gaiters and snowshoes.

After the elements, getting lost is the next major concern. Most day hikes are well signed and visitors are numerous, but you should always take some sort of map. If you plan on going into the backcountry, definitely take a topographic (topo) map and a

compass. You can pick up detailed maps in most visitor centers; National Geographic's *Trails Illustrated* series is generally excellent.

At lower elevations and in desert parks, always inquire about ticks, poison oak, poison ivy and rattlesnakes before heading out. Most day hikes are on well-maintained trails, but it's good to know what's out there.

And all hikers, solo or not, should always remember the golden rule: let someone know where you are going and how long you plan to be gone.

Rafting, Kayaking & Canoeing

Rafts, kayaks, canoes and larger boats are a wonderful way to get to parts of the parks that landlubbers can't reach. River-running opportunities abound in the parks, but none stand out quite like the **Colorado River**. The most famous trip along the Colorado is a three-week odyssey through the Grand Canyon – arguably the best possible way to visit – though you can also take a heart-thumping multiday excursion further upstream through the desert wilds of the Canyonlands. The **Snake River** in Grand Teton National Park has rafting for all skill levels, as does the **Pigeon River** in the Smokies.

If larger bodies of water are more your speed, one of the best parks to explore in a canoe or kayak is **Voyageurs** on the Minnesota–Canada border, which consists of over 30 lakes and 900 islands. Another northern park offering kayaking trips is **Isle Royale**, the largest island in Lake Superior. Many of the campgrounds in both of these parks are only accessible by boat.

In Glacier National Park, the lake paddling is excellent and accessible, thanks to boat ramps and rentals on several lakes. In Grand Teton, **String** and **Leigh Lakes** are great for family and novice paddlers, and you can rent boats at Colter Bay. In Yosemite, **Tenaya Lake** makes for spectacular paddling. Yellowstone's **Shoshone Lake** is the largest backcountry lake in the Lower 48, and offers boat-in access to some of the remotest areas of the park.

Boat Tours & Snorkeling

Both the Atlantic and the Pacific have a handful of marine-based parks – many accessible only by boat, and several perfect for underwater adventures. Boat trips exploring the vast **Everglades** are de rigueur in the dry season, while only 5% of **Biscayne**, Florida's largest stretch of undeveloped Atlantic coastline, is land – glass-bottom boats and snorkeling tours are obligatory to check out the coral reefs offshore. Southern California's **Channel Islands** are another prime destination for snorkeling, diving and boat tours.

If you're prepared to leave the continental US, the **Dry Tortugas**, **Virgin Islands** and **American Samoa** are certainly the best options for snorkeling and diving in sapphire-blue waters.

And of course, at the other end of the spectrum, there's Alaska: **Glacier Bay's** calving icebergs and humpback whales are generally visited on a cruise (though you can kayak if you prefer), while volcanic **Katmai** offers innumerable river-running, lake paddling and sea kayaking options. Daily boat tours also explore the inlets and islands at **Kenai Fjords**, Alaska's 'smallest' park.

Rock Climbing & Mountaineering

There's no sport quite like rock climbing. From a distance it appears to be a feat of sheer strength, but balance, creativity, technical know-how and a Zen-like sangfroid are all parts of the game. Clinging by your fingertips 2000ft up on one of Yosemite's renowned big walls? Not the place to lose your cool. Thankfully, there are plenty of options for climbers of all ages and levels that don't require the mind control of a Jedi. Sign up for a day of guided climbing – the **Yosemite Mountaineering School** is a great place to start. Other world-renowned destinations include Joshua Tree, Zion, Acadia and the Black Canyon of the Gunnison.

Closely related to rock climbing is mountaineering: the technical ascent of a summit, involving ropes, climbing equipment, and, when there are glaciers, ice axes and crampons. Mountaineering routes are a dime a dozen out West; some of the most famous summits include **Longs Peak** (Rocky Mountain), **Grand Teton**, **Mt Ranier**, and, of course, **Denali**. Other incredible locales to rope up include the awe-inspiring peaks of the **North Cascades** and **Glacier National Park**. Because of the exposure and high altitude on these routes, the risks can be high. Like rock climbing, you'll want to hire a guide if you don't already have significant experience.

Cycling & Mountain Biking

As a general rule, expect more options for two-wheeled fun just outside park boundaries. There are, however, some exceptions: in Yosemite the 12 miles of paved pathways along the **Loop Trails** make for incredibly scenic and leisurely pedaling. In Zion, you can rent a bike and ride the 6.2-mile **Zion Canyon Scenic Drive** (closed to cars most of the year), which connects with the paved Pa'rus Trail. In Bryce, the 34-mile **Bryce Canyon Scenic Drive** makes for an excellent longer ride. Many parks have bicycle rental shops close to the main entrance.

Adventurous Tales

John Wesley Powell led the first recorded descent of the Colorado River in 1869 – with only one arm. The ten-man survey team took four 21ft boats from Wyoming to Nevada in three months, passing through the Grand Canyon. One boat, many supplies and three men were lost along the way.

In 2014 the Spaniard Kilian Jornet summited Denali's West Buttress route in an incredible 9 hours 45 minutes, climbing 13,000ft over 16 miles of glacial terrain. He then skied down to base camp in two hours.

In January 2015, climbers Tommy Caldwell and Kevin Jorgeson became the first to free-climb El Capitan's 3000ft Dawn Wall in Yosemite, a feat long thought impossible. The pair spent 19 days on the cliff face, sleeping on portaledges and documenting their progress with their phones.

★ So Much to Do...

For those that want to try it all, here's some more fodder for fun:

Stargazing It's especially outstanding in Capitol Reef and Bryce.

Soaking Submerge your sore muscles in thermal hot springs at Yellowstone, Olympic (pictured) or Hot Springs.

Canyoneering Descend into Utah's mesmerizing slot canyons; with a guide, no experience is necessary.

Glissading Take your ice axe and slide down the snow fields on Mt Ranier.

Tide pooling Olympic, Acadia and the Channel Islands are tide-pool heaven.

Sand surfing Rent a board or simply slide on your butt in Colorado's Great Sand Dunes.

Caving Join a subterranean tour at Mammoth Cave, Wind Cave or Carlsbad.

On the downside, cycling within national parks can sometimes be challenging due to heavy traffic and steep grades. Anyone who's been grazed by an RV mirror can attest to that.

Mountain biking on trails is largely prohibited in the national parks, but some parks have dirt roads that substitutes. **Canyonlands National Park** is particularly full of them, and there are several gravel roads in **Great Smoky**. In Utah, you won't have to stray very far for some of the best mountain biking in the world, found on the desert slickrock outside **Arches** and **Zion**.

Winter Sports

Cross-Country Skiing & Snowshoeing

Come winter, trails and roads in many parks get blanketed with snow and the crowds disappear. It's a magical time to visit, and those willing to step into skis or snowshoes and brave the elements will be rewarded. The best parks for both activities are Glacier, Yellowstone, Grand Teton, Rocky Mountain, Yosemite, Voyageurs, Olympic, Mt Rainier and Denali, though this is far from a comprehensive list. Surprisingly, there's even cross-country skiing at the Grand Canyon.

In most of these parks, rangers lead snowshoe hikes, which can be an excellent entry to the sport and a great way to learn about the winter environment. Visitor centers are the best place to check for information.

Downhill Skiing & Snowboarding

Most of the best downhill skiing takes place outside the parks. Three parks, however, do have downhill ski resorts: **Badger Pass** in Yosemite National Park is an affordable, family-friendly resort and, just inside the border of Olympic National Park, **Hurricane Ridge** has only three lifts and is the westernmost ski resort in the Lower 48. At Ohio's Cuyahoga Valley, the **Boston Mills/Brandywine Ski Resort** offers about a dozen short trails. The most notable skiing adjacent to parks covered in this guide is **Jackson Hole**, Wyoming, which has long runs, deep powder and a screeching 4139ft vertical drop.

Swimming

With the exception of the higher-elevation parks (like Glacier and Rocky Mountain) and northern parks like Denali, summer means heat, and heat means swimming. Alpine lakes make for wonderful but often frigid swimming, and many of the larger lakes have beaches and designated swimming areas.

As river rats the world over will attest, nothing beats dipping into a swimming hole and drip-drying on a rock in the sun. But be careful – every year, swimmers drown in national park rivers. Always check with visitor centers about trouble spots and the safest places to swim. Unless you're certain about the currents, swim only where others are swimming.

Top places to get wet are Zion's **Virgin River**, the **Merced River** in Yosemite Valley, **Sedge Bay** in Yellowstone, **Leigh Lake** in Grand Teton, **Midnight Hole** in Great Smoky and **Sol Duc Hot Springs** in Olympic.

Fishing

For many, the idea of heading to the national parks without a fishing rod is ludicrous. Yellowstone offers some of the best fly-fishing in the country. Olympic's **Hoh** and **Sol Duc Rivers** are famous for their runs of salmon and winter steelhead. Waters in Yosemite's high country, particularly the **Tuolumne River**, can be great for small, feisty trout. **Glacier**, **Grand Teton** and, of course, most of Alaska's parks all offer outstanding fishing. **Great Smoky** has exceptional fishing for trout and bass.

Wherever you fish, read up on local regulations. Fishing permits are always required, and those caught fishing without one will be fined. (Children under 15 are generally not required to have a license.) Some waters, including many streams and rivers, are catch-and-release only, and sometimes bait-fishing is prohibited. Certain native fish, such as bull trout, kokanee salmon and wild steelhead, are often protected, and anglers in possession of these can be heavily fined. The best place to check regulations is online. For details on regulations, check the park's NPS website (www.nps.gov) and refer to the respective state's department of fish and game website. Find the latter by searching for the state plus 'fish and game.'

Horseback & Mule Riding

The most time-tested form of transport still makes for a wonderful way to experience the great outdoors. Horseback riding is possible in many of the parks, and outfitters within or immediately outside the parks offer everything from two-hour rides to full- and multiday pack trips. Rides run around $40 per hour or $80 per half-day.

In **Great Smoky**, over 550 miles of trails are open to horses, and outfitters abound. Popular horseback excursions such as the descent into the **Grand Canyon** or the **High Sierra Camps** in Yosemite require reservations far in advance.

Gray wolf, Yellowstone National Park (p364)

Wildlife Watching

It's no coincidence that the establishment of many of the earliest national parks coincided with the first wave of near mass extinctions in the United States: by the 1890s the passenger pigeon, bison, eastern elk, wolf, mountain lion and grizzly bear – along with their habitats and numerous less heralded species – were all on the verge of disappearing forever. Today, some of these animals have made a comeback, thanks in large part to the protection afforded by the national parks.

Bison, Moose & Other Grazers

The continent's largest land mammal is the American bison (or buffalo). Some 60 million bison once roamed North America, but Euro-American settlers, in one of the saddest chapters of US history, reduced their numbers to about 300. Beginning in the 1860s, the US government and army encouraged the slaughter in order to deprive the Plains Indians of their primary means of survival. But for many Americans traveling West, killing bison was done for the sheer pleasure of sport. By the 1890s, Yellowstone's bison herd was the only one remaining in the country, with poachers successfully reducing its numbers one by one.

What could have been a disaster instead became a turning point. Thanks to the determined intervention of George Bird Grinnell, editor of *Forest and Stream* and founder of the

Audubon Society, and a young politician by the name of Theodore Roosevelt, Congress passed an 1894 law granting national parks the power to protect all wildlife within their boundaries. Previous to this, poachers were simply expelled from park lands; now they could be arrested. Yellowstone's bison were gradually bred back from the brink of extinction, and today an estimated 4500 roam the park.

Other large grazers are commonplace throughout many parks. Moose, the largest of the world's deer species, stand 5ft to 7ft at the shoulder and can weigh up to 1000lb. They're common in Yellowstone, Glacier, Rocky Mountain, Grand Teton, Voyageurs and Denali. The same parks are home to elk, which grow antlers up to 5ft long and weigh up to 700lb. These majestic herbivores graze along forest edges and are commonly sighted. They were reintroduced to Great Smoky in 2001.

Bighorn sheep are synonymous with the Rocky Mountains, and have made a slow but steady comeback after nearing extinction in the 1800s. Today they are sighted throughout the Rockies, and in Joshua Tree, Zion and Bryce Canyon. During late-fall and early-winter breeding seasons, males charge each other at 20mph and clash their horns so powerfully that the sound can be heard for miles.

The fuzzy, sure-footed mountain goat, actually a species of antelope, lives at high altitudes throughout the year and has a habitat spread across the Rockies, Cascades and parts of Alaska. On the Western plains, the pronghorn antelope is North America's fastest land animal, capable of reaching speeds of 55mph.

Bears

If you see a bear on your trip, odds are it will be a black bear. These mostly vegetarian foragers are much more common than their larger, more elusive cousins, grizzly (brown) bears. Black bears are very adaptable and in some places, such as Yosemite, have become so accustomed to humans that they regularly roam campsites and break into cars at night for food.

Black bears, which are sometimes brown or cinnamon colored, roam montane and subalpine forests throughout the country and are surprisingly common. The Rockies and the Sierras have the highest populations, but it's also possible to spot them in the Great Smoky Mountains, Shenandoah, Voyageurs and even parts of Florida. Black bears are usually not aggressive unless there are cubs nearby, but they will go after food or food odors. Make sure to store your food and trash properly, and use a bear canister if you plan on backpacking.

The grizzly bear once ranged across the western US, but today its population in the Lower 48 is estimated to be around 1500 to 1800. In the continental US, grizzlies are only found in the mountainous regions of Montana, Idaho, Wyoming and Washington. In Alaska, of course, they are much more common – Katmai's Brooks Falls is an iconic bear fishing hole. Of the national parks within the Lower 48, Yellowstone has the most grizzlies, with a population of around 750 bears; you can sometimes spot them at dawn in the Lamar Valley (take a telescope or binoculars). Grizzlies can reach up to 800lb and can be distinguished from black bears by their concave snout, rounded ears and prominent shoulder hump.

Grizzly attacks in national parks are rare, but they do happen. Most occur because people surprise them or inadvertently come between a mother and her cub. The National Park Service (www.nps.gov) has excellent information on bears and how to handle encounters.

Wolves & Coyotes

The gray wolf was once the Rocky Mountains' main predator, but relentless persecution reduced its territory to a narrow belt stretching from Canada to the Northern Rockies. The last wolf pack in Yellowstone was killed in 1924, but wolves were successfully reintroduced to the park beginning in 1995. The last official count in 2016 showed 108 wolves, though

TOM TIETZ/SHUTTERSTOCK ©

there are an estimated 500 in the Greater Yellowstone Ecosystem. The Lamar Valley is your best chance for a wolf sighting, and you can sign up for a wolf-watching excursion with a tour company.

Coyotes and foxes are common in many of the parks. When it comes to coyotes, you're far more likely to hear them than see them. Listening to them howl at night as you doze off to sleep is an eerie yet wonderful experience.

Cats

North America's largest cat is the mountain lion (also known as a puma or cougar), an elusive and powerful predator. Highly adaptable, mountain lions are present in many parks, including Yellowstone, Grand Teton, Glacier, Yosemite, Joshua Tree and Grand Canyon. It's highly unlikely you'll spot one, as they avoid human contact. If you're camping, however, you may hear one scream – it's an utterly terrifying sound in the darkness and a virtual guarantee that you won't fall back asleep until dawn. Adult males can measure over 7ft nose to tail and weigh up to 220lb, though they are usually smaller. Though they rarely trouble humans, there are sporadic attacks every couple of years, usually involving children and joggers.

Bobcats and lynx are also present in most of these parks and are equally hard to spot.

Small Mammals

Small mammals often get short shrift on people's watch lists, but animals like beavers, pikas, marmots and river otters are a delight to see. Beavers (and their dams) are found in Rocky Mountain, Yellowstone, Grand Teton, Voyageurs and Glacier National Parks, and are particularly fun to watch. Marmots, despite being little more than glorified ground squirrels, are enjoyable to watch hopping around on rocks in the high country. They are found in the subalpine regions of both the Rockies and the Sierras. Other critters you might come across include bats, squirrels, voles, mice, chipmunks, raccoons, badgers, skunks, shrews and martens.

Birds

Everglades National Park is the national park most famous for its birds. Over 360 species have been spotted there, including 16 different wading birds and dozens of terns, gulls and other shorebirds. Acadia National Park is close behind with 338 species on record.

Needless to say, bird-watching in both parks is outstanding. But don't rule out the inland parks. In Yellowstone, nearly 300 bird species have been sighted. Most of the NPS park websites (www.nps.gov) have complete bird lists – bring binoculars for the best experience.

Birds of prey – including eagles, falcons, hawks, owls and harriers – are common in the parks, especially the Western ones. Osprey, which nest and hunt around rivers and lakes, are a commonly spotted raptor. Keep your eyes peeled for bald eagles, which can be seen throughout Voyageurs and the Rockies, as well as in Mt Rainier, Olympic and the North Cascades. Extremely rare, California condors are sometimes spotted in Pinnacles, the Grand Canyon and Zion. There are 225 known wild California condors, spread throughout California, Utah and Arizona.

Amphibians & Reptiles

Frogs, toads and salamanders thrive in and around streams, rivers and lakes in several of the parks. With 24 species of salamanders, Great Smoky Mountains is often deemed the salamander capital of the world. The creepy-looking Pacific giant salamander, which can reach up to 12in in length, is found in Olympic and Mt Rainier. The incredible tiger salamander has adapted to life in the barren Great Sand Dunes.

When it comes to reptiles, Everglades National Park reigns supreme. Not only is it home to crocodiles, alligators and caiman, but also over 20 species of snakes, including the eastern coral snake, diamondback rattlers and boa constrictors. Everglades is also home to 16 turtle and tortoise species.

Return of the Wolf

The wolf is a potent symbol of America's wilderness. This smart, social predator is the largest species of canine – averaging more than 100lb and reaching nearly 3ft at the shoulder. An estimated 400,000 once roamed the continent from coast to coast, from Alaska to Mexico.

Wolves were not regarded warmly by European settlers. As 19th-century Americans moved west, they replaced the native herds of bison, elk, deer and moose with domestic cattle and sheep, which wolves found equally tasty. To stop wolves from devouring the livestock, extermination soon became official government policy. Up until 1965, for $20 to $50 an animal, wolves were shot, poisoned, trapped and dragged from dens, until in the Lower 48 states only a few hundred gray wolves remained, in northern Minnesota and Michigan.

In 1944 naturalist Aldo Leopold called for the return of the wolf. His studies showed that wild ecosystems need their top predators to maintain biodiversity.

Protected and encouraged, wolf populations made a remarkable recovery, however in 2011 heavy pressure from ranchers resulted In the lifting of federal protections for wolves in six states—Montana, Idaho, Wyoming, Minnesota, Wisconsin, and Michigan. The Center for Biological Diversity estimates that, since 2011, in these states, over 3500 wolves have been killed. More recently, wolves have had their federal protection reinstated in some states.

Love 'em or hate 'em, snakes are here to stay in most of the parks – but snakebites are rare (in Yellowstone, the NPS reports two in the history of the park). Western and prairie rattlesnakes are common, but they are generally docile and would rather rattle and scram than bite. Gopher and garter snakes are the most common of all.

Trees & Plants

If you were to travel to every national park in this guide, you'd experience a vast array of plant life, from the salty mangroves of the Everglades to the bizarre Joshua trees of the Mojave Desert, and the colorful tropical flowers of Hawaii to the arctic tundra in Alaska.

In the Realm of Giants

Yosemite, Sequoia, and Kings Canyon are home to the world's largest living things: giant sequoias. Although they aren't the tallest trees, nor the thickest, they are the biggest in terms of sheer mass. Living up to 3000 years, giant sequoias are also among the oldest living organisms. The General Sherman tree, in Sequoia, stands 275ft tall and measures 102ft around, making it the largest living single-specimen organism on earth. Think of it this way: according to the National Park Service, its trunk alone is equivalent to 15 blue whales or 25 military battle tanks. Now that's a big tree.

Trees

The national parks protect some of the greatest forests in the world. Redwood has the planet's tallest trees, Yosemite's Mariposa Grove of giant sequoias is home to some of the planet's largest trees, while the park's high country holds subalpine forests that are nothing short of high-altitude fairylands. North of the Sierra Nevada, in the Cascade Range, Mt Rainier National Park protects thick forests of western hemlock, Douglas fir, cedar, true firs, and western white pine. West of the Cascades, Olympic National Park is home to some of the greatest stands of temperate rainforest and old-growth forest.

In the Rockies, sparse piñon-juniper forests cover the drier, lower elevations, while the sweet-scented ponderosa pines dominate the montane zone. One of the Rockies' most striking trees is the quaking aspen, whose leaves flutter and shimmer in the mountain breeze and turn entire hillsides golden yellow in fall. The stunted, gnarled bristlecone pine, the oldest living life form on the planet, grows throughout the West in stands just below treeline. Many are thousands of years old.

In the drier, hotter climates of Zion, Bryce Canyon and Grand Canyon, trees are fewer, but still common. Many Zion visitors are surprised to find a lush riparian zone along the Virgin River that supports beautiful stands of cottonwoods and gorgeous bigtoothed maples. In the Mojave Desert is the strange Joshua tree, actually a giant yucca.

As far as biological diversity goes, however, the Great Smoky Mountains are king. The old-growth forests of the Smokies are home to more native tree and plant species than anywhere else in the United States. Drive 900 miles south from Great Smoky and you end up in Everglades National Park, home to vast mangroves forests and tropical hardwoods.

Smaller Plants

When it comes to the smaller plants of the national parks, none seem to make an impression like wildflowers do. If you're traveling in spring or summer, it's always worth doing a little research on your park of choice to find out what's blooming when. For example, wildflowers put on a spectacular show in Death Valley every spring, usually in late February and March, and on good years it's worth planning a trip around them. Throughout the Rockies, June and July are prime wildflower months. In the Sierras, wildflowers bloom in spring at lower elevations, in early summer up around Tuolumne Meadows, and as late as mid-July at the highest elevations.

On the Colorado Plateau (Zion, Bryce, Grand Canyon), wildflowers such as desert marigolds and slickrock paintbrush bloom for a short period in early spring. The plateau's most interesting plants are arguably the cacti and desert succulents that make this mostly desert region so unique. Although many plants are specific to the plateau, others are drawn from adjacent biological zones such as the Great Basin, Mojave Desert and Rocky Mountains.

In the Southern Appalachians, the Great Smoky Mountains boast an incredible 1500 flowering plants, including nine native species of rhododendron and azalea (blooming late May through June).

Joshua Tree National Park (p62)

DENNIS SILVAS/SHUTTERSTOCK ©

Conservation

Protecting the national parks has been a challenge since the day Yellowstone was created in 1872. Thanks to the efforts of passionate individuals, the parks now safeguard some of the greatest natural treasures on the planet. But they face new, often concurrent, threats. Climate change, invasive species, overuse and irresponsible land use on park peripheries all jeopardize the national parks today.

Climate Change

Major voices within the national parks service, in agreement with scores of eminent scientists and climatologists, worry that climate change poses a significant threat to the health of the network's diverse ecosystems. Although park biologists are only just beginning to understand its impact, nearly all agree that it is taking a toll.

Scientists worry, for example, that due to rising temperatures in the Mojave Desert, Joshua trees may disappear almost entirely from Joshua Tree National Park within the next 60 to 90 years. Glacier National Park may be devoid of glaciers by 2030 if melting continues at current rates (in 1850 the park contained 150 glaciers; today there are 25). And in Sequoia and Kings Canyon National Parks, there is concern that changing temperatures and rainfall patterns may threaten the giant sequoias.

Invasive Species

Invasive species pose a severe threat to the national parks. In the Southern Appalachians, a non-native insect called the hemlock woolly adelgid is decimating eastern hemlock forests. In Great Smoky Mountains National Park, where the insect was discovered in 2003, trees are already beginning to die. In Shenandoah, where the insect has been present since 1980, nearly 95% of the hemlocks have perished.

In Glacier National Park, botanists have identified over 125 non-native plants that are reducing food sources for local wildlife. In Sequoia and Kings Canyon National Parks, non-native trout have practically wiped out the mountain yellow-legged frog population, landing the frog on the candidate list for endangered species. In Hawai'i Volcanoes National Park, invasive species, including feral animals, mongooses and numerous plant species, pose tremendous threats to native flora and fauna.

Of course, we can hardly remove ourselves from the list of invasive species. Each year, nearly 300 million visitors clock up more than a billion cumulative hours in the parks. Traffic, auto emissions, roads and the simple fact of human presence in sensitive wildlife areas all take their toll on park ecosystems.

Park Peripheries

Aside from the impact visitors make on the parks, humans are putting immense pressure on many locations by operating high-impact businesses outside park boundaries. Conservationists battled for more than two decades to prevent Kaiser Ventures from creating the nation's largest landfill on the edge of Joshua Tree National Park. In Alaska mining companies attempted to create the continent's largest open-pit gold and copper mine only miles from Clark Lake National Park. Great Smoky Mountains, Grand Canyon and Big Bend National Parks are all affected by emissions from coal-fired power plants, which drift over the parks and contaminate the air. Sensitive riparian areas along the Grand Canyon's Colorado River have long been impacted by upriver damming and water holding. And on Washington's Olympic Peninsula, logging companies have clear-cut forests right up to the borders of the park, which has displaced the northern spotted owl from the region.

Sustainable Visitation

As magnificent as they are, only a tiny percentage of the US national budget is put aside for the benefit of the nation's national parks. Despite this, park visitors can make a positive impact by traveling sustainably and getting involved with park associations. Whenever you can, ride park shuttles instead of driving your car. Skip high-impact park activities such as snowmobiling in Yellowstone and flight-seeing trips over the Grand Canyon. Conserve water in the desert parks and prevent erosion by always staying on trails. If you're backpacking, use biodegradable soaps (or skip them altogether) and follow the principles of Leave No Trace (lnt.org).

Nearly every national park has an associated foundation or other nonprofit that supports its parent park. These organizations, which include Yellowstone Park Foundation (www.ypf.org), the Yosemite Conservancy (www.yosemiteconservancy.org) and Friends of the Smokies (www.friendsofthesmokies.org), conduct everything from trail maintenance to habitat restoration. Members can volunteer or donate to programs that are critical to the parks' well-being.

The National Parks Conservation Association (www.npca.org) covers all of the parks. Since 1919, this nonprofit organization has been protecting and preserving America's national parks through research, advocacy and education.

WIN-INITIATIVE/GETTY IMAGES ©

★ **Did you know?**

More than 200 national parks and monuments contain at least one endangered species.

BENNY MARTY/SHUTTERSTOCK ©

Top: Mountain yellow-legged frog in Kings Canyon; Bottom left: Barren hemlock trees in Great Smoky Mountain; Bottom right: A Colorado River dam

Everglades National Park (p448)

Landscapes & Geology

Tectonic collisions, glaciation, volcanic eruptions, erosion – the forces of nature and time have worked wonders on the continent, and nowhere is that geological history more beautifully evident than in the national parks. Each park tells its own ancient story through landscapes that are as unique as they are complex.

New England & the Mid-Atlantic

The eastern United States is defined by the Atlantic Ocean and the Appalachian Mountains, which run parallel to the coastline from Maine to Alabama. The sedimentary Appalachians are the continent's oldest mountains, dating back some 300 million years, to a time when North America was part of the supercontinent Pangaea.

The northern Appalachians, with numerous peaks over 5000ft, were further sculpted by the Ice Age: Acacia's Mt Desert Island, for example, was created some 20,000 years ago, when glacial ice sheets sheared it from the mainland. Peaks in the central Appalachian region in Virginia, usually referred to as the Blue Ridge Mountains, top out around 4000ft. Some of the rocks in Shenandoah are over one billion years old.

The South

The peaks in the Southern Appalachian are the range's highest, topping out at 6684ft-high Mt Mitchell in North Carolina. Nearby is the wet, heavily forested Great Smoky Mountains, the USA's most visited national park with 16 summits over 5000ft. Steep elevation gradients, deep V-shaped valleys, ridges, abundant rainfall and high summertime humidity make the Appalachians one of the most diverse ecosystems in all of the USA.

Heading south, things get wetter and warmer, passing through the floodplain forests in South Carolina's Congaree, famous for its large tracts of old-growth deciduous forest.

Florida

Heading further south, you enter the flatter, sub-tropical and tropical domain of Florida, the US state with the lowest high-point and the longest coastline (outside Alaska). Southern Florida is characterized by its swamps. Protected today in the Everglades National Park, they comprise the largest subtropical wilderness in the US. With an average elevation of only 6ft, the park is an expansive wetland atop an ancient seabed, with a tremendous variety of coastal and marine ecosystems.

Great Lakes & Plains

In geological terms, the Great Lakes area represents the southern part of what is known as the Canadian Shield. Consisting mainly of igneous (volcanic) and metamorphic rock 2.5 to 3.5 billion years old (by comparison, the Jurassic dinosaurs were lumbering about only 200 million years ago), this region was profoundly shaped during the Ice Age. The most obvious remnants of the massive glaciers here are the five Great Lakes, which represent the greatest expanse of fresh water on the continent, consisting of 20% of the world's supply. Both Isle Royale and Voyageurs are defined by their lakes, marshes and boreal forest – a mix of conifers and hardwoods adapted to the short growing season of the far north.

The Great Plains is the relatively flat prairie that extends over much of the Central United States. Once an inland sea, it eventually became fertile grassland, which was most recently developed for agriculture. Originally home to millions of bison, you can get some sense of what parts of the prairie looked like in the Badlands, Theodore Roosevelt and Wind Cave National Parks, all in the Dakotas.

Rocky Mountains

Nearly 1000 miles west of the Appalachians, the Rocky Mountains begin their dramatic ascent from the western reaches of the Great Plains and climb to over 14,000ft. Much younger than the Appalachians, the Rockies were created by tectonic uplift between 70 million and two million years ago. The mountains were carved and eroded by water and wind and finally, during the Ice Age two million years ago, hewn by glaciers into the landscapes we see today.

Yellowstone was shaped by the same Ice Age, but what really differentiates it from other parks in the range is its volcanic activity. Yellowstone sits on a geological 'hot spot,' a thin piece of the earth's crust that is essentially floating atop a massive, 125-mile-deep plume of molten rock. Fueled by this underground furnace, Yellowstone bubbles like a pot on a hot stove to produce over 10,000 geothermal features – more than all other geothermal areas on the planet combined.

★ **National Park Extremes**

Highest point Denali, 20,310ft

Lowest point Death Valley, -282ft

Tallest tree Redwood, 379ft

Biggest tree Sequoia, 52,500 cubic ft

Wettest region Olympic (pictured), annual rainfall 11.25ft

Largest park Wrangell–St Elias, total area 20,500 sq miles

Yellowstone, Grand Teton, Glacier, Rocky Mountain, Black Canyon and the Great Sand Dunes together protect some 3 million acres of the Rockies. Rocky Mountain has the highest point in these parks, its iconic Longs Peak punching 14,259ft into the sky.

Southwest

At the southwest end of the Rockies, the mountains descend to the Colorado Plateau, a 130,000-sq-mile region centered on the arid Four Corners area of the United States. Home to Grand Canyon, Zion and Bryce Canyon – among numerous other parks – the Colorado Plateau is one of the world's densest concentrations of exposed rock. Arizona's Petrified Forest is a trove of Late Triassic-era fossils, which date back 225 million years.

Unlike the Rocky Mountains to the east and the Sierras to the west, the plateau has remained stable for millions of years, during which water and wind slowly eroded the landscape, forming the spectacular canyons, arches, hoodoos and other rock formations you see today. From an aerial perspective, the plateaus and cliffs form a remarkable staircase that steps downward from the pink cliffs of Bryce Canyon, to the white and red cliffs of Zion, and finally to the chocolate cliffs abutting the Grand Canyon – each color represents a different geological era. This so-called Grand Staircase exposes the hundreds of millions of years of layered rock that make the region so visually awesome.

California

South of Zion, the Colorado Plateau meets the Mojave Desert, which is home to the hottest, driest places in North America. Here you'll find Death Valley, which protects over 5000 sq miles of what is no less than a crazy quilted geological playground. Encompassing far more than Death Valley itself, the park contains giant sand dunes, marbled canyons, extinct volcanic craters and palm-shaded oases.

At the southernmost edge of the Mojave lies Joshua Tree, which straddles both the Mojave and the Sonoran Deserts. The Mojave section of the park is home to a particularly striking member of the yucca family, the namesake Joshua tree.

Northwest of the California deserts, the Sierra Nevada is a 400-mile-long mountain range with tremendous biological and geological diversity. The Sierras are an uplifted, westward-tilting slab of granite that broke off from the Earth's crust and thrust upward roughly 10 million years ago.

Between two million and 10,000 years ago, glaciers 'flowed' from high-elevation ice fields, scouring out canyons and valleys and sculpting the range into a granite masterpiece. In Yosemite, evidence of glaciation is everywhere and is what makes the park so spectacular.

The Sierras' highest peaks stand within the areas protected by Yosemite, Sequoia, and Kings Canyon, with Mt Whitney (14,505ft; in Sequoia), standing taller than any other peak in the Lower 48.

Although located in northern California, the coastal Redwoods and Lassen Volcanic National Parks are more closely related to the temperate rainforests and fiery peaks of the Pacific Northwest.

Pacific Northwest

North of the Sierra Nevada stands the Cascade Range, a volcanic mountain range stretching from northern California into British Columbia. The range's highest peak is 14,411ft Mt Rainier, a massive strato-volcano protected by Mt Rainier National Park. The volcano is 'episodically active' and is considered the most hazardous volcano in the Cascades. The mountain is covered in snow for much of the year and contains expansive ice fields and 25 glaciers. It last erupted in 1854. Other major parks in the range include Oregon's Crater Lake – an extinct volcano whose caldera filled with water 7700 years ago and is today the deepest (and clearest) lake in the US – and the North Cascades, a rugged swathe of glacier-bound jagged peaks, featuring both temperate rainforest on the west side of the range and drier ponderosa forests on the east.

West of the Cascades, on Washington's Olympic Peninsula, the Olympic Mountains plunge dramatically into the Pacific Ocean. They are a separate range entirely and, unlike the volcanic Cascades, were formed five to 15 million years ago during convergence of the Juan de Fuca and North American plates. Between the Olympic's highest peaks, which top out at 7965ft, and the ocean below, Olympic National Park protects a landscape drenched in rain, hammered by wind and pounded by waves.

Subterranean Wonders

The national parks' caves are often overlooked by road-tripping families on summer vacations. After all, is walking around in a chilly, pitch-black tunnel really as appealing as spotting bears in Yellowstone or hugging giant trees in Sequoia? Maybe not on the surface, but the thrill of exploring the underworld's bizarre formations should not be overlooked. Three enormous cave systems in the US have been protected as national parks: Mammoth Cave (Kentucky), Carlsbad Caverns (New Mexico), and Wind Cave (South Dakota). Rangers lead tours of all three, plus you can hike down into Carlsbad's Big Room on your own. Mammoth is the world's largest known cave system, with over 400 miles of labyrinths. Interested in spelunking? Sign up for their challenging Wild Cave Tour. Other parks with smaller caves to explore include Pinnacles, Kings Canyon and Sequoia in California.

Alaska

Dramatic mountain ranges arch across the landmass of Alaska. The Pacific Mountain System, which includes the Alaska, Aleutian and St Elias Ranges, as well as the Chugach and Kenai Mountains, sweeps along the south before dipping into the sea southwest of Kodiak Island. Most of Alaska's seven national parks are located here, including the granddaddy of them all, Denali – its namesake mountain is North America's tallest peak (20,310ft). Further north looms the imposing and little-visited Brooks Range, skirting the Arctic Circle, where you'll find the wild and remote Gates of the Arctic.

In between the Alaska and Brooks Ranges is interior Alaska, an immense plateau rippled by foothills, low mountains and magnificent rivers; among them the third

Fun Facts

The largest national park is Alaska's Wrangell–St Elias. Bigger than Switzerland, it's also home to the second-tallest peak in the US, Mt St Elias (18,008 ft), whose dizzying climb from sea level occurs in just 10 miles.

The 2663-mile Pacific Crest Trail, which extends from Canada to Mexico, passes through seven national parks. Similar in nature, the Appalachian (2160 miles) and Continental Divide (3100 miles) Trails follow the USA's other main north–south mountain ranges, passing through an additional five national parks.

Colorado's Great Sand Dunes are composed of 29 different rocks and minerals – from obsidian and sulphur to amethyst and turquoise – and cover an incredible 30 sq miles of land, with dunes as tall as 700ft.

longest in the US, the mighty Yukon River, which runs for 2300 miles. At the state's far southeasern corner is Glacier Bay – the perfect place to observe glacial retreat in action.

In geological terms Alaska is relatively young and still very active. The state represents the northern boundary of the chain of Pacific Ocean volcanoes known as the Ring of Fire and is the most seismically active region of North America. In fact, Alaska claims 52% of the earthquakes that occur in the country and averages more than 13 each day. Most are mild shakes, but some are deadly. Three of the six largest earthquakes in the world – and seven of the 10 largest in the US – have occurred in Alaska.

Hawaii

The Hawaiian archipelago embraces more than 50 volcanoes (and 137 islands and atolls), part of the larger, mostly submerged Hawaiian–Emperor Seamount chain that extends 3600 miles across the ocean. Hawaii's volcanoes are created by a rising column of molten rock – a hot spot – under the Pacific Plate. As the plate moves northwest a few inches each year, magma pierces upward through the crust, creating volcanoes.

Each new volcano slowly creeps northwest past the hot spot that created it. As each volcanic island moves off the hot spot, it stops erupting and instead of adding more new land, starts eroding. Wind, rain and waves add geologic character to the newly emerged islands, cutting deep valleys, creating sandy beaches and turning a mound of lava into a tropical paradise. For a first-hand look at the different ecosystems that a volcano's slopes harbor, explore Haleakalā, which rises over 10,000ft up from near sea level.

Straddling the hot spot today, the Hawai'i Volcanoes' Kilauea, on the Big Island, is the world's most active volcano. All Hawaiian volcanoes are shield volcanoes that erupt with effusive lava to create gently sloped, dome-shaped mountains, but they can also have a more explosive side, as Kilauea dramatically reminded onlookers and scientists in 2018.

Behind the Scenes

Acknowledgements

Climate map data adapted from Peel MC, Finlayson BL & McMahon TA (2007) 'Updated World Map of the Köppen-Geiger Climate Classification', *Hydrology and Earth System Sciences*, 11, pp1633–44.

Images pp44–5 (clockwise from top left): Mark Read/Lonely Planet ©; NaughtyNut, Lukas Proszowski, Sean Pavone, Liga Cerina, Amineah, ivvv1975, Sundry Photography, Michael Rosebrock/Shutterstock ©

Cover photograph: Rocky Mountain National Park, Cathy & Gordon Illg/AWL ©

Send Us Your Feedback

We love to hear from travelers – your comments keep us on our toes and help make our books better. Our well-traveled team reads every word on what you loved or loathed about this book. Although we cannot reply individually to postal submissions, we always guarantee that your feedback goes straight to the appropriate authors, in time for the next edition. Each person who sends us information is thanked in the next edition, the most useful submissions are rewarded with a selection of digital PDF chapters.

Visit lonelyplanet.com/contact to submit your updates and suggestions or to ask for help. Our award-winning website also features inspirational travel stories, news and discussions.

Note: We may edit, reproduce and incorporate your comments in Lonely Planet products such as guidebooks, websites and digital products, so let us know if you don't want your comments reproduced or your name acknowledged. For a copy of our privacy policy visit lonelyplanet.com/privacy.

This Book

This second edition of Lonely Planet's *USA's National Parks* was curated by Anita Isalska and Brendan Sainsbury, and researched and written by Amy Balfour, Loren Bell, Greg Benchwick, Jade Bremner, Jennifer Rasin Denniston, Michael Grosberg, Bradley Mayhew, Carolyn McCarthy, Christopher Pitts and Regis St Louis. This guidebook was produced by the following:

Destination Editors Ben Buckner, Trisha Ping, Sarah Stocking

Senior Product Editors Grace Dobell, Kate Mathews, Vicky Smith

Design Development Katherine Marsh

Cartographic Series Designer Wayne Murphy

Product Editor Hannah Cartmel

Senior Cartographer Alison Lyall

Book Designer Mazzy Prinsep

Assisting Editors Sarah Bailey, Andrew Bain, James Bainbridge, Katie Connolly, Kate Daly, Melanie Dankel, Carly Hall, Trent Holden, Anita Isalska, Lou McGregor, Anne Mulvaney, Lauren O'Connell, Sarah Reid, Fionnuala Twomey

Assisting Cartographers Laura Bailey, Anita Banh, Hunor Csutoros

Assisting Book Designers Gerilyn Attebery, Clara Monitto, Virginia Moreno, Wibowo Rusli

Production Development Liz Heynes, Dianne Schallmeiner, John Taufa, Juan Winata

Cover Researcher Katherine Marsh

Thanks to Imogen Bannister, Kate Chapman, Evan Godt, Victoria Harrison, Andi Jones, Sandie Kestell, Anne Mason, Karyn Noble, Claire Naylor, Martine Power, Lyahna Spencer

A–Z
Index

A

Acadia National Park 13, 28-9, 41, 402-11, **403**
accessible travel 164, 327, 432
activities 43, 488-93, *see also individual activities*
acute mountain sickness 25
Alaska 230-317, **231**
Aleutian WWII National Historic Area 252
animals, *see individual animals*
alligators 39
antelope 391
Antiquities Act 486
Arches National Park 28-9, 140-5, **141**
Ashland 236
avalanches 25

B

Badlands National Park 28-9, 380-1, **381**
Bartlett Cove 262
bears 27, 39, 270, 495
bicycle travel, *see cycling*
Big Bend National Park 28-9, 146-51, 156, **147**
birds 458, 496-7
birdwatching 148, 458
Biscayne National Park 28-9, 444-5, **445**
bison 390, 494-5
Black Canyon of the Gunnison National Park 28-9, 322-3, **323**
boat tours 444, 490-1
books 23
Brooks Camp 39, 268
Brooks Falls 268
Bryce Amphitheater 14

Bryce Canyon National Park 14, 28-9, 158-67, **159**
Bryce Point 158
bushwalking, *see hiking*

C

Cades Cove 422-3
Cadillac Mountain 13, 403, 410
California 48-135, **49**
canoeing & kayaking 15, 16, 490
  Congaree 420
  Glacier Bay 16, 260, 262
  Grand Teton 338
  Katmai 270
  Kenai Fjords 275-6
  Kobuk Valley 256
  Lake Clark 278
  Mammoth Cave 439
  Redwood 98
canyoneering 43, 218
Canyonlands National Park 28-9, 170-5, **171**
Capitol Reef National Park 28-9, 176-83, **177**
Carlsbad Caverns National Park 28-9, 184-5, **185**
Cascades Pass Trail 37
Cathedral Lakes 126-7, **127**
caves 41, 505
  Balconies Cave 94
  Boulder Cave 290
  Carlsbad Caverns 184-5
  Lehman Caves 196
  Mammoth Cave 438
  Wind Cave 394
Chain of Craters Road 469
Channel Islands National Park 28-9, 50-5, 93, **51**
Chapin Mesa 206
Charlies Bunion 434-5, **435**
children, travel with 41, 160
Chilkoot Trail 252
Chiricahua National Monument 213

Civilian Conservation Corps (CCC) 485
Cliff Palace 16, 204
climate 20-2, **18**
climate change 499
clothing 26-7
Cody Stampede 22
Congaree National Park 28-9, 420-1, **421**
costs 19
coyotes 495-6
Crater Lake 238
Crater Lake National Park 30-1, 232-41, **233**
Cuyahoga Valley National Park 30-1, 382-3, **383**
cycling 62, 215, 245, 356, 425, 491-2

D

Death Valley National Park 30-1, 56-61, **57**
deer 390
Delicate Arch 140-2
Denali 247
Denali National Park 30-1, 242-51, **243**
Diablo Lake 294
diving 445
driving tours
  Acadia 408-11, **409**
  Big Bend 152-7, **153**
  Bryce Canyon 162-3, **163**
  Capitol Reef 180-1, **181**
  Crater Lake 236-41, **237**
  Going-to-the-Sun Road 333, **333**
  Great Smoky Mountains 430, 431, **430, 431**
  Grand Teton 342-3, **343**
  Great Basin 197
  Joshua Tree 68-73, **69**
  Hawai'i Volcanoes 468
  Highway 24 180-1, **181**

Hole-in-One 342-3, **343**
Kings Canyon 130-5, **131**
Mt Rainier 284-91, **285**
Newfound Gap Road 430, **430**
Newton B Drury Scenic
  Parkway 97
Olympic Peninsula 304-9,
  305
Palm Springs 68-73, **69**
Redwood Coast 102-7, **103**
Roaring Forks Motor Nature
  Trail 431, **431**
Sequoia 130-5, **131**
Shenandoah 412
Yosemite 130-5, **131**
Zion Canyon 222-3, **222**
Dry Tortugas National Park 30-1,
  446-7, **447**

E

economy 480-1
El Capitan 120
elk 391
Emerald Pools 218
environmental issues 262, 481,
  499-501
equipment 26-7
events 20-2
Everglades National Park 15,
  30-1, 448-51, **449**
Exit Glacier 274-5

F

Fairyland Loop Trail 160
Federation Forest State Park 291
festivals 20-2
films 23
fishing 271, 493
Florida 442-51, **443**
Forks 308
Fort Jefferson 446

G

galleries, see museums &
  galleries

Gates of the Arctic National
  Park 30-1, 254-9
Gateway Arch National Park
  384-5, 481, **385**
General Grant Grove 74-6
General Sherman Tree 108
geography 351, 502-6
geology 176, 190, 199, 212-13,
  395, 502-6
geothermal features 374-5
geysers 374
giant sequoias 498
Glacier Bay National Park 16,
  30-1, 260-7, **261**
Glacier National Park 6, 30-1,
  39, 324-35, **325**
Glen Canyon National
  Recreation Area 212
Going-to-the-Sun Road 6, 329,
  333, **333**
Golden State Heritage Site 240
Grand Canyon National Park 7,
  30-1, 186-95, **187**
Grand Prismatic Spring 364-5
Grand Teton Music Festival 22
Grand Teton National Park 8,
  30-1, 336-45, **337**
Grandview Trail 37
Great Basin National Park 30-1,
  196-7, **197**
Great Lakes 378-97, **379**
Great Plains 378-97, **379**
Great Sand Dunes National Park
  30-1, 348-53, **349**
Great Smoky Mountains
  National Park 30-1, 422-33,
  423
Guadalupe Mountains National
  Park 30-1, 198-203, **199**
Gustavus 262

H

Haleakalā National Park 32-3,
  456-65, **457**
Halemaʻumaʻu Crater 468
Half Dome 118-20
Hawaii 454-77, **455**

Hawaiʻi Volcanoes National Park
  32-3, 466-75, **467**
health 24-5
hiking 24-5, 37, 488-9
  Arches 142
  Big Bend 148
  Bryce Canyon 168-9, **169**
  Bunsen Peak Trail 370-1, **371**
  Capitol Reef 177
  Charlies Bunion 434-5, **435**
  Chilkoot Trail 252
  Congaree 420
  Crater Lake 232-3
  Death Valley 58
  Denali 243-4
  Everglades 39, 448
  Glacier 330, 331, 332, **330**,
    331, **332**
  Grand Canyon 7, 186, 192, 193,
    192, **193**
  Grand Teton 346-7, **347**
  Great Smoky Mountains
    423-5, 428, 429, **428**, **429**
  Guadalupe Mountains 198-9
  Haleakalā 462-3
  Hawaiʻi Volcanoes 472
  Joshua Tree 62
  Katmai 270
  Kenai Fjords 276
  Kephart Loop 434-5, **435**
  Kings Canyon 80-1, **81**
  Kobuk Valley 254-6
  Lake Clark 279
  Lassen Volcanic 88-91
  Mist Falls 80-1, **81**
  Mt Rainier 282, 288
  Narrows, the 226-7, **227**
  North Cascades 292-4
  Olympic 302
  Pinnacles 94-5, **95**
  Rae Lakes Loop 84-7, **85**
  Redwood 96-7, **97**
  Rocky Mountain 37, 330, 331,
    332, 356, **330**, **331**, **332**
  Saguaro 214-15
  Sequoia 112-15, **113**, **115**

hiking *continued*
Shenandoah 413
Teton Crest Trail 37, 346-7, **347**
Theodore Roosevelt 388
Under the Rim Trail 168-9, **169**
Wind Cave 394-5, **395**
Wrangell-St Elias 313
Yellowstone 365-6, 367, 368-9, 370-1, **369**, **371**
Yosemite 37, 125-7, **125**, **127**
Zion 37, 218
history 53, 188, 201, 252-3, 326, 482-7
Hoh Rain Forest 15, 41, 298-9, 306
Holzwarth Historic Site 355
hoodoos 213
horseback riding 426, 493
Hot Springs National Park 32-3, 436-7, **437**
Hurricane Ridge 300-1

I

Iñupiat Heritage Center 253
Island in the Sky 170
Isle Royale National Park 32-3, 386-7, **387**

J

Jenny Lake 338
Joshua Tree Music Festival 21
Joshua Tree National Park 8, 32-3, 62-7, **63**
Joshua trees 65

K

Kalahaku Overlook 458-9
Kalaupapa National Historical Park 477
Kaloko-Honokohau National Historical Park 476

Katmai National Park 32-3, 268-73, **269**
kayaking, *see* canoeing & kayaking
Kenai Fjords National Park 32-3, 274-7, **275**
Kennecott 312
Kennicott Glacier 315
Kilauea Iki Overlook 469
Kilauea volcano 469
Kings Canyon National Park 32-3, 74-83, **75**
Kobuk Sand Dunes 256
Kobuk Valley National Park 30-1, 254-9, **255**

L

Lake Clark National Park 32-3, 278-9, **279**
Lake Crescent 301
Lake Quinault 299-300
Lassen Peak 90
Lassen Volcanic National Park 32-3, 88-91, **89**
Lava Beds National Monument 92
Leleiwi Overlook 458
Logan Pass 324-6
Longs Peak 10, 356-7

M

Mammoth Cave National Park 32-3, 438-9, **439**
Mammoth Hot Springs 365
Maze, the 171
McCarthy 310-12
Medford 236
Mesa Arch 171
Mesa Verde National Park 16, 32-3, 204-9, **205**
Mid-Atlantic, the 400-15, **401**
mining 312
Mission 66 486
Monarch Lakes 112, **113**
moose 495

mountain biking 491-2
Canyonlands 172
Great Sand Dunes 351
Rocky Mountain 356
mountain lions 496
mountaineering 43, 341, 357, 491
Mt LeConte 423
Mt Mazama 233
Mt McKinley 247
Mt Rainier National Park 17, 32-3, 280-3, **281**
Mt Washburn 368-9, **369**
Muir, John 484
Muir Woods National Monument 93
museums & galleries
Abbe Museum 408
Douglas County Museum 240
El Paso Holocaust Museum 152
El Paso Museum of Art 152
Longmire Museum 281
Schneider Museum of Art 236
Volcano Art Center 469
Yavapai Point & Geology Museum 190
music 23

N

Narrows, the 11, 216, 226-7, **227**
national parks 28-35, **44-5**
Natural Bridges National Monument 158, 213
Needles, the 170-1
nene 458
New England 400-15, **401**
North Cascades National Park 32-3, 292-7, **293**

O

Old Faithful 362-4
Olympic National Park 15, 32-3, 298-303, **299**
Oregon Vortex 240

P

Pacific Northwest 230-317, **231**
Paradise 280-1
Park Loop Road 402
Park Road 242-3
Petrified Forest National Park 34-5, 210-11, **211**
petroglyphs 179, 471
Pinnacles National Park 34-5, 94-5, **95**
planning
  budgeting 19
  calendar of events 20-2
  clothing 26-7
  equipment 27
  national parks basics 18-19, 28-35
  safety 24-5
Point Reyes National Seashore 93
politics 480-1
prairie dogs 391
Pronghorn antelopes 391
Prospect 236
Puebloan people 188, 206
Pu'uhonua o Honaunau National Historical Park 476
Pu'u'ula'ula (Red Hill) Overlook 459, 462

R

rafting 43, 186, 245, 424, 425, 490
Rainbow Bridge National Monument 212
Redwood Canyon 76
Redwood National Park 34-5, 96-101, **97**
Reflection Lake 288
rock climbing 8, 41, 491
  Grand Teton 336-8, 341
  Joshua Tree 65
  Pinnacles 95
Rocky Mountain National Park 10, 34-5, 354-61, **355**

Rocky Mountains 320-75, **321**
Roosevelt, Franklin Delano 485
Roosevelt, Theodore 389, 485
Roseburg 240
Ross Lake 294

S

safe travel 24-5
Saguaro National Park 34-5, 214-15, **215**
saguaros 215
sand sledding 41
Santa Monica Mountains National Recreation Area 92
Scenic Bryce Canyon 162-3, **163**
Sequoia National Park 34-5, 108-17, **109**
Shenandoah National Park 34-5, 412-15, **413**
Shoshone Lake 367
Sitka National Historical Park 253
skiing & snowshoeing 20, 43, 492-3
  Cliff Palace Loop Rd 206
  Crater Lake 233
  Grand Teton 338
  Rocky Mountain 359
Snake River 8, 338
snorkelling 490-1
snowshoeing, see skiing & snowshoeing
southern USA 418-39, **419**
southwest USA 138-227, **139**
St Mary Lake 326
stargazing 148, 185, 197, 461, 492
Sunrise 281-2
swimming 493

T

Tenaya Lake 120
Theodore Roosevelt National Park 34-5, 388-9, **389**
Thurston Lava Tube 469

Toketee Falls 240
tortoises 221
trees 110, 210, 497-8
Trees of Mystery 106
Tuolumne Meadows 121
Twilight saga 308

V

Valley of Ten Thousand Smokes 270
Voyageurs National Park 34-5, 392-3, **393**

W

Waikamoi Preserve 458
water 25
waterfalls 76, 120-1, 286, 382
weather 20-2
Wetherill Mesa 206
Wild Horse Sanctuary 91
wildflowers 17, 20, 22, 498
wildlife watching 12, 39, 270, 364, 390-1, 494-8
Wind Cave National Park 34-5, 394-7, **395**
wine 240
wolves 495-6, 497
Wrangell-St Elias National Park 34-5, 310-17, **311**
WWII Valor in the Pacific National Monument 477

Y

Yellowstone National Park 12, 34-5, 362-73, **363**
Yosemite National Park 4, 34-5, 118-29, **119**
Yosemite Valley 4, 118

Z

Zion Canyon 218
Zion National Park 11, 34-5, 216-25, **217**

Christopher Pitts

Born in the year of the Tiger, Chris's first expedition in life ended in failure when he tried to dig from Pennsylvania to China at the age of six. Hardened by reality but still infinitely curious about the other side of the world, he went on to study Chinese in university, living for several years in Kunming, Taiwan and Shanghai. A chance encounter in an elevator led to a Paris relocation, where he lived with his wife and two children for over a decade before the lure of Colorado's sunny skies and outdoor adventure proved too great to resist. Visit him online at www.christopherpitts.net.

Regis St Louis

Regis grew up in a small town in the American Midwest – the kind of place that fuels big dreams of travel – and he developed an early fascination with foreign dialects and world cultures. He spent his formative years learning Russian and a handful of Romance languages, which served him well on journeys across much of the globe. Regis has contributed to more than 50 Lonely Planet titles, covering destinations across six continents. His travels have taken him from the mountains of Kamchatka to remote island villages in Melanesia, and to many grand urban landscapes. When not on the road, he lives in New Orleans. Follow him @regisstlouis on Instagram.

Contributing Writers

Brett Atkinson, Carolyn Bain, Sara Benson, Alison Bing, Catherine Bodry, Cristian Bonetto, Celeste Brash, Nate Cavalieri, Gregor Clark, Ashley Harrell, Mark Johanson, Adam Karlin, Virginia Maxwell, Hugh McNaughtan, Becky Ohlsen, Josephine Quintero, Kevin Raub, Andrea Schulte-Peevers, Helena Smith, John Vlahides, Benedict Walker, Greg Ward, Karla Zimmerman

Symbols & Map Key

These symbols and abbreviations give vital information for each listing:

☍ Sustainable or green recommendation
FREE No payment required

&#9742;	Telephone number	&#9641;	Swimming pool
&#9733;	Opening hours	&#9641;	Bus
P	Parking	&#9641;	Ferry
❋	Air-conditioning	&#9641;	Tram
&#9745;	Wi-fi access	&#9641;	Train
		&#9641;	Family-friendly

Find your best experiences with these Great For... icons.

&#9786;	Beaches	&#9786;	Photo Op
&#9786;	Cycling	&#9786;	Scenery
&#9786;	Family Travel	&#9786;	Walking
&#9786;	History	&#9786;	Winter Travel
&#9786;	Wildlife		

Points of Interest

- Beach
- Camping
- Canoeing/Kayaking
- Drinking & Nightlife
- Eating
- Hut/Shelter
- Lookout
- Mountain/Volcano
- Monument
- Museum/Gallery/Historic Building
- Park
- Ruin
- Shopping
- Skiing
- Sleeping
- Walking
- Zoo/Wildlife Sanctuary
- Other Sight
- Other Activity
- Other Point of Interest
- Pass
- Picnic Area
- Springs/Waterfall

Information & Transport

- Airport
- Border crossing
- Bus
- Cable car/Funicular
- Cycling
- Detour
- Ferry
- Metro station
- Parking
- Petrol station
- Toilet
- Tourist Information
- Train station/Railway
- Other Information/Transport

Amy Balfour

Amy practiced law in Virginia before moving to Los Angeles to try to break in as a screenwriter. After a stint as a writer's assistant on *Law & Order,* she jumped into freelance writing, focusing on travel, food and the outdoors. She has hiked, biked and paddled across Southern California and the Southwest, and recently criss-crossed the Great Plains in search of the region's best burgers and barbecue. Books authored or co-authored include Lonely Planet's *Los Angeles Encounter, Los Angeles & Southern California, Caribbean Islands, California, California Trips, USA, USA's Best Trips* and *Arizona.* Amy's essays have appeared in the *Los Angeles Times* and *Southern Living,* and the travel anthologies *Go Your Own Way* and *The Thong Also Rises.*

Loren Bell

When Loren first backpacked through Europe, he was in the backpack. That memorable experience corrupted his 6-month old brain, ensuring he would never be happy sitting still. His penchant for peregrination has taken him from training dogsled teams in the Tetons to chasing gibbons in the jungles of Borneo – with only brief pauses for silly 'responsible' things such as earning degrees. When he's not demystifying destinations for Lonely Planet, Loren writes about science and conservation news. He basecamps in the Rocky Mountains where he probably spends too much time on his mountain bike and skis.

Greg Benchwick

Greg has been drifting across the high plains of the Colorado Plateau for most of his life – he calls it a 'true spiritual home'. As a kid, he canoed desolate river canyons with his family, while in his wilder college days he pushed the limits on classic rock-climbing routes like Castleton Tower and the Moonlight Buttress. He's backpacked lost canyons, hitchhiked to Zion, mountain-biked Moab, and found solitude and peace in the lost corners of this desert wonderworld.

Jade Bremner

Jade has been a journalist for more than a decade. She has lived in and reported on four different regions. Wherever she goes she finds action sports to try, the weirder the better. Jade has edited travel magazines and sections for *Time Out* and *Radio Times,* and has contributed to *The Times,* CNN and *The Independent.* She feels privileged to share tales from this wonderful planet we call home and is always looking for the next adventure.

Jennifer Rasin Denniston

Jennifer's love for travel began with a 10-week family trip through Europe when she was eight. By 21, she had traveled independently in Australia, New Zealand, Africa, China and the US, and soon after graduation from college she began writing for Lonely Planet. Though her professional career focuses on the US, with a graduate degree in American Studies and multiple Lonely Planet titles on US destinations, her personal travel focuses on extended travel with children and multi-generational travel. Today, she lives in Iowa with her husband and two daughters, and they spend their summers on the road.

Michael Grosberg

Michael has worked on over 50 Lonely Planet guidebooks. Other international work included development on Rota in the western Pacific; South Africa where he investigated and wrote about political violence and trained newly elected government representatives; and Quito, Ecuador, to teach. He received a Masters in Comparative Literature and taught literature and writing as an adjunct professor.

Bradley Mayhew

Bradley has been writing guidebooks for 20 years now. He started traveling while studying Chinese at Oxford University, and he is the co-author of Lonely Planet's *Tibet, Nepal, Trekking in the Nepal Himalaya, Bhutan, Central Asia* and many others. Bradley has also fronted two TV series for Arte and SWR, one retracing the route of Marco Polo via Turkey, Iran, Afghanistan, Central Asia and China, and the other trekking Europe's 10 most scenic long-distance trails.

Carolyn McCarthy

Carolyn specializes in travel, culture and adventure in the Americas. She has written for *National Geographic, Outside, BBC Magazine, Sierra Magazine, Boston Globe* and other publications. A former Fulbright fellow and Banff Mountain Grant recipient, she has documented life in the most remote corners of Latin America. Carolyn has contributed to 40 guidebooks and anthologies for Lonely Planet, including *Colorado, USA, Argentina, Chile, Trekking in the Patagonian Andes, Panama, Peru* and *USA National Parks* guides. For more information, visit www.carolynmccarthy.org or follow her Instagram travels @mccarthyoffmap.

Our Story

A beat-up old car, a few dollars in the pocket and a sense of adventure. In 1972 that's all Tony and Maureen Wheeler needed for the trip of a lifetime – across Europe and Asia overland to Australia. It took several months, and at the end – broke but inspired – they sat at their kitchen table writing and stapling together their first travel guide, *Across Asia on the Cheap*. Within a week they'd sold 1500 copies. Lonely Planet was born.

Today, Lonely Planet has offices in Franklin, London, Melbourne, Oakland, Dublin, Beijing, and Delhi, with more than 600 staff and writers. We share Tony's belief that 'a great guidebook should do three things: inform, educate and amuse'.

Our Writers

Anita Isalska

Anita is a travel journalist, editor and copywriter. After several merry years as a staff writer and editor – a few of them in Lonely Planet's London office – Anita now works freelance between Australia, the UK and any Alpine chalet with good wi-fi. Anita writes about France, Eastern Europe, Southeast Asia and off-beat travel. Read her stuff on www.anitaisalska.com.

Brendan Sainsbury

Born and raised in the UK in a town that never merits a mention in any guidebook (Andover, Hampshire), Brendan spent the holidays of his youth caravanning in the English Lake District and didn't leave Blighty until he was 19. Making up for lost time, he's since squeezed 70 countries into a sometimes precarious existence as a writer and professional vagabond. In the last 11 years, he has written more than 40 books for Lonely Planet about places ranging from from Castro's Cuba to the canyons of Peru.

More Writers

STAY IN TOUCH LONELYPLANET.COM/CONTACT

AUSTRALIA The Malt Store, Level 3, 551 Swanston St, Carlton, Victoria 3053
☏ 03 8379 8000,
fax 03 8379 8111

IRELAND Digital Depot, Roe Lane (off Thomas St), Digital Hub, Dublin 8, D08 TCV4

USA 124 Linden Street, Oakland, CA 94607
☏ 510 250 6400,
toll free 800 275 8555,
fax 510 893 8572

UK 240 Blackfriars Road, London SE1 8NW
☏ 020 3771 5100,
fax 020 3771 5101

 twitter.com/
lonelyplanet

 facebook.com/
lonelyplanet

 instagram.com/
lonelyplanet

 youtube.com/
lonelyplanet

 lonelyplanet.com/
newsletter